Contributions to Economics

Deborah Winkler

Services Offshoring and its Impact on the Labor Market

Theoretical Insights, Empirical Evidence, and Economic Policy Recommendations for Germany

Physica-Verlag
A Springer Company

Dr. Deborah Winkler
Faculty of Business, Economics and Social Sciences
University of Hohenheim
70593 Stuttgart
Germany
deborahs@uni-hohenheim.de

ISSN 1431-1933
ISBN 978-3-7908-2806-1 e-ISBN 978-3-7908-2199-4
DOI: 10.1007/978-3-7908-2199-4
Springer Heidelberg Dordrecht London New York

Softcover reprint of the hardcover 1st edition 2009

Cover design: WMXDesign GmbH, Heidelberg

Printed on acid-free paper

Physica-Verlag Berlin Heidelberg (www.springer.com)

Acknowledgements

First, I would like to express my deep gratitude to my advisor Prof. Harald Hagemann (University of Hohenheim), whose guidance and encouragement were of critical importance to me throughout my doctoral studies. I enjoyed his continuous mentorship and benefited greatly from his sage advice and depth of knowledge.

Special thanks go to Prof. Hans-Michael Trautwein (University of Oldenburg) for early comments on my research and for agreeing to be on my thesis committee. Likewise, I thank Prof. Ansgar Belke (University of Duisburg-Essen) for sparking my interest in international trade, for his continuous support, and for helpful comments on the empirical part of my work.

I thank Prof. William Milberg (New School for Social Research) for his cooperation on other projects, for valuable comments on my thesis, and for his encouraging support. Also, I would like to thank Prof. Catherine Mann (Brandeis University) for our inspiring discussion and for her friendly helpfulness, as well as Prof. Gerhard Wagenhals (University of Hohenheim) and Prof. Bertrand Koebel (Université Louis Pasteur Strasbourg) for important suggestions concerning my empirical work.

I owe thanks to the Evangelisches Studienwerk Villigst e.V. for granting me a graduate scholarship, which facilitated my doctoral studies and research stays abroad. I also thank the Landesbank Baden-Württemberg-Stiftung for kindly supporting the publication of this book.

My thanks go to my colleagues and friends Patricia Hofmann, Julia Spies, and Ralf Rukwid. I enjoyed very much our discussions, economic and otherwise, as well as their company at various conferences, and I am thankful for their support. I am very grateful to our diligent assistant, Christine Eisenbraun, who has a heart of gold. I also benefited from discussions with my other colleagues at the department.

I sincerely thank my good friends, especially Marina Kühn, Alexandra Kalthoff, Miriam Kuhn, and Julia Kaiser, for their caring encouragement, good humor, and prayers for many years.

My heartfelt thanks go to my parents Erich Schöller and Tiagon Aritonang-Schöller and my sister Christina Schöller, whose love, tireless encouragement, wise support, and continuous prayers have carried me throughout my life.

I want to express my deep gratitude to my husband, Stephan Winkler, who knows me, understands me, and empathizes with me. I thank Stephan for his love, his moral support, and his belief in me. Saya cinta kamu.

Finally, I thank God for his countless blessings. No words can express my gratitude. S.D.G.

Preface

The German economy has exhibited strong export performance over many years, which, nonetheless, has failed to translate into higher economic growth and better employment performance during the last decade. This has often been attributed to a reduction in domestic manufacturing production linked to a greater fragmentation or unbundling of production activities, sometimes called the "bazaar-effect". However, fragmentation, outsourcing, and offshoring reflect an overall trend in international trade which has raised fears in the more advanced economies of job losses due to globalization.

Deborah Winkler focuses on the growing phenomenon of services offshoring, which is driven by information and communication technologies as well as by trade liberalization. Her investigation is a well-balanced synthesis of theoretical analysis, detailed empirical studies, and a good sense for economic policy relevance. She has already applied the findings to a study of globalization, offshoring, and economic insecurity in industrialized countries for the U.N. Department of Economic and Social Affairs (co-authored with William Milberg).

Particularly innovative and of greater value to the international research community is the rich empirical material on German services offshoring in an international comparison which Winkler presents in Chap. 3, and the empirical evidence on the labor market effects of services offshoring on productivity, labor demand, and the relative demand for less-skilled labor in Chap. 5. The econometric findings in the three subsections of this chapter, which are based on input-output data for the Federal Republic of Germany for the period 1991–2004, can well be regarded as the core and most innovative contribution of the book. Whereas Winkler's findings for the period 1991–2000 could be expected, namely that services offshoring has reduced relative demand for less-skilled labor, her results for the period 1995–2004 – which indicate a relative demand shift away from high-skilled labor – might be more surprising, although it is too early to identify a new trend. Nevertheless it may foster concern over the new phenomenon of skilled-labor offshoring. I do hope that Deborah Winkler's study will contribute to a more dispassionate and critical analysis of an important topic which, in the public domain, very often leads to overheated controversies.

Prof. Harald Hagemann
Director
PhD Program "Globalization and Employment"
University of Hohenheim, Stuttgart

Contents

Abbreviations

2SLS	Two-stage least squares
AIC	Akaike Information Criterion
ASEAN	Association of Southeast Asian Nations
B	Billion
BDA	Bundesvereinigung der Deutschen Arbeitgeberverbände (Confederation of German Employers' Associations)
BDI	Bundesverband der Deutschen Industrie e.V. (Federation of German Industries)
BJP	Bharatiya Janata Party
BMBF	Bundesministerium für Bildung und Forschung (Federal Ministry of Education and Research)
BPM5	Balance of payments manual, fifth edition
BPO	Business process outsourcing
c.i.f.	Cost, insurance, freight
CAGR	Compound annual growth rate
CARICOM	Caribbean Community
CD-ROM	Compact disc read-only memory
CEE	Central and Eastern Europe
CEEC	Central and Eastern European country
CEO	Chief executive officer
CER	Closer economic relations trade agreement between Australia and New Zealand
CMM	Capability maturity model
CMMI	Capability maturity model integration
CPF	Consumption possibility frontier
DBB	Deutsche Bundesbank (Federal Reserve Bank of Germany)
DEV	Developing countries
DGB	Deutscher Gewerkschaftsbund (Confederation of German Trade Unions)
DIHK	Deutscher Industrie- und Handelskammertag (Association of German Chambers of Industry and Commerce)

EC	European Community
EPL	Employment protection legislation
EU	European Union
FDI	Foreign direct investment
FOC	First order condition
FPE	Factor price equalization
FTA	Free trade agreement between Canada and the United States
FY	Financial year
GATS	General Agreement on Trade in Services
GDP	Gross domestic product
H_0	Null hypothesis
IAB	Institut für Arbeitsmarkt- und Berufsforschung (Institute for Employment Research)
ICT	Information and communication technology
IMF	International Monetary Fund
IPR	Intellectual property rights
ISDN	Integrated Services Digital Network
ISIC	International Standard Industrial Classification
ISP	Internet services provider
IT	Information technology
ITES	Information technology-enabled services
IV	Instrumental variables
LDC	Less developed country
LHS	Left-hand side
Log	Logarithmic
LP	Labor productivity
Ltd	Limited
M&A	Merger and acquisition
M	Million
m.f.n.	Most-favored-nation
MERCOSUR	Mercado Común del Sur
MII	Ministry of Information Industry
MINT	Mathematics, informatics, natural sciences, and technical engineering
MNC	Multinational company
MOFCOM	Ministry of Commerce
MPT	Ministry of Posts and Telecommunications
n.i.e.	Not included elsewhere
NAFTA	North American Free Trade Agreement
NMA	Northern and Middle America
NTP	National telecom policy
OIN	Other industrialized countries
OLS	Ordinary least squares
PCR	Privatization, competition and independent regulation

PhD	Doctor of Philosophy
PPF	Production possibility frontier
Prob	Probability
R&D	Research and development
resp.	Respectively
RHS	Right-hand side
RTA	Regional trade agreement
s.t.	Subject to
SNA	System of National Accounts
SSP	Specialized services provider
TAC	Transaction cost
TFP	Total factor productivity
Translog	Transcendental logarithmic
TRIPS	Trade-Related Aspects of Intellectual Property Rights
TWA	Temporary work agency
UK	United Kingdom
UN	United Nations
UNCTAD	United Nations Conference on Trade and Development
US	United States
WEU	Western Europe
WTO	World Trade Organization
ZDH	Zentralverband des Deutschen Handwerks (Association of German Craft and Trade Enterprises)

Variables

A	Sector A
a	Unit labor requirement = $1/\pi$
a_{HS}	Unit high-skilled labor requirement; amount of high-skilled labor used to perform a typical HS-task
a_{LS}	Unit less-skilled labor requirement; amount of less-skilled labor used to perform a typical LS-task
B	Sector B
C	Costs
C	Cost function
c_i	Unobserved time-constant sector-specific effect
CT	Total cost function
CV	Variable unit cost function, variable costs
DOM	Domestic materials outsourcing (= proportion of domestically purchased material inputs in total non-energy inputs)
DOS	Domestic services outsourcing (= proportion of domestically purchased service inputs in total non-energy inputs)
D	Good's demand
D_t	Unobserved cross-sector year fixed effect
EX	Exports
HS-tasks	Tasks performed by high-skilled labor
i	Sector dimension
IM	Imports
IM/Y	Import share = imports/output
INP	Non-energy inputs
j	Homogeneous input factor
K	Capital
K^{equip}	Capital spending on equipment
K^{build}	Capital spending on buildings
K/L	Capital intensity or capital-to-labor-ratio = capital/labor input
K/Y	Capital coefficient = capital/output
L	Labor

L_{HS}	High-skilled labor
L_{LS}	Less-skilled labor
LS-tasks	Tasks performed by less-skilled labor
M	Material input
MPK	Marginal product of capital
MPL	Marginal product of labor
OSM	Materials offshoring intensity (= proportion of imported material inputs in total non-energy inputs)
OSS	Services offshoring intensity (= proportion of imported service inputs in total non-energy inputs)
P	Output price
p	Input price
P^{TOT}	Terms-of-trade; relative price; price of export good/price of import good
P_j	Price of homogeneous input factor j
π	Labor productivity = output/labor input = $1/a$
r	Rental rate on capital
RD/Y	Research and development intensity = cumulated R&D-expenditures/output
S	Service input
$S_{HS} = L_{HS}/\mathrm{CV}$	Cost share of L_{HS} in variable costs CV
$S_{LS} = L_{LS}/\mathrm{CV}$	Cost share of L_{LS} in variable costs CV
T	Technology shifter
t	Time dimension
U	Utility
W	World
w	Wage
w_{HS}	Wage of high-skilled labor
w_{LS}	Wage of less-skilled labor
w^r	Real wage, i.e. wage divided by the unit price of output w/P
x	Some explanatory variable
X_j	Amount of homogeneous input factor j
Y	Output, good
Z_j	Quasi-fixed input factor
α	Demand elasticity of utility
$\varepsilon_{\mathrm{it}}$	Idiosyncratic error term (time- and sector-specific effect)
η_L	Price elasticity of demand for labor
η_Ω	Cross-elasticity of demand for labor due to a change in other input prices
η_Y	Employment-output elasticity
I	Index of the marginal task; fraction of LS-tasks performed abroad
σ	Elasticity of substitution
τ	Task

φ	Feasibility of offshoring (a higher feasibility is reflected by a lower φ)
Ω	Vector of input factors other than labor
ω	Vector of input prices other than wages
NB:	* as a superscript refers to the corresponding foreign variable. *A* or *B* as a subscript refer to the corresponding sector.

List of Figures

List of Tables

List of Boxes

Chapter 1
Introduction

Abstract Since the new tradability of services has made services vulnerable to relocation, the public awareness of services offshoring and its potential labor market effects has increased strongly. People's uncertainty and ignorance about the effects of services offshoring on the domestic labor market often encounter pessimistic press articles and contradictory statements by CEOs, politicians, and economists. Therefore, measuring the influence of services offshoring on the German labor market is extremely important. Socially, this study meets the interest of wide parts of the population, whose jobs have become vulnerable to relocation. Scientifically, our study remedies the lack and deficiencies of economic studies on this subject. The first chapter introduces three kinds of labor market effects: productivity, employment, and employment structure. Section 1.1 presents the development of each labor market effect in Germany, which is followed by a literature survey of existing studies that relate this effect to offshoring. Deficiencies of existing research, notably the lack of studies on services offshoring, are pointed out, motivating our own empirical analysis. Section 1.2 outlines the structure, contents, and methodology of this work. Although our focus is put on the specific German case, many insights of our work are also applicable to other developed countries.

1.1 Motivation

Intensifying globalization processes have coincided with low economic growth rates and high unemployment in Germany, especially in the 1990s. Globalization in the economic sense comprises the transnational movement of factors of production, goods, and services, which results in a higher degree of integration of international goods, money, and capital markets (Reining 2003). Trade and investment flows in particular have increased, which often leads to the one-sided conclusion that growing globalization causes negative labor market effects.

The latent fear of globalization is reflected in the German press. When German unemployment marked its historical peak of 5 M unemployed in 2004, the weekly

D. Winkler, *Services Offshoring and its Impact on the Labor Market*,
Contributions to Economics, DOI: 10.1007/978-3-7908-2199-4_1,

magazine *Stern* tried to brighten the "felt depression" and entitled the whole issue "Made in Germany – We are better than we believe" (Stern 2004). Although the number of unemployed has decreased over the subsequent years, mainly due to the recovering economy in Germany, the weekly magazine *Der Spiegel* titled its first June issue "Globalization: Winners–Losers" (Der Spiegel 2007). Globalization remains a subject of widespread concern, as the financial crisis of 2008, the catalyst for the worldwide economic downturn that has followed, shows. The popular belief that globalization may harm developed countries demands academic clarification.

Globalization processes have an impact on domestic labor markets via three main channels. First, integrated product markets intensify the *international goods and services trade*, which influences the labor market at home. Second, domestic labor markets can also be affected by economic integration via *foreign direct investment* (FDI) and the *fragmentation of production*. Both channels have an indirect effect on national labor markets, whereas the third channel addresses the direct labor market integration via *migration* (Landesmann 2000). Offshoring focuses a priori on the second channel, when multinational companies (MNCs) undertake parts of their production abroad. If the foreign production is followed by reimports to the country of origin, the first channel must also be considered. Regarding offshoring-induced labor market effects, economists distinguish between *quantitative labor market effects* e.g., the overall level of domestic employment, and *qualitative aspects* such as the distribution of employment or income. Concerning the latter, Anderton et al. (2002) note:

> "The notion of [...] [offshoring] [...] tends to find a significant impact of trade on the relative employment and wages of unskilled workers in industrialised countries (Anderton et al. 2002, p. 1)."

In Germany, the discussion of offshoring-induced labor market effects has gained momentum in recent years. Some "economic experts" put foreign investments on a level with German job exports, whereas many economists praise the development of falling market barriers, expecting increased economic efficiency. The following developments have contributed to a growing awareness of offshoring in Germany. First, the geographical and cultural proximity of the new Central and Eastern European Countries (CEECs) that have joined the European Union (EU) has fostered the offshoring discussion, since many of these countries provide workers, often German-speaking, at a lower wage level. At the political level, the president of the Association of German Chambers of Industry and Commerce (DIHK), Ludwig Georg Braun, recommended to domestic companies that they take advantage of the opportunities of the EU enlargement in March 2004. Former chancellor Gerhard Schröder blamed this as an "unpatriotic act".

A second novelty is the scope of activities being offshored. In recent years, it has extended to high-skilled jobs, while in the 1990s, cost-oriented offshoring focused on less-qualified activities. Newspaper headlines, such as "Long ago the Czech Republic was only subcontracting" published in *Die Welt* refer to this phenomenon (Schmidt 2004). Third, employment-related topics, such as the debate on minimum wages, are often associated with potential job relocations. Fourth, the shortage of skilled specialists in Germany in certain sectors is addressed by issuing Green Cards. Besides migration, offshoring constitutes the only short-term solution for domestic firms to counter the shortage of human capital. And fifth, economic slowdown like the current recession might incite domestic companies to cut costs by moving jobs offshore.

In the US, this public controversy reached a peak in the course of the presidential campaigns in 2004. Thus, globalization advocate N. Gregory Mankiw, former Chairman of the President's Council of Economic Advisers, outlined the positive aspects of international job relocations, whereas democratic candidate John Kerry criticized US firms that shift jobs abroad. Nobel prize laureate Samuelson (2004) argued with a theoretical Ricardian model that offshoring might provoke negative domestic labor market effects when the trade partner has productivity gains in its initially import-competing sector. That means that the trade partner gains some of the comparative advantage that was previously limited to the domestic economy. In this case, technological innovation could permanently reduce the per capita income in the country of origin (Samuelson 2004).

In more recent years, the newer phenomenon of *services offshoring* seems to dominate the offshoring debate. Services are of particular interest, since their significance has grown in terms of both quantity and quality. First, services trade has been fostered by a number of global drivers that have appeared simultaneously. One and a half decades ago, most services were considered non-tradable, but the emergence and development of new information and communication technologies (ICTs) has contributed to overcoming geographical distance. The move towards liberalization of international services trade has further accelerated this process. Second, offshoring of services appears to be much faster and less costly compared to offshoring of manufactured inputs, as neither large factory buildings nor assembly lines are needed.

The tradability of certain services, however, made negative labor market effects possible within the formerly inviolable service sector. Therefore, the above-mentioned concerns about traditional materials offshoring are also relevant for services. In the words of Gregory Mankiw:

> "We're very used to goods being produced abroad and being shipped here on ships or planes. What we are not used to is services being produced abroad and being sent here over the Internet or telephone wires. But does it matter from an economic standpoint whether values of items produced abroad come on planes and ships or over fiber-optic cables? Well, no, the economics is basically the same (Andrews 2004; taken from Bhagwati et al. 2004, pp. 93–94)."

In Germany, services offshoring is discussed in newspaper articles such as "High-tech jobs are migrating, too", which reports that domestic services in the information and technology (IT) sector, as well as call centers and accounting services, are relocated to less-developed countries (LDCs) in Asia and Eastern Europe. Jörg Menno Harms, then Chief Executive Officer (CEO) of Hewlett-Packard Germany, is quoted in this article predicting that the offshoring of software and services follows the manufacturing sector to low-income countries, but at a much faster pace

(Stuttgarter Zeitung 2004). "IG-Metall: 10,000 jobs threatened – Siemens Group also wants to use cheap locations for administration and engineering jobs" indicates the new quality of services offshoring (Magenheim-Hörrmann 2004). In the US, free trade advocate Alan Blinder's (2007b) estimations on the potential offshorability of 30–40 M American service jobs is quoted in newspaper articles, such as "Pain from free trade spurs second thoughts" in the *Wall Street Journal* (Wessel and Davis 2007) or "Free trade's great, but offshoring rattles me" in the *Washington Post* (Blinder 2007a).

People's uncertainty and ignorance about the effects of services offshoring on the domestic labor market often encounter pessimistic press articles and contradictory statements by CEOs, politicians, and economists. Therefore, measuring the influence of services offshoring on the German labor market is extremely important. Socially, this study meets the interest of wide parts of the population, whose jobs have become vulnerable to relocation. Scientifically, our study remedies the lack and deficiencies of economic studies on this subject, as highlighted in the following.

Empirical research on services offshoring and its potential labor market effects can give valuable insights into the direction and the extent to which offshoring has influenced domestic labor markets. Scientifically, the services offshoring debate in Germany is not yet well established. Even in the Anglo-Saxon countries there is a shortage of economic research. German studies dealing with labor market effects suffer from four main deficits. First, German empirical research focuses more on materials offshoring and has not yet integrated tradable services. Second, to our knowledge, there are only a few empirical studies for Germany at a sectoral level. Third, most studies focus either on the effects of offshore outsourcing or on FDI. Only a few studies consider both simultaneously in their empirical analyses. Fourth, German studies including service inputs stress some aspects but neglect others. For example, Görzig and Stephan (2002) do not differentiate between domestic and foreign service purchases when studying the effects of services outsourcing on firm-level performance. The McKinsey Global Institute measures the welfare gain of services offshoring for the US, Germany, and France, but does not clearly reveal the underlying method. According to this study, Germany experiences a welfare loss of 26% (Farrel 2004; McKinsey Global Institute 2005). Falk and Koebel (2002) only consider the impact of domestically purchased services and imported material inputs on the domestic labor demand structure. Moreover, they use data from 1978 to 1990, which do not cover the relevant ICT-period.

In the following subsections, we focus on three labor market effects: productivity, employment level, and employment structure. Each subsection presents the development of the corresponding labor market effect in Germany, which is followed by a literature survey of existing studies that relate this effect to offshoring. Deficiencies of existing research, notably the lack of studies on services offshoring, are pointed out, motivating our own empirical analysis.

The main contributions of our empirical studies are the following. First, we use newly published revised input–output data for the period from 1995 to 2004, making this the first study, to our knowledge, that reflects the relevant ICT-period. Using current data is very important: Hutzschenreuter et al. (2007) find that the bulk of offshored corporate functions in German firms took place between 1999 and 2005. Second, we differentiate not only between imported service and material inputs but also between domestically produced service and material inputs, which has not so far been done in other studies. Thus, we are able to detect the individual effects of services and materials offshoring as well as domestic services and materials outsourcing. Third, our calculations of German offshoring intensities are based on published German import matrices, whereas many other studies only use proxy variables for imported inputs. Fourth, we measure the effects of services offshoring on productivity, labor demand, and the relative demand for less-skilled labor.

1.1.1 Productivity

Figure 1.1 plots the development of German productivity, measured as total factor productivity (TFP) and labor productivity (LP) between 1991 and 2003. TFP is measured as TFP growth rates in percentage points (see bars in Fig. 1.1). Except for 1993, TFP growth was always positive, with fluctuations. The measure of LP uses volume indices with 1995 as the base year (1995 = 100). LP per person rose from a level of 91.8 in 1991 to a level of 110.5 in 2003, which represents an increase of 18.7 percentage points (see grey line in Fig. 1.1). LP per hour started at 90.4 and rose to the level of 118.5 in 2003, which translates into an increase of 28.1 percentage points over the period (see black line in Fig. 1.1). The rise in TFP and LP could be due to an increase in offshoring intensity; consequently, the first empirical study of this work is dedicated to assessing the link between German productivity growth and offshoring.

Remarkably, there is no empirical research on potential *productivity effects* of German services offshoring, especially at a sectoral level. Even the Anglo-Saxon

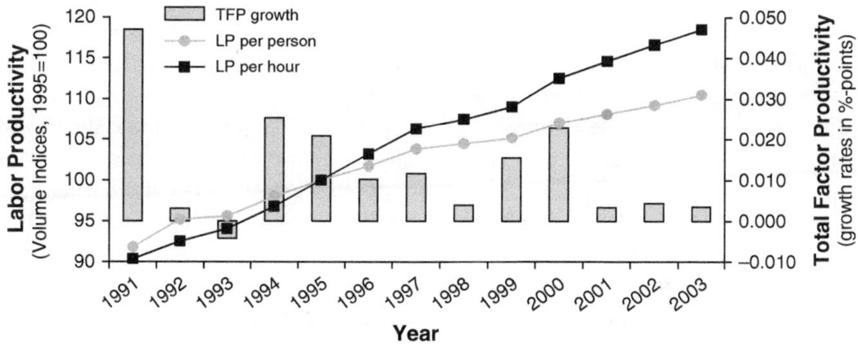

Fig. 1.1 German productivity development
Source: own illustration. Data: labor productivity: Groningen growth and development centre, 60-industry database, March 2006, http://www.ggdc.net, updated from O'Mahony and van Ark (2003); Total factor productivity: Timmer et al. (2003), Appendix tables, updated June 2005

countries show few empirical studies. In the US, Mann (2003) calculates the productivity effect of services offshoring in the IT industry between 1995 and 2002. She finds that real GDP growth increased by 0.3 percentage points per year. The aforementioned McKinsey Global Institute report (2005) finds a welfare gain of services offshoring for the US of around 14–17%. Amiti and Wei (2006) find positive evidence of services offshoring on TFP and LP in the manufacturing sectors. Thus, services offshoring had a significantly positive impact on US productivity between 1992 and 2000, which is estimated at a sectoral level. Görg and Hanley (2003) analyze the impact of services offshoring on LP for Ireland using plant level data. The effect was positive in the electronics industry between 1990 and 1995.[1] In a more recent plant-level study, Görg, Hanley, and Strobl (2008) evaluate the productivity effects of materials and services offshoring for Irish manufacturing for the period 1990–1998, differentiating between exporting and non-exporting firms. They find a significantly positive impact of services offshoring on TFP of exporting firms.

Schöller (2007b) finds that services offshoring significantly increased TFP and LP in German manufacturing between 1995 and 2004. Our study therefore contributes to the scarce empirical literature and is, to our knowledge, the first German study at a sectoral level. Table 1.1 gives a literature survey of offshoring-induced labor market effects.

1.1.2 Employment Level

Considering the development of the overall employment level, i.e., the absolute number of employees in Germany, would not be meaningful. A better approach is to calculate the absolute number of employees relative to a reference number. The employment-to-population ratio constitutes one alternative. A second option would be to use the economy's total civilian labor force as denominator. The unemployment rate, defined as the number of unemployed (instead of employees) relative to the total civilian labor force, is a modification of the second alternative and is the most commonly used measurement of employment.

Figure 1.2 shows the development of the seasonally adjusted annual unemployment rate for Germany between 1969 and 2007. Unemployment rose strongly as a result of the first and second oil price shock in 1973 and 1979–1980 and German reunification in 1990. The unemployment rate for unified Germany increased from 5.7% in 1991 to the level of 9.0% in 2007, which constitutes an average compound annual growth rate (CAGR) of 3.0%. Thus, the German unemployment rate follows a growing trend (see dashed trend line) since the mid-1970s, while other EU countries such as Ireland, Sweden, Finland, Denmark, the UK, and Spain were

[1]For a literature survey of more recent contributions on the relationship between outsourcing, efficiency, and productivity, see, e.g., Heshmati (2003).

Table 1.1 Labor market effects of offshoring – survey of literature

Source	Country	Industry	Sectors	Years	Effects of offshoring		
Dependent variable: productivity					Materials	Services	Overall
Mann (2003)	US	IT		1995–2002		+	
Görg and Hanley (2003)[a]	Ireland	Electr.[b]		1990–1995	No ev.	+	
Amiti and Wei (2004, 2006)[a]	US	Mfg.	96	1992–2002	+	+	
Schöller (2007a)[a]	Germany	Mfg.	35	1995–2004	+	+	
Görg et al. (2008)[c]	Ireland	Mfg.[b]		1990–1998	No ev.	+	
Dependent variable: labor demand					Materials	Services	Overall
Amiti and Wei (2006)[a]	US	Mfg.	450	1992–2001	+	–	
			96		+	+	
Amiti and Wei (2005)[a]	UK	Mfg.	69	1995–2001	+/–	+	
		Service	9		–	–	
Schöller (2007c)[a]	Germany	Mfg.	36	1991–2000	–	–	
Schöller (2007a)[a]	Germany	Mfg.	35	1995–2004	–	–	
OECD (2007)[a]	12 OECD	Mfg.	26	1995, 2000			–
		Service					–
Dependent variable: relative demand for less-skilled labor					Materials	Services	Overall
Falk and Koebel (2002)[d]	Germany	Mfg.	26	1978–1990	No ev.		
Geishecker (2002)[d]	Germany	Mfg.	22	1991–2000	–		
Strauss-Kahn (2003)[e]	France	Mfg.	Not rep.	1977–1993	–		
Hijzen et al. (2005)[d]	UK	Mfg.	50	1982–1996	–		
Ekholm and Hakkala (2006)[d]	Sweden	Mfg.	20	1995–2000	–[f]		
Geishecker (2006)[d]	Germany	Mfg.	23	1991–2000	–[g]		
Schöller (2007b)[a]	Germany	Mfg.	28	1991–2000	–	–	

(*continued*)

Table 1.1 (continued)

Source	Country	Industry	Sectors	Years	Effects of offshoring		
Dependent variable: relative demand for high-skilled labor					Materials	Services	Overall
Feenstra and Hanson (1996)[a]	US	Mfg.	450	1977–1993	+		
Feenstra and Hanson (1999)[d]	US	Mfg.	450	1979–1990	+		
Falk and Koebel (2002)[d]	Germany	Mfg.	26	1978–1990	No ev.		
Ekholm and Hakkala (2006)[d]	Sweden	Mfg.	20	1995–2000	+[h]		
					+[i]		

Source: own illustration
[a]Imported inputs/total (non-energy) inputs
[b]Firm-level study
[c]Imported inputs/total wage bill
[d]Imported inputs from same sector/output
[e]Vertical specialization
[f]Medium-skill employment
[g]To CEECs
[h]To low-income countries
[i]Inhouse–offshoring

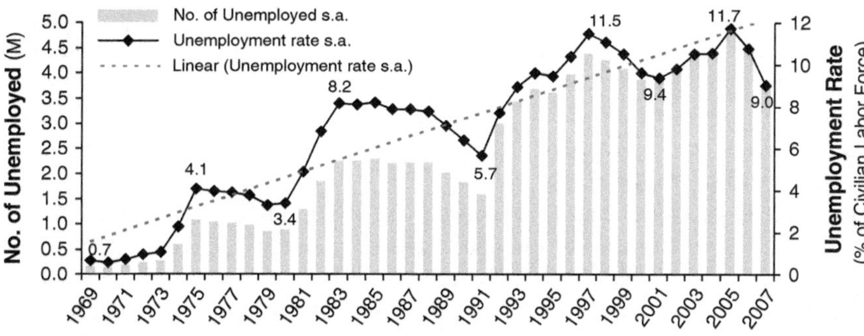

Fig. 1.2 Annual unemployment rates in Germany (seasonally adjusted)
Source: own illustration. Data: OECD labor statistics. NB: unemployment data are seasonally adjusted. Unemployment rates are measured as number of unemployed as a percentage of the civilian labor force (the dependant civilian labor force, the self-employed and family workers)

able to reduce their unemployment rates from the beginning of the 1990s onward (see Hagemann and Rukwid 2007).

The reasons for the increase in German unemployment are numerous. Keynesian unemployment is caused by a lack of aggregate demand for goods and services, and thus for labor, due to a downturn of the business cycle. Classical unemployment occurs when real wages are higher than the market-clearing level. Here, market forces are unable to swing, for instance due to public interventionism and strong regulations in (setting) work conditions and wages. Structural unemployment can be caused by a failure of the labor force to adapt rapidly to new challenges, such as globalization and technological progress. Since the process of increasing globalization seems to be accompanied by growing unemployment in industrialized countries, economists have analyzed the linkage between globalization-related processes like offshoring and labor demand. Studies are scarce, and there are only a few studies that evaluate the effect of offshoring on domestic employment.

The impact of services and materials offshoring on the *employment level* has been empirically measured for the US by Amiti and Wei (2006). At a highly disaggregated sectoral level (450 industries), they derive a significantly negative effect, whereby services offshoring reduced manufacturing employment by 0.4–0.7% per year between 1992 and 2001. At a more aggregated level (96 industries), the negative effect disappears. The authors explain this phenomenon with the potential of services offshoring to increase efficiency in certain sectors which leads to the creation of new jobs in other sectors. Amiti and Wei (2005) test the impact of services and materials offshoring on home employment for the UK between 1995 and 2001. Examining 69 manufacturing industries, they find a significantly positive correlation between services offshoring and employment, and cite the same explanation as in their US study. Thus, a 1% increase of services offshoring led at least to a 0.085% increase in employment. The impact of materials offshoring was ambiguous and insignificant.

Schöller (2007a) analyzes the impact of services offshoring on German employment between 1991 and 2000 for 36 manufacturing industries and finds evidence of a negative impact. Materials offshoring also had a negative influence in some specifications. In a second study, Schöller (2007b) finds that services offshoring reduced manufacturing employment (35 industries), using revised input–output data from 1995 to 2004.

The OECD (2007) measures the effects of offshoring for 12 OECD countries (Austria, Belgium, Denmark, Finland, France, Germany, Greece, Italy, Korea, Norway, Sweden, United States). Three types of models are estimated, which all cover 26 manufacturing and service industries for the two years 1995 and 2000, i.e., growth rates from 1995 to 2000 are used in the regressions. The results indicate a significantly negative effect of offshoring on manufacturing and service employment, respectively. They use an overall offshoring intensity measure that includes both imported service and material inputs.

1.1.3 Employment Structure

The overall employment level considers labor as a homogeneous input factor, whereas employment structure differentiates between different types of heterogeneous labor. Labor can be classified, e.g., according to its level of qualification. In Germany and in other developed countries, less-skilled workers face a higher risk of unemployment or wage cuts compared to their high-skilled counterparts. The development of German qualification-specific unemployment rates is shown in Fig. 1.3. Three qualification levels, namely primary, secondary, and tertiary education, are taken into account. Obviously, people with tertiary education – the highest educational attainment – have the lowest risk of unemployment. Thus, their unemployment rates remained stable at around 4% between 1991 and 2004.

Employees with secondary education, i.e., vocational education and training, faced a slightly higher unemployment rate of 5.6% in 1991, which rose steadily to 9.9% in 2004. Hence, their unemployment rate increased by 4.3 percentage points over the period, or by on average 4.5% per year. People with primary education, the lowest educational attainment, do not possess any vocational education. In 1991, their unemployment rate averaged 14.5% and climbed to 24.6% in 2004. This constitutes a growth of more than ten percentage points over the period, or a CAGR of 4.1%.

While the higher jobless rate among less-skilled labor is generally not questioned, the underlying causes for that fact are not unanimously accepted. What explains a rise in the relative remuneration of high-qualified labor? The debate centers around two main arguments. *Increase in internal trade* was named as the main reason. Empirical studies often denied that international trade had harmed less-qualified jobs in the 1980s. Newer studies provide evidence of an increased risk to less-skilled labor in developed countries due to trade during the 1990s. Since the relative appreciation of human capital is observed more strongly within than

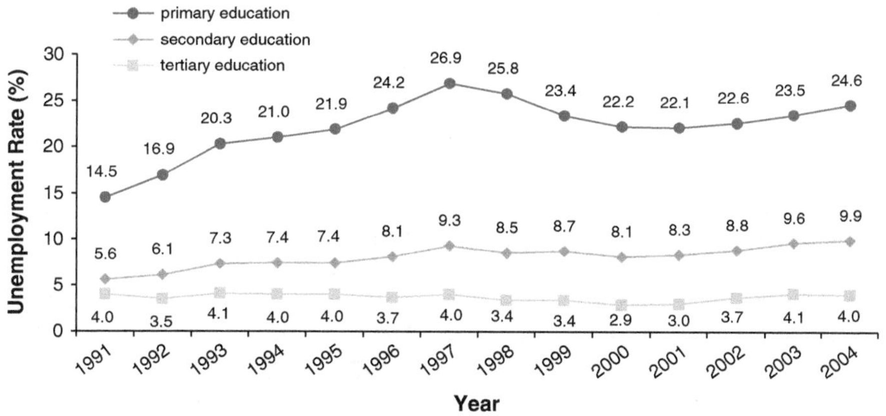

Fig. 1.3 Qualification-specific unemployment rates in Germany 1991–2004
Source: own illustration. Data: Reinberg and Hummel (2005). Unemployment rates are calculated as a percentage of civilian labor force (without apprentices) of the same qualification. Employees without any information on educational attainment according to the micro-census are proportionally distributed to all qualification levels. Primary education includes people without vocational qualification. Secondary education includes people with vocational education and training. Tertiary education includes people with a master's (and other university degrees) or bachelor's (and Fachhochschulabschluss) degree

between industries, economists suggested *skill-biased technological progress* as a main driver. This initiated the *trade versus technology debate* in the mid-1990s.

Under the assumption of downward wage rigidities, the intra-industrial appreciation of human capital does not preclude the results of standard trade theory, whereby less-qualified labor is systematically squeezed out of the labor market (Geishecker 2002). According to this reasoning, international trade is still considered a possible explanation for the appreciation of high-skilled labor. Feenstra and Hanson (2001) also argue for international trade as the main driver behind the appreciation of high-skilled labor:

> "The argument against trade is based, in part, on a misreading of the data. Stable trade to GDP ratios, an apparent increase in the relative price of skill-intensive goods, and employment shifts towards skilled workers that occur mainly within, rather than between, industries are all cited as evidence that trade cannot have contributed to rising [. . .] inequality. This line of reasoning emphasizes trade in final goods and ignores the globalization of production and recent dramatic increases in trade in intermediate inputs (Feenstra and Hanson 2001, p. 46)."

Advocates of the skill-biased technological progress argue primarily with arguments based on trade in *final goods*. However, the globalization of production has resulted in growing international trade flows in *intermediate goods*. Relating to offshoring in general and services offshoring in particular, imported intermediate goods and services could substitute for less-skilled labor in certain industries, which would explain the appreciation of human capital within industries. The sourcing of intermediate inputs to labor-abundant low-wage countries would indeed yield a skill-bias within industries, as activities with lower skill-intensities are more likely produced abroad. Besides skill-intensity, offshoring depends on the industries' structure and the offshorability of certain activities. Services offshoring in particular can lead to an intra-industrial downward shift of less-skilled labor, because services are expected to have a sector-specific influence on employment. Like skill-biased technological progress, services offshoring could lead to intra-sectoral rather than inter-sectoral appreciation of human capital. Besides trade and technological progress, Rukwid (2007) lists the insufficient skill-adaptation of labor supply, increased labor participation of women, institutional changes, and a decreasing relevance of the manufacturing sectors as factors that contribute to the worsening employment and income situation of less-skilled labor (Rukwid 2007).

Studies on the effects of offshoring on *employment structure* focus on the relative demand for heterogeneous labor, which is determined by the cost share of specific labor in the sector's total wage bill wL, where w denotes the wage rate and L labor input. If we consider less-skilled labor L_{LS} as specific labor input, its cost share would be $S_{LS} = w_{LS}L_{LS}/wL$. This cost share S_{LS} can be interpreted in a twofold way. On the one hand, it reflects the relative demand for less-skilled labor L_{LS}, while on the other hand, it also reflects the relative wage of less-skilled labor w_{LS}. The following studies focus on the first interpretation and analyze the impact of offshoring on the *relative demand for less-skilled labor* (see Table 1.1).

Falk and Koebel (2002) studied the effects of materials offshoring on the relative demand for less-skilled labor in Germany. The authors found no evidence that imported materials substituted for unskilled labor in the 26 manufacturing sectors between 1978 and 1990. Geishecker (2002) finds that materials offshoring had a negative impact on the relative demand for less-skilled workers in 22 German manufacturing sectors between 1991 and 2000, but skill-biased technological change is at least as important as offshoring to explain the decrease of the relative demand for less-skilled labor. In a more recent study, Geishecker (2006) finds evidence of a significantly negative effect of offshoring to CEECs on the relative demand for less-skilled labor. In addition to materials offshoring, Schöller (2007c) also includes services offshoring in her study. Her results show that services offshoring significantly reduced the relative demand for less-skilled labor. Materials offshoring also shows negative (but in absolute terms rather smaller) coefficients, which are significant in many specifications.

Strauss-Kahn (2003) finds that imported material inputs had a negative impact on the relative demand for unskilled workers in French manufacturing sectors in the period from 1977 to 1993. Hijzen et al. (2005) demonstrate a strongly negative materials offshoring-induced effect on unskilled labor in 50 manufacturing sectors for the UK between 1982 and 1996. Ekholm and Hakkala (2006) analyze the impact of offshoring on manufacturing workers with different educational attainments for Sweden between 1995 and 2000. They distinguish between offshoring to low-income and high-income countries, and include 20 manufacturing industries in their study. Offshoring to low-income countries tends to shift labor demand away from domestic workers with an intermediate level of education.

Some of the studies mentioned above explicitly measure the effect of offshoring on the *relative demand for high-skilled labor*. Falk and Koebel (2002) find no evidence of substitutability between materials offshoring and high-skill employment in German manufacturing, whereas Ekholm and Hakkala (2006) show that materials offshoring to low-income countries and in-house-offshoring both significantly increased the relative demand for high-skilled labor in Swedish manufacturing. Other studies that only consider the two variable inputs less-skilled and high-skilled labor (e.g., Geishecker 2002, 2006; Schöller 2007c; Strauss-Kahn 2003), implicitly measure the effects of offshoring on high-skill employment, since only one cost share is linearly independent (see Sect. 5.3.1.1). Feenstra and Hanson (1996, 1999) focus on the second interpretation of the cost share, namely the relative wage. They find that imported material inputs significantly increased the relative wage of high-skilled labor in 450 US manufacturing sectors. They consider the period from 1977 to 1993 in their study from 1996, and the period from 1979 to 1990 in their study from 1999.

Except for Schöller (2007c), none of the aforementioned studies consider the effects of services offshoring. Our contribution is to distinguish between services and materials offshoring when analyzing the impact on the demand for heterogeneous labor. To our knowledge, this is the first study for Germany at a sectoral level that evaluates the impact of services offshoring on the relative demand for less-skilled labor.

1.2 Outline and Methodology

The following section outlines the structure, contents, and methodology of this work. Chapter 2 is subdivided into the two sections: Sects. 2.1 and 2.2. Section 2.1 examines how services offshoring is defined, which forms it can take, and which service activities are involved. In Sect. 2.1.1, we compare and contrast outsourcing and offshoring before deriving our own working definition of services offshoring. Section 2.1.2 focuses on the *service* part of services offshoring. First, we define services and the uno-actu-principle. Then, we describe the implications of the new tradability of services. Second, we classify services trade depending on the geographical location of the agents on the one hand, and the classification of the General Agreement on Trade in Services (GATS) by modes of supply on the other hand. Third, we categorize the relevant service activities, starting with an overview of several classification possibilities and then differentiating between business activities, other commercial services, other business services, technological services, and information technology and business process outsourcing (BPO) services. Section 2.1.3 focuses on the *offshoring* part of services offshoring and stresses the fact that offshoring can take two generic forms: in-house production and external procurement from independent suppliers. The decision for either one is theoretically discussed in efficiency-based, resource-based, and transaction costs-based theories of the firm.

Section 2.2 explains the main reasons why the phenomenon of services offshoring has rapidly gained in importance. It is subdivided into three subsections. Section 2.2.1 describes changes in the global environment, namely developments in ICTs as well as multilateral and regional liberalization of trade in services, which have been driving services offshoring. Section 2.2.2 focuses on the decision-making unit in the offshoring process – the firms. Firms have various offshoring motives, which are mainly classified as market-oriented, cost-oriented, and procurement-oriented. The latter motive originally referred to the provision of raw materials and other intermediate products, but has now been extended to the procurement of human capital or strategic assets. Section 2.2.3 focuses on the host countries, i.e., the local environment of the foreign production plant, which functions as a pull-factor for services offshoring. Here, the availability of human capital in LDCs, the presence of MNCs, and the liberalization of services sectors need to be mentioned.

In Chap. 3, we use descriptive statistics to identify the position of German services offshoring relative to other countries, the main service sectors being offshored as well as the main destination countries. Section 3.1 gives an overview of the largest offshoring countries in both absolute and relative terms (Sect. 3.1.1). For this purpose, import data of the selected four services categories "computer and information services", "other business services", "communication services", and "financial services" for the year 2005 are used as a proxy for services offshoring. The data are based on the IMF Balance of Payments statistics. Since the worldwide comparison only captures a single point of time, we further compare the development of German services offshoring to selected OECD countries, namely France, Japan, the UK, and the US, applying the same methodology as previously described (Sect. 3.1.2). Finally, we use the calculation of services offshoring intensities based on input–output data as a more sophisticated measure of services offshoring (Sect. 3.1.3). Services offshoring intensities measure the proportion of imported service inputs in total non-energy inputs used in home production and are calculated at a sectoral basis. German offshoring intensities are then compared to previously available offshoring intensities for the UK and the US.

Section 3.2 identifies the main offshoring sectors as well as the kind of service activities that are most commonly being offshored. First, we discuss the global development (Sect. 3.2.1) before moving on to specific trends in Germany (Sect. 3.2.2). We use import data from the Deutsche Bundesbank, which are based on the German Balance of Payments statistics as well as input–output data. Section 3.3 presents the major destination countries from a global and a German perspective. We detect the "Destinations of Global Services Offshoring" (Sect. 3.3.1) from existing studies and from IMF Balance of Payments data, and identify "Destinations of German Services Offshoring" (Sect. 3.3.2) by using import data from the Deutsche Bundesbank.

Chapter 4 evaluates how existing classical and neoclassical theories have modeled offshoring with a focus on the labor market and national welfare effects. Section 4.1 begins with "Offshoring of Final Goods". Precisely, we focus on offshoring in the Ricardian, Heckscher–Ohlin, and Specific-Factors models.

We use the Samuelson model (2004) as an example of a Ricardian trade model with final goods (Sect. 4.1.1). The model begins with "Offshoring in a Two-Goods Model with Autarky" and shows numerically how two countries – a developed and a developing country – gain from trade compared to their autarky equilibrium. In a next step, Samuelson (2004) evaluates how "Technological Progress in the Two-Goods Model" changes the initial trade equilibrium, distinguishing between technological progress in the developing country's export sector and its import sector. Section 4.1.2 focuses on "The Heckscher–Ohlin Model". We introduce the basic model before moving on to the "Free Trade Equilibrium and Four Theorems" in a second step. Finally, Sect. 4.1.3 centers on "The Specific-Factors Model" presenting the model of Bhagwati et al. (2004). We begin with "Offshoring in a Two-Goods Model" before turning to "The Welfare Effects of Offshoring".

Section 4.2 focuses on "Offshoring of Intermediate Goods". We present the general equilibrium model of Grossman and Rossi-Hansberg (2006a, b), which includes a continuum of intermediate inputs and allows for two, three, or many factors of production. In a first step, we introduce "The Basic Model" (Sect. 4.2.1). Hereby, we show how trade in tasks is modeled before evaluating the effects of falling offshoring costs. In a next step, Grossman and Rossi-Hansberg (2006a, b) study "Different Scenarios"(Sect. 4.2.2) focusing on the effects of offshoring low-skill-intensive tasks in a small and in a large economy, the labor-supply effect, and offshoring of skill-intensive tasks.

Chapter 5 constitutes the major contribution of this work. It comprises a collection of three empirical studies: "Services Offshoring and its Impact on Productivity in Germany", "Services Offshoring and its Impact on Labor Demand in Germany", and "Services Offshoring and its Impact on the Relative Demand for Less-Skilled Labor in Germany". The studies are all divided into the three subsections "Basics of the Empirical Analysis", "Estimations with Unrevised Input–Output Data: 1991–2000", and "Estimations with Revised Input–Output Data: 1995–2004". Dividing our estimations into two periods is necessary due to the revision of the German input–output data and the resulting structural break. The estimations focus on the labor market effects in the manufacturing sectors. We include 36 manufacturing sectors of the input–output classification in all studies except for Sect. 4.3.2, where the sectors are aggregated to 28. We use two different estimation methods for all of our studies, which increases the reliability of our estimation results. In a first step, we use the consistent fixed effects estimators. Second, we apply the instrumental variables two-stage least squares fixed effects estimator to address the potential endogeneity of some variables.

Section 5.1 studies the effects of services offshoring on TFP and LP. Section 5.1.1 begins with the theoretical and empirical model. According to the Solow growth decomposition, a firm's linearly homogeneous production function can be subdivided into the growth rates of the input factors and the growth rate of an unexplained residual, called TFP. Besides efficiency, the rate of technology T is considered the most important part of TFP, defined as a function of services and materials offshoring, domestic services and materials outsourcing as well as research and development (R&D)-intensity. Output is assumed to depend on T and other factors of production, namely labor, capital, service inputs, and material inputs, which are estimated in log-linear form. We hypothesize that services offshoring increases productivity, before moving to the description of the data. Section 5.1.2 gives first indications in support of our conjecture, then turns to the estimation results. The results indicate that services offshoring significantly increased TFP between 1991 and 2000. One possibility to address the potential endogeneity of labor, real services, and real materials is to choose LP as the dependent variable. The estimation results show that services offshoring had a positive impact on LP between 1991 and 2000. The same structure is used for our "Estimations with Revised Input–Output Data: 1995–2004" (Sect. 5.1.3), which confirm the positive productivity effects.

Section 5.2 starts with "The Basics of the Empirical Analysis" (Sect. 5.2.1). The theoretical model derives the labor demand specification of Hamermesh (1993) from a linearly homogeneous cost function of a firm, applying Shephard's Lemma. The conditional labor demand function depends on output, wages, and other input prices as exogenous variables. The empirical model concretizes other input prices and uses services and materials offshoring intensities, domestic services and materials outsourcing intensities as well as R&D-intensity as inverse proxies for the input prices of foreign and domestically purchased service and material inputs as well as technology. We also present an unconditional labor demand function where the output price is substituted for the profit-maximizing output level. We conjecture that services offshoring affects labor demand negatively and describe the data used to test our hypothesis. Section 5.2.2 shows that services offshoring was negatively related to manufacturing employment in Germany between 1991 and 2000. Section 5.2.3 follows the same methodology and confirms the negative employment effects, which are stronger and more significant.

Section 5.3 considers two types of labor. Section 5.3.1 presents a static partial equilibrium model, which is based on a variable unit cost function as introduced by Brown and Christensen (1981) allowing for quasi-fixed input factors. Applying Shephard's Lemma to the general transcendental logarithmic form of the variable unit cost function yields the corresponding factor demand, which is the factor's share in total variable costs, as the cost function is in logarithmic form. We distinguish between production and non-production workers, defining the first as less-skilled labor. The share of less-skilled labor in total variable costs constitutes the dependent variable, while output, relative wages, capital intensity, services and materials offshoring intensities, domestic services and materials outsourcing intensities, as well as R&D-intensity are the explanatory variables. The predictions from the model lead to the conjecture that services offshoring is expected to release rather less-skilled than high-skilled labor. Section 5.3.2 begins with preliminary predictions before moving on to the empirical results. Our estimation results show that services offshoring significantly reduced the relative demand for less-skilled labor in the German manufacturing sectors between 1991 and 2000. The "Estimations with Revised Input–Output Data: 1995–2004" follow the same structure, but indicate a shift towards a decline in the relative demand for high-skilled labor due to services offshoring.

Chapter 6 is subdivided into the two sections: Sects. 6.1 and 6.2. The first section summarizes the main findings of our study. The second section deduces possible implications and economic policy recommendations for Germany. Our own results, combined with the literature survey, indicate that besides Germany, other developed countries have also experienced negative labor market effects due to offshoring. Therefore, we consider labor market insecurity (Sect. 6.2.1) one of the most important implications of services offshoring. We compare the "Perceptions of Labor Market Insecurity" and the development of "Unemployment, Inequality, and the Burden of Risk" in Germany with Denmark, France, Japan, the United Kingdom, and the United States.

Section 6.2.2 addresses two aspects of labor markets, namely security and flexibility. "Different Country Models" are identified with respect to labor support and labor market flexibility. Section 6.2.2.2 analyzes different measures and reforms to promote flexicurity, i.e., high labor support and low to medium labor market flexibility, in Germany. Section 6.2.3 addresses the necessity of an "Effective Education Policy" to counteract the shortage of human capital in Germany. We first describe the measures that have been taken in the last years to reduce the "Shortage of Workers with Vocational Education". We also show that less measures have been taken to face the "Shortage of Workers with Tertiary Education".

References

Amiti M, Wei S-J (2005) Fear of service outsourcing: is it justified? Economic Policy 20(42): 308–347

Amiti M, Wei S-J (2006) Service offshoring, productivity and employment: evidence from the US. CEPR Discussion Paper, No. 5475, February 2006

Anderton B, Brenton P, Oscarsson E (2002) Outsourcing and inequality. CEPS Working Document, No. 187, October 2002

Andrews, Edmund L (2004) Democrats criticize bush over job exports, New York Times, 11 February 2004, p. A26

Bhagwati J, Panagariya A, Srinivasan TN (2004) The muddles over outsourcing. J Econ Perspect 18(4):93–114

Blinder AS (2007a) Free trade's great, but offshoring rattles me. Washington Post

Blinder AS (2007b) How many U.S. jobs might be offshorable? CEPS Working Paper Princeton University, No. 142, March 2007

Brown RS, Christensen LR (1981) Estimating elasticities of substitution in a model of partial static equilibrium: an application to US agriculture, 1947–1974. In: Berndt ER, Field BC (eds) Modeling and measuring natural resource substitution. MIT Press, Cambridge, MA, pp 209–229

Der Spiegel (2007) Globalisierung: gewinner – verlierer. Der Spiegel, 23

Ekholm K, Hakkala K (2006) The effect of offshoring on labour demand: evidence from Sweden. CEPR Discussion Paper, No. 5648, April 2006

Falk M, Koebel BM (2002) Outsourcing, imports and labour demand. Scand J Econ 104(4):567–586

Farrel D (2004) Can Germany win from offshoring, July 2004. McKinsey Global Institute

Feenstra RC, Hanson GH (1996) Globalization, outsourcing and wage inequality. Am Econ Rev 86(2):240–245

Feenstra RC, Hanson GH (1999) The impact of outsourcing and high-technology capital on wages: Estimates for the United States, 1979–1990. Quart J Econ 114(3):907–940

Feenstra RC, Hanson GH (2001) Global production sharing and rising inequality: a survey of trade and wages. NBER Working Paper, No. 8372, July 2001

Geishecker I (2002) Outsourcing and the demand for low-skilled labour in German manufacturing: new evidence. DIW Discussion Paper, No. 313, November 2002

Geishecker I (2006) Does outsourcing to central and eastern Europe really threaten Manual Workers' Jobs in Germany? The World Econ 29(5):559–583

Görg H, Hanley A (2003) International outsourcing and productivity: evidence from plant level data. Research Paper Series: globalisation, productivity and technology, No. 20/2003. University of Nottingham

Görg H, Hanley A, Strobl E (2008) Productivity effects of international outsourcing: evidence from plant-level data. Can J Econ 41(2):670–688

Görzig B, Stephan A (2002) Outsourcing and firm-level performance. DIW Discussion Paper, No. 309, October 2002

Grossman GM, Rossi-Hansberg E (2006a) The rise of offshoring: it's not wine for cloth anymore. Paper presented at The New Economic Geography: Effects and Policy Implications. Federal Reserve Bank of Kansas City, Jackson Hole, pp 59–102

Grossman GM, Rossi-Hansberg E (2006b) Trading tasks: a simple theory of offshoring. NBER Working Paper, No. 12721, December 2006

Hagemann H, Rukwid R (2007) Perspectives of workers with low qualifications in Germany under the pressures of globalization and technical progress. Hohenheim Discussion Papers, No. 291. University of Hohenheim, Stuttgart

Hamermesh D (1993) Labor demand. Princeton University Press, Princeton, NJ

Heshmati A (2003) Productivity growth, efficiency and outsourcing in manufacturing and service industries. J Econ Surv 17(1):79–112

Hijzen A, Görg H, Hine RC (2005) International outsourcing and the skill structure of labour demand in the United Kingdom. Econ J 115(506): 860–878

Hutzschenreuter T, Dressel S, Ressler W (2007). Offshoring von Zentralbereichen, Von den Erfahrungen deutscher und amerikanischer Unternehmen lernen. Springer, Berlin

Landesmann M (2000). Migration und Arbeitsmarkteffekte der EU-Erweiterung. Die Union – Vierteljahreszeitschrift für Integrationsfragen 3:15–40

Magenheim-Hörrmann T (2004) IG-Metall: 10,000 Arbeitsplätze bedroht. Stuttgarter Zeitung, 23 March 2004

Mann C (2003) Globalization of IT services and white collar jobs: the next wave of productivity growth. Int Econ Policy Briefs, (PB03–11): Institute for International Economics. Retrieved from http://www.iie.com/publications/pb/pb03–11.pdf

McKinsey Global Institute (2005) How offshoring of services could benefit France, June 2005: McKinsey Global Institute

O'Mahony M, van Ark B (2003) EU productivity and competitiveness: an industry perspective can Europe resume the catching-up process? Luxembourg: Office for Official Publications of the European Communities

OECD (2007) Offshoring and employment: trends and impact. OECD, Paris

Reining A (2003) Lexikon der Außenwirtschaft. München, Wien, Oldenburg

Reinberg A, Hummel M (2005) Vertrauter Befund – Höhere Bildung schützt auch in der Krise vor Arbeitslosigkeit, IAB Report No. 9, Data Attachment. http://doku.iab.de/kurzber/2005/kb0905_anhang.pdf

Rukwid R (2007) Arbeitslosigkeit und Lohnspreizung, Empirische Befunde zur Arbeitsmarktsituation gering Qualifizierter in Deutschland. Schriftenreihe des Promotionsschwerpunkts Globalisierung und Beschäftigung, No. 24/2007

Samuelson PA (2004) Where Ricardo and Mill Rebut and confirm arguments of mainstream economists supporting globalization. J Econ Perspect 18(3):135–146

Schmidt H-J (2004) Tschechien ist schon lange nicht mehr verlängerte Werkbank. Die Welt, 2 April 2004

Schöller D (2007a) Service-Offshoring: Eine Herausforderung für die Beschäftigung in Deutschland? Wirtschaftsdienst 87(4):249–257

Schöller D (2007b) Service offshoring and its impact on productivity and labor demand in Germany: evidence from revised input–output data. Paper presented at the ICEG European Center Annual Conference, Budapest, Hungary, pp 20–55

Schöller D (2007c) Service offshoring and the demand for less-skilled labor: evidence from Germany. Hohenheim Discussion Papers, No. 287. University of Hohenheim, Stuttgart

Stern (2004) Made in Germany – Wir sind besser, als wir glauben. Stern, 27

Strauss-Kahn V (2003) The role of globalization in the within-industry shift away from unskilled workers in France. NBER Working Paper, No. 9716, May 2003

Stuttgarter Zeitung (2004) Auch Hightech-Arbeitsplätze wandern ab. Stuttgarter Zeitung, 22 April 2004

Timmer MP, Ypma G, van Ark B (2003) IT in the European union: driving productivity convergence? Research Memorandum GD-67, October 2003. Groningen Growth and Development Centre

Wessel D, Davis B (2007) Pain from free trade spurs second thoughts. Wall Street Journal, 28 March 2007

Chapter 2
Framework of Services Offshoring

Abstract In this second chapter, we develop a "Framework of Services Offshoring", which contains a thorough analysis of the classification and drivers of services offshoring. The classification, in Sect. 2.1, examines how services offshoring is defined, which forms it can take, and which service activities are involved. First, we compare and contrast outsourcing and offshoring before deriving our own working definition of services offshoring. Second, we focus on the *service* part of services offshoring, defining services and describing the implications of their new tradability. We also classify services trade and the relevant service activities. Third, we focus on the *offshoring* part of services offshoring and discuss the make-or-buy decision in efficiency-based, resource-based, and transaction costs-based theories of firms. Section 2.2 identifies the main drivers of services offshoring. We first describe changes in the global environment, namely developments in ICTs as well as multilateral and regional liberalization of trade in services. We then discuss market-oriented, cost-oriented, and procurement-oriented services offshoring motives of firms, also including newer developments. Finally, we focus on developments in the destination countries, namely the availability of human capital, the presence of multinational companies, and the liberalization of service sectors.

2.1 Classification of Services Offshoring

The classification of services offshoring explains what services offshoring means and which forms it can take. The forms can vary with respect to the offshored services and the organizational form offshoring can take. We contribute to the growing services offshoring literature in a number of ways. First, we clearly distinguish outsourcing from offshoring, and offer a general and a special working definition of services offshoring in Sect. 2.1.1, which constitutes a contribution in the light of the existence of many misleading definitions. Second, many technical papers, such as econometric estimations or theoretical models, reduce services to a technical input

D. Winkler, *Services Offshoring and its Impact on the Labor Market*,
Contributions to Economics, DOI: 10.1007/978-3-7908-2199-4_2,

factor. In the "real world", however, services can take different forms and can be provided in different ways, which is taken into account in Sect. 2.1.2. Third, outsourcing and in-house production are often assumed to be given, when, however, they are the result of a previous make-or-buy decision and are thus endogenous. Section 2.1.3 explains the make-or-buy decision in efficiency-based, resource-based, and transaction cost-based theories of firms.

2.1.1 Definition of Services Offshoring

Despite the public debate on the advantages and disadvantages of buying goods and services from abroad, it seems that neither a terminology nor a definition of the phenomenon has become universally accepted. Often, terms such as outsourcing, international outsourcing, offshoring, offshore outsourcing, and even fragmentation of production or FDI, are used interchangeably to refer to this phenomenon but, strictly speaking, they do not mean the same thing. Different economists use different definitions and nuances, and thus a clear definition of offshoring is essential for our study. In the following two sections, we define the terms outsourcing (Sect. 2.1.1.1) and offshoring (Sect. 2.1.1.2) and distinguish them from each other. The third sub-subsection derives our own general and special working definition of services offshoring (Sect. 2.1.1.3).

2.1.1.1 Definitions of Outsourcing

Traditionally, firms produce a large percentage of their goods in-house and thus posses a *high degree of value added*. Such firms are also called vertically integrated. In the extreme case they encompass all levels of the value chain, from R&D via the procurement of inputs and their logistics, the production process and assembly, the logistics of the products and services, and marketing and sales to after-sales services. Supporting processes for all stages of the value chain include human resources, accounting and finance, call centers, and IT. Complete vertical integration often results in immobile and inflexible firms that struggle to adapt to the requirements of globalization. Especially, the pace of information flows is reduced within such a corporate structure. Therefore, manufacturing firms have, since the 1960s, started to *break the value chain down* by delegating parts of their value chain to specialized external contractors. In particular, non-core activities not considered decisive for the firm's performance were contracted out. This phenomenon was called outsourcing, a neologism which is made-up of the terms *outside resource using*. The written-out form indicates that resources from an external supplier outside the firm are used, be it from the domestic country or from abroad.

Box 2.1 presents selected definitions of (services) outsourcing published in recent years which emphasize different aspects of outsourcing. The definition of Abramovsky et al. (2004) corresponds to the general meaning of outsourcing derived above, which includes material and service inputs as well as domestic and foreign inputs, provided they are purchased and not produced in-house. Bhagwati et al. (2004) underline the meaning of *services* within the outsourcing discourse. They show that, at the beginning of the 1980s, the term outsourcing describes the external procurement of physical inputs, while in 2004, the same term has a completely different meaning. Their focus on international service inputs constrains the more general definition. Pujals (2005) and Kirkegaard (2004) also concentrate on services, and define outsourcing as the provision of services from an *outside specialist provider*, whereby the former points out that the nationality of the provider is irrelevant.

Some authors relate "outside" to resources outside the *frontier* of a country, which also comprises in-house production. Amiti and Wei (2005) remark:

> "Some people interpret 'outside' to mean outside the firm, and others outside the country. Both usages are common (Amiti and Wei 2005, p. 311)."

Amiti and Wei (2005) use the specific term "international outsourcing" to make sure that they include only the procurement of foreign inputs. Their definition of international outsourcing comprises both the external and in-house provision of goods and services. The definition of Anderton et al. (2002) focuses on the international relocation of low-skill-intensive parts of production and thus limits outsourcing, to low-wage labor-abundant countries.

In our opinion, the definition of outsourcing meaning the relocation of formerly in-house-produced inputs to an external firm has become more widely accepted. Hence, outsourcing in our study relates to this definition. A special sort of outsourcing is BPO, which can be defined as "a contractual service to completely

Box 2.1: Selected definitions of outsourcing

"Outsourcing is specialisation outside the firm. This occurs when firms opt to 'buy' rather than 'make' in-house. That is, outsourcing involves greater specialisation as firms switch from sourcing inputs internally to sourcing them from separately owned suppliers (Abramovsky et al. 2004, p. 7)."

"It [outsourcing] referred now to a specific segment of the growing international trade in services. This segment consists of arm's length [or what Bhagwati (1984) has called "long-distance] purchase of services abroad, principally, but not necessarily, via the electronic mediums such as telephone, fax and internet and includes, for example, phone call centers staffed in Bangalore to serve customers in New York and X-rays transmitted digitally from Boston to be read in Bombay (Bhagwati et al. 2004, p. 2)."

"Outsourcing refers to firms purchasing services from outside specialist providers. Conversely, the Word "Insourcing" refers to the production of something inside a company. Outsourcing can be domestic or abroad (Pujals 2005, p. 4)."

"Outsourcing refers to companies (or governments) purchasing services from outside specialist providers at arms length. This may include a wide range of services, such as cleaning, catering, security, building maintenance, as well as business services such as IT support, consulting, advertising, payroll management, accounting or specialist design (Kirkegaard 2004, p. 22)."

"In this paper, we focus on international outsourcing, defined as the procuring of service or material inputs by a firm from a source in a foreign country. This term includes both intra-firm international outsourcing (by which the foreign provider of the input is still owned by the firm) and arm's-length international outsourcing (by which the foreign provider of the input is independent from the firm using the input). International outsourcing is part of a country's imports (of goods and services) (Amiti and Wei 2005, p. 313)."

"Outsourcing occurs where firms take advantage of both the low-wage costs of relatively labour abundant countries and modern production techniques – whereby the process of manufacturing a product can be broken-down, or fragmented, into a number of discrete activities – and move the low-skill-intensive parts of production abroad, but continue to carry out the high-skill intensive activities themselves.

'Moving the low-skill-intensive parts of production abroad' does not necessarily mean that the firm is involved in outward foreign direct investment, it can also mean that the low-skill parts of production are closed-down and replaced by imports – of either intermediate or finished goods – from low-wage countries (Anderton et al. 2002, p. 3)."

Source: own illustration

manage, deliver, and operate one or more (typically IT-intensive) business processes or functions" (Mattoo and Wunsch-Vincent 2004, p. 767). *Insourcing*, on the other hand, means the opposite – that externally purchased inputs get vertically integrated into the value chain and are produced in-house.

2.1.1.2 Definitions of Offshoring

In the following, the notion of offshoring is defined. Originally, the term was used in financial economics, since many offshore financial centers are former British colonial islands located off-shore of the mainland such as Singapore, Hong Kong, and the Caribbean Islands. Today, offshoring in the financial context must rather be understood in juridical than geographical terms. That means offshore financial centers describe locations with zero or very low tax rates, weak financial regulation, as well as strict banking secrecy and anonymity. Another feature is that financial institutions in offshore centers are engaged primarily in business with non-residents (IMF 2000).

The term offshoring has extended from its solely financial meaning to the term materials (or goods) offshoring and more recently also services offshoring. The starting point is a firm which is located in the domestic country. Offshoring is used as a general term to describe all kinds of entrepreneurial activities in a country other than the domestic one in order to support a company's business. The foreign activities can happen for several reasons, but a main motive of firms is to exploit wage differentials between countries.

Box 2.2 presents selected definitions of offshoring, which are more homogeneous than in the case of outsourcing. Garner (2004) and Abramovsky et al. (2004) describe probably the most general definition, where offshoring means the relocation of jobs and production abroad. Garner (2004) outlines the two forms of offshoring, namely within or outside the MNC, and distinguishes offshoring from the term outsourcing. Abramovsky et al. (2004) stress that offshoring can be undertaken to serve foreign markets or to use the output back in the home country. They thereby refer to the existence of several offshoring motives. The definitions of Erber and Sayed-Ahmed (2005) and Sinn (2005) focus on cost-savings as the main motive.

As mentioned in the previous sub-subsection, Amiti and Wei (2005) define international outsourcing as the procurement of inputs from abroad, whereas Anderton et al. (2002) define outsourcing as the relocation of in-house-produced goods to low-wage countries. Strictly speaking, their definitions of outsourcing should be considered definitions of offshoring. In the context of his "bazaar hypothesis", which has spawned a large debate among economists not only in Germany, Sinn (2005) on the one hand limits offshoring to the relocation of internal services to a foreign subsidiary, while on the other hand, he calls the provision from foreign suppliers, which is the complementary aspect of the term offshoring, foreign outsourcing. Probably the clearest definition is given by Grossman and Rossi-Hansberg (2006a) who distinguish the term offshoring from outsourcing. The former thus focuses on the geographical scope of the activities, while the latter captures the organizational form.

As in the case of outsourcing, there exists no general definition of offshoring, but many economists understand it to mean the relocation of production processes to another country, be it in-house or externally. A specific form of offshoring is

Box 2.2 Selected definitions of offshoring

"The term "offshoring" refers to the relocation of jobs and production to a foreign country. The relocated jobs and production could be at a foreign office of the same multinational company or at a separate company located abroad. In contrast, the term "outsourcing" does not necessarily imply that jobs and production are relocated to another country (Garner 2004, p. 6)."

"Offshoring occurs when firms move production overseas. This could be to serve foreign markets – for example to substitute for exports – or to import overseas produced imports for use back [. . .] (Abramovsky et al. 2004, p. 7)."

"Offshoring can be defined as relocation of business processes (including production, distribution, and business services, as well as core activities like research and development) to lower-cost locations outside national borders. This term assumes the perspective of the country of origin (Erber and Sayed-Ahmed 2005, p. 4)."

"Offshoring is the practice by which companies outsource processes, chiefly IT-based services, across large distances to other parts of the world, often low-wage countries (Schaaf 2004, p. 3)."

"The Bazaar-Hypothesis acts on the assumption that more and more German manufacturing companies relocate labor-intensive parts of their value chains to foreign subsidiaries (offshoring) or purchase them from providers abroad (foreign outsourcing) in order to escape from high labor costs (own translation of Sinn 2005, p. 5)."

"The terms offshoring and outsourcing are sometimes used interchangeably, but we believe that such usage is confusing. We prefer to use "offshoring" to mean the performance of tasks in a country different from where a firm's headquarters are located and reserve "outsourcing" for the performance of tasks under some contractual arrangement by an unrelated party. Thus, offshoring can be conducted in-house or at arms-length, while outsourcing can be performed in a domestic or foreign location (Grossman and Rossi-Hansberg 2006a, p. 3)."

Source: own illustration

nearshoring which includes the relocation to countries that are geographically closer to the country of origin. In the German case, the move to CEECs would be subsumed under nearshoring. Accordingly, Schaaf's (2004) definition of offshoring mentions the feature of large distances between the domestic and the foreign firms. A new buzzword used by service providers and consulting firms is *bestshoring*, reflecting the experience of firms that not all offshoring decisions are satisfactory and strategically effective. Finally, the term *onshoring* describes the shift of production processes that have formerly been performed abroad back to the domestic country.

2.1.1.3 Working Definition of Services Offshoring

Outsourcing asks for the "source" of production, i.e., whether the input is produced by an internal source (self-production or subsidiary) or an external source

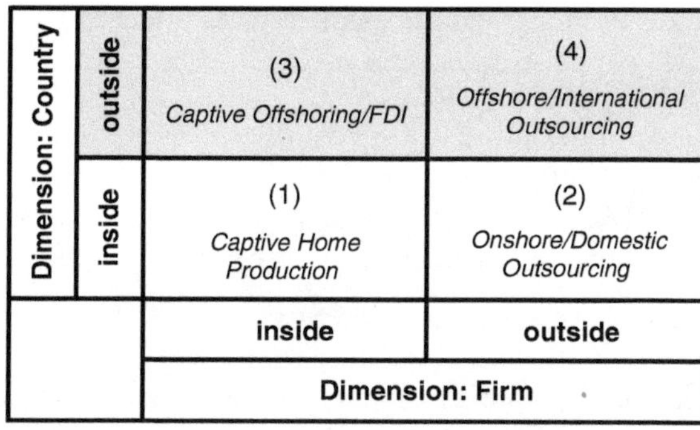

Fig. 2.1 Classification of offshoring
Source: own illustration

(independent supplier/subcontractor), wherever the source might be located geographically. Offshoring, on the other hand, asks for the "shore", or country of production, i.e., whether the input is produced at home or abroad regardless of the source. The matrix in Fig. 2.1 presents the synthesis of outsourcing and offshoring.

There are four possible combinations of both criteria:

1. An internal source of production in the home country (*captive home production*),
2. An external source of production in the home country (*onshore* or *domestic outsourcing*),
3. An internal source of production abroad (*captive offshoring* or *FDI*), and
4. An external production abroad (*offshore* or *international outsourcing*)

Offshoring comprises both the internal (3) and external production (4) in a foreign country.

There are three possibilities for firms that start out as exclusively domestic producers to arrive at offshoring. First, firms that already practice onshore outsourcing begin to recruit foreign providers (from 2 to 4). Second, firms that have not yet outsourced start to consult foreign suppliers (from 1 to 4). And third, some firms that are not yet engaged in foreign production might start to build up a subsidiary abroad (from 1 to 3) (Abramovsky et al. 2004).[1]

Many authors focus either exclusively on materials offshoring or do not explicitly distinguish services offshoring. Exceptions are, for example, Kirkegaard (2004), Bhagwati et al. (2004), and Amiti and Wei (2005). Due to the increased relocation of business services, our definition seeks to reduce offshoring to services offshoring. To sum up, our working definition must so far meet three main criteria. First, the country of production plays the decisive factor, as only foreign production is concerned. Second, the boundary of the firm is neglected, so that both internal and

[1]Theoretically, one could also imagine a firm that previously outsourced to a domestic supplier and instead builds a subsidiary abroad (from 2 to 3). Practically, however, this might rarely be the case, as the foreign subsidiary requires internal knowledge about processes and services that are no longer performed in-house.

Box 2.3 Working definitions of services offshoring

General definition of services offshoring:
"Services offshoring *in the broader sense* comprises all kinds of foreign service activities of a multinational company that are aimed at supporting its domestic production, and include both captive offshoring and offshore outsourcing."

Special definition of services offshoring:
"Services offshoring *in the narrower sense* designates the provision of service inputs from a foreign supplier that are produced abroad mainly for cost reasons and re-imported to the home country. The foreign purchase either happens externally, via an independent supplier (offshore outsourcing), or internally within the multinational company (captive offshoring)."

Source: own illustration

external production are considered simultaneously. And third, the working definition focuses on services. These three criteria are reflected in our *general definition* of services offshoring (or services offshoring in the broader sense) in Box 2.3.

The motives behind an offshoring decision can be mainly market-oriented, cost-oriented, or procurement-oriented (see Sect. 2.2.2). Services offshoring is expected to have the potential for harming domestic labor markets when formerly home-produced services are relocated for cost reasons and re-imported to the country of origin. Hence, the previous domestic production and the offshore production are substitutes. Therefore, the *special definition* of services offshoring (or services offshoring in the narrower sense) focuses on cost-oriented motives (see Box 2.3). In most cases, these re-imports are composed of intermediate inputs that are further processed into final goods in the home country. However, they could also consist of final goods, as global corporations in the major industrialized countries are not strictly involved in assembly (see Sect. 4.1).

The combination of captive offshoring and offshore outsourcing in our working definitions has at least two advantages over definitions that only focus on one aspect. First, the decision for in-house production or external procurement has become increasingly determined by cost-oriented motives rather than by strategic reasons. Thus, FDI might be chosen due to tax benefits in the destination country. Moreover, FDI often arises in the form of mergers and acquisitions (M&As), where already existing foreign companies are bought up, and the foreign production is not really self-performed (Abramovsky et al. 2004). Focusing solely on FDI could therefore be misleading.

Second, many studies only center on one aspect of offshoring when analyzing possibly related labor market effects. In the 1980s, economists focused on the impact of growing international trade flows on domestic labor markets, whereas in the 1990s, many studies measured the effects of FDI on home employment. Our working definition in the narrower sense has the advantage of integrating both.

Services offshoring and subsequent re-imports of intermediate or final goods from the offshore-location (within or outside the MNC) to the country of origin can be considered a special form of international trade. Hence, an integrated definition protects against possibly misleading conclusions when evaluating the labor market effects of offshoring.

2.1.2 *Services and their Tradability*

Services are of particular interest, since their significance has grown in terms of both quantity and quality, which also applies to Germany. In *quantitative* terms, services clearly dominate the *structural distribution of German FDI*. In 2005, the share of service investments in the worldwide stock of German outward FDI constituted more than 70.6% compared to 58.7% in 1995. This corresponds to a growth rate of 480% over the period compared to a total growth rate in outward FDI stocks of 399%. One could object that large parts are composed of investment companies, but the share excluding the latter nevertheless reached 59.4% in 2005 compared to 53.2% in 1995 (Deutsche Bundesbank, several time series). Service investments appear to be much faster and less costly compared to manufacturing investments, as neither large factory buildings nor assembly lines are needed.

The *foreign employment of German MNCs* also reflects the process towards the tertiarization of the economy. In 2005, 41.7% of the employees in foreign subsidiaries were occupied in the service sector, while this share was only 28.1% in 1995. Thus, services employment grew by 260% over the period, while total employment increased by 176% (Deutsche Bundesbank, several time series). Not only the foreign in-house production, but also the external procurement of services abroad is expected to grow. An analysis of the Deutsche Bank Research predicts that the *process of relocating IT-services abroad* will yield an enormous growth potential for the German economy, especially for small- and medium-sized firms. The study expects that offshoring will reduce the prices of IT-services, which will lead to a further ICT penetration of the German economy (Schaaf 2004).

In *qualitative* terms, services have undergone a tremendous change. One and a half decades ago, most services were considered non-tradable, but the emergence and development of new ICTs has contributed to overcoming geographical distance. This development has started to break down the prior universality of the uno-actu-principle, which is elaborated in the following sub-subsection (Sect. 2.1.3.1). Services are further classified into their modes of provision (Sect. 2.1.3.2), before presenting several classifications of service activities (Sect. 2.1.3.3).

2.1.2.1 Services and the Uno-Actu-Principle

The first classifications of services are found among the classical economists, who distinguished productive from unproductive labor depending on whether the worker was involved in the production of goods or services. T.P. Hill's "On Goods and Services" (1977) traces this distinction back to Adam Smith's *Wealth of Nations* (1776):

> "[...] in the chapter on capital accumulation Smith was at pains to distinguish a labour service which "fixes and realizes itself in a particular subject or vendible commodity" from labour services which "generally perish in the very instant of their performance". The first kind of labour service was described as "productive" and the second as "unproductive" (Hill 1977, p. 330)."

Hill points out that the classical view restricts the concept of wealth to material goods, where labor is only considered productive when it materializes in goods. However, some classical economists recognized the potential of certain services to raise LP, such as J.S. Mill's *Principles of Political Economy* (1852) that categorizes service industries in productive labor (e.g., education and health) and unproductive labor. According to Mill, services that raise LP contribute indirectly to the production of goods.

> "Such labour may be said to be productive indirectly or mediately, in opposition to the labour of the ploughman and the cotton spinner, which are productive immediately (Mill 1852, p. 60, taken from Hill 1977, p. 331)."

Hill further mentions that "the distinction between productive and unproductive labor has been perpetuated through Marx's influence in the distinction drawn in the MPS (material product system) between the material and non-material spheres of production" (Hill 1977, p. 311).

> "The non-material sphere embraces all activities directed towards rendering services to the population in order to satisfy certain personal and social needs of people. The features of services are, first, that the time they are rendered is, as a rule, the same as the time they are consumed, and second, that the object of the application of labour is man himself, while the object of the application of labour in the production of material goods are natural things and natural forces (UN 1974, p. xxix, taken from Hill 1977, p. 329)."

Neoclassical economists, however, find little relevance in distinguishing between goods and services. "Marshall, for example, dismissed services as "immaterial products" while present day economists tend to describe them as "immaterial goods" or simply as "goods" (Hill 1977, p. 315). As, according to Hill, services and goods are basically different, he provides his own definition of services (see Box 2.4). When one person agrees to a service, she orders it. This leads to the activity of another economic agent, which in turn results in the change in the condition of the person and of goods, respectively. Thus, Hill differentiates between the change of a person and of a good. The condition of a person can be changed physically by services such as passenger transportation, hairdressing, and medical treatment or mentally by services such as education and communication. Services that affect goods are, for example, transportation of goods, postal deliveries, repairs, cleaning and maintenance.

> "This definition accords with the meaning of the word "service" as used in ordinary speech and by economists. It is consistent with the underlying idea which is inherent in the concept of a service, namely that one economic unit performs some activity for the benefit of another. In this way, one unit "serves" the other (Hill 1977, p. 318)."

Box 2.4: Selected definitions of services

> "A service may be defined as a change in the condition of a person, or of a good belonging to some economic unit, which is brought about as a result of the activity of some other economic unit, with the prior agreement of the former person or economic unit (Hill 1977, p. 318)."
> "Services are not separate entities over which ownership rights can be established. They cannot be traded separately from their production. Services are heterogeneous outputs produced to order and typically consist of changes in the condition of the consuming units realised by the activities of the producers at the demand of the customers. By the time their production is completed they must have been provided to the consumers (UN 2002, p. 7)."
> "Services are usually perceived as intangible, invisible, perishable and requiring simultaneous production and consumption, while goods are tangible, visible and storable, and do not require direct interaction between producers and consumers (UNCTAD 2004, p. 145)."

Source: own illustration

The 'Manual on Statistics of International Trade in Services' which has been developed and published jointly by the WTO, the European Commission, the IMF, the OECD, UNCTAD, and the UN, respects the 1993 System of National Accounts' (SNA)[2] definition of services (see UN 2002, in Box 2.4). This definition refers to the above definition of Hill by mentioning the changes in the conditions of the involved parties. It further outlines the impossibility of establishing ownership rights over services and the non-separability of services from their production when being traded (UN 2002).

It might be reasonable to contrast goods and services when formulating a general definition of services, as both singly and in combination constitute the only outputs in the value-adding production process of the economy. Due to the limited durability of services, they are considered not storable or transferable. Hence, *direct contact* between the producer and consumer of a service is required, which is called the *uno-actu-principle*. The Latin term *uno actu* in the ablative case can be translated into the English term 'through/with one action' and implies that a service must be produced and consumed on site. According to the uno-actu-principle, either the consumer of a service has to seek the producer out or vice versa. A typical example is the service of a haircut, where the person that wishes a haircut (consumer) has to seek out the hairdresser (producer). Goods, contrariwise, do not demand direct interaction between producer and consumer due to their tangibility, visibility, and storability (see UNCTAD 2004, in Box 2.4).

[2]The Manual conforms with and explicitly relates to the SNA 1993 and the fifth edition of the IMF's Balance of Payments Manual.

This distinction between services and goods should not be understood in a strict sense. First, some services have features of goods and are tangible (e.g., books or the printed report of a management consultant), visible (e.g., theatre), and storable (e.g., music or voice-mail). Second, most goods have the purpose to provide a service or function. Third, goods and services are mostly interacted, since in the majority of cases goods depend on service inputs in their production and vice versa. And fourth, goods and services are often consumed simultaneously (e.g., airline travel requires aircraft) (UNCTAD 2004).

The 'Manual on Statistics of International Trade in Services' quotes the 1993 SNA on this issue and lists service sectors that have many characteristics of goods, such as services "concerned with the provision, storage, communication and dissemination of information, advice and entertainment in the broadest sense of those terms – the production of general or specialized information, news, consultancy reports, computer programs, movies, music, etc. The outputs of these industries, over which ownership rights may be established, are often stored on physical objects – paper, tapes, disks, etc. – that can be traded like ordinary goods. Whether characterized as goods or services, these products possess the essential characteristic that they can be produced by one unit and supplied to another, thus making possible division of labour and the emergence of markets" (UN 2002, pp. 7–8).

This ambiguity makes it difficult to give a general definition of services. Even the GATS renounces such and defines only services trade in terms of four different modes of supply (see Sect. 2.1.2.2). The 'Manual on Statistics of International Trade in Services' and the UNCTAD (2004) outline the difficulties of a general definition of services:

> "These and other complications make it difficult to formulate a clear-cut definition of services. No commonly accepted definition exists (UNCTAD 2004, p. 145)."

Recent developments in ICTs, however, have made it possible to uncouple information from its physical memory, rendering the transfer of huge amounts of data possible within a few seconds (see Sect. 2.2.1.1). Thus, the universality of the uno-actu-principle has been called into question. Henneberger and Ziegler (2001) differentiate between three services categories which is based on the classification of Bhagwati (1987). In the first two categories, the universality of the uno-actu-principle holds, which is shown in Fig. 2.2. The first category contains services where the provider seeks out the user (e.g., transport sector, waste disposal) and pays the transaction costs (TACs), at least the preliminary ones. Hence, this category is characterized by a mobile provider, but immobile user. The inverse case happens, when the user (consumer) needs to seek out the provider (e.g., retail, wholesale, tourism sector) and thus pays the TACs in the second category. Bhagwati (1987) also mentions a further case where both the provider and the user are mobile, so that the service (e.g., haircuts, tailor's suits, lectures, etc.) can be provided in either's location. This hybrid case should be excluded from our consideration as, in reality, this general case specializes into either the first or the second category. The third category does not require personal contact between the provider and the user, as the emergence of ICTs has contributed to overcoming

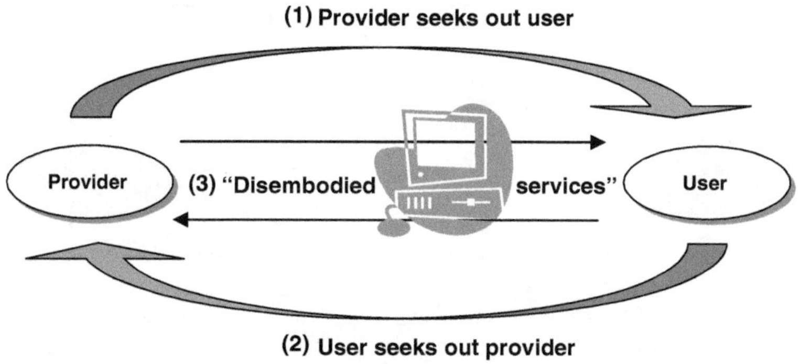

Fig. 2.2 Disembodied services
Source: own illustration based on Bhagwati (1987) and Henneberger and Ziegler (2001)

geographical distance in the formerly inviolable service sector. As the physical proximity becomes inessential, this services category is called *disembodied services* or "long-distance" services (Bhagwati 1987, pp. 552–553).

2.1.2.2 Classification of Services Trade

Classification of Service Provision according to the Geographical Location of Agents

A proposition of service classification is made by Henneberger and Ziegler (2001) who classify tradable services according to the *geographical location of the consumer and producer*. Although the authors focus on FDI as the only form of foreign production, their classification can easily be extended to the form of offshore-outsourcing. Figure 2.3 shows the four different combinations of service provision. Let us start with the situation where the producer is located in the domestic country (on the left side). If the consumer is situated in the home country, both the production and the provision of the service occur at home. If the consumer is situated abroad, the domestic producer must export its services to the foreign location.

Let us now assume that the producer is located abroad (on the right side). This could be either in the form of an affiliated branch or in the form of an independent service provider. If the producer abroad has to serve a consumer in the home country, the services are produced abroad and (re)imported to the domestic country. If the producer abroad serves the foreign market, the production and the provision of services happen on site abroad. Services trade flows are only included in the two grey-shaded areas, i.e., the producer and the consumer are located in different countries. Thus, this matrix only covers the flows of disembodied services, but not services embodied in people. The latter is included in the next classification of services trade.

Location of the Consumer		Location of the Producer: Home Country	Location of the Producer: Abroad
	Home Country	Production and provision of services in the home country.	Service production abroad and (re)imports to the home country.
	Abroad	Service production in the home country and exports to the foreign location.	Production and provision of services abroad.

Fig. 2.3 Classification of service provision
Source: own illustration, taken and modified from: Henneberger and Ziegler (2001), p. 21

Classification of Services Trade According to the Modes of Service Supply in the GATS

The GATS, which entered into force on 1 January 1995, was reached in the Uruguay Round and constitutes the first attempt to extend internationally agreed rules and commitments on international trade to services trade (see Sect. 2.2.1.2). The WTO designates this achievement as "perhaps the most important single development in the multilateral trading system since the GATT (General Agreement on Tariffs and Trade) itself came into effect in 1948" (WTO 1999, p. 1). Besides the scope of the GATS, the first article out of 29 defines services trade in terms of four different modes of supply, namely cross-border supply, consumption abroad, commercial presence in the consuming country, and presence of natural persons. The categorization is subject to the mode or place of service supply and has become widely accepted.

The *cross-border supply of services* is the first mode, which describes the supply of a service "from the territory of one [WTO] Member [country] into the territory of any other Member" (UN 2002, p. 11). It allows the supplier and buyer to remain at their respective locations, as the services can be transferred mostly electronically via ICTs. Bhagwati et al. (2004) note that ICTs only facilitate the transfer of tremendous amounts of data and information, while the transfer would principally also be possible via conventional communication methods. This mode of supply is equivalent to the normal form of trade in goods and is also considered the most direct form of services trade, as it corresponds to the GATT in many ways, e.g., the clear geographical distance of both agents. A major difference is the fact that this form of services trade cannot yet be submitted to customs examinations. One can distinguish between individual suppliers, such as freelance designers, architects, and advisors, on the one hand, and suppliers that belong to a company, such as call centers, back offices, and software programmers, on the other hand (Bhagwati et al. 2004; UN 2002; WTO 1999).

Consumption abroad constitutes the second mode of supply and covers the supply of services "in the territory of one [WTO] Member to the service consumer of another Member" (UN 2002, p. 11). Tourism is the prime example of where the service is consumed at the location of the supplier. Other examples include medical treatments of non-residents, the provision with education of foreign students (e.g., language courses), as well as ship or aircraft repair, where only the property of the consumer is located abroad (UN 2002; WTO 1999).

In the third mode of supply, the provision happens "by a service supplier of one [WTO] Member, through *commercial presence* in the territory of any other Member" (UN 2002, p. 11). This mode allows for direct contact between the producer and consumer through the establishment of a foreign branch, which is decisive for services, such as banking, legal advice, and communications. It embraces various stages of the value chain, such as production, distribution, marketing, sales, and delivery. Medical services by a foreign-owned hospital and courses in a foreign-owned school are further examples. Foreign workers are not necessarily employed if a local workforce is sufficient (UN 2002; WTO 1999).

In the fourth mode of supply, the service procurement is effected "by a service supplier of one [WTO] Member, through *presence of natural persons* of a Member in the territory of any other Member" (UN 2002, p. 11), i.e., individuals move to another location where they provide services. This could either be in combination with mode 3 or without the necessity of a commercial presence. The former includes domestic managers or specialists that are sent to a foreign branch, while the latter includes individuals that are employed by a foreign firm or that are self-employed. Mode 4 implies temporary migration, as only non-permanent employment is covered. Since the GATS does not define "non-permanent", the concretization depends on the countries' commitments, which generally involves between 2 and 5 years. Services in the domain of construction and consulting as well as in the medical and educational sector are further examples of mode 4 services (Bhagwati et al. 2004; UN 2002; WTO 1999).

The four modes can be classified according to the territorial presence of the transactors beginning with the consumers (UN 2002, p. 22):

1. Consumer outside the territory of residence: consumption abroad (mode 2).
2. Consumer inside the territory of residence:
    (a) Supplier outside the territory of the consumer: cross-border supply (mode 1).
    (b) Supplier inside the territory of the consumer:
        - Through commercial presence (mode 3).
        - Through the presence of natural persons (mode 4).

Offshoring is often seen as a substitute for mode 4, since jobs move to foreign workers and not vice versa. Services that were formerly only provided by the presence of natural persons can now be traded electronically according to mode 1. In India, for instance, the share of on site exports through temporary movement of service suppliers (mode 4) in total IT exports has declined, while at the same time, the share of cross-border exports (mode 1) has risen. This is especially the case for low value and high volume activities, such as call center and other back office services (Chanda 2006). Nevertheless, the relationship between mode 1 and mode 4 is considered complementary, since the presence of foreign workers in a country stirs up the firms' awareness of more available talent abroad (van Welsum 2004). Thus, one can argue that the presence of many Indian IT-specialists in the US has influenced the offshoring decisions of American firms in India.

The relationship between mode 1 and mode 3 can likewise be considered complementary, if the commercial presence abroad leads to an increase in cross-border supply. This could be the case when international relocation goes along with growing service imports from the foreign location to the country of origin. Alternatively, international relocation could increase exports from the country of origin to the destination country, which is studied by Pain and van Welsum (2004), but their results are considerably heterogeneous with respect to different services categories. Analyzing further possible relationships among different modes of supply, Chanda (2006) finds that "[t]he most common linkage that emerges is that between modes 3 and 4, where temporary movement of service providers complements commercial presence, and there is a supporting and intermediary role played by mode 1 in this process" (Chanda 2006, p. 4).

Our working definitions of services offshoring comprise mode 1 service supplies, where services can be traded despite the physical distance between the producer and the consumer. The cross-border supply of services can happen in the form of external service providers abroad or in the form of in-house provision. Despite the possibility of FDI, mode 3 services are not considered, as we focus on users in the country of origin and not in the destination country.

2.1.2.3 Classification of Service Activities

As a clear definition of services does not exist, the "pragmatic approach" simply selects activities that are considered services. Even this approach has its difficulties, as the boundaries between the economic sectors are no longer clear cut when the complexity of production processes grows. Kalmbach et al. (2005) show that the terms business services, production-related services, and industry-related services are often used as synonyms. They come to the conclusion that no classification has become universally accepted, but that a multitude of different definitions co-exist (Kalmbach et al. 2005). Therefore, we present several approaches of service classifications in the first part. Since we focus on tradable business services with a potential for offshoring, business activities, commercial services, other business services, technological services, as well as IT and BPO services are defined in a second step.

Several Approaches of Service Classifications

In the *residual approach*, all activities that do not belong to the primary and secondary sector are assigned to the residual service sector. This approach results in ambiguous classifications, where some activities, such as construction, repair or electricity, gas, and water supply, are sometimes classified as in the secondary and sometimes in the tertiary sector. A second approach distinguishes *consumer services* from *producer services*, whereby the first describe final services and the latter constitute intermediate services. A third and early attempt was made by Browning and Singelmann (1975), who differentiated between *distribution services* (transport, storage, retail, wholesale trade), *producer services* (banking, finance, insurance, real estate, engineering, architectural, accounting, legal), *social services* (education, health, welfare and religious services, postal services, governmental services), and *personal services* (domestic, repair, barber and beauty shops, hotels, restaurants, entertainment). A fourth possibility is the classification of services according to their factor- and knowledge-intensity. One can distinguish between *capital-intensive services* (e.g., electricity, telecommunications, and transport), *human-capital-intensive services* (e.g., call centers) or *knowledge-intensive services* (e.g., insurance and professional business services) (UNCTAD 2004).

Related to the last classification is the fifth approach that classifies services according to their required skill-intensity. Barth (1998) distinguishes between *primary services*, including more simple office work, trade and sales, while *secondary services* subsume more qualified activities, such as R&D, management, consulting, and the provision of information (Barth 1998, p. 18). A more detailed classification can be found in the World Investment Report 2004 of the UNCTAD (2004), differentiating low-skill, medium-skill, and high-skill services. While Barth (1998) includes all kinds of service activities, the UNCTAD (2004) focuses only on tradable services. *Low-skill services* "are services with the lowest entry barriers in terms of skills, scale and technology. [...] They tend to need general – but not very high – levels of formal education, a working knowledge of the relevant language and/or basic computer skills" (UNCTAD 2004, p. 151). Examples are data entry and call centers, although some call centers demand a higher skill-intensity. *Medium-skill services* "are complex services that require more advanced skills" (UNCTAD 2004, p. 151). Examples include financial and accounting services, standardized programming work, routine data analysis and processing or back-office services such as ticketing and billing. Specialized training would generally be required (and so also the necessary training institutions). *High-skill services* are "the most creative and skill-intensive end of offshored services, with the most stringent entry requirements. [...] These require advanced skills at high levels of specialization, often with strong educational institutions" (UNCTAD 2004, p. 151). Such services encompass, for instance, R&D, design services, architectural drawings, new software development, animation, medical testing or analysis, and technology systems design (UNCTAD 2004).

Finally, we present the approach of Abramovsky et al. (2004), where the service classification depends on the demand side. Business services are demanded by

Table 2.1 Service classification

Services		
Other services	Business services	
	IT–enabled services	IT–computer services
– Wholesale and retail trade	– Renting of machinery equipment and other	– Software consultancy
– Financial activities	– Research and development	– Data processing and database activities
– Transportation and communication	– Legal activities	– Hardware consultancy
– Real estate	– Market research and management consultancy[a]	– Maintenance and repair of computing machinery
– Hotel and restaurants	– Architectural activities and technical consultancy[b]	
– Public administration	– Advertising	
– Health	– Other business services[c]	
– Education		
– Other services		

Source: own illustration. Based on: Abramovsky et al. (2004, p. 9)
[a]Business and management consultancy, market research and public opinion polling, management activities of holding companies
[b]Architectural and engineering activities and consultancy, technical testing and analysis
[c]Labor recruitment and provision of personnel, investigation and security activities, industrial cleaning, photographic activities, packaging activities, secretarial and translation services, other business activities

private and public companies, while other services are demanded by individuals (see Table 2.1). *Other services* consist of miscellaneous services, such as trade, financial services, transportation and communication, personal services, and social services. *Business services* are further subdivided into IT-enabled services and IT-computer services. The latter "consist of hardware and software consultancy, maintenance and repair of computers, and data processing and database activities. *IT-enabled services* include professional services (legal, accountancy, market research, technical, engineering, architectural, advertising, and consultancy), but also other more diverse activities such as labour placement agencies, renting of machinery, R&D, and call centres" (Abramovsky et al. 2004, p. 9). The smaller category *IT-computer services* thus comprises such services that are in direct contact to information technologies. The larger and expanding category IT-enabled services covers all services that are only enabled by information technologies (Abramovsky et al. 2004).

The Definition of Business Activities

Kalmbach et al. (2005) select eight services out of 27 from the German input-output tables, which they define as *business activities* in the broader sense.

Consumer-related[3] and social services[4] are not considered, since the former in general do not represent typical offshoring services and the latter are not tradable. Business activities comprise 'other business activities' in a narrower sense (sector 62), as well as the following seven sectors: 'wholesale, trade and commission excl. motor vehicles', 'post and telecommunications', 'financial intermediation' (except insurance and pension funding), 'activities related to financial intermediation', 'renting of machinery and equipment', 'computer and related activities', research and development (sectors 46, 54, 55, 57, 59–61). We exclude 'wholesale, trade and commission excl. motor vehicles' services from the original definition, since they do not represent typical offshoring services to our opinion. Abramovsky et al. (2004), for instance, classify them among non-business services (see Table. 2.1). In opposition to Abramovsky et al. (2004), however, we follow Kalmbach et al.'s (2005) approach to include financial intermediation and related activities. Banking, insurance, and finance represent 35% (and thus the largest part) of the total services offshoring market as will be shown in Sect. 3.2.1.1, which justifies our selection.

The calculation of services offshoring intensities (Sect. 3.1.3) as well as the econometric part of this study (Chap. 5) both rely on the definition of business activities according to Kalmbach et al. (2005), while the structure of German services offshoring (Chap. 3) is mainly based on services trade data from the IMF and German Balance of Payments statistics. In the following, the relevant service classifications are described and reviewed and then matched with the definition of business activities according to Kalmbach et al. (2005).

Other Commercial Services

The service classification of the International Trade Statistics of the WTO (2004) is based on the fifth edition of the IMF Balance of Payments Manual (BPM5). In the BPM5, the current account is subdivided into goods, services (including government services, n.i.e.), income (investment income and compensation of employees), and current transfers. Commercial services are defined as services minus government services, n.i.e. and are further sub-divided into transport, travel, and other commercial services. *Other commercial services* comprise the following components as defined in the BPM5:

(1) Communication services, (2) construction services, (3) insurance services, (4) financial services, (5) computer and information services, (6) royalties and license fees, (7) other business services, and (8) personal, cultural, and recreational services (WTO 2004).

Other commercial services are of special interest for our study, as they contain four services categories that match the definition of business activities according to

[3]Sectors within the classification of the German Federal Statistical Office: 45, 47–53, 56, 58, 69–71.
[4]Sectors within the classification of the German Federal Statistical Office: 63–68.

Kalmbach et al. (2005), namely (1) communication services, (4) financial services, (5) computer and information services, and (7) other business services.

The following definitions of these four services categories are taken from the 'Manual on Statistics of International Trade in Services' (see Sect. 2.1.2.1). The first category *communication services* is further subdivided into postal and courier services and telecommunication services. *Postal and courier services* focus on the pick-up, transport, and delivery of printed matter (e.g., letters, newspapers, periodicals, brochures), parcels and packages, including post office counter and mailbox rental services. Telecommunication services comprise the transmission of sound, images, or other information by telephone, telex, telegram, radio, and television cable and broadcasting, satellite, electronic mail, facsimile services, etc., as well as cellular telephone services, internet backbone services, and on-line access services, including provision of access to the internet. The second category *financial services* covers financial intermediation and auxiliary services that are provided by banks, stock exchanges, factoring enterprises, credit card enterprises, and other enterprises. Life insurance enterprises and pension funds are not included.

The third category *computer and information services* is subdivided into computer services, news agency services, and other information provision services. *Computer services* consist of hardware and software-related services and data-processing services, such as: hardware and software consultancy and implementation services; maintenance and repair of computers and peripheral equipment; disaster recovery services, provision of advice and assistance on matters related to the management of computer resources; analysis, design and programming of systems ready to use (also web page development and design), and technical software consultancy; system maintenance; and data-processing services (data entry, tabulation, processing, web page hosting services) to name some of them.[5] *News agency services* comprise the provision of news, photographs, and feature articles to the media. *Other information provision services* include database services, database conception, data storage, and the dissemination of data and databases, both online and through magnetic, optical, or printed media; and web search portals (UN 2002).

The fourth category *other business services* consists of trade related services, operational leasing (rentals), and miscellaneous business, professional, and technical services. Due to their diversity, other business services are described more precisely in the following paragraph.

Other Business Services

The category *other business services* include merchanting and other trade-related services, operational leasing services as well as miscellaneous business,

[5]Besides the provision of packaged (non-customized) software, non-specific computer training courses are excluded from computer services, as the first is classified as goods and the latter belongs to *other personal, cultural, and recreational services*. The download of software via the internet was being discussed during the preparation of the Manual.

professional, and technical services. *Merchanting* means the purchase of a good by a resident of the compiling economy from a non-resident and the subsequent resale of the good to another non-resident. *Other trade-related services* cover commissions on goods and service transactions between *residents* (merchants, commodity brokers, dealers, and commission agents) and *non-residents*. *Operational leasing services* include resident/non-resident leasing (rental) and charters of ships, aircraft and transportation equipment, such as railway cars, containers and rigs, without operators and crew. *Legal services* cover, for instance, legal advisory and representation services in any legal, judicial, and statutory procedures.

Accounting, auditing, bookkeeping, and tax consulting services include the recording of commercial transactions for businesses and others, examination services of accounting records and financial statements, business tax planning and consulting, and preparation of tax documents. *Business and management consulting and public relations services* cover advisory, guidance, and operational assistance services provided to businesses for business policy and strategy, and the overall planning, structuring, and control of an organization. *Advertising, market research, and public opinion polling* comprise, e.g., the design, creation and marketing of advertisements by advertising agencies. *Research and development services* cover services that are associated with basic research, applied research, and experimental development of new products and processes.

Further services within the category of other business services are architectural, engineering, and other technical services, waste treatment and de-pollution services, agricultural, mining, and other on-site processing services. Finally, 'other business services' include the placement of personnel, security and investigative services, translation and interpretation, photographic services, building cleaning, real estate services, and the distribution of electricity, water, gas, and other petroleum products, while 'services between related enterprises, n.i.e.' comprise services that cannot be classified to another sub-category (UN 2002).

Technological Services

Every two years, the German Federal Reserve Bank (*Deutsche Bundesbank, DBB*) publishes the Special Statistical Publication No. 12 "Technological Services in the Balance of Payments" (*Technologische Dienstleistungen in der Zahlungsbilanz*), which contains international trade flows of *technological services* between Germany and all other countries. The data are based on the balance of payments statistics, especially on the *Deutsche Bundesbank* statistics on external payments, which in turn is based on the Foreign Trade and Payments Act (*Außenwirtschaftsgesetz*) of 28 April 1961, and supplementary provisions, especially section 59 et seq. of the Foreign Trade and Payments Regulation (*Außenwirtschaftsverordnung*). According to this regulatory framework, only financial transactions of more than 12,500 € are considered, which hence does not cover gratuitous foreign exchange of technological transfer, which is mainly important for patents and licenses (Deutsche Bundesbank 2006a, b). This publication aims to map Germany's receipts of and expenditures for "technological knowledge", and consists of patents and licenses, R&D, and computer services, as well as 'engineering and other technical services'.

Patents and licenses include the usage, purchases and sales of patents, inventions, processes, and intellectual property rights. *R&D* mainly contains payments for the research and development of new products and processes including scientific advice. *Engineering and other technical services* cover payments for the planning and design of manufactured products and aggregates (e.g., engineering and construction, maintenance and inspection, and technical consulting and planning) as well as payments for information, consulting, and training in the scientific and medical area.

Finally, *computer services* include the development and maintenance of software and the installation of hardware, unless such services are not covered under 'system development' in R&D. Examples are payments for data processing, analysis, planning and programming of ready-for-use systems (including the development and design of websites), as well as technical software-consulting, development, production, provision, and documentation of customer-specific software (including customer-specific operating systems), maintenance and other supporting services, such as training courses within the scope of consulting services, basic R&D in technical computing, and the payments for licenses. One specialty is the treatment of software. If standardized software is traded in the form of data storage carriers (CD-ROM, floppy disk, DVD, etc.), the value of both the software and the data storage carrier must be registered as trade in goods in the foreign trade statistics of the German Federal Statistical Office. If software is traded online via the internet, these payments are classified as computing services (Deutsche Bundesbank 2006b).

Three of the four technological services categories match the definition of business activities used in this study, namely R&D, 'engineering and other technical services', as well as computer services. Patents and licenses, contrariwise, are of less interest, as they are certainly not offshored for cost reasons. Other services categories of interest that are not part of the technological services, but reported separately in the German Balance of Payments statistics, are *financial services*, i.e., essentially payments for bank commissions, as well as *other business services*, such as commercial services, communication services, which consist of postal and courier services and telecommunication services, commissions, and rental and leasing services.

Information Technology and Business Process Outsourcing Services

Statistics on services especially in India mostly focus on IT and BPO services. Mattoo and Wunsch-Vincent (2004) present the following list of IT and BPO services, whereby the categories can mutually overlap. *IT services* are generally computer-related services and include software development and implementation services, data processing and database services, IT support services, application development and maintenance, business intelligence and data warehousing, content management, e-procurement and business-to-business marketplaces, enterprise security, package implementation, system integration, enterprise application integration, total infrastructure outsourcing, web services (internet content preparation, etc.), web-hosting, and application service providers.

BPO services can be subdivided into customer interaction services, back-office operations, and more independent professional or business services. *Customer interaction services* comprise sales support, membership management, claims, reservations for airlines and hotels, subscription renewal, customer services helpline, handling credit and billing problems, telemarketing, and marketing research services. *Back-office operations* include data entry and handling, data processing and database services, medical transcriptions, payment services, financial processing (financial information and data processing/handling), human resource processing services, payroll services, warehousing, logistics, inventory, supply chain services, ticketing, insurance claims adjudication, and mortgage processing. *More independent professional or business services* consist of human resource services (hiring, benefit planning, and payroll, etc.), finance and accounting services (including auditing, bookkeeping, taxation services, etc.), marketing services, and product design and development (Mattoo and Wunsch-Vincent 2004).

IT and BPO services match the definition of business activities according to Kalmbach et al. (2005) only incompletely. While 'computer and related activities' as well as 'other business activities' in the narrower sense are covered, the following services categories are missing: 'post and telecommunications', 'financial intermediation and related activities', 'renting of machinery and equipment', and R&D.

2.1.3 Offshoring – A Make-or-Buy Decision

The following subsection addresses the two generic organizational forms of offshoring, theoretically discussed as the make-or-buy decision. Firms thus decide endogenously whether to "make" certain levels of the value chain (in-house production) or "buy" them from an external firm (outsourcing), which implies a vertical view of the value chain. Heshmati (2003), however, notes that "[...] in practice, outsourcing is not a make-or-buy decision, but rather makes previous investments a sunk cost to the firms and this negatively affects the outsourcing decision" (Heshmati 2003, pp. 94–95). In the last decade, a host of theoretical literature modeled the make-or-buy decision abroad to determine when a firm should vertically integrate or purchase inputs at arm's length (see e.g., Antràs 2003; Antràs et al. 2006; Antràs and Helpman 2004; Grossman and Helpman 2002, 2004, 2005; Marin and Verdier 2003a, b; McLaren 2000).

The expanded tradability of services raises the question why in-house production is still relevant. Figure 2.4 shows, for instance, that the majority of German services offshoring seems to take the form of foreign affiliates or joint ventures, according to a survey of 119 German firms based on 159 offshoring actions. External provision is most important in Eastern Europe (26%) and Asia (24%)

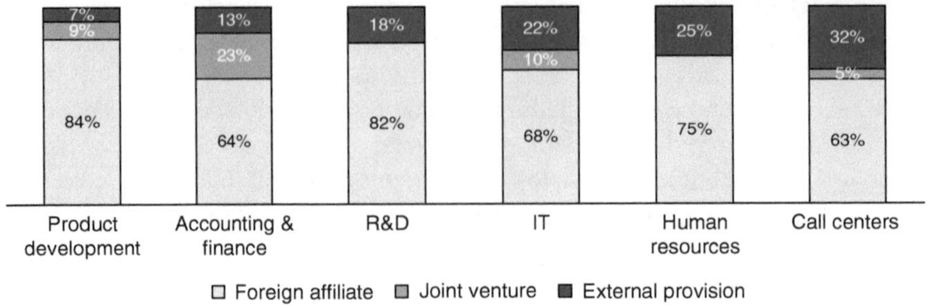

Fig. 2.4 Modes of provision of German firms by type of service
Source: own illustration. Data: Hutzschenreuter et al. (2007), p. 95. Based on 159 offshoring actions of 119 German firms

(Hutzschenreuter et al. 2007). As the discussion on make-or-buy decisions – which was originally related to goods – had already started some decades ago, the arguments must evidently go beyond the sheer tradability of services. Long before make-or-buy models appeared, the firms had discussed the make-or-buy question theoretically. Three main lines of thinking are relevant to our discussion, namely efficiency-based, resource-based, and transaction cost-based.

Efficiency-based motives, such as cost savings, are used to explain why firms buy inputs externally via the market. They are based on neoclassical economic theory that understands firms primarily as a production function. External purchases are made to save on labor costs, to raise flexibility, to focus on core competencies, or to gain learning advantages. The *resource-based view of the firm* constitutes a second stream of theories, where productive resources and competencies of a firm are the center of interest. Generally, firms have an incentive to diversify and thus grow in order to be less vulnerable in a dynamic environment. Strongly diversified firms, however, risk being involved in unfamiliar business areas, which increases the potential for business mistakes. Therefore, outsourcing helps firms to focus on their core competencies and resources. Finally, a firm's make-or-buy decision in *transaction cost-based theories* is made according to the criterion of TACs. In-house production is advantageous, when TACs are high, e.g., in the case of uncertainties, market failure, imperfect contracts, and information asymmetries. Thus, the following sub-subsections analyze efficiency-based (Sect. 2.1.3.1) and resource-based motives for outsourcing (Sect. 2.1.3.2) and transaction cost-based motives for in-house production (Sect. 2.1.3.3).

2.1.3.1 Efficiency-Based Motives for Outsourcing

There is generally no single motive that dominates a firm's decision to outsource. In most cases, many motives are simultaneously decisive. The early study of Abraham and Taylor (1996) thus states that "[t]he picture of employers' motives for contracting out that emerges from our analysis is rather more complex than that given in the typical popular account" (Abraham and Taylor 1996, p. 417). Many of the commonly stated advantages from outsourcing reveal an efficiency-oriented view of the firm without explicitly naming it as such.

One of the main outsourcing motives is the *search for flexibility or risk-sharing*. Due to changes in the external environment, such as changing market opportunities in a globalizing world or technological changes, firms are exposed to greater uncertainty. Thus, uncertainty combined with risk averse behavior promotes the search for pooling or sharing risk and thus the search for more flexibility (Deavers 1997). According to Abraham and Taylor (1996) outsourcing gives firms the possibility of smoothing the work load of the regular work force. Firms might favor a relatively stable work flow, since more volatility on the demand side can raise costs, e.g., due to the need to vary the number of regular workers or to employ more workers than necessary in off-peak seasons.

Outsourcing work to subcontractors or rescheduling work to off-peak periods helps firms to vary the number of regular workers in peak periods. Note that the costs of outsourcing exceed the costs of in-house production for a certain number of activities, otherwise a firm would outsource all activities. But even if the unit costs of outsourcing are higher, outsourcing could still remain beneficial to the firm if other costs can be reduced. A steady workflow can also be attained by extending the number of workers, so that the demand in peak seasons can be satisfied. In off-peak seasons, however, too many workers would be employed, which lowers productivity and/or the firm would have to pay high hiring and firing costs. Outsourcing thus reduces costs if the internal adjustment costs of the workforce exceed the contracting costs (Abraham and Taylor 1996). Besides labor flexibility, other types of flexibility, e.g., in corporate strategy, technology, and product range, can be increased due to outsourcing (Deavers 1997).

A second outsourcing motive is the *search for lower costs*. Abraham and Taylor (1996) explain how wage and benefit savings are possible when firms practice outsourcing. If firms subcontract less-skilled work to external providers, who pay lower wages and benefit packages, they can save partially high costs. How can external providers or subcontracting firms offer lower wages, even if they are located in the same country? One explanation given by the authors is the possibility that firms are unionized and thus pay higher wages than the firm's real willingness to pay. In such a case, outsourcing to non-unionized firms immediately reduces wage payments. A second explanation is related to "efficiency wages" which are higher than actual market wages. Efficiency wages increase the willingness of employees to improve their job performance, reduce the labor turnover rate, attract human capital, and intensify the good will of employees towards their employers. Efficiency wages are only appropriate for employees who belong to the firm's core activities, but less for employees who do not and/or who can easily be monitored and replaced. Since it is impossible to pay efficiency wages to the core workforce, while compensating the remaining employees with lower market wages, even non-unionized firms will take outsourcing into consideration (Abraham and Taylor 1996). As outsourcing to a domestic supplier can already lower wages, offshore-outsourcing to low-wage countries contains a much higher potential for wage savings.

Besides wage savings, Sharpe (1997) argues that "outsourcing mainly arose as a means to reduce the adjustment costs of responding to economic change – change that affects both organizations and workers" (Sharpe 1997, p. 536). Economic change includes technological innovation, rapid growth, changes in customer and worker preferences, and other shifts in supply and demand. Lowering the cost of adjusting to economic change can be achieved, for instance, when a firm absorbs general skills and technologies through outsourcing without directly investing in their development. Furthermore, external service providers have a greater motivation to hire and promote their employees at market prices compared to firms that keep these services in-house. The latter are more likely to employ workers at above market wages. By outsourcing these activities, firms are able to purchase support services at current market prices. Finally, outsourcing enables firms to simplify their management in highly growing areas or sectors with fast-paced changes. "Fast growth technology companies in highly competitive markets such as Apple, Nike, Intel, Microsoft, and Motorola outsource extensively and were among the earliest users of outsourcing. Newly emerging technology companies such as 3COM are following in their footsteps with regard to outsourcing (Sharpe 1997, p. 543)."

A third reason for outsourcing is that firms might benefit from *specialization advantages*, since external suppliers dispose of special equipment or knowledge. Specialized providers can generate scale effects, which depend on technological conditions, but also on their "ability to aggregate performance-related data horizontally across the same function at a number of different companies" (Sharpe 1997, p. 542). Linked to that argument is the capability of outsourcing suppliers to aggregate among many customers. It is, for example, easier for specialized firms to produce at the optimal scale for efficient production. For years, large firms have benefited more strongly from economies-of-scale. This advantage has been reduced due to the use of technology and outsourcing (Abraham and Taylor 1996).

Specialized services providers (SSPs) can generate higher scale-effects than non-specialized companies for the following reasons. First, one service activity can be used by more employees simultaneously without relevant cost increases. Imagine that a non-specialized company needs an instructor for its computer specialists. SSPs can reduce their fixed costs, because the instructor can teach more specialists at the same time. Second, some employees in the non-specialized companies do not work to full capacity, since they are not often or only irregularly needed in the companies (e.g., training, repair, maintenance, bookkeeping). SSPs can perform these tasks in different companies at different times, which saves fixed costs, because the same employee works continuously to full capacity. Third, not all companies introduce a new technology simultaneously, because there are early and late adopters of the same technology. SSPs could thus spread their fixed costs over a longer period of time than the companies that produce a specific service in-house (Bartel et al. 2005).

Specialization advantages are also generated due to the expertise of SSPs. Especially small or medium sized firms should outsource computer-based activities in order to increase cost efficiency, because their own computer specialists could be inexperienced if a more complex problem occurs that they rarely face. Specialized firms can deal faster and more efficiently with complex problems due to their expertise, e.g., in more quickly identifying inefficient work patterns and processes. Finally, firms are likely to lack adequate specialists, who are expensive or difficult to attract. Thus, Sharpe (1997) argues that in-house employees working in non-core areas of the firm have lower promotion chances. If such employees provide their services to a specialized firm, their chances to pursue a career rise. High-skilled specialists thus rather tend to work in specialized firms, otherwise they might demand a skill-premium (Abraham and Taylor 1996; Sharpe 1997).

2.1.3.2 Resource-Based Motives for Outsourcing

The Basics of Resource-Based Theories

Focusing on productive resources and competencies of a firm, *resource-based theories* constitute the dominant contemporary stream of theories in the field of strategy. Edith Penrose established this approach in her book "The Theory of the Growth of the Firm" (1959), although the author maintained a certain distance towards the developing and not completely homogeneous resource-based theories of the firm. Some authors "think of Penrose as re-stating, refining, and sometimes radicalizing the basic conceptualization of the firm that can be found in the work of Marshall and his later followers [. . .]" (Foss 1998, p. 3). Thus, Penrose like Marshall emphasizes not only the feature of firms to generate productive knowledge, but also their capability to develop and manage knowledge. Developing and managing knowledge, in particular, is difficult to separate, which is the essential Penrosian point according to Foss (1998). The year 1984 marked a milestone of the modern resource-based theories with Wernerfelt's "A Resource-Based View of the Firm" (1984) and Rumelt's "Towards a Strategic Theory of the Firm" (1984). Many other contributions have followed since then (Foss 1997).

The Penrosian firm represents a collection of *productive resources* that have the capability to generate services. Productive resources are managed within an administrative organization, which can determine the amount and type of these services. Penrose hereby outlines the necessity for firms to create a sustainable *competitive advantage* over the competitors, such as technological superiority, strong marketing, and operational scale effects, by building up new resources, maintaining them, and renewing them. Productive resources thus become the unit of analysis and must have the following features. First, they must be heterogeneous in order to render rents. Second, they must be obtained at a lower price than the current discounted net value, otherwise rents are absorbed by higher costs. Third, these resources should be difficult to imitate and non-substitutable. Fourth, productive resources must be firm-specific. The main question for a firm is, hence, how to receive the highest value out of its resources. However, the *real* input factors in the production process are not the resources but the productive services which can be obtained from them (Penrose 1959; Wernerfelt 1984; Foss 1997, 1998).

According to Penrose, "[a] firm may achieve rents not because it has better resources, but rather the firm's distinctive competence involves making better use of its resources (Penrose 1959, p. 54)."

Learning processes with regard to these productive services enable firms to diversify. *Diversification* in this context means (1) that productive possibilities of the firm can be expanded, and (2) that excess managerial resources can be used in related business fields (Foss 1998). Concerning (1), a firm is diversified when it offers new and sufficiently different products in addition to its already existing product range of intermediate and final goods. The "diversification of [...] activities, sometimes called 'spreading of production' or 'integration'" increases the variety of final goods, vertical integration, and the number of basic business areas (Penrose 1959, p. 104).

Concerning (2), firms gradually accumulate physical resources, but are unable to use all of them at the same time due to coordination problems. Hence, the firm always disposes of *excess resources* which render additional revenues possible without increasing the costs. Since there are no opportunity costs for unused resources, firms have an endogenous incentive for diversification and growth. The process of diversification produces new knowledge and further excess resources, which in turn induces the managers to develop new business areas, and so forth (Best and Garnsey 1999). This process seems to require no optimal size of the firm. Anyhow, the main limitation on a firm's growth is the shortage of managerial resources, which Slater (1980) models as the so-called "Penrose effect" (Slater (Slater 1980, p. 521). One has to further stress that firms are primarily interested in profits; therefore, only an increase in expected total profits and not the full utilization of resources or the stabilization of rents justify diversification (Penrose 1959).

Why should firms diversify? According to Penrose (1959), *efficient production* at a given product variety is only possible for large firms with strong diversification and integration for the following reasons. First, highly specialized firms are vulnerable in a dynamic environment due to technological progress and changes in consumer preferences. Only high product variety can protect a firm from major demand shifts – neither monopoly power nor technological progress alone will do. Distributing productive resources to a larger variety of goods can thus be more profitable in certain periods. Second, and more important, is the fact that diversification extends the production and investment possibilities into new areas, while maintaining or even expanding the present production lines (Penrose 1959).

Penrose (1959) accepts other explanations for integration, but criticizes their scope of explanation. "A variety of ad hoc explanations ranging from market imperfections and uncertainty to the dead hand of the past have been presented, and are true enough so far as they go, but they do not go very far (Penrose 1959, pp. 104–105)." Especially, *competition* requires strong diversification by firms. Expected actions of external competitors lead to internal adaptations in order to maintain a firm's position, which in turn increases the internal supply of productive services and knowledge. "The Schumpeterian process of 'creative destruction' has not destroyed the large firm; on the contrary, it has forced it to become more 'creative' (Penrose 1959, p. 106)."

The Decision for Outsourcing

The possibility of purchasing and selling business areas supports "excessive" diversification, but also restrains it. In the process of increasing diversification, firms are confronted with unfamiliar business areas, in which they commit errors and in which expectations cannot be fulfilled. The stronger the diversification, the higher the number of mistakes. Firms can correct mistakes by selling unfamiliar business areas, and thus can reduce the risk of making losses. For this purpose, firms need to control whether a business area is still successful. Penrose (1959) recommends selling these business areas that a firm does not fully control in order to specialize in their *core competencies* and exploit learning effects. Selling "inefficient" businesses to specialized producers leads to *learning and efficiency effects* as a consequence of specialization, which can be increased through the adoption of a decentralized type of organization. Penrose's arguments for selling less profitable aspects of the firm can also be applied to the make-or-buy question. To sum up, generally the necessary productive resources are produced in-house and should only be purchased externally if the firm cannot provide the necessary knowledge. Although there is no general need to produce resources in-house that can also be purchased via markets, market purchases are limited due to TACs (Penrose 1959).

While Penrose (1959) treats the subject of specialization on core competencies more implicitly, *knowledge-based theories* address this issue more directly. Knowledge-based theories form a separate school of thought among the resource-based theories. Prahalad and Hamel (1990) thus put their focus on core competencies, defined as "the collective learning in the organization, especially how to coordinate diverse production skills and integrate multiple streams of technologies" (Prahalad and Hamel 1990, p. 82). A *core competence* should at least have three features. "First, a core competence provides access to a wide variety of markets. [...] Second, a core competence should make significant contribution to the perceived customer benefits of the end product. [...] Finally, a core competence should be difficult for competitors to imitate (Prahalad and Hamel 1990, pp. 83–84)."[6]

While knowledge is considered *one* important resource besides others in the literature mentioned above, Grant (1996), Liebeskind (1996), and Spender (1996) were among the first authors that explicitly outline knowledge as the most important resource of competitive advantage. "Since the origin of all tangible resources lies outside the firm, it follows that competitive advantage is more likely to arise from the intangible firm-specific knowledge which enables it to add value to the incoming factors of production in a relatively unique manner (Spender 1996, p. 46)." Knowledge can be considered the Ricardian comparative advantage or competitive

[6]Mahoney and Pandian (1992) also outline that *unique capabilities* in the strategic management literature "are important sources of heterogeneity that may result in sustained competitive advantage" (Mahoney and Pandian, 1992, p. 365).

advantage in business terms, as pointed out by Liebeskind (1996) when relating knowledge to rents. Specializing in less tasks, individuals can concentrate on learning new techniques and instruments, which will increase their efficiency (Smith 1776). Therefore, firms should specialize in the production of such goods where they possess a competitive learning advantage (Vang 2003). Only implicitly included in most knowledge-based theories is the notion that other areas should be purchased from external suppliers (outsourcing) who work more efficiently, contain learning advantages, and produce more cost-effectively due to specialization (Vang 2003).

2.1.3.3 Transaction Cost-Based Motives for In-House Production

The Basics of Transaction Cost-Based Theories

According to transaction cost-based approaches, TACs incur with external procurement and can outweigh efficiency advantages. The ideas of TACs have been elaborated in TAC-based theories of the firm, where opportunistic potential of the involved parties is stressed as the major reason for TACs. TAC-based theories are part of the *New Institutional Economics*, the latter representing more a bundle of multiple institutional theories rather than a general theory with a focus on social and legal norms and rules.[7] Contrary to neoclassical consideration, firms are not reduced to a production function, but represent an organizational construction, i.e., a governance structure of contractual relations that focus on attracting orders, reducing conflicts, and realizing mutual profits. The basics of the TAC-based approach are found in Coase's article "The Nature of the Firm " (1937), where he evaluates "why a firm emerges at all in a specialized exchange economy" (Coase 1937, p. 3):

> "The main reason why it is profitable to establish a firm would seem to be that there is a cost of using the price mechanism. The most obvious cost of "organizing" production through the price mechanism is that of discovering what the relevant prices are (Coase 1937, p. 4)."

Without such a price mechanism of the market, the so-called TACs, firms would not have a "raison-d'être" (Coase 1937, p. 5). Thus, transactions become the unit of analysis. Although TACs can lead to opportunistic behavior of the agents before signing the contract (ex ante), the focus is especially put on ex post possibilities (Coase 1937). TACs comprise all sacrifices and disadvantages that arise for the

[7]According to Williamson (2000), four levels of social analysis can be distinguished, namely the *social theory* at the first level, the *property rights theory* at the second level, the *TAC-based approach* at the third level, and the *principal-agent-theory* at the fourth level. Our study is largely interested in the TAC-based approach, which extends the informal rules of the first level (e.g., sanctions, customs, traditions, codes of conduct) and formal rules of the second level (e.g., constitutions, laws, property rights) by also integrating contractual relationships (Williamson 2000).

involved parties when exchanging goods and services. They include all information and communication costs that are associated ex ante with the initiation (e.g., travel, communication, and consulting costs), the agreement (e.g., arrangement costs, legal advice), and transaction (e.g., management costs for leadership and coordination) and ex post with the control (e.g., control of quality and date) and adjustment (extra costs due to subsequent changes in amount and dates) of an exchange that is perceived as fair (e.g., Picot 1982, 1991).

TAC-based theories are based on *human factors* of the agents, whose conduct corresponds to a large extent to reality. *Bounded rationality* of the agents, the result of information asymmetries, is assumed. "Bounded rationality refers to rate and storage limits on the capacities of individuals to receive, store, retrieve, and process information without error (Williamson 1973, p. 317)." Especially, contractual incompleteness in combination with the assumption of opportunism creates large problems. "*Opportunism* [!] is an effort to realize individual gains through a lack of candor or honesty in transactions (Williamson 1973, p. 317)." Opportunism thus designates the possibility of selfish individuals to maximize their individual utility at the expense of thirds, which is reflected in adverse selection, moral hazard, and other strategic behavior. Agents are further endowed with *conscious foresight* which enables them to detect possible prospective events, in order to integrate them ex ante in their contracts and thus to dispose of advantages (Williamson 2000).

Williamson (1975) completes the behavioral analysis of the agents with further *transactional factors*. First, transactions have a *specificity* which can be measured by means of singularity of the provision or use of the resource. The author differentiates specialized physical assets, specialized human assets, site specificity, dedicated asset specificity, and brand capital. Specific transactions thus depend on site-specific facilities, specialized machines and technologies, and specialized and qualified employees, or on buyer-specific investments. Second, agents are subject to *uncertainty*, which measures the predictability or frequency of change during a transaction (Williamson 1975).

Note that the risk of uncertainty has already been addressed by Coase (1937). Generally, agents prefer a long-term contract to a sequence of short-term contracts in order to reduce costs and risks. A long-term contract, however, contains the risk of *uncertainty* to the agents, especially to the buyer as regards future efforts of the seller. For this reason, the detailed modalities of the seller, on the one hand, are deliberately unpredicted to allow for future adjustment possibilities. The buyer, on the other hand, finalizes the details after having concluded the contract. According to Coase, "[a] firm is likely therefore to emerge in those cases where a very short-term contract would be unsatisfactory" (Coase 1937, p. 5).

Transaction Costs with Market Purchases of Services

In the following paragraph, possible TACs that occur with market purchases of services are discussed. According to Cronin et al. (2004), firms might face search, transition, coordination and exchange costs, and the costs for strategic capabilities.

First, *search costs* emerge from sacrificing time or effort to find the range of different market prices for the respective services. Since only the processes and not the services themselves can be standardized, Cronin et al. (2004) estimate search costs to be relatively high. If market prices do not represent the single criterion of utility and/or if products are not standardized, these prices might become even higher (Douma and Schreuder 1998). Due to their heterogeneity, services transactions are often uncertain. Thus, search costs constitute between 1 and 10% of the total contract value in the IT-sector (Overby 2003).

Second, *transition costs* include the training and integration of new service providers to guarantee a minimum service quality. The more national boundaries, such as cultures and business environments, are crossed, the higher are transition costs. 2–3% of the total contract price in the IT-sector are used to become familiar with the provider. Layoffs and other associated costs, such as the costs for reorganization and retraining, might lead to further 3–5%. Beyond that, during the first two years, firms have experienced a decrease in productivity of 20%, which constitutes further transition costs (Overby 2003).

Third, *coordination costs* with respect to the outsourced activities can also occur, even if the firm buys (costly) insurance against several disturbances, e.g., on the supply side. Other coordination costs comprise, for instance, sufficient telecommunication links between the purchaser and the buyer. Thus, 1–10% of the contract value can be dedicated to coordination costs in IT (Overby 2003). Fourth, *exchange costs* or contract management costs are spent to guarantee the terms of exchange, which are likely to increase for complex international contracts or long delivery periods (Hill 2003). In the IT-sector, these costs account for 6–10% of the contract value (Overby 2003).

Fifth, *the costs for strategic capabilities* comprise the risk of loss of proprietary information, which can be lowered through detailed contract specification. Moreover, asset specificity also creates additional costs, if these assets (e.g., specific training software) cannot be used for other purposes, as outlined by Williamson (1985). Finally, the infrastructural capacity is reduced, when former in-house-produced services are outsourced, since knowledge and technical capabilities, and with them several options, will disappear. Thus, keeping several activities in-house maintains a certain flexibility and protection towards future events (Cronin et al. 2004).

The Decision for In-House Production

According to Williamson (1996), markets can be distinguished from in-house production, also called hierarchy, by three main features. First, markets are characterized by a stronger intensity of incentives and limited bureaucratic burdens. Second, markets offer possibilities for economies-of-scale and scope due to an aggregated demand. Third, hierarchies possess internal control mechanisms (Williamson 1996). In various studies, Williamson explains a firm's decision for in-house production (vertical integration) with *market failure*, especially of product and capital markets.

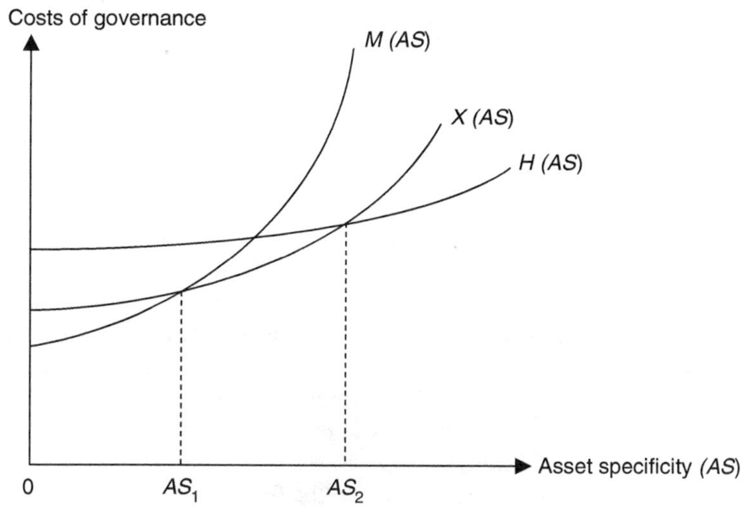

Fig. 2.5 Comparative costs of governance
Source: own illustration. Modified from: Williamson (2002, p. 181)

Firms exist because they have the capacity to solve internal tasks more efficiently than markets, whereas markets, especially product or capital markets, discipline inefficient firms insufficiently.[8] Inefficient firms are firms that do not maximize profits due to uncompetitive structures on the product markets, such as oligopolies or monopolies, but also due to failure of the capital market. Williamson emphasizes this latter point. According to Williamson, the corporate head office would coordinate the firm's divisions more efficiently than the capital market would do if the divisions were independent firms. This is explained with information disadvantages (e.g., concerning the efficiency of a firm) and based on the thesis of separation of ownership and control according to Berle and Means (1932).

Thus, firms occur when the internal *comparative costs of governance* are more cost-efficient than the comparative costs of governance of the market solution. Figure 2.5 maps the comparative costs of governance in markets, $M(AS)$, and in hierarchies, $H(AS)$, both being functions of asset specificity AS. When AS is zero, the costs of governance with hierarchy are higher due to bureaucratic barriers compared to the market solution, i.e., $H(AS) > M(AS)$. The more AS increases, the more the initial cost advantage of the market solution falls, and it may even reverse itself for very large AS, where the comparative costs of governance with hierarchy are smaller than the market costs. $X(AS)$ represents a hybrid of "market-preserving credible contracting modes that possess adaptive attributes located between classical markets and hierarchies" (Williamson 2002, p. 181). For $0 \leq AS < AS_1$, the market solution dominates the two other options. If $AS = AS_1$, the market

[8]Williamson rejects the neoclassical model, where competition promotes efficiency on product and capital markets by squeezing inefficient firms out of the markets.

and hybrid solution show the same costs of governance. For $AS_1 < AS < AS_2$, the hybrid solution is preferred, while for $AS = AS_2$ hierarchy is as good as the hybrid solution. Finally, if $AS > AS_2$, hierarchy is the best option (Williamson 2002).

Besides market failure, hierarchy can be more efficient than the external market solution due to the existence of *incomplete contracts*.[9] According to Williamson (2002), "[a]ll complex contracts are unavoidably incomplete. For this reason, parties will be confronted with the need to adapt to unanticipated disturbances that arise by reason of gaps, errors and omissions in the original contract" (Williamson 2002, p. 174). Thus, the transaction environment with uncertainty and bounded rationality makes a complete contract impossible, since adjustments are always required. Moreover, a detailed contract ex ante would prevent the contract from being flexible enough for prospective adjustments. The central question is whether investments of a party lead to a *hold-up*, which is a possibility for the contracting party of a short-term change or break-up of the contract. Such a hold-up possibility would turn the own specific investments into sunk-costs (Vang 2003).

Let us assume a fully specified contract in the following. In the beginning, both parties formulate the contract and integrate the exact modalities such as prices, delivery conditions, and so forth. Nevertheless, adjustments and changes are possible afterwards. After completion of the contract, the subcontractor needs to make specific investments, which reduces his bargaining power, since his specific investments could turn into sunk-costs. In such a situation, the subcontractor would have to accept any price between the originally negotiated price and zero in order to reduce total losses. Since the subcontractor can already anticipate such a situation, he is tempted to make more general investments, which could be used more widely (i.e., with a lower asset-specificity), but would be less efficient than the optimal investment. Note that the customer can have a worse bargaining position, too, e.g., if his production depends on certain irreplaceable inputs of the subcontractor.

Time-specificity can constitute a hold-up for both parties, when the customer (resp. subcontractor) depends on the punctual delivery. The subcontractor (resp. customer) could threaten the customer (resp. subcontractor) with a delay of delivery (resp. change of subcontractor) in order to increase (resp. reduce) prices. The subcontractor will only undertake optimal investments when he has sufficient incentives, which is more likely with reduced hold-up possibilities, for instance, when the customer owns shares of the subcontractor's firm or contracts to buy a minimum amount. If such supplementary conditions cannot be achieved, firms have an incentive for integration (Vang 2003).

> "To sum up integration occurs either because the subcontractor needs to make specific investments that allow the customer to make or hold on him (or vice versa) or because the

[9]Incomplete contracts have been used in several models to explain the make-or-buy decision of a firm (e.g., Antràs 2003). Among these, Ethier (1986) stresses the aspect of information asymmetries between firms, that make it difficult for firms to control the amount of research endeavours of the adverse party and to formulate an incentive-compatible contract. Besides, the required quality is difficult to integrate into a contract.

subcontractor can make a hold up because of the customer's losses, if he does not receive the good at a certain time (or vice versa) (Vang 2003, p. 7)."

2.2 Drivers of Services Offshoring

The international trading environment has changed over the last 20 years.[10] The changes reflect technological, political, and economic changes that have together encouraged more international trade and foreign investment, altered the structure of trade, and changed the relation between trade and foreign direct investment. These changes in the international economy began decades ago and have emerged gradually. Thus, we are not seeing a sudden shift in economic relations, but there has been enough change in the amount of internationalization of production to justify our designation of the past 20 years as comprising a "new wave" of globalization. This new wave of globalized production has involved a quantitative and a qualitative shift in the role of international trade.

Economists describe the new arrangements as no longer involving only trade in goods and services, but as a "trade in tasks" (Grossman and Rossi-Hansberg 2006a, b). Levy (2005) sees offshoring as driven not by comparative advantage but by firms' ability to "coordinate a geographically dispersed network of activities". He notes that offshoring "decouples the linkages between economic value creation and geographic location" (Levy 2005, p. 685). In other words, offshoring has altered the traditional link between trade and value added. Higher imports, which can lower costs considerably, can thus raise (lead) firm profits and contribute to the rising share of corporate profits in national income.

The massive expansion of supply chains internationally, with lead firms investing abroad or subcontracting with foreign producers in search of cost reductions or to better serve local markets, has been given its most important boost by *developments in ICTs* (see Sect. 2.2.1.1), in particular with the integration of computers into mass production, including product design, the management of the supply chain, the monitoring of inventory, sales and distribution, and payroll, finance, and accounting. Developments in ICTs have also led to a decline in communication costs and thus fostered offshoring, which Baldwin (2006) describes as the "second unbundling":

"Rapidly falling transportation costs – a trend which has been going on since the late nineteenth century – caused the first unbundling, namely the end of the necessity of making goods close to the point of consumption. More recently, rapidly falling communication and coordination costs have fostered a second unbundling – the end of the need to perform most manufacturing stages near each other. Even more recently, the second unbundling has spread from factories to offices with the result being the offshoring of service-sector jobs. In a nutshell, the first unbundling allowed the spatial separation of factories and consumers. The second unbundling spatially unpacked the factories and offices themselves (Baldwin 2006, p. 7)."

---

[10] The introductory notes on the following two pages have been taken and modified from Milberg and Schöller (2008).

A political development affecting the volume and direction of international trade and investment is the wave of multilateral and regional trade agreements, covering more countries than ever in history, that have reduced tariff and non-tariff barriers and most importantly have provided protection for foreign investors. The WTO has multiplied its membership over the original GATT by a factor of six, hundreds of bilateral investment treaties have been signed, and numerous regional trade agreements have come into effect. These agreements have contributed to the ongoing process of reducing tariffs and non-tariff barriers, but they have also significantly aided the globalization of production by creating protection for foreign investors. Concerning services trade, the progress of multilateral (Sect. 2.2.1.2) and regional (Sect. 2.2.1.3) trade agreements are being reviewed with regard to their scope and achievements.

Trade occurred increasingly through sophisticated global value chains, as companies in developed countries went offshore to perform both manufacturing and services. There are several motives why firms go offshore. We distinguish between market-oriented motives (Sect. 2.2.2.1), cost-oriented motives (Sect. 2.2.2.2), and procurement-oriented motives (Sect. 2.2.2.3). More recently, the latter also include the search for agglomeration advantages and the search for skilled labor abroad. While, for a long time, market-oriented motives dominated the (captive) offshoring decisions, newer studies confirm the trend towards cost-orientation not only in Germany. This has resulted in greater reliance on imports from low-income countries.

Politically, perhaps the most significant development of this period was the entry of former communist and other largely-closed economies into the capitalist world economy. The collapse of the Soviet Union and of communist governments throughout Eastern Europe and East Asia, the capitalist turn of communist China's economic plan, and even the opening and liberalization of India's economy, have all served to expand global productive capacity, international trade, foreign investment, and international subcontracting. Freeman (2007) has characterized this development as "the great doubling" of the world capitalist system's labor force as it had added 1.3B people to the pool of labor seeking work under competitive conditions (see Sect. 2.2.3.1). The role of multinational companies in this development for the host countries is analyzed in Sect. 2.2.3.2. Finally, we focus briefly on the liberalization efforts in two selected developing countries, namely India and China (see Sect. 2.2.3.3).

2.2.1 *Global Developments*

2.2.1.1 Developments in Information and Communication Technologies

The Age of Information and Telecommunications

The fast pace of services offshoring was mainly fostered by the development and distribution of *information and communication technologies*, i.e., technologies that enable information and communication flows.

> "Information and communication technologies encompass all those technologies that enable the handling of information and facilitate different forms of communications among human actors, between human beings and electronic systems, and among electronic systems. These technologies can be sub-divided into: [c]apturing [...,] [s]torage [...,] [p]rocessing [...,] [c]ommunications [...,] [and d]isplay technologies [...] (Hamelink 1997, p. 3)."

This 'electronic-digital revolution' initiated the *age of information and telecommunications* (and biotechnology), also called information economy, and started in the early 1990s. The age of information and telecommunications represents the fifth Kondratieff-wave[11] and follows the age of electronics, computers, and robots (fourth Kondratieff) that started in the 1950s, as well as the age of oil, the automobile, electricity, and chemical innovations (third Kondratieff), that was initiated at the beginning of the twentieth century.

The age of information and telecommunications builds on partially simultaneous *developments in telecommunications and IT* during the preceding one and a half centuries. Thus, the development of telecommunication technologies can be traced back to the invention of the telegraph in 1844, followed by the telephone in 1870, the mobile phone in 1979, the Integrated Services Digital Network (ISDN) in 1987, and the broadband in 1990 (Hutzschenreuter et al. 2007). Developments in IT began with the invention of the first computer, Zuse Z3, in 1941. By 1960, there were around 7,000 computers worldwide. The first precursor of today's personal computer was invented in 1968, followed by the predecessor of the internet – the Arpanet – in 1969. In 1971, the first micro-chip was presented to the public, which transformed the large computers into desktop computers. The first Apple computer was sold in 1976, the internet was developed in 1983, and the world wide web in 1989. In 1994, more computers than automobiles were sold worldwide for the first time (Hutzschenreuter et al. 2007; Mosdorf 1998).

More than three decades ago, Helleiner (1973) was already reporting on an early form of services offshoring to low-income countries:

> "The variety of activities now being performed for export on this basis in the less-developed countries is already very large. It may be worth listing some examples in order to show the flavour of these developments. [. . .] Data are flown to Southeast Asia and the West Indies for punching upon tape by low-wage key punch operators, following which the tapes are flown back again (Helleiner 1973, p. 29)."

This example shows us that, in a strict sense, ICTs did not enable services offshoring, but rendered services offshoring less difficult. Developments in ICTs have eliminated technical restrictions of some former uno-actu services that theoretically would have been transferable (e.g., data in books and printed reports), but economically could not be traded quickly enough or at low costs. The elimination of such technical restrictions include the following advantages.

First, *digitization* allows the users of ICTs to store enormous amounts of data, which otherwise would have used lots of space in the form of data in printed reports,

[11]The Kondratieff-waves, also called grand supercycles, have a length of between 45 and 60 years.

books, and folders, or in form of CDs and tapes. Second, developments in ICTs have made it possible to *uncouple information from its physical storage*, enabling the transfer of huge amounts of data within a few seconds ('disembodied services') and creating a new space–time structure (Boes 2004; UNCTAD 2004).

A third advantage is the possibility of *data separation*, which enables individuals to communicate independently from their physical movement, i.e., e-mails can be stored in the mailbox and then read at any point of time, whereas telephone calls require the physical presence of both actors. Fourth, the use of ICTs generates twofold externalities, which are both characterized by non-rivalry. *Content-related externalities* give users access to information (e.g., on the internet). Moreover, enlarging the ICT-network creates *network externalities*. Thus, new users of the system can benefit from the information and network structure through the exchange of information, which also increases the advantages for existing users. Fifth, ICTs represent a *general purpose technology* (GPT) that can potentially be used by any subject and any sector (Bedi 1999).

Sixth, the use of electronic media changes *customs and traditions*. Before the age of information and telecommunications, it was common to produce some traditional functions, such as accounting, archiving, and design, in-house. The use of ICTs no longer requires face-to-face contact, since formerly in-house-produced services can now be externalized. Finally, knowledge has become available in codified, standardized and digitized form, making fragmentation of services into smaller components and thus global sourcing possible (UNCTAD 2004).

The so-called *productivity-bias* is a consequence of the new tradability of services. Empirically, the manufacturing sector has been considered more productive than the service sector, with the share of manufactured products in GDP remaining constant despite a reduction of manufacturing workers. Due to the increased use of ICTs, productivity gains were also recorded in the service sector. Especially, service sectors with significant innovation potential, such as banking and insurance and the ICT-sector itself, have caught up in productivity (Barth 1998).

Thus, the use of (circular) e-mails in a firm can raise productivity, as e-mails hold a *control function*. First, accountability is always given, because everything is documented in written and not only in oral form. Second, public commitment via circular e-mail better disciplines the responsible person and entails higher productivity compared to an agreement only made between two persons. Third, public interaction through circular e-mails better prevents workers from being passive. Besides the control function, e-mails are also characterized by a *long-term memory*. The documentation of information in form of e-mails counteracts a repeated problem-solving of the same issue, which raises productivity. This effect is eased by the development of (desktop) search engines. There might be more channels through which the use of e-mails in particular and of ICTs in general increases productivity.

Information and Communication Technologies in Developing Countries

The process of developments in ICTs might go hand in hand with an increased services offshoring potential, especially to developing countries. As early as 1996, the Economist stated that "[f]irms in the rich world have "outsourced" all manner of things to developing countries – from computer programming and airline revenue accounting to processing hospital patients' records and insurance claims. [. . .] As IT expands the scope for trade in services, it will inevitably expose workers in previously sheltered sectors to international competition, including skilled workers" (The Economist 1996, p. 32, taken from Deavers 1997, p. 517). The following paragraph focuses on *information and communication technologies in developing countries* and evaluates how well the latter are prepared to absorb the services that have previously been performed in developed countries.

The *distribution of internet users* around the world reveals for the period from 2001 to 2005 that high-income countries showed an increase from 378 to 523 internet users per 1,000 inhabitants, middle-income countries from 35 to 114, and low-income countries from five to 44 users. The ratio of internet users in middle-income countries relative to high-income countries rose sharply from 3% in 2001 to almost 22% in 2005. The ratio of users in low-income countries relative to high-income countries increased from 1.3 to 8.4%. Thus, low-income countries showed the highest growth rates between 2001 and 2005, while middle-income countries are also catching up. Note that the worldwide distribution of fixed line and mobile phone subscribers is very similar (World Bank 2007).

Nevertheless, the number of ICT users is not always a reliable indicator for the technological development of a country, as the case of India demonstrates. With on average 128 fixed line and mobile phone subscribers and 55 internet users per 1,000 people in 2005, India's ICT penetration is smaller than China's with 570 fixed line and mobile phone subscribers and 85 internet users (World Bank 2007). Since India is a larger exporter of computer and information services (see Sect. 3.3.1.2), this difference in ICT penetration indicates a stronger digital divide in India between the rural and urban populations.

The trend described above is confirmed by the *Networked Readiness Index* of the World Economic Forum (2007). This index measures the degree of preparation of a nation or community to participate in and benefit from ICT developments. 122 countries are ranked in the Networked Readiness Index 2006–2007 (see Appendix A). Our interpretation of the ranking is the following. The best-ranked quarter of the 122 countries includes almost exclusively high-income or upper-middle income countries according the grouping of the World Bank. The second best quarter contains countries that have already become or are becoming important offshore destinations, such as India or China. The third best quarter includes countries with a high potential to become the next generation of offshore destinations. Some of them have already established themselves as offshore destinations for countries from the second best quarter, such as the Philippines for India. The countries in the lowest quarter are unlikely to become offshore destinations for services in the near future. Note also that Appendix A clearly indicates a correlation between a country's income and ICT penetration.

Another important issue in the context of services offshoring is the existence of sufficient internet connection between developed and developing regions. *Total interregional internet bandwidth* grew by on average 96% p.a. between 1999 and 2005. The interregional distribution clearly shows that developing regions, especially Africa, are insufficiently connected to the developed regions in Europe and North America. Despite this fact, there is evidence of a catching up of some interregional connections, especially between Latin America and the US and Canada, but also between Asia and Europe. The connections Africa–Europe, Asia–Europe, and Latin America–US and Canada all grew more than the average. Only the connection Latin America–Europe experienced negative growth. The interregional internet bandwidth between Asia and the developed regions Europe and North America represents around a third of the total interregional internet bandwidth, with 33% in 1999 and 30% in 2005 (UNCTAD 2006).

We conclude that less-developed countries and regions seem to catch up in terms of ICT penetration and interregional internet bandwidth, but there is still a long way to go for the poorest among them. In particular, the group of lower-middle income countries could become interesting offshore destinations, as they dispose of both a relatively stable ICT infrastructure, that could be further improved, and the advantage of very low costs. Note that ICTs are not only beneficial to developed countries in terms of growing services offshoring potentials, but also play an important role in economic development.

Bedi (1999) discusses a variety of potential advantages for organizations, markets, and institutions that occur with the *adoption or increased use of ICTs* in developing countries. First, as the costs for the provision, processing, and production of information decrease and the quality of information rises, the decision making process within organizations can be facilitated. Second, the increase in information flows will reduce market insecurity, which will lead to a higher participation rate in factor and goods markets and finally to higher output. Third, institutional inefficiencies are more likely to be identified and improved, when ICT-based institutional models are used. Possible negative effects of ICTs could include the increase in the wage gap between qualified (ICT-using) and less-qualified workers (Bedi 1999).

2.2.1.2 Multilateral Liberalization of Trade in Services

From the establishment of GATT in 1947 through the Tokyo Round (1973–1979), the multilateral trading system focused exclusively on goods. Services were covered first in the Uruguay round (1986–1994) and the establishment of the WTO in January 1995. The WTO replaced the GATT as an organization, but the latter still exists under the umbrella of the WTO, which at present consists of 153 member countries. The range of trade negotiations currently covers around 60 agreements and separate commitments made by individual members in specific areas. Their scope has been extended to goods, services, and intellectual property, which are covered by the Multilateral Agreements on Trade in Goods (including the GATT 1994), the GATS, and the Trade-Related Aspects of Intellectual Property Rights (TRIPS), all established in Annex 1 of the Uruguay Round agreements.

The *General Agreement on Trade in Service* constitutes the first and only set of multilateral agreements covering international trade in services. Its main objectives correspond to the ones of the GATT, which are "creating a credible and reliable system of international trade rules; ensuring fair and equitable treatment of all participants (principle of non-discrimination); stimulating economic activity through guaranteed policy bindings; and promoting trade and development through progressive liberalization" (WTO[12]). The GATS consists of two parts, namely the framework of general obligations and disciplines and the individual countries' commitments on access to their national service markets. A summary of the main contents of the GATS can be found in Box 2.5.

Box 2.5: The general agreement on trade in services

"The Services Agreement which forms part of the Final Act rests on three pillars. The first is a framework agreement containing basic obligations which apply to all member countries. The second concerns national schedules of commitments containing specific further national commitments which will be the subject of a continuing process of liberalization. The third is a number of annexes addressing the special situations of individual services sectors.

Part I of the basic agreement defines its scope [...].

Part II sets out general obligations and disciplines. A basic most-favoured-nation (m.f.n.) obligation states that each party "shall accord immediately and unconditionally to services and service providers of any other Party, treatment no less favourable than that it accords to like services and service providers of any other country". However, it is recognized that m.f.n. treatment may not be possible for every service activity and, therefore, it is envisaged that parties may indicate specific m.f.n. exemptions. Conditions for such exemptions are included as an annex and provide for reviews after 5 years and a normal limitation of 10 years on their duration. [...]

Part III contains provisions on market access and national treatment which would not be general obligations but would be commitments made in national schedules. Thus, in the case of market access, each party "shall accord services and service providers of other Parties treatment no less favourable than that provided for under the terms, limitations and conditions agreed and specified in its schedule". The intention of the market-access provision is to progressively eliminate the following types of measures: limitations on numbers of service providers, on the total value of service transactions or on the total number of service operations or people employed. Equally, restrictions on the kind of legal entity or joint venture through which a service is provided or any foreign capital limitations relating to maximum levels of foreign participation are to be progressively eliminated. [...]

[12]See http://www.wto.org/english/tratop_e/serv_e/gatsqa_e.htm

Part IV of the agreement establishes the basis for progressive liberalization in the services area through successive rounds of negotiations and the development of national schedules. It also permits, after a period of 3 years, parties to withdraw or modify commitments made in their schedules. Where commitments are modified or withdrawn, negotiations should be undertaken with interested parties to agree on compensatory adjustments. Where agreement cannot be reached, compensation would be decided by arbitration.
Part V of the agreement contains institutional provisions, including consultation and dispute settlement and the establishment of a Council on Services. The responsibilities of the Council are set out in a Ministerial Decision."

Source: A summary of the final act of the Uruguay Round, WTO legal texts, taken from: http://www.wto.org/english/docs_e/legal_e/ursum_e.htm#mAgreement

The agreement covers all traded services and defines four different modes of supply (see Sect. 2.1.2.2). *General obligations* comprise the most-favored-nation (m.f.n.) treatment and transparency. The m.f.n. treatment prohibits discrimination by requiring from member countries to treat their trading partners equally, which applies to all services with only a few temporary exemptions. This includes, for instance, that all WTO members receive equal opportunities, when a country opens a service sector. Transparency is assured through the obligation of member countries to publish all relevant regulations and laws and to establish inquiry points. The *individual countries' commitments* to open their markets and the measures to be taken are specified in the "schedules" listing the respective sectors, the extent of market access (e.g., limitations on the number of service providers, service operations, or employees in the sector), and possible limitations on national treatment (i.e., whether or not rights to local firms are granted to foreign firms).

Setting up of a framework for a multilateral trading system that covers services is seen as the major achievement of the GATS. Nevertheless, some weaknesses of the GATS slowed down the progress of liberalizing the service sectors in the five subsequent years except for the financial and telecommunications sectors (for a discussion of the weaknesses and suggestions of new rules, see Mattoo 2001). One of the weaknesses is that members have not agreed whether an electronic services provision should be considered cross-border trade (mode 1) or consumption abroad (mode 2). Another weakness is the 'positive list' approach pursued in the GATS, i.e., measures concerning trade liberalization only apply to listed services (Mattoo and Wunsch-Vincent 2004).

According to Article XIX of the GATS, a *new services round* should start not later than five years from the date of entry into force. Thus, the first phase of negotiations began in January 2000. It was concluded in March 2001 with the agreement of the member countries on the guidelines and procedures of the service round, which have been incorporated into the Doha Development Agenda. Another part of negotiations is related to the m.f.n. treatment. The GATS 1995 allowed exemptions of more favorable treatments, which should be limited to ten years. All exemptions are now being reviewed with regard to the question if the conditions for their first application exist to date and should remain part of the new negotiations. In addition, an agreement of March 2003 takes into account the liberalization efforts of member countries on their own initiative when negotiating market access in services.[13]

To sum up, the process of liberalizing the service sectors seems to have accelerated with the new services round, but the achievements of the GATS are still difficult to estimate. This might be largely linked to the nature of trade in services and its measurement.

> "International trade in services requires, unlike trade in goods, no physical package to cross borders, frequently has no description of content, or information on quantity, origin or destination, and critically has no administrative system based on customs duty collection measuring it. [...] International service trade data [...] are collected through both business accounting and recordkeeping systems, administrative sources, regular surveys of businesses as well as numerical estimations by statistical agencies (Kirkegaard 2004, p. 24)."

2.2.1.3 Regional Liberalization of Trade in Services

Besides the GATS, the liberalization of trade in services is also fostered by endeavors of *regional trade agreements* (RTAs). In the late 1980s and early 1990s, the first RTAs, promoting the liberalization of services trade, entered into force, such as the Australia–New Zealand Closer Economic Relations trade agreement (CER) in 1983, the European Community's Single Market in 1987, the Canada–United States Free Trade Agreement (FTA) in 1989, and the North American Free Trade Agreement (NAFTA) in 1994 (Hoekman and Sauvé 1994). In the 1990s, approaches towards services liberalization have been undertaken, for instance, by the Association of Southeast Asian Nations (ASEAN) in 1997, the Mercado Común del Sur (MERCOSUR) in 1997, the Andean Community in 1998, and the Caribbean Community (CARICOM) in 1998 as well as by numerous bilateral RTAs (Stephenson 2002).

The EU shows the deepest regional initiative concerning trade liberalization of services. Progress has mainly been made through the further clarification and development of the two "fundamental freedoms" of the European Community (EC) Treaty – the freedom of establishment and the freedom to provide cross-border services – through specific legislation in fields such as financial services, telecommunications, and broadcasting, and through the recognition of professional qualifications (EU 2008).

Although the 1992 Single Market initiative proposed actions to integrate the service markets, segmentation still exists due to national regulations defining

---

[13]Most of the information is retrieved from the homepage of the WTO (http://www.wto.org).

the qualifications, competition, and control of firms, which constitute barriers to trade (Hoekman 2006). As a result, the Lisbon summit of EU leaders in March 2000 asked for a strategy to remove cross-border barriers to services. This included the publication of a report on the State of the Internal Market for Services, identifying obstacles to free intra-EU services trade in July 2002. Another important result is the Services Directive, proposed by the European Commission in January 2004. After revision, it was adopted by the European Parliament and the Council in December 2006 (see Box 2.6) and must be implemented by the member states by the end of 2009 (EU 2008).[14]

Box 2.6: Final legislative act of the EU services directive (extracts)

"The key elements of the Directive can be summarised as follows:

1. *General provisions*

The Directive establishes the general provisions for facilitating the freedom of establishment for service providers and the free movement of services. [...] The scope of the Directive is very specific. It will not apply to: *non-economic* services of general interest; (the Directive later specifies that certain economic services of general interest will also be excluded from the Directive. They include, inter alia: postal services; the electricity sector; the gas sector; water distribution and waste water services); financial services; electronic communication services and networks; transport services; temporary work agencies; healthcare services; audiovisual services; gambling activities; activities connected to official work; social services; private security services; and services provided by notaries and bailiffs.

In cases where service sectors are already regulated under EU legislation then existing provisions will prevail over the provisions set out in this Directive. The Directive will not concern rules of private international law.

2. *Administrative simplification*

To date, one of the main causes of market fragmentation has been overly cumbersome administrative procedures. One of the key aspects of this Directive, therefore, is to provide for administrative simplification. As a result, the Directive provides that in future, application forms will be based on a standard European form, which will be developed by the Commission in accordance with comitology procedures. Service providers seeking the cross-border establishment of their activities will be able to apply through a national "Single Contact Point". The single contact points will: provide applicants with all the necessary information needed to establish themselves abroad; set up a system whereby all procedures and formalities can be easily completed; and allow for applications to be submitted at a distance and by electronic means.

[14]See http://ec.europa.eu/internal_market/top_layer/index_19_en.htm

3. *Freedom of establishment*
Those seeking "the right of establishment" will not be subject to authorisation schemes. Authorisations will only be permitted on condition that they are non-discriminatory; they are justified on the grounds of public interest; and the objective can not be achieved by less restrictive measures (i.e. an inspection would take place too late). Any authorisation that fulfils these criteria must, in any case, be reported to the Commission.
4. *Free movement of services*
Member States must respect the right of service providers to operate in a country other than the one in which they are established. As such, service providers will not need: to be established in the territory in which they are seeking to work; to obtain an authorisation; to register with a professional body or association; or be banned from setting up a certain type of infrastructure which they may need to supply the services in question. Only requirements concerning public policy, public security, public health or the protection of the environment may be imposed on a service provider.

The above, however, will not apply to services of economic interest such as, the postal sector; the electricity sector; the gas sector; water distribution services etc.
5. *Quality of services*
In order to protect consumers, the Directive lists a number of provisions, applicable to the service industry. For example, service providers must provide the Member States with their name; legal status; geographic address of establishment; registered trade number; authorisation scheme (where relevant); VAT number; after sales guarantees etc. They must also, where necessary, subscribe to a professional liability insurance.
6. *Administrative co-operation*
The Directive obliges Member States to offer each other mutual assistance and to put in place measures for effective co-operation in order to ensure the correct supervision of providers and the services they provide. An "alert" mechanism is also set out.
7. *Convergence programme*
The Member States will, in co-operation with the Commission, take accompanying measures to encourage the drawing up, at a Community level, of codes of conduct which seek to facilitate the provisions of a service.
Entry into Force: 28 December 2006.
Transposition: 28 December 2009.

Source: 12/12/2006 – final legislative act (COD/2004/0001), taken from: http://www.europarl.europa.eu/oeil/resume.jsp?id = 240902&eventId = 980998&back-ToCaller = NO&language = en

Kox and Lejour (2006) stress that the policy heterogeneity within the EU causes different fixed market-entry costs for service providers. They find that these policy heterogeneity costs in the EU affect services trade and FDI negatively.

According to this study, the 2004 Services Directive could have counteracted this negative effect by reducing the fixed market-entry costs. Due to the adoption of the revised Services Directive in 2006, which excludes the acceptance of home country regulation, the authors, however, expect less positive trade effects (as reported by Hoekman 2006). Hoekman (2006) notes that similar cost reduction effects might be generated for a non-EU country by accession to the EU or by adopting parts of the *acquis communautaire*.

As a consequence, the multilateral form of trade liberalization is sometimes considered superior or equal to regional trade agreements (e.g., Hoekman and Sauvé 1994). Thus, Hoekman (2006) concludes that "[t]he resistance inside the EU to fully liberalizing intra-EU services trade, and the length of time it has taken EU members to open intra-EU trade in services, also illustrates that the challenges to services liberalization may not be that much easier to address regionally than multilaterally" (Hoekman 2006, p. 39).

Stephenson (2002), however, discusses why RTAs have been more successful than the GATS in terms of transparency, stability, and liberalization of trade in services. First, many RTAs have surpassed the GATS in establishing disciplines for trade in services by using a different approach. Unlike the GATS, whose disciplines apply separately to goods, services, and intellectual property, some RTAs – inspired by the NAFTA – have adopted an integrated approach, where disciplines (e.g., on investments, on technical barriers to trade, on the movement of natural persons) apply simultaneously to goods and services.

Second, many RTAs apply a 'negative list' of services in contrast to the 'positive list' approach of the GATS. In the first perspective, all services are subject to the obligations of trade liberalization, unless they appear in the negative list. Either approach can lead to equal results in terms of services liberalization, but the negative list approach requires the members to reveal all non-conforming measures and excluded sectors.

Third, transparency is increased in some RTAs (e.g., Andean Community, CARICOM, MERCOSUR) by requiring member countries to publish their national inventories of measures affecting trade in services, which serves as the basis for removal of such restrictions. Other indicators for the superiority are the possibility of RTAs of a deeper integration due to stricter disciplines for services trade (e.g., an unconditional m.f.n. and national treatment in the MERCOSUR and the Andean Community) or due to their smaller size (Stephenson 2002).

To sum up, the number of regional and especially bilateral trade agreements has increased enormously in the last two decades, fostering the liberalization of trade in services. The deepest regional initiative has been made in the EU, but free intra-EU trade in services has still not been reached. Based on the arguments of Stephenson (2002), we believe that regional trade agreements are probably more effective than the GATS in promoting the liberalization of services. Another advantage is the greater flexibility of RTAs, since only a fraction of countries is included compared to the large number of WTO-members.

2.2.2 Services Offshoring Motives of Firms

This subsection examines the diverse *offshoring motives of firms and their expected domestic employment effects*. Traditionally, captive-offshoring (FDI) motives have been classified market-oriented, cost-oriented, and procurement-oriented. Newer motives can often be allocated to the traditional motives. The search for human capital abroad, for instance, which is clearly a newer phenomenon, can basically be considered a procurement-oriented motive. Remember that captive-offshoring is not the only form of offshoring. Firms might choose the form of offshore-outsourcing, motivated by advantages of SSPs abroad. We have already discussed motives why firms prefer external service provision to in-house production (Sect. 2.1.3). Thus, efficiency-based motives (Sect. 2.1.3.1) included e.g., the search for flexibility, while resource-based motives (Sect. 2.1.3.2) outlined the focus on firms' core competencies related to marketing, finance, R&D, and design. However, these motives do not reveal why outsourcing firms decide to go offshore. Offshore-outsourcing basically happens for the same motives as captive-offshoring, but the search for lower cost and the shortage of domestic inputs are more likely in this category than market-oriented motives.

The expected employment effects of an offshoring decision depend on the relationship between domestic and foreign production. First, the *substitutionality hypothesis* claims that offshore production replaces home production due to cheaper re-imports, which leads to negative domestic employment effects in the short term. Second, if domestic and foreign production are complementary, offshoring affects domestic employment positively according to the *complementarity hypothesis*. Third, since home and foreign production have no relationship in the *neutrality hypothesis*, offshoring has a neutral impact on domestic employment (modified from Henneberger, Graf, and Vocke 2000). For a long time, the relationship between offshore and domestic service production was supposed to be neutral due to the non-tradability of services. The tradability of disembodied services and the possibility of cheaper re-imports, however, made negative employment effects possible within the formerly inviolable service sector. Before defining and analyzing each of the three main offshoring motives, further offshoring motives and their relative importance are shown.

Single market-oriented motives are chosen to evade trade barriers, notably import restrictions (e.g., high import duties) by a local presence. Often, third countries try to benefit from reduced or eliminated internal tariffs in integrated regions through foreign affiliates. Free trade zones protect themselves from the possibility that companies import their goods via the member country with the lowest external tariff by imposing "local content requirements", which force firms to produce on site (Roling 1999; Tüselmann 1998). Single market-oriented motives become less important in view of globally falling import tariffs. The average tariffs for goods to the EU15 and the US have been cut by half between 1991 and 2005. Especially, import tariffs on goods from countries in transition were reduced by approximately three-quarters (UNCTAD GlobStat Database).

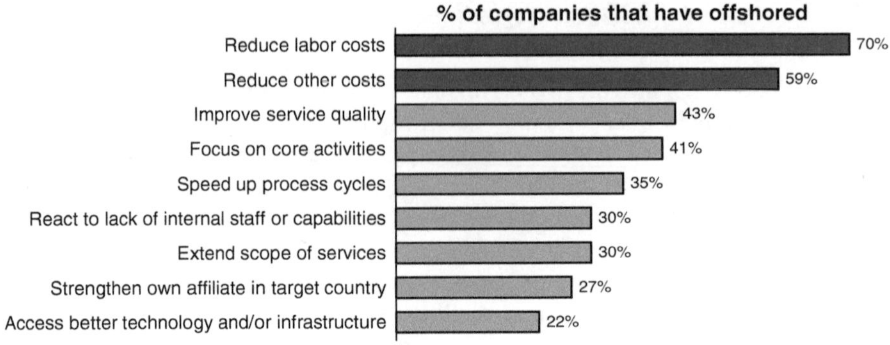

Fig. 2.6 Expected benefits from services offshoring
Source: own illustration. Based on UNCTAD and Roland Berger (2004), p. 9. NB: multiple answers possible

The *relative importance* of the different motives for services offshoring is shown in Fig. 2.6. The UNCTAD and Roland Berger Strategy Consultants (2004) analyzed a representative sample of the top 500 European firms on their services offshoring strategies, which constitutes the first survey on services offshoring in Europe. The company sample accounts for more than a fifth of the revenue of Europe's top 500. Asked on their expected benefits from services offshoring, the majority of the respondents first mentioned the reduction of labor costs (70%) and the reduction of other costs (59%). Besides cost-oriented motives, a variety of other expected benefits encourages firms to relocate services. The survey ranks the improvement of service quality third (43%) and the focus on core activities fourth (41%). Other motives include the search for staff and capabilities or better technology (UNCTAD and Roland Berger 2004). Another study surveyed 119 German firms, based on 144 offshoring arrangements, on their most important offshoring motives. They are ranked as follows: skill-level in the offshoring country, search for low costs, quality of the infrastructure, existing business experiences, political stability, and linguistic aspects (Hutzschenreuter et al. 2007).

2.2.2.1 Market-Oriented Motives

Traditional offshoring motives can be *market-oriented* in order to build up, maintain, or increase a company's market share abroad (Trabold et al. 2001), especially in the presence of stagnating domestic demand for goods and services. Market-oriented motives also integrate aftersales activities, such as customer service, sales and distribution, marketing, and so forth. A local presence abroad – be it an affiliate or an external sales company – directly or indirectly increases the company's local know-how, which in turn helps to attract new customers and to adopt quickly to changing customers' needs and tastes. Especially, large markets with huge current

Table 2.2 Tradability of services and main offshoring motive

		Main offshoring motive		
		Market-oriented	Cost-oriented	Procurement-oriented
Tradability of services	Non-tradable	*Neutrality hypothesis:* firms serve foreign markets via a local presence. (No export solution)	*Neutrality hypothesis:* domestic procurement of services. (No import solution)	*Neutrality hypothesis:* no procurement of imported services
	Tradable	*Substitutionality hypothesis:* foreign production substitutes for domestic service production (exports) *Complementary hypothesis:* foreign production reinforces domestic service exports (e.g., of intermediate inputs) *Neutrality hypothesis:* foreign production accompanies domestic service exports	*Substitutionality hypothesis:* foreign production (imports) substitutes for domestic production	*Complementarity hypothesis:* procurement of imported services renders domestic production possible

Source: own illustration

or potential growth and a high degree of trade integration, such as China or India, represent attractive offshore destinations.

What are the effects of market-oriented offshoring on domestic employment? In a first step, services need to be subdivided into non-tradable and tradable services. Table 2.2 classifies services with respect to their tradability and their main offshoring motive. Let us focus on market-oriented offshoring. When *non-tradable* services are considered (upper part of the table), foreign markets can only be served by a local presence. As an export solution from the country of origin to the destination country is not possible, domestic and foreign production have a neutral relationship with no impact on domestic employment (neutrality hypothesis).

If services are *tradable* (lower part of the table), market-oriented offshoring motives can affect domestic employment in a threefold manner, depending on the relationship between offshoring and exports. *Export-substituting* offshoring is expected to replace home produced goods and services, thereby reducing labor demand at home (substitutionality hypothesis). *Export-boosting* offshoring is anticipated to stimulate home production and increase home employment (complementarity hypothesis). *Export-accompanying* offshoring decisions are presumed to have a neutral domestic employment effect (neutrality hypothesis). The overall employment effect of market-oriented motives is assumed to be generally positive in the short and medium term (Roling 1999).[15]

2.2.2.2 Cost-Oriented Motives

While earlier studies detected market-oriented motives as the principal driver behind (captive) offshoring, more recent studies reveal a shift towards *cost-oriented motives* for Germany (see, e.g., Beyfuß and Eggert 2000; Jungnickel and Keller 2003). Cost-oriented motives aim at exploiting lower costs abroad, such as lower prices and other related advantages. Services contain a high offshoring potential, as their production is generally labor-intensive. In most cases, MNCs apply the "mixed calculation" strategy, relocating labor-intensive parts of their value chain and maintaining (human) capital-intensive parts at home.

One can distinguish between production-oriented, location-oriented, and scale-effect-oriented cost motives. *Production-oriented cost motives* include the direct search for lower wages, non-wage labor costs, construction and transport costs, or land prices. Production-oriented cost motives are driven by so-called *pull-factors*, i.e., attractive conditions in the destination country with respect to the production, but *push-factors* in the home country, such as high wages, can also provoke or accelerate the relocation process (Henneberger and Ziegler 1998). Thus, some authors find evidence for a positive impact of high domestic wages on offshoring and outsourcing. Hatzius (2000) detects a positive relationship between high unit labor costs in Germany and the UK and outward FDI-flows between 1982 and 1993. Girma and Görg (2003) show that high domestic wages are positively related to outsourcing. Görzig and Stephan (2002) find that, for Germany, the main motivation for outsourcing is the saving of internal resources, especially the costs for labor and capital investments.

Potential *cost savings* from offshoring IT services up to 40–60% are often communicated, but real savings seem to be lower. Indian IT service providers report savings of 20–25% (Boes 2004). According to a recent study including 119 German firms (based on 104 offshoring implementations), offshoring led to cost savings of 32% in IT, 26% in product development, 23% in call centers, and 20% in human resources, as well as 16% in accounting and finance and in R&D. Many firms reported a high discrepancy between planned and achieved savings, which was highest in call centers, accounting and finance, and IT. Most of the cost savings could be reaped within 12 months, but some activities still generated a large part of

[15]Note that the tradability of services also contains the possibility of closing down a foreign presence or of reducing foreign production by serving the foreign market with increased domestic exports.

their cost savings after twelve months, e.g., accounting and finance (66%), human resources (50%), and R&D (41%) (Hutzschenreuter et al. 2007).

Labor cost savings are high when qualified jobs are offshored, but even higher when less-skilled tasks are relocated. According to the National Association of Software and Service Companies (NASSCOM), which constitutes the chamber of commerce and is considered the "voice" of the IT software and services industry in India, an Indian call-center employee earns only a tenth of its British counterpart, whereas and IT programmer with five years work experience already earns a quarter (The Economist 2003). Nevertheless, hourly rates for computer programmers in India and the Czech Republic were around a seventh of German rates in 2004 (Schaaf 2004). The *average annual salary in IT and BPO* for 2005 as well as the projected average for 2010 are shown in Fig. 2.7. According to these forecasts, India is expected to experience the most significant wage increase. Industry maturity, increasing competition, growing complexity of offshoring projects, or stable demand are identified among the key drivers (neoIT 2006). Since Indian wages and other costs grow by 10–15% per year, IT and BPO providers in India face the challenge to cut total costs in order to maintain the 40% cost advantage for their customers (NASSCOM and McKinsey Global Institute 2005).

Location-oriented cost motives focus on a business-friendly environment, such as subsidies, tax incentives, fewer environmental requirements, less regulation, or a more liberal redundancy protection abroad. Contrary to production-oriented motives, location-oriented motives aim at cutting costs in a more indirect way. The pull-factor here is the attractive business environment in the destination country, but domestic push-factors such as high regulation and taxes can speed up the offshoring process. Ireland, for instance, has been attracting enormous amounts of FDI-flows for two decades thanks to its low corporate tax of initially 10%. Ireland's European neighbors put pressure on its tax policy, so Ireland raised corporate taxes to 12.5% in 2003. Gaston and Nelson (2001) find that labor costs are only indirectly included in captive-offshoring decisions, as the majority of

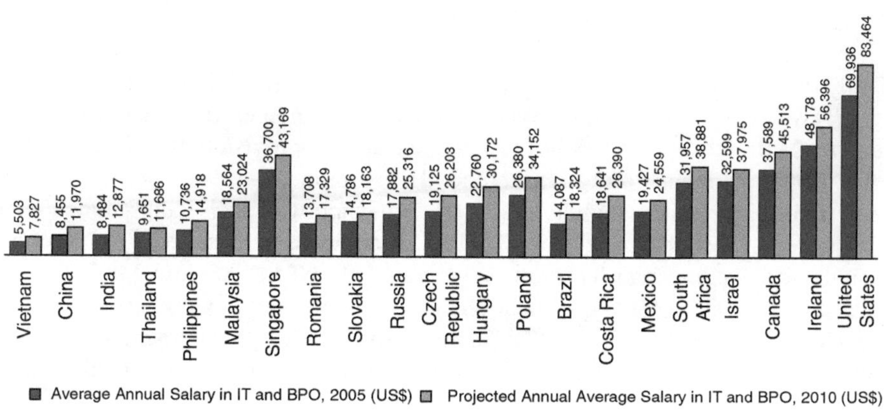

Fig. 2.7 Average annual salary in IT and BPO, 2005 versus 2010 (US$)
Source: own illustration. Data: neoIT (2006), p. 21

worldwide FDI goes to high-income countries. Although FDI flows to the US are directed towards states with a lower wage level, this is considered rather a consequence of low levels of labor laws, trade union activities, and centralized wage settings.

Scale-effect-oriented cost motives can be categorized into motives at the company level and motives at the operational level. *Scale-effects at the company level* are generated when foreign subsidiaries can benefit from specific knowledge of the parent company or another part of the company without significant extra costs. This includes technical, marketing, organizational, and other knowledge. Relocation to low-income countries can thus reduce fixed R&D costs (Borrmann 2001). Another advantage is the possibility to work in several shifts around the globe. American firms with subsidiaries in India, for instance, benefit from these time shifts when they order a service today and receive it tomorrow. Recently, the disadvantages of such time-differences have come to light, since Indian employees have started to complain about bad working hours and night-shifts. *Scale effects at the operational level* are a result of technical cost-advantages due to mass production (Borrmann 2001).

In a next step, the implications of *cost-oriented offshoring* for domestic employment are evaluated (see Table 2.2). When services are *non-tradable*, there is *no import solution* and the services must be produced in the home country even if a company wishes to relocate in order to cut costs. Hence, domestic employment is not influenced here. In the case of *tradable services*, foreign production substitutes for domestic production and offshored services are re-imported to the home county. This results in direct negative employment effects in the short term, because specific segments are affected by layoffs or wage reductions. However, this "job export" can only be considered avoidable if an alternative domestic solution exists. Some argue that the provision of cheaper re-imports through offshoring helps MNCs to save or even strengthen the productive jobs at home by relocating less productive jobs abroad (Roling 1999; Trabold et al. 2001).

2.2.2.3 Procurement-Oriented Motives

Third, the *procurement of inputs* which are rare or unavailable in the home country (e.g., raw materials, preliminary products) represents another traditional offshoring motive. More recent motives in this category are the provision of human-capital, know-how, and technology from abroad. The form of captive-offshoring is often preferred to guarantee a regular and secure provision with such inputs. Jungnickel and Keller (2003) show that the relevance of strategic *asset-seeking* for German manufacturing companies has grown, especially when TACs are low. Marin (2004) finds that the high average qualification and R&D intensity of German affiliates in the CEECs reflect the *search for human capital*. The procurement of foreign services is one option to counteract the decreasing demographic trend and the talent shortage in many developed countries.

The effects of procurement-oriented services offshoring on domestic employment are shown in Table 2.2. *Non-tradable* service inputs cannot be provided from abroad (neutrality hypothesis), and domestic employment is thus not affected. When services are *tradable*, the procurement of foreign inputs enables domestic production, which raises the demand for domestic labor (complementarity hypothesis) (e.g., Roling 1999). Henneberger et al. (2000) estimate that the substitutionality hypothesis is applicable to more than 50% of all services, for instance in the banking, assurance or marketing sector. Developments in ICTs could further raise this share (Henneberger et al. 2000).

Procurement of Agglomeration Advantages

A first and more recent procurement-oriented offshoring motive is the provision of *agglomeration advantages*. Agglomeration advantages can be understood as Krugman's theoretical"core" of the New Economic Geography, a geographical accumulation of different firms from different sectors which are concentrated in agglomerations due to scale-effects and external effects. The latter include the presence of human capital and suppliers as well as knowledge or technology spill-over effects (Soci 2003). Generally, such spill-over effects cannot be transferred via markets. According to Jungnickel and Keller (2003), agglomeration advantages can be subdivided into *asset-seeking*, e.g., knowledge and technological potential, and *efficiency-seeking*, e.g., scale-effects and favorable conditions abroad. Agglomeration advantages become more relevant when TACs for trade and FDI are falling, since firms are then rather located in the most competitive agglomerations, where they can similarly benefit from knowledge effects, scale-effects and external effects.

Jungnickel and Keller (2003) show that market-oriented offshoring is still important for German firms, but observe a shift towards cost- and agglomeration-oriented offshoring, especially asset-seeking. The change of strategy towards asset-seeking and efficiency-seeking is evoked by diverse changes on the supply and on the demand side. First, the development of a more deregulated single market and the opening of domestic markets attract more foreign competitors. Second, technological progress leads to shorter life-cycles and greater uncertainty about the competitive situation in the future, which requires rapid innovation and the tapping of external, complementary knowledge. Third, developments in ICTs facilitate the coordination within and between firms. As a consequence, firms face both greater competitive pressure and more opportunities and possibilities.

These changes go along with the following two trends. First, the share of greenfield investments relative to M&As has continuously decreased. Second, integrated capital markets and investment banks put a higher pressure on firms to become more efficient and innovative (Jungnickel and Keller 2003). Since the costs of trade in services have been reduced due to trade liberalization (Sects. 2.2.1.2 and 2.2.1.3) and developments in ICTs (Sect. 2.2.1.1), we expect a growing importance of asset-seeking and efficiency-seeking services offshoring.

The pressure of increased competitiveness requires firms to search for efficiency and assets at specialized locations. Therefore, agglomeration-oriented offshoring should not be considered a substitute for trade. Domestic employment effects are not expected to be negative, since agglomeration-oriented offshoring rather supports the firms' competitiveness and assures domestic jobs in the parent company. Schaaf (2004) describes the *specialization patterns* of the most important offshore destinations (agglomerations) for IT and BPO services. The study shows that maintaining high-quality production in developed countries while offshoring lower-quality processes to less-developed countries does *not* apply to IT and BPO services (for more details, see Sect. 3.3.1.4). Thus, firms can benefit from agglomeration advantages both in developed Ireland and in developing India.

Procurement of Human Capital

The procurement of human capital, a more recent offshoring motive, could also be considered part of asset-seeking. However, a small but important difference remains. While the procurement of agglomeration advantages focuses on the *spill-over effects* due to the presence of human capital in agglomerations, the procurement of human capital centers purely on its supply. The *shortage of skilled labor* in developed countries, combined with the relative abundance of human capital in less-developed countries, contributed strongly to the services offshoring wave. The annual growth rates of the German human capital stock (per capita) increased by 0.85% between 1960 and 1980, fell to 0.75% between 1980 and 1990, and then fell further to 0.18% between 1990 and 1997 (Koman and Marin 2000; Marin 2004).

On the other hand, the demand for qualified labor rose in the 1990s due to increased trade integration with the CEECs and developments in ICTs, resulting in a shortage of human capital. In its annual report of 2001/2002, the German Council of Economic Experts (*Sachverständigenrat*) reports on the shortage of human capital, especially in Western Germany, but also notes that the shortage of skilled labor is not a new phenomenon in Germany. Involuntary job vacancies were mainly found in smaller knowledge- and technology-intensive service companies and in the manufacturing sectors. The lack of suitable candidates, but also exceeded wage expectations, represented the main reasons for the shortage of qualified labor (Sachverständigenrat zur Begutachtung der gesamtwirtschaftlichen Entwicklung 2001).

Recently, the DIHK published a survey on the shortage of human capital in Germany. One-third (33%) of the 20,000 companies had job vacancies in 2007 compared to 16% in 2005, whereby the share increased with the size of the company. At the sectoral level, 40% of the manufacturing companies were affected, out of which 83% had difficulties in finding engineers and technicians. 32% of the service companies could not fill vacancies, out of which 39% had vacant service jobs, 32% vacant commercial jobs, 30% vacant engineering/technical jobs, and 22% vacant IT jobs. 85% of the data processing firms with job vacancies had immense difficulties in finding IT-specialists. Germany has a bottleneck of graduates in mathematics, informatics, natural sciences, and technical engineering (MINT). Vacancies in IT and engineering require skilled workers with tertiary education (DIHK 2007).

Marin (2004) relates the German human capital shortage to offshoring decisions of domestic firms. Her study includes 2,200 investment projects of 660 German and Austrian firms to Eastern Europe and covers the period between 1990 and 2001. One of the main findings was that firms offshored the most skill-intensive parts to the CEECs as a response to the human capital shortage in Germany and Austria. Thus, the shares of high-skilled employees in the total affiliates' workforce was on average two to three times higher than the share in the German parent company. Likewise, the average share of employees in R&D and engineering in the Central and Eastern European affiliates was slightly higher than in the German parent company (Marin 2004).

However, a higher quantity of human capital in Eastern Europe does not necessarily reflect a better quality of services. Hutzschenreuter et al. (2007) surveyed 119 German firms and found that, for 74% of the 126 offshoring implementations, the planned service quality was obtained within twelve months, and for further 16% after twelve months. However, 39% of the offshoring projects to Eastern European locations required more than a year to achieve the planned service quality level, compared to only 22% in Asia, 23% in Western Europe, and 18% in North and Central America (Hutzschenreuter et al. 2007).

If Germany responds to its human capital shortage of engineers or IT-specialists by performing such services in Eastern Europe or India, one could expect positive domestic employment effects, since otherwise the domestic production requiring these services could not be maintained at home. The provision of human capital through imports of intermediates (indirect provision) and immigration of skilled labor (direct provision) can counteract the shortage of skilled labor and the decreasing demographic trend in developed countries, at least in the short term. If politics constrain the first and second possibilities, a last medium- or long-term option would be an effective education policy to produce enough talent at home (see Sect. 6.2.3).

2.2.3 Developments in the Destination Countries

2.2.3.1 Availability of Human Capital in Less-Developed Countries

As we have seen in the previous sub-subsection, offshoring to less-developed countries with a relative abundance of human capital could solve the problem of human capital shortage at home. Thus, the number of graduates per year in mathematics, computer sciences, and natural sciences reached 66,000 in Germany, compared to a talent pool of 250,000 in China and 320,000 in India (Moczadlo 2004). In the following, the *availability of skilled labor in the destination countries* with a focus on developing countries is evaluated, starting with India.

Figure 2.8 shows that the *total number of knowledge professionals in the Indian IT sector* grew from around 56,000 in 1990–1991 to 284,000 in 1999–2000, and reached almost 1.3M in 2005–2006 (NASSCOM 2006b, c). The employment share

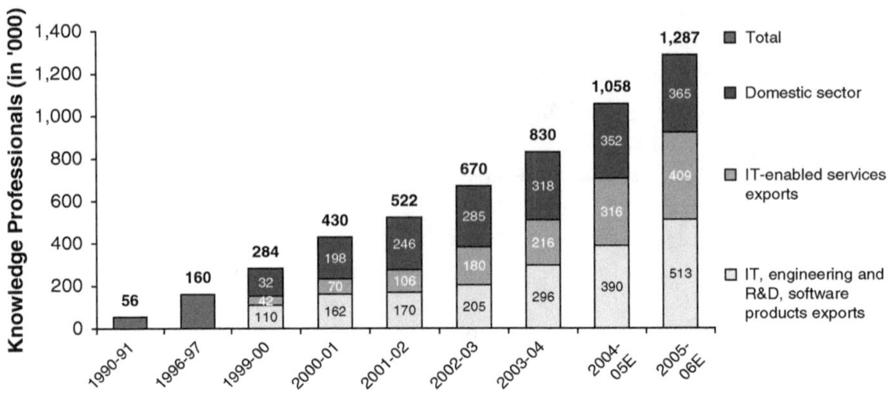

Fig. 2.8 Knowledge professionals employed in the Indian IT sector
Source: NASSCOM (2006b, c). NB: numbers do not include employees in the hardware sector

of the IT export sector in total IT employment was 54% in 1990–1991, which expanded to 72% in 2005–2006. Accordingly, the employment share of the domestic IT sector fell from 46 to 28% over this period. Within the IT export sector, "IT, engineering and R&D, and software products" play a larger role than IT-enabled services, but the latter have caught up in terms of employees. Recently, the NASSCOM reported that the number of BPO-IT professionals exceeded 1.6 million in 2007, mainly due to India's demographic profile and the network of high-quality academic institutions (NASSCOM 2007a). The advantages of India's talent pool are characterized as follows:

> "From India's young demographic profile (an inherent advantage), to its vast network of academic infrastructure that churns out 3.1 million graduates annually, to its English-speaking workforce, the country offers an unmatched mix of human-power benefits to organizations (NASSCOM 2007a).

However, recent estimates of the NASSCOM reveal that India's technology sector created 50,000 fewer jobs in 2008 than in the preceding year due to the downturn of its economy, but still added 200,000 employees. Thus, captive offshoring operations in the financial sector, such as American Express and Goldman Sachs, laid off part of its workforce. On the other hand, many Indian service providers such as Infosys, who strongly depend on banks and other financial clients, must also cut back (Kahn 2008).

India stands out not only in terms of quantity but also of quality since, in 2002, most companies worldwide with the Capability Maturity Model (CMM®) Level 5 were located in India. The CMM® is a capability model, developed and instituted by the Software Engineering Institute at Carnegie Mellon University, that helps buyers to find reliable software suppliers by identifying a supplier's processes and understanding their maturity level. Level 5 is the highest level possible. The 2007 Strategic Review of the NASSCOM states that as of December 2006 over 440

Indian companies had acquired quality certifications, out of which 90 were CMM® Level 5 certifications (NASSCOM 2006a).

India's total fresh IT labor supply grew from 150,000 professionals in 2003–2004 to 180,000 in 2006–2007 (NASSCOM 2006b). The former president of the NASSCOM, Kiran Karnik, reported that 200,000 professionals in engineering and computer science were added to the IT sector in 2007. A similar number accounts for the BPO sector. Nevertheless, first concerns about a possible *human capital shortage* in India itself are being mentioned, with a national engineering capacity of around 550,000 jobs and an IT sector selection ratio of only 30%. This already constitutes a problem today and could rise in the future. In order to improve the selection ratio, the NASSCOM proposes measures to expand professional education, which should be accompanied by curriculum and pedagogic changes (NASSCOM 2007b).

One initiative in the IT–BPO industry is the *employment pyramid approach*, which has been initiated by a partnership of the NASSCOM, the Indian government, and academia. The base of the pyramid stands for simple technical skills, the middle of the pyramid represents mainstream skills, and the top of the pyramid stands for high-end technology skills. One of the largest challenges is the top of the pyramid, as India aims to produce more PhDs and research scientists. The middle part of the pyramid will account for the majority of the shortage in the future, whereby measures are implemented to improve the fit between employees and employers. Workers in the bottom part of the pyramid should be equipped with hard and soft skills in order to ensure their employability (NASSCOM 2007a).

Besides India, other countries also dispose of a large amount of IT supply. According to Tschang and Xue (2005), the number of IT graduates in China rose from 29,000 to 41,000 between 1999 and 2001 (taken from Arora and Gambardella 2004). However, according to a report in 'The Economic Times' of 17 September 2007, China faces shortages, notably the low number and quality of PhDs, which impedes its progress in becoming a global science and technology leader. A new program was established in collaboration with the US which encourages PhD students at Chinese universities to spend 12–24 months at a US faculty. During their stay, the research proposal is defined and a major part of the research work is undertaken, before the students finish their dissertation back at the Chinese home university. The advantages include that students use current technologies and create links with US laboratories. In the 2007–2008 academic year, approximately 4,000 Chinese PhD students received such a fellowship, which costs about 40,000 US$ per person. These students work on a J1-visa that obliges them to return to their home country immediately after completion of the program for at least 1 year. This restriction and the fact that the students only obtain their PhD degrees at their home universities are incentives to make them return (Srivasta and Jalote 2007).

According to Botelho et al. (2005), Brazil had 18,000 graduates in 2000, which relative to the total population is more than in India or China (taken from Arora and Gambardella 2004). To give an example for a developed country, Ireland produces 34,000 graduates p.a. and has one of the highest proportions of adults with tertiary education in the total population. 30% of these degrees are in science

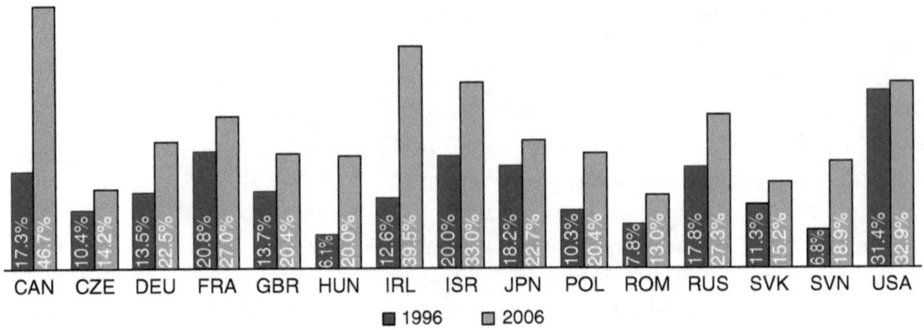

Fig. 2.9 Share of tertiary educated in the economically active population (%)
Source: own illustration. Data: ILO LABORSTA yearly statistics. Tertiary education includes the third level, first stage, leading to a first university degree or equivalent qualification, and the third level, second stage, leading to a higher tertiary degree. NB: 1995 instead of 1996 figures for Slovakia. 2002 instead of 1996 figures for the US. 2002 instead of 2006 figures for Canada. 2003 instead of 2006 figures for Slovenia. 2005 instead of 2006 figures for the Czech Republic, France, and the United Kingdom

and technology (Arora and Gambardella 2004). Figure 2.9 shows the *share of tertiary educated in the economically active population* for some selected countries. In 2006, Ireland's share (39.5%) was the second largest after Canada (46.7%), followed by Israel (33.0%) and the US (32.9%). Germany (22.5%) and the UK (20.4%) have a relatively small share of tertiary educated among the developed countries. The CEECs including Russia all increased their shares between 1996 and 2006, but still did not catch up except for Russia.

According to Arora and Gambardella (2004) an *excess supply of human capital* was driving the immense growth of the software industry in the 3I-countries India, Israel, and Ireland. Although all 3I-countries did not have the highest number of specialists, they had an excess supply of engineering and technology graduates in the 1980s and early 1990s relative to the demand-side. Moderate annual growth rates of 2 to 3% between 1970 and 1990 resulted in low opportunity costs of working in the software industry, contrary to the Asian Tigers, South Korea, Taiwan, and Singapore. The reasons for the abundance of skilled workers are not yet well analyzed, but the high level as well as the elasticity of supply of human capital represented two decisive factors (Arora and Gambardella 2004).

This rapid increase in human capital was fuelled by *private and public investments*. In India, new capacity was created mainly in the private sector. In 2003, 80% of the accredited intake capacity for engineering students at the undergraduate level was absorbed by privately financed colleges. Ireland, Israel, and China benefit from public investments. Ireland, for instance, used around 40% of its EU structural funds for human capital investments between 1989 and 1999 (see Fig. 2.10), while other net recipients like Greece and Portugal invested predominantly in physical capital (Arora and Gambardella 2004). In comparison, the remaining EU11 countries invested less than 30% in human capital.

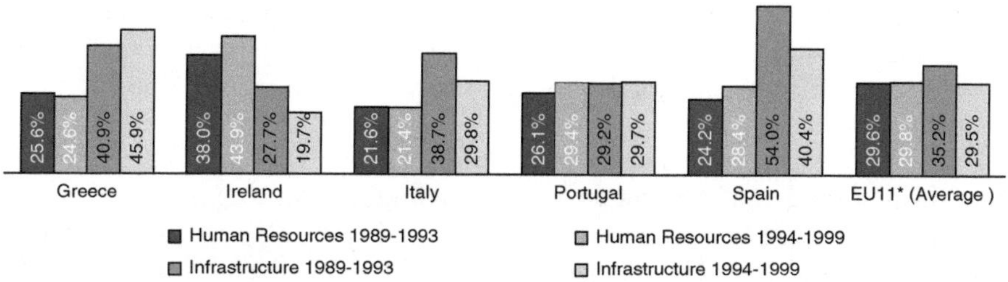

Fig. 2.10 Distributions of EU structural funds 1989–1993 and 1994–1999 (%)
Source: first report on economic and social cohesion 1996 DG XVI EC Brussels, p. 147. The 11 EU countries comprise Austria, Belgium, Germany, France, Greece, Ireland, Italy, Netherlands, Portugal, Spain, and United Kingdom

One important reason for the acceleration of this process lies in the *diaspora*, i.e., a large part of the talent pool emigrated to industrialized countries. Qualified immigrants can share their knowledge and expertise when returning to their home country, which is expected to increase quality and the stock of human capital there. The US in particular has absorbed a high number of immigrants from India, Ireland, and Israel, as well as from China and Brazil. Arora and Gambardella (2004) refer to a study of Kapur and McHale (2005) which shows that Indians and Chinese received most of the H-1B visas, which are approved for a limited stay. Indians obtained 42% of these visas, out of which more than a half were for computer-related areas. Despite high returning numbers to China and India, only Ireland shows an unambiguous relationship between the return and the growth of human capital in the home country (Arora and Gambardella 2004).

2.2.3.2 Presence of Multinational Companies

The following sub-subsection studies the *role of multinational companies* in the development and growth of domestic industries. An empirical study of Görg and Strobl (2002) finds evidence that the presence of MNCs in Ireland significantly contributed to the entry of indigenous firms. The study focuses on the Irish manufacturing sectors, since the domestic industries, that were focused on traditional and food-sector industries, experienced a shift towards high-tech sectors due to heavy investments of MNCs. Although we are primarily interested in the role of MNCs in the development of domestic service sectors, the study gives us general insights into the potential effects of MNCs on the host economy.

Görg and Strobl (2002) name three main *linkages* that are based on the theoretical model of Markusen and Venables (1999). First, MNCs compete with domestic final goods producers. Thus, the aggregated higher output lowers prices and pushes some domestic firms out of the market (competition effect). Second, MNCs create additional demand for domestically produced intermediates. Assuming imperfectly competitive intermediate supplier industries, average costs decrease and profits rise, which attracts new intermediates producers. And third, due to the second effect, intermediates' prices decline as well, which can be an incentive for indigenous or multinational final goods producers to enter the market (Görg and Strobl 2002).

The presence of multinational companies played an important role not only for the growth of the manufacturing sector but also for the *software industry* in non-G7 countries. Arora and Gambardella (2004) showed that the 3Is as well as China and Brazil were characterized by a large presence of MNCs in the software sector. "At the risk of some exaggeration, one can say that MNCs came to Israel to do R&D, to India for inexpensive skilled workers, and to Ireland to leverage tax incentives and access the European market (Arora and Gambardella 2004, p. 12)." Often, the case of Ireland, which still benefits from an extraordinarily low corporate tax rate of 12.5%, is cited as evidence that MNCs stimulated the sectoral growth of domestic firms, while in Israel and India, MNCs and the domestic sector started to grow *simultaneously* in the 1990s.

The authors refer to a study of Giarratana et al. (2005) who show that 57% of the MNCs in the ICT-sector were already present in Ireland before 1990, compared to 44% in India and 37% in Israel. Ireland's leading role becomes even more obvious in the software industry. Here, 55% of the MNCs have been built up before 1990 compared to only 18% in India and 16% in Israel. In addition, two-thirds of the patents for MNCs in Ireland have already been assigned before 1994 in comparison to 37% in Israel and 32% in India, suggesting that MNCs have undertaken R&D investments earlier in Ireland. Citing Botelho et al. (2005), the study also shows that MNCs, especially Siemens and Ericsson, are contributing to the development of the local competencies of the Irish software industry (Arora and Gambardella 2004). To sum up, we can see indications of a linkage between the presence of MNCs in the software industry and the development and growth of the domestic service sector.

2.2.3.3 Liberalization of Service Sectors

As part of the broad liberalization process, the developing world emerged from the era of import substitution to embrace policies promoting export growth within a growing network of international supply chains. For example, export processing zones have expanded in scope and number, offering foreign firms long tax holidays on corporate profits and unrestricted profit repatriation.[16] Arora and Gambardella (2004) identify two different development patterns, namely the export-led model and the development-led export model. Among the 3Is, Brazil, and China, only India depended heavily on exports at the beginning of its software industry development. The other countries rather followed the development-led export model,

[16] See Milberg (2007) for an overview of the expansion of EPZs in the 2000s.

Box 2.7: Liberalization of the telecommunication services market in India

India's past was influenced by Mahatma Gandhi's call for self-sufficiency, which for instance became visible in a law of 1976 that restricted foreign ownership to 40%. Former prime minister Rajiv Gandhi identified ICTs as a core sector, but only after the establishment of the National Telecom Policy (NTP) 1994, the government monopoly of the telecommunications sector was opened. Despite the opening, progress was slow with only 1.217 mobiles and 29.985 mainlines per 1,000 inhabitants by 1998. With the election of the Bharatiya Janata Party (BJP) in 1997, ICTs again became a center of attention. The NTP 1999 was enacted and led to a decrease of mobile license fees (15% profit sharing). Falling capital and handset costs, increased competition from wire line operators and newcomers, prepaid calling, and calling-party pays contributed to a fast growth of the mobile sector. By 2003, the number of mobiles per 1,000 people has increased to 24.747. The wire line market has grown to 46.284 per 1,000 inhabitants in 2003, but private wire line services are still lacking and rural areas are still insufficiently reached.

A similar picture could be found in the Indian internet sector. Based on the Indian Telegraph Act 1885, the Indian government did not allow private Internet Services Providers (ISPs) to operate, and thus the Ministry of Communication had a monopoly over commercial ISP services. After the 1997 elections, the BJP set up a National Taskforce on IT and Software Development in May 1998 to map out an IT policy. Just two months later, the National Taskforce published a 108-step IT action plan and released a second action plan on the development, manufacture and export of IT hardware in October 1998. A long-term national IT policy was released in April 1999, which resulted in an increase in the number ISP licenses that were issued. As a result, the total number of internet subscribers increased from 25,000 in 1997 to 6.674 M in 2005. Since most of Indian's ICT growth is experienced in urban areas, there is major concern of increased digital divide between rural and urban areas.

Source: UNCTAD (2006)

where the domestic software industry was nurtured by domestic demand first before focusing on exports (Arora and Gambardella 2004).

The cases of export growth described above were enabled by the *transformation from protectionist to open market economies* in the last one to two decades due to constant privatization, competition, and independent regulation. This sub-subsection studies the *liberalization of the telecommunication services market* with a focus on the success stories of India (see Box 2.7) and China (see Box 2.8). The telecommunications sector has been chosen, since it has largely attributed to the rise in the worldwide services offshoring development.

Box 2.8: Liberalization of the telecommunication services market in China

China's success was mainly reached by the combination of three developments, namely the economic opening, the government support of the telecommunications sector, and the introduction of competition. Since the late 1980s, when China began to open its markets, exports, imports, FDI, and GDP per capita increased tremendously. During the 1990s, China's industrial policy started to focus on infrastructure and high technology. The Chinese State Council decided to permit entry to the internet in 1996, and one year later every provincial capital had competing ISPs.

Interestingly, China's government stimulates the *competition* by the strategy of allocating resources to state-owned companies. The establishment of China Unicom as a competitor of China Telecom constitutes such an example, the latter being part of the Ministry of Posts and Telecommunications (MPT). Since the MPT was in charge of both competing and regulating, a new regulatory system was required. Therefore, the MPT and the Ministry of Electronic Industry merged in 1998 to become the Ministry of Information Industry (MII), which is responsible for the development strategy, the regulation of telecommunications, broadcasting, satellites, and the internet, as well as the establishment of a multimedia network that prevents duplication of investments. In 1999, the MII subdivided China Telecom into four independent groups (China Telecom, China Mobile, China Satellite, and Guo Xin Paging Company, for radio paging) in order to facilitate the competition between and the regulation of its state-owned companies.

The Chinese ISP sector was characterized by a *mixed ownership* between state-owned companies and local ISPs, the former controlling the backbone networks, and the latter ensuring the local access. ISPs competed like free market organizations. China's internet exchange points, too, followed the mixed-ownership principle. Routed by the US backbone in earlier years, the government encouraged the establishment of own internet exchange points that are in charge of the domestic traffic. The Chinese government also encourages the adoption of new technologies, such as voice-over internet protocol, as it considers low communication costs beneficial for companies and individuals.

Source: UNCTAD(2006)

In 1997, 69 industrialized and emerging WTO member states signed the agreement to open their telecommunication services markets. By the end of 1998, this number had gone up to 90. The opening of the markets has increased competition and thus the number of facilities-based international carriers and mobile operators, which led to lower ICT prices. By 2001, 43% of the countries allowed competition on local calls, 38% on international calls, 37% on long-distance calls, 78% on mobile calls, and 86% on the internet. The worldwide experience showed that a *combination of privatization, competition, and independent regulation* is most likely to be successful (UNCTAD 2006).

Most developing countries that are now attracting large amounts of FDI in the service sector were characterized by protectionist policies before opening up to foreign ownership of companies. The Digital Divide Report of the UNCTAD (2006) identifies six successful countries with regard to the liberalization of the ICT sector, namely India, China, Singapore, Chile, Botswana, and the US. The process towards liberalization in these countries included privatization, competition, and independent regulation, and the governments played an important role in planning, investing, and procuring.

However, there are also *limits to privatization, competition, and independent regulation*, such as ineffective government agencies, the resistance from operators, and corruption. There might also be limits to market freedom due to problems linked to the market structures, vertical integration, or the infrastructure of the country. The success stories of developing countries have shown the necessity of a strong and independent regulator. Specifically, "[t]he regulator must have the resources to audit providers and create and enforce regulations that mitigate any inequity arising from integration and imperfect competition" (UNCTAD 2006, p. 34).

We conclude that constant privatization, competition, and independent regulation during the last two decades have fostered the liberalization process of the telecommunications sector, especially in India and China. While public policy focused on privatization in India, China's success was predominantly driven by public policy that emphasized competition.

References

Abraham KG, Taylor SK (1996) Firms' use of outside contractors: theory and evidence. J Labor Econ 14(3):394–424

Abramovsky L, Griffith R, Sako M (2004) Offshoring of business services and its impact on the UK economy. November 2004. Advanced Institute of Management Research, London Business School, London

Amiti M, Wei SJ (2005) Fear of service outsourcing: is it justified?. Econ Policy 20(42):308–347

Anderton B, Brenton P, Oscarsson E (2002) Outsourcing and inequality. CEPS Working Document, No. 187, October 2002

Antràs P (2003) Firms, contracts, and trade structure. Quart J Econ 118(4):1375–1418

Antràs P, Helpman E (2004) Global sourcing. J Political Econ 112(3):552–580

Antràs P, Garicano L, Rossi-Hansberg E (2006) Offshoring in a knowledge economy. Quart J Econ 121(1):31–77

Arora A, Gambardella A (2004) The globalization of the software industry: perspectives and opportunities for developed and developing countries. NBER Working Paper, No. 10538, June 2004

Baldwin R (2006) Globalisation: the great unbundling(s). Paper for the Finnish Prime Minister's Office, September 2006. Economic Council of Finland

Bartel A, Lach PS, Sicherman N (2005) Outsourcing and technological change. NBER Working Paper, No. 11158, February 2005

Barth D (1998) Perspektiven des internationalen Dienstleistungshandels. Friedrich Ebert Stiftung, Bonn

Bedi AS (1999) The role of information and communication technologies in economic development, a partial survey. ZEF Discussion Papers on Development Policy, No. 7, May 1999

Berle AA, Means GC (1932) The modern corporation and private property. Harcourt, Brace & World, New York [1932] 1968

Best M, Garnsey E (1999) Edith Penrose, 1914–1996. Econ J 109(453):187–201

Beyfuß J, Eggert J (2000) Auslandsinvestitionen der deutschen Wirtschaft und ihre Arbeitsplatzeffekte: Aktuelle Trends, Ergebnisse einer Unternehmensbefragung und die Bedeutung der staatlichen Förderung. Beiträge zur Wirtschafts- und Sozialpolitik 258 (4):

Bhagwati J (1987) Trade in services and the multilateral trade negotiations. World Bank Econ Rev 1(4):549–569

Bhagwati, Jagdish (1984) Splintering and disembodiment of services and developing nations, World Economy 7(2):133–144

Bhagwati J, Panagariya A, Srinivasan TN (2004) The muddles over outsourcing. J Econ Perspect 18(4):93–114

Boes A (2004) Industrialisierung und Internationalisierung von IT-Dienstleistungen, Voraussetzungen und Konsequenzen von Offshoring. Arbeitspapier 7 des Projekts ARB-IT 2, March 2004. München: ISF

Borrmann C (2001) Standort Deutschland im internationalen Verbund. Nomos, Baden-Baden

Botelho AJ, Stefanuto G, Veloso F (2005) The Brazilian software industry, in from underdog to tigers: the rise and growth of the software industry in some emerging economies, Arora A and Gambardella A (eds.), pp 99–130, Oxford University Press, Oxford UK

Browning HL, Singelmann J (1975) The emergence of a service society: demographic and sociological aspects of the sectoral transformation of the labor force in the U.S.A. National Technical Information Service, Springfield, VA

Chanda R (2006) Intermodal linkages in services trade. OECD Trade Policy Working Paper, No. 30, January 2006

Coase RH (1937) The nature of the firm. Economica 4(16):386–405

Cronin B, Catchpowle L, Hall D (2004) Outsourcing and offshoring. CESifo Forum 2:17–21

Deavers KL (1997) Outsourcing: a corporate competitiveness strategy, not a search for low wages. J Labor Res 18(4):503–519

Deutsche Bundesbank (2006a) Balance of payments by region. Special statistical publication, No. 11, August 2006

Deutsche Bundesbank (2006b) Technologische Dienstleistungen in der Zahlungsbilanz. Special Statistical Publication, No. 12, June 2006

DIHK (2007) Kluge Köpfe – vergeblich gesucht! Fachkräftemangel in der deutschen Wirtschaft, Ergebnisse einer DIHK-Unternehmensbefragung. Fall 2007

Douma S, Schreuder H (1998) Economic approaches to organizations. Prentice-Hall, Englewood Cliffs, NJ

Erber G, Sayed-Ahmed A (2005) Offshore outsourcing, a global shift in the present IT industry. Intereconomics 40(2):100–112

Ethier WJ (1986) The multinational firm. Quart J Econ 101(4):805–833

EU (2008) A single market for services. Retrieved from http://ec.europa.eu/internal_market/top_layer/index_19_en.htm

Foss NJ (1997) Equilibrium vs evolution in the resource-based perspective: The conflicting legacies of Demsetz and Penrose. DRUID Working Paper, No. 97–10, October 1997

Foss NJ (1998) Edith Penrose and the Penrosians – or, why there is still so much to learn from the theory of the growth of the firm. January 1998. Denmark: Department of Industrial Economics and Strategy, Copenhagen Business School

Freeman R (2007) The expansion of the global labor supply. In: Paus E (ed) Global capitalism unbound: winners and losers from offshore outsourcing. Palgrave Macmillan, London

Garner CA (2004) Offshoring in the service sector: economic impact and policy issues. Econ Rev Q3:5–37. Federal Reserve Bank of Kansas City

Gaston N, Nelson D (2001) Multinational location decisions and the impact on labour markets. ZEF-Discussion Papers on Development Policy, No. 37, May 2001

Giarratana M, Torrisi S, Pagano A (2005) The Role of multinational companies, in from underdog to tigers: The rise and growth of the software industry in some emerging economies, Arora A and Gambardella A (eds.), pp 207–235, Oxford University Press, Oxford UK

Girma S, Görg H (2003) Outsourcing, foreign ownership and productivity: evidence from UK establishment level data. DIW Discussion Papers, No. 361, August 2003

Görg H, Strobl E (2002) Multinational companies and indigenous development: an empirical analysis. Eur Econ Rev 46(7):1305–1322

Görzig B, Stephan A (2002) Outsourcing and firm-level performance. DIW Discussion Paper, No. 309, October 2002

Grant RM (1996) Toward a knowledge-based theory of the firm. Strategic Manage J 17:109–122

Grossman GM, Helpman E (2002) Integration versus outsourcing in industry equilibrium. Quart J Econ 117(1):85–120

Grossman GM, Helpman E (2004) Managerial incentives and the international organization of production. J Int Econ 63(2):237–262

Grossman GM, Helpman E (2005) Outsourcing in a global economy. Rev Econ Stud 72 (1):135–159

Grossman GM, Rossi-Hansberg E (2006a) The rise of offshoring: it's not wine for cloth anymore. Paper presented at The New Economic Geography: Effects and Policy Implications. Federal Reserve Bank of Kansas City, Jackson Hole, pp 59–102

Grossman GM, Rossi-Hansberg E (2006b) Trading tasks: a simple theory of offshoring. NBER Working Paper, No. 12721, December 2006

Hamelink, Ceese (1997) New information and communication technologies, social development and cultural change. UNRISD Discussion Paper No. 86, June 1997

Hatzius J (2000) Foreign direct investment and factor demand elasticies. Eur Econ Rev 44 (1):117–143

Helleiner GK (1973) Manufactured exports from less-developed countries and multinational firms. Econ J 83(329):21–47

Henneberger F, Ziegler A (1998) Beschäftigungseffekte von Direktinvestitionen: Die gewählte Methodik beeinflusst das Ergebnis. Wirtschaftspolitische Blätter 45(6):554–563

Henneberger F, Ziegler A (2001) Internationalisierung der Dienstleistungserstellung: Konsequenzen für den schweizerischen Arbeitsmarkt. HWWA Discussion Paper, No. 149

Henneberger F, Graf S, Vocke M (2000) Globalisierung und Arbeitsmarkt: Auslandsinvestitionen von Dienstleistungsunternehmen und ihre Auswirkungen auf die Beschäftigung (1st ed.). Baden-Baden

Heshmati A (2003) Productivity growth, efficiency and outsourcing in manufacturing and service industries. J Econ Surv 17(1):79–112

Hill TP (1977) On goods and services. Revi Income Wealth 23(4):315–338

Hill CWL (2003) International business: competing in the global marketplace. McGraw-Hill, New York

Hoekman B (2006) Trade in services, trade agreements and economic development: a survey of the literature. CEPR Discussion Paper, No. 5760, July 2006

Hoekman B, Sauvé P (1994) Regional and multilateral liberalization of trade in services: complements or substitutes?. J Common Market Stud 32(3):283–317

Hutzschenreuter T, Dressel S, Ressler W (2007) Offshoring von Zentralbereichen, Von den Erfahrungen deutscher und amerikanischer Unternehmen lernen. Springer, Berlin

IMF (2000) Offshore financial centers. IMF Background Paper, June 2000. Prepared by the Monetary and Exchange Affairs Department

Jungnickel R, Keller D (2003) German FDI and integration of production in the EU. HWWA Discussion Paper, No. 232

Kahn J (2008) Recession trickles to India, New York Times, 3 December 2008

Kalmbach P, Franke R, Knottenbauer K, Krämer H (2005) Die Interdependenz von Industrie und Dienstleistungen, Zur Dynamik eines komplexen Beziehungsgeflechts. Berlin

Kapur D, McHale J (2005) Sojourns and Software: Internationally mobile human capital and high-tech industry development in India, Ireland, and Israel, in from underdog to tigers: The rise and growth of the software industry in some emerging economies, Arora A and Gambardella A (eds.), pp 236–274, Oxford University Press, Oxford UK

Kirkegaard JF (2004) Offshore outsourcing – much ado about what? CESifo Forum 2/2004:22–29

Koman R, Marin D (2000) Human capital and macroeconomic growth: Austria and Germany 1960–1997. Münchner Wirtschaftswissenschaftliche Beiträge

Kox H, Lejour A (2006) The effects of the services directive on intra-EU trade and FDI. Revue Econ 57(4):747–769

Levy DL (2005) Offshoring in the new global political economy. J Manage Stud 42(3):685–693

Liebeskind JP (1996) Knowledge, strategy, and the theory of the firm. Strategic Manage J 17:93–107

Mahoney JT, Pandian JR (1992) The resource-based view within the conversation of strategic management. Strategic Manage J 13(5):363–380

Marin D (2004) A nation of poets and thinkers – less so with eastern enlargement? Austria and Germany. CEPR Working Paper, No. 4358, March 2004

Marin D, Verdier TA (2003a) Globalization and the empowerment of talent. CEPR Discussion Paper, No. 4129

Marin D, Verdier TA (2003b) Globalization and the new enterprise. J Eur Econ Assoc 1 (2–3):337–344

Markusen JR, Venables AJ (1999) Foreign direct investment as a catalyst for industrial development. Eur Econ Rev 43(2):335–356

Mattoo A (2001) Shaping future GATS rules for trade in services. World Bank Policy Research Working Paper, No. 2596, April 2001

Mattoo A, Wunsch-Vincent S (2004) Pre-empting protectionism in services: The WTO and outsourcing. World Bank Policy Research Working Paper, No. 3237, March 2004

McLaren JE (2000) 'Globalization' and vertical integration. Am Econ Rev 90(5):1239–1254

Milberg W (2007) Export processing zones, industrial upgrading and economic development. International Labor Organization, Geneva

Milberg W, Schöller D (2008) Globalization, offshoring and economic insecurity in industrialized countries. World Economic and Social Survey 2008 Background Paper. Department of Economic and Social Affairs, United Nations, New York

Mill JS (1852) Principles of political economy. N Am Rev 98(202):270–273

Moczadlo R (2004) Chancen und Risiken des Offhore-Development, Empirische Analyse der Erfahrungen deutscher Unternehmen. Retrieved from http://www.verdi-it.de/it-fachtagung/r-moczadlo_verdi-fachtagung-it-offshoring-12032004.pdf

Mosdorf S (1998) Arbeit 21, Gesellschaft der Zukunft – Information und Dienstleistung. In: Mangold K (ed), Die Welt der Dienstleistung – Perspektiven für Arbeit und Gesellschaft im 21. Jahrhundert (reprint of 1st ed) Frankfurt am Main, pp 171–183

NASSCOM (2006a) 2007 strategic review, executive summary. Retrieved from http://www.nasscom.in/upload/51054/Executive%20Summary.pdf

NASSCOM (2006b) Knowledge professionals. Retrieved from http://www.nasscom.in/Nasscom/templates/NormalPage.aspx?id = 6314

NASSCOM (2006c) Knowledge professionals in India. Press Information Note. Retrieved from http://www.nasscom.in/upload/5216/nasscom%20knowledge%20professionals%20factsheet%202006.pdf

NASSCOM (2007a) NASSCOM's education initiatives, Sustaining India's talent edge to fuel the next wave of IT–BPO industry growth. Press Information Note. Retrieved from http://www.nasscom.in/upload/5216/July%205%202007%20%20Education%20Initiatives-Final.doc

NASSCOM (2007b) Planting seeds, growing PhDs, Economic Times. Retrieved from http://www.nasscom.in/Nasscom/templates/NormalPage.aspx?id = 52468

NASSCOM, McKinsey Global Institute (2005) The NASSCOM-McKinsey Report 2005: Outlining a success strategy for India's offshore IT–BPO industries! NASSCOM Newsline, 50. Retrieved from http://www.nasscom.in/Nasscom/templates/NormalPage.aspx?id = 11075

neoIT (2006) Offshore insights. Market Rep Ser 4(4), pp 1–23

Overby S (2003) The hidden costs of offshore outsourcing. CIO Mag. Retrieved from http://www.cio.com/article/29654

Pain N, van Welsum D (2004) International production relocation and exports of services. OECD Economic Studies, No. 38, 2004/1. OECD, Paris

Penrose ET (1959) The theory of the growth of the firm, 1st ed. Basil Blackwell, Oxford

Picot A (1982) In der Organisationstheorie – Stand der Diskussion und Aussagewert. Die Betriebswirtschaft 42:267–284

Picot A (1991) Ein neuer Ansatz zur Gestaltung der Leistungstiefe. Zeitschrift für betriebswirtschaftliche Forschung 43:336–357

Prahalad CK, Hamel G (1990) The core competence of the corporation. Harv Bus Rev 68(3):79–91

Pujals G (2005) Offshore outsourcing in the EU financial services industry, Special policy issue – EUROFRAME-EFN Report, Spring 2005: OFCE

Roling J (1999) Bedeuten deutsche Direktinvestitionen im Ausland einen Export' deutscher Arbeitsplätze?. Zeitschrift für Wirtschaftspolitik 48(2):147–167

Rumelt RP (1984) Towards a strategic theory of the firm. In: Lamb R (ed.) Competitive strategic management. Prentice-Hall, Englewoods Cliffs, NJ, pp 556–570

Sachverständigenrat zur Begutachtung der gesamtwirtschaftlichen Entwicklung (2001) Für Stetigkeit – gegen Aktionismus, Annual Report 2001/2002

Schaaf J (2004) Offshoring: globalisation wave reaches services sector, digital economy and structural change No. 45, 27-Sep-04: Deutsche Bank Research

Sharpe M (1997) Outsourcing, organizational competitiveness, and work. J Labor Res 18(4):335–349

Sinn HW (2005) Basarökonomie Deutschland: Exportweltmeister oder Schlusslicht? ifo Schnelldienst, No. 6, March 2005

Slater M (1980) The managerial limitation to the growth of firms. Econ J 90(359):520–528

Smith A (1776) An inquiry into the nature and causes of the wealth of nations

Soci A (2003) FDI and the process of European integration: a brief overview. J Econ Integr 18 (4):642–660

Spender JC (1996) Making knowledge the basis of a dynamic theory of the firm. Strategic Manage J 17:45–62

Srivasta J, Jalote P (2007) Pump priming with US horsepower. Econ Times, 17 September 2007

Stephenson SM (2002) Regional versus multilateral liberalization of services. World Trade Rev 1(2):187–209

The Economist (1996) 28 Septemer 1996

The Economist (2003) Relocating the back office, Special report offshoring. The Economist, 13 December 2003

Trabold H, Bach S, Franzmeyer F, Schultz S, Schumacher D, Weise C (2001) Herausforderung Globalisierung: Konsequenzen für die Bildungs-, Steuer- und Arbeitsmarktpolitik. Schüren, Marburg

Tschang T, Xue L (2005) The Chinese software Industry: The implications of a changing domestic market for software enterprises, in from underdog to tigers: The rise and growth of the software industry in some emerging economies, Arora A and Gambardella A (eds.), pp 131–170, Oxford University Press, Oxford UK

Tüselmann HJ (1998) Deutsche Auslandsinvestitionen in den neunziger Jahren: Abwanderung der deutschen Industrie und Abbau von Arbeitsplätzen?. WSI Mitteilungen 5:292–303

UN (1974) Yearbook of national accounts statistics, Vol. 1. p. xxix

UN (2002) Manual on statistics of international trade in services. Statistical Papers, Series M No. 86. United Nations, Geneva, Luxembourg, New York, Paris, Washington, DC

UNCTAD (2004) The shift towards services, World Investment Report 2004. United Nations, New York and Geneva

UNCTAD (2006) ICT diffusion index 2005, The digital divide report. United Nations, New York and Geneva

UNCTAD, Roland Berger (2004) Service offshoring takes off in Europe – in search of improved competitiveness, service offshoring, June 2004

van Welsum D (2004) In search of 'off shoring': evidence from U.S. imports of services. Birbeck Working Papers in Economics & Finance, No. 0402, September 2004

Vang J (2003) Organization of the news industry, the case of 'making-or-buying' articles. DRUID Working Paper, No. 3–13

Wernerfelt B (1984) A resource-based view of the firm. Strategic Manage J 5(2):171–180

Williamson OE (1973) Markets and hierarchies: some elementary considerations. Am Econ Rev 63(2):316–325

Williamson OE (1975) Markets and hierarchies: analysis and antitrust implications, a study in the economics of internal organization. New York, London

Williamson OE (1985) The economic institutions of capitalism: firms, markets, relational contracting. Simon & Schuster, New YorkSimon

Williamson OE (1996) Transaktionskostenökonomik. In: Dietl H, Erlei C, Erlei M, Leschke M (eds). Ökonomische Theorie der Institutionen, 2nd ed, vol 3. Hamburg

Williamson OE (2000) The new institutional economics: taking stock, looking ahead. J Econ Lit 38(3):595–613

Williamson OE (2002) The theory of the firm as governance structure: from choice to contract. J Econ Perspect 16(3):171–195

World Bank (2007) World development indicators 2007. http://www.worldbank.org/

World Economic Forum (2007) The global information technology report 2006–2007, Connecting to the networked economy, 6th ed. Palgrave MacMillan, New York

WTO (1999) An introduction to the GATS. Trade in Services Division, WTO Secretariat, Geneva

WTO (2004) International trade statistics 2004. http://www.wto.org/english/res_e/statis_e/its2004_e/its04_toc_e.htm

Chapter 3
The Structure of Services Offshoring

Abstract This third chapter uses descriptive statistics to analyze the "Structure of Services Offshoring". We identify the position of German services offshoring relative to other countries. We also look at the sectoral and regional structure of services offshoring. The analysis is based on balance of payments statistics, input–output data, and existing studies. Section 3.1 gives an overview of the largest offshoring countries at absolute and relative consideration, followed by the development of services offshoring in selected OECD countries. We then calculate services offshoring intensities as a more sophisticated measure of services offshoring. Services offshoring intensities measure the proportion of imported service inputs in total non-energy inputs used in home production. German offshoring intensities are then compared to previously available offshoring intensities for other countries. The sectoral structure of services offshoring in section 3.2 identifies the main offshoring sectors as well as the kind of service activities that are most commonly being offshored. First, the global development is discussed before moving on to specific trends in Germany. Finally, the regional structure of services offshoring in section 3.3 presents the major destination countries from a global and a German perspective.

3.1 German Services Offshoring in an International Comparison

3.1.1 Services Offshoring in a Worldwide Comparison

The following subsection identifies the largest services offshoring countries in a worldwide comparison. For this purpose, imports of services are used as a proxy for services offshoring, while services exports serve as a proxy for onshoring. Amiti and Wei (2005) choose computer and information services as well as other business services, since cost-oriented services offshoring followed by re-imports seems to be

D. Winkler, *Services Offshoring and its Impact on the Labor Market*, Contributions to Economics, DOI: 10.1007/978-3-7908-2199-4_3,

most probable in these services categories. We additionally select communication services and financial services, which better match the definition of tradable business activities, according to Kalmbach et al. (2005).

3.1.1.1 The Largest Offshoring Countries by Services Category

Table 3.1 gives an overview of the *largest offshoring countries* by services category in 2005, in both absolute and relative terms. The upper part of the table presents the ten biggest offshoring countries plus other selected, mostly developing countries, measured in M US$. Taking the size of the economy into account, the lower part of the table measures service imports as percentage of GDP and lists the top five countries plus other selected economies. The absolute top ten importers across the four services categories were all developed countries except for Brazil ranked tenth in computer and information service imports. The US, the UK, and Germany were the largest, but other European economies (e.g. Spain, France, Italy, Netherlands) and Japan were mostly ranked among the top ten importers. Interestingly, Germany's imports of computer and information services (8,472M US$) were more than double those of the next country, UK (3,840M US$), which could indicate a shortage of skilled labor in this field. Note also that Luxembourg was the largest absolute importer of financial services in 2005. The table shows that developing countries, especially China and other Asian countries, but also CEECs were often ranked among the top 20 in terms of service imports.

Using a relative measure, we find mostly smaller and often developing economies among the top five importers. Luxembourg's service imports in GDP was always among the top five worldwide, but other European countries, such as Ireland in other business and financial services and Finland, Netherlands, and Belgium in computer and information services, were also represented. Germany and the UK were the two largest importers among the five large developed countries, France, Germany, Japan, UK, and US, across all services categories. Japan and the US had relatively small import shares and France was situated in the middle. Note that India and Russia showed larger import shares than Japan and the US, and even China was ranked higher in computer and information services and other business services. For the *largest absolute and relative onshoring countries* per services category in 2005 see Sect. 3.3.1.2, Table 3.16.

3.1.1.2 The Largest Surplus and Deficit Countries by Services Category

The balance in Table 3.2 reveals the *largest surplus and deficit countries*, measured as exports minus imports, by services category. The five largest surplus and deficit countries are listed for 2004 and 2005, respectively. The 2004 figures are shown to highlight Germany's deficit position in other business services. The UK and the US were always listed among the largest surplus countries except for communication services, where only the UK ranked among the top five. Other large developed

Table 3.1 Largest absolute and relative offshoring countries per services category in 2005 (M US$ and % of GDP)

Rank	Country	Computer & information services	Rank	Country	Other business services	Rank	Country	Communication services	Rank	Country	Financial services
1.	Germany	8,472	1.	United States	50,190	1.	United States	5,292	1.	Luxembourg	13,539
2.	United Kingdom	3,840	2.	Germany	46,506	2.	Germany	4,957	2.	United Kingdom	8,860
3.	Netherlands	3,697	3.	Italy	30,894	3.	United Kingdom	4,851	3.	United States	6,549
4.	United States	2,469	4.	United Kingdom	29,900	4.	Netherlands	3,194	4.	Germany	4,262
5.	Japan	2,432	5.	Ireland	28,832	5.	Italy	3,105	5.	Belgium	3,545
6.	Canada	2,101	6.	France	28,253	6.	France	2,099	6.	Ireland	3,311
7.	Spain	1,979	7.	Japan	26,497	7.	Spain	1,709	7.	Spain	2,739
8.	Belgium	1,855	8.	Netherlands	25,861	8.	Canada	1,704	8.	Japan	2,687
9.	France	1,766	9.	Austria	23,260	9.	Sweden	1,570	9.	France	2,382
10.	Brazil	1,713	10.	Spain	19,797	10.	Belgium	1,327	10.	Canada	2,251
11.	China	1,623	11.	China	16,287	12.	Hong Kong[b]	1,124	11.	Taiwan	1,370
18.	India[a]	659	16.	Indonesia	10,526	14.	Ireland	810	15.	Hong Kong[b]	1,165
19.	Indonesia	561	17.	Saudi Arabia	9,620	15.	Russia	746	18.	Czech Republic	906
21.	Hungary	510	18.	Taiwan	8,669	17.	Malaysia	680	19.	Russia	892
22.	Russia	482	19.	India[a]	8,088	20.	India[a]	610	21.	Singapore	788
Rank	**Country**	**Computer & information services/GDP**	**Rank**	**Country**	**Other business aservices/ GDP**	**Rank**	**Country**	**Communication services/ GDP**	**Rank**	**Country**	**Financial services/ GDP**
1.	Luxembourg	1.86%	1.	Lebanon	15.32	1.	Luxembourg	3.20	1.	Luxembourg	4.75
2.	Aruba	0.74%	2.	Ireland	14.29	2.	Guyana	2.47	2.	Swaziland	1.64

(*continued*)

Table 3.1 (continued)

Rank	Country	Computer & information services	Rank	Country	Other business services	Rank	Country	Communication services	Rank	Country	Financial services
3.	Finland	0.60%	3.	Suriname	12.12	3.	Samoa	1.02	3.	Ireland	1.22
4.	Netherlands	0.59%	4.	Luxembourg	10.14	4.	Moldova	0.94	4.	Malta	1.03
5.	Belgium	0.50%	5.	Aruba	9.10	5.	Netherl. Antilles	0.73	5.	Panama	1.00
19.	Germany	0.30%	35.	Germany	1.66	45.	United Kingdom	0.22	17.	United Kingdom	0.40
38.	United Kingdom	0.17%	41.	United Kingdom	1.36	51.	Germany	0.18	47.	Germany	0.15
58.	France	0.08%	42.	France	1.33	83.	France	0.10	56.	Russia	0.12
59.	India[a]	0.08%	53.	India[a]	1.01	84.	Russia	0.10	59.	France	0.11
60.	China	0.08%	58.	Russia	0.84	96.	India[a]	0.08	78.	India[a]	0.06
64.	Russia	0.06%	59.	China	0.82	109.	United States	0.04	80.	Japan	0.06
71.	Japan	0.05%	66.	Japan	0.58	112.	China	0.03	84.	United States	0.05
88.	United States	0.02%	72.	United States	0.40	119.	Japan	0.01	102.	China	0.01

Source: own calculations. Data: IMF Balance of Payments, retrieved from: UNCTAD
[a]Most recent available figures for India are for 2003
[b]Most recent available figures for Hong Kong are for 2004

Table 3.2 Largest surplus and deficit countries per services category in 2004 and 2005

Rank	Country	Computer & information services	Rank	Country	Other business services	Rank	Country	Communication services	Rank	Country	Financial services
2005		M US$	2005		M US$	2005		M US$	2005		M US$
Largest surplus			Largest surplus			Largest surplus			Largest surplus		
1.	Ireland	18,240	1.	United Kingdom	24,635	1.	France	1,381	1.	United Kingdom	33,435
2.	India[a]	10,706	2.	United States	22,847	2.	Kuwait	1,199	2.	United States	22,732
3.	United Kingdom	6,740	3.	Hong Kong[b]	17,575	3.	Belgium	882	3.	Luxembourg	11,631
4.	United States	3,570	4.	China	6,996	4.	United Kingdom	678	4.	Switzerland	9,379
5.	Luxembourg	1,650	5.	Switzerland	5,089	5.	Netherlands	568	5.	Hong Kong[b]	3,389
Largest deficit			Largest deficit			Largest deficit			Largest deficit		
86.	Germany	−339	75.	Saudi Arabia	−3,703	113.	Hong Kong[b]	−272	92.	Czech Republic	−482
87.	Indonesia	−414	76.	India	−5,487	114.	Spain	−286	93.	Canada	−486
88.	Italy	−898	77.	Korea, Rep. of	−6,154	115.	Ireland	−302	94.	Russia	−502
90.	Japan	−1,306	78.	Indonesia	−7,645	116.	Italy	−915	95.	Norway	−504
91.	Brazil	−1,626	79.	Ireland	−16,720	117.	Germany	−1,530	96.	France	−960
Rank	Country	Computer & information services	Rank	Country	Other business services	Rank	Country	Communication services	Rank	Country	Financial services
2004		M US$	2004		M US$	2004		M US$	2004		M US$
Largest surplus			Largest surplus			Largest surplus			Largest surplus		
1.	Ireland	18,394	1.	United Kingdom	26,037	1.	France	1,142	1.	United Kingdom	29,847
2.	India[a]	10,706	2.	United States	20,163	2.	United Kingdom	1,031	2.	United States	19,876

(continued)

Table 3.2 (continued)

Rank	Country	Computer & information services	Rank	Country	Other business services	Rank	Country	Communication services	Rank	Country	Financial services
3.	United Kingdom	7,988	3.	Hong Kong	17,575	3.	Belgium	632	3.	Luxembourg	8,957
4.	United States	4,755	4.	Singapore	8,315	4.	Indonesia	476	4.	Switzerland	8,568
5.	Luxembourg	1,692	5.	China	6,041	5.	India[a]	455	5.	Hong Kong	3,389
Largest deficit			Largest deficit			Largest deficit			Largest deficit		
94.	Austria	−227	115.	Germany	−4,394	124.	Ireland	−346	101.	Italy	−347
95.	Indonesia	−330	116.	Korea, Rep. of	−5,037	125.	Spain	−350	102.	Russia	−425
96.	Italy	−643	117.	Indonesia	−5,315	126.	United States	−381	103.	Czech Republic	−527
97.	Japan	−1,145	118.	India[a]	−5,487	127.	Italy	−778	104.	Canada	−944
98.	Brazil	−1,228	119.	Ireland	−16,371	128.	Germany	−1,411	105.	France	−1,039

Source: own calculations. Data: IMF Balance of Payments, retrieved from: UNCTAD

[a]Most recent available figures for India are for 2003

[b]Most recent available figures for Hong Kong are for 2004

countries showed a more heterogeneous pattern. France constituted the largest net exporter of communication services, but the largest net importer of financial services. In 2005, Germany belonged to the five largest deficit countries in computer and information services as well as communication services, and in 2004 also in other business services. Japan was only found among the largest net importers of computer and information services.

There are also service-specific differences. Not surprisingly, Ireland and India were by far the largest surplus countries of *computer and information services*, while the performance of Luxembourg as the fifth largest net exporter is quite surprising. The largest net exporters of *other business services* included Hong Kong, China, and Switzerland besides the UK and the US, while Ireland and India belonged to the largest deficit countries, reflecting their specialization in computer and information services. The largest surplus countries of *communication services* besides France and the UK included Kuwait, Belgium, and the Netherlands. Finally, the biggest net exporters of *financial services* besides the UK and the US were Luxembourg, Switzerland, and Hong Kong.

We conclude that on the one hand the UK, the US, and small economies such as Luxembourg and Switzerland showed a relatively strong net export performance. On the other hand, there are countries, such as Germany, Italy, and Indonesia that were only found among the largest net importers in more than one services category. Other countries, however, showed a clear specialization pattern, being a large net exporter in one or two services categories, while they were found among the largest deficit countries in another services category. These include Hong Kong, Ireland, India, and France. Note also that China constituted the fourth largest net exporter of other business services.

3.1.1.3 The Largest Overall Services Offshoring and Onshoring Countries

In the following, we add the four services categories computer and information services, other business services, information services, and financial services to identify the ten *largest overall services offshoring and onshoring countries* in 2005. The left column of Table 3.3 represents absolute values (M US$), while the right column shows the values as percentage of GDP. The main trends of Tables 3.1 and 3.2 can be confirmed.

Concerning *services offshoring*, the top ten importers were solely developed countries. The US and Germany were the largest overall service importers with a comparable value (~64,000M US$), followed by European countries plus Japan. There were also three developing countries among the top 20, namely China, Indonesia, and Taiwan. Measured as percentage of GDP, Luxembourg, Ireland, and Austria belonged to the top five offshoring countries. Among the large developed countries, Germany constituted the largest service importer relative to its size, followed by the UK, France, Japan, and the US. Note again that Russia, China, and India imported relatively more services than Japan and the US.

Table 3.3 Largest offshoring and onshoring countries in 2005

Rank	Country	Total (M US$)	Rank	Country	Total/GDP (%)
Total imports			Total imports/GDP		
1.	United States	64,500	1.	Luxembourg	52.33
2.	Germany	64,197	2.	Ireland	16.54
3.	United Kingdom	47,451	3.	Lebanon	16.01
4.	Italy	36,754	4.	Aruba	10.82
5.	France	34,499	5.	Austria	8.37
6.	Netherlands	33,762	30.	Germany	2.30
7.	Ireland	33,374	31.	United Kingdom	2.16
8.	Japan	32,232	38.	France	1.62
9.	Spain	26,224	45.	India[a]	1.23
10.	Austria	25,626	47.	Russia	1.12
13.	China	18,672	51.	China	0.94
17.	Indonesia	12,121	60.	Japan	0.71
18.	Taiwan	10,859	62.	United States	0.51
Total exports			Total exports/GDP		
1.	United States	113,390	1.	Luxembourg	87.47
2.	United Kingdom	112,940	2.	Lebanon	22.00
3.	Germany	64,259	3.	Ireland	18.38
4.	Netherlands	37,463	4.	Cyprus	15.90
5.	Ireland	37,092	5.	Austria	12.05
6.	Japan	33,844	12.	United Kingdom	5.14
7.	Italy	32,283	23.	Germany	2.30
8.	France	32,220	31.	India[a]	1.93
9.	Luxembourg	31,900	40.	France	1.51
10.	Hong Kong[b]	27,448	44.	China	1.30
17.	India[a]	15,425	52.	United States	0.90
18.	Taiwan	13,892	54.	Russia	0.88
21.	Brazil	7,554	56.	Japan	0.74
Largest surplus			Largest surplus/GDP		
1.	United Kingdom	65,488	1.	Luxembourg	35.14
2.	United States	48,890	2.	Cyprus	11.90
3.	Hong Kong[b]	20,541	3.	Lebanon	9.51
4.	Luxembourg	12,815	4.	United Kingdom	6.00
5.	China	7,081	5.	Costa Rica	2.98
Largest deficit			Selected countries		
60.	Austria	−2,647	6.	Ireland	1.84
61.	Kazakhstan	−3,080	22.	United States	0.39
62.	Italy	−4,471	35.	Japan	0.04
63.	Korea, Rep. of	−5,114	36.	Germany	0.00
64.	Indonesia	−7,727	38.	France	−0.11
Largest surplus in 2004			Largest surplus/GDP in 2004		
1.	United Kingdom	64,903	1.	Luxembourg	28.27
2.	United States	44,413	2.	Hong Kong	11.90
3.	Hong Kong	20,541	3.	Netherl. Antilles	9.92

(continued)

Table 3.3 (continued)

Rank	Country	Total (M US$)	Rank	Country	Total/GDP (%)
4.	Luxembourg	10,311	4.	Cyprus	9.18
5.	China	6,350	5.	Barbados	6.81
Largest deficit in 2004			Selected countries		
77.	Austria	−3,734	7.	United Kingdom	2.95
78.	Italy	−4,069	27.	United States	0.35
79.	Germany	−4,210	46.	Japan	−0.05
80.	Korea, Rep. of	−4,402	48.	France	−0.10
81.	Indonesia	−5,466	52.	Germany	−0.15

Source: own calculations. Data: IMF Balance of Payments, retrieved from: UNCTAD
[a]Most recent available figures for India are for 2003
[b]Most recent available figures for Hong Kong are for 2004

Concerning *services onshoring*, the US and the UK represented the largest service exporters with comparable export values (~113,000M US$). Germany (64,259M US$) was ranked third, followed by other developed countries except for Hong Kong. Among the top 21 service exporters, we also found the developing countries India, Taiwan, and Brazil. The five largest exporters at relative consideration were almost identical to the top five importers including Luxembourg, Ireland, and Austria. Considering large developed countries, the UK had the lead, followed by Germany, France, the US, and Japan.

Finally, the largest overall *surplus and deficit countries* are identified. The UK, the US, Hong Kong, Luxembourg, and – surprisingly – China represented the largest surplus countries in services. Thus, China does not only have an advantage in exporting goods, but also in exporting services. Taking GDP into account, Luxembourg was by far the largest surplus country, but the UK was also found among the top five. Indonesia constituted the largest deficit country, followed by South Korea, Italy, Kazakhstan, and Austria. Note that in 2004 Germany also was among the five largest deficit countries. The shares of surpluses and deficits in GDP reveal that Germany and Japan reversed their deficits of 2004, while France still constituted a deficit country.

3.1.2 Development of Services Offshoring in Selected OECD Countries

The following subsection focuses on five selected large developed countries, namely France, Germany, Japan, the UK and the US. Like in the previous section, import data and export data are used as a proxy for offshoring and onshoring, respectively. Again, the four services categories computer and information services, other business services, communications and financial services are considered. To reflect the development in these countries, four years (1991, 1996, 2001 and 2005) are taken into account. 1991 is selected as the starting point, since earlier years are unavailable for most of the four services categories.

3.1.2.1 Offshoring Development by Services Category

The imports of the four selected services categories are shown in Fig. 3.1. Regarding *computer and information services*, all countries showed two-digit annual growth rates except for Japan with stagnating growth. This might reflect developments in ICTs. German imports unambiguously dominated other imports, especially in 2001 and 2005, while the other countries showed more comparable import values. The CAGR was highest for the UK and the US, which is due to their low starting value in 1991. Regarding *other business services*, all countries experienced positive growth between 1991 and 2005. Germany, the UK, and the US showed a constant upward trend, while France and Japan experienced a drop in 2001. In absolute terms, the US displaced Germany to rank two in 2005. The CAGR is two-digit for the UK and the US, lower in Germany and in France, and almost zero in Japan.

Concerning imports of communication services, all countries showed positive growth rates except for the US (−2.0%). Growth was constant over the four years in France, Germany, and the UK, whereas Japan and the US experienced a decline in 2001 and 2005. Despite the fact that imports fell in the US, it still maintained its status as the largest absolute importer, followed by Germany and the UK, both showing a similar trend. The last category – *financial services* – had a more heterogeneous pattern, but all countries except for France experienced positive growth rates. Imports grew constantly in Germany, the UK, and the US, the Anglo-Saxon countries mostly being the largest importers. Germany and the UK showed the highest CAGR, and especially the latter grew strongly in the last years.

We conclude that Germany and the UK had positive growth rates in all categories, while France and the US experienced negative growth in one category. Imports to Japan, however, stagnated between 1991 and 2005 except for financial services. For the *absolute onshoring development per services category* see Appendix B.

Table 3.4 presents the *shares of service imports in total imports of other services* for the selected services categories. This gives an indication of the relative importance of each type of service. "Other services" are defined as the difference between "total services" minus "transportation" and "travel". From 1991 to 2005, France's import shares increased in all categories except for financial services. The share of other business services grew by 12.6 percentage points. Germany's import shares increased in all categories except for other business services that experienced a weak decline. Especially the shares of computer and information services and financial services grew rapidly. This indicates a possible shortage of IT specialists. Japan's share of other business services imports fell strongly, while the other shares remained more or less constant. The UK enlarged its share in all categories, especially in other business services (by 15.5 percentage points), except for communication services that dropped by four percentage points. Finally, the US shares of computer and information services grew weakly, while the shares of other

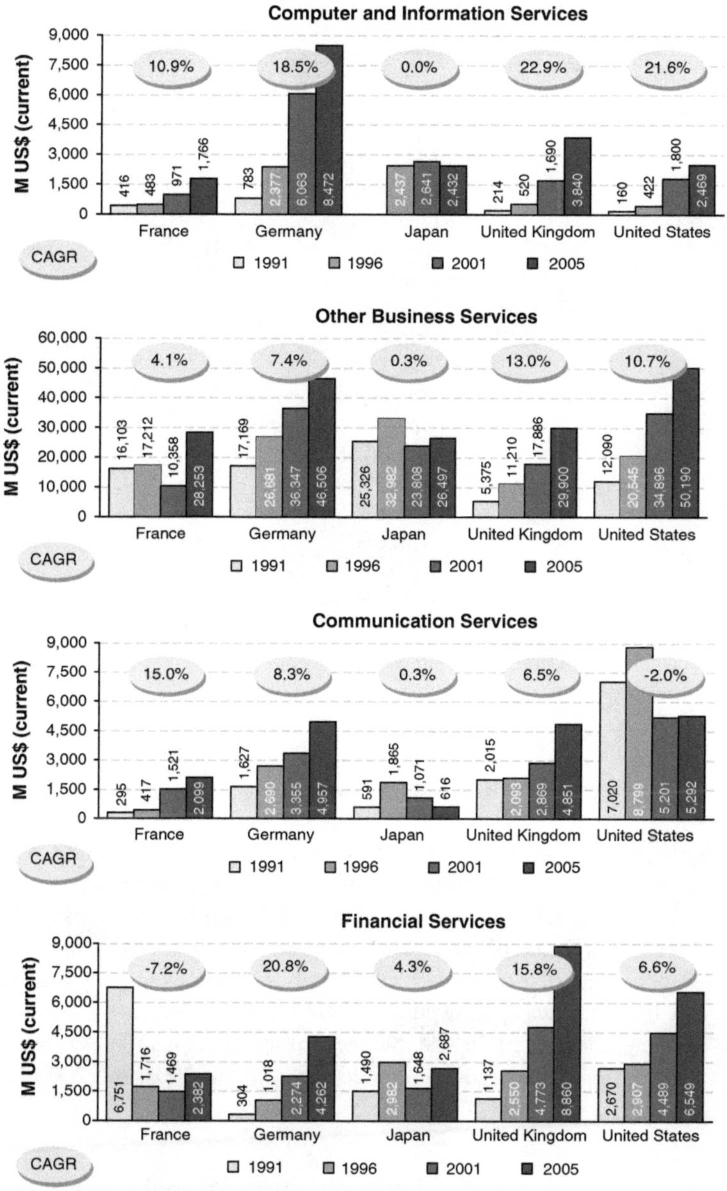

Fig. 3.1 Absolute offshoring development per services category (M US$)
Source: own calculations. Data: IMF Balance of Payments, retrieved from: UNCTAD

business services expanded strongly. The shares of communication and financial services, however, fell. For the relative onshoring development per services category see Appendix C.

Table 3.4 Relative offshoring development by services category (% of other services)

		1991	1996	2001	2005
Computer and information services	France	1.3	1.7	4.5	3.8
	Germany	2.5	4.6	9.3	9.8
	Japan	n.a.	4.1	5.4	4.3
	United Kingdom	1.2	1.8	4.4	6.0
	United States	0.3	0.7	1.8	1.6
Other business services	France	48.4	59.5	48.3	61.0
	Germany	55.6	52.2	56.0	53.6
	Japan	69.9	55.6	48.3	47.1
	United Kingdom	31.1	39.4	46.1	46.6
	United States	25.8	34.4	35.7	32.8
Communication services	France	0.9	1.4	7.1	4.5
	Germany	5.3	5.3	5.2	5.7
	Japan	1.6	3.1	2.2	1.1
	United Kingdom	11.6	7.4	7.4	7.6
	United States	15.0	14.7	5.3	3.5
Financial services	France	20.3	5.9	6.9	5.1
	Germany	1.0	2.0	3.5	4.9
	Japan	4.1	5.0	3.3	4.8
	United Kingdom	6.6	9.0	12.3	13.8
	United States	5.7	4.9	4.6	4.3

Source: own calculations. Data: IMF Balance of Payments, retrieved from: UNCTAD. NB: other services correspond to "total services" minus "transportation" and "travel"

3.1.2.2 Changes in the Trade Balance by Services Category

The *development of the trade balance by services category* is presented in Table 3.5. France showed no clear trend, being a surplus or deficit country across all services categories. Germany and Japan were clear deficit countries across all services categories except for financial services. However, Germany has managed to reduce its deficit in other business services in 2005, while Japan even generated a surplus. The UK and the US always showed a growing surplus except for communication services. Despite the deficit in the balance of communication services, the US reduced its deficit, while the UK generated a surplus in 2001 and 2005.

3.1.2.3 Overall Development of Services Offshoring and Onshoring

Finally, we add the four services categories in Table 3.6 to analyze the development of total offshoring, total onshoring, and the balance for our five countries. Germany and the US have become the leading offshoring countries from the mid-1990s on. Regarding total onshoring, the US and especially the UK performed the largest overall exports from the mid-1990s on. France constituted a net service exporter, but showed a net deficit in 2005, which is reflected in the growing share of service

Table 3.5 Balance development per services category (M US$)

		M US$			
		1991	1996	2001	2005
Computer and information services	France	−325	27	152	−72
	Germany	−423	−776	−1,258	−339
	Japan	n.a.	−1,215	−1,227	−1,306
	United Kingdom	534	1,186	2,993	6,740
	United States	2,020	2,353	3,623	3,570
Other business services	France	9,073	5,303	11,446	−2,628
	Germany	−2,931	−4,409	−10,469	−100
	Japan	−9,255	−11,006	−7,563	782
	United Kingdom	6,216	10,475	17,886	24,635
	United States	8,630	12,742	17,419	22,847
Communication services	France	−79	165	55	1,381
	Germany	−454	−667	−1,586	−1,530
	Japan	−354	−490	−352	−221
	United Kingdom	−240	−440	59	678
	United States	−3,540	−5,248	−611	−259
Financial services	France	−662	166	−375	−960
	Germany	621	1,767	961	2,031
	Japan	−1,401	−146	1,062	2,357
	United Kingdom	5,339	10,299	17,743	33,435
	United States	2,340	5,322	11,009	22,732

Source: own calculations. Data: IMF Balance of Payments, retrieved from: UNCTAD

imports in other services by almost five percentage points between 1991 and 2005. Germany and Japan were net importers, but became net exporters in 2005. The share of Germany's service imports in other services increased from 1991 to 2005, and more drastically the share of its exports. Contrary, Japan's export and especially import shares fell between 1991 and 2005. The UK and the US both represented net exporters with a growing trend over time. The share of service imports in other services increased strongly over the period in the UK, while the share decreased in the US. However, both countries had growing export shares between 1991 and 2005.

3.1.3 Calculation of Services Offshoring Intensities

3.1.3.1 Input–Output Tables

Input–output tables focus "on the interrelationships between industries in an economy with respect to the production and uses of their products and the products imported from abroad. In a table form [...] the economy is viewed with each industry listed across the top as a consuming sector and down the side as a

Table 3.6 Overall development of services offshoring and onshoring

	M US$				CAGR	% of other services			
	1991	1996	2001	2005		1991	1996	2001	2005
Total offshoring									
France	23,566	19,828	14,318	34,499	2.8	70.9	68.6	66.8	74.5
Germany	19,883	32,766	48,039	64,197	8.7	64.4	64.1	74.0	74.0
Japan	27,407	40,266	29,168	32,232	1.2	75.6	67.9	59.1	57.2
United Kingdom	8,740	16,372	27,218	47,451	12.8	50.5	57.5	70.1	73.9
United States	21,940	32,673	46,385	64,500	8.0	46.8	54.6	47.5	42.2
Total onshoring									
France	31,573	25,488	25,597	32,220	0.1	75.6	72.8	75.6	69.0
Germany	16,696	28,681	35,686	64,259	10.1	49.3	62.2	71.4	73.2
Japan	16,397	27,409	21,087	33,844	5.3	68.8	65.2	56.7	54.6
United Kingdom	20,590	37,892	65,900	112,940	12.9	70.8	72.6	78.7	81.0
United States	31,390	47,842	77,826	113,390	9.6	46.5	43.8	52.6	53.6
Balance									
France	8,007	5,661	11,278	−2,280					
Germany	−3,187	−4,085	−12,353	62					
Japan	−11,010	−12,857	−8,080	1,611					
United Kingdom	11,849	21,520	38,682	65,488					
United States	9,450	15,169	31,440	48,890					

Source: own calculations. Data: IMF Balance of Payments, retrieved from: UNCTAD. NB: Total offshoring and onshoring services include computer and information, other business, communications, and financial services. CAGR refers to 1991–2005

supplying sector" (UN 1999, p. 3). For a historical background of input–output tables see Box 3.1.

Box 3.1: Historical background of input–output tables

"Input–output (I/O) analysis as a theoretical framework and an applied economic tool in a market economy was developed by Wassily Leontief with the construction of the first input–output tables for the United States for the years 1919 and 1929 which were published in 1936. Since then, tables describing the interrelationships among various producers of an economy have been constructed for over 90 countries.

For the development of input–output methodology and its application to important economic issues, Leontief was honored with a Nobel prize in Economic Science in 1973. The integration of an input–output framework into the system of national accounts was developed and published in 1968 by the United Nations as a *System of National Accounts, Studies in Methods*. The integrated work earned Professor Richard Stone a Nobel prize in Economic Science in 1984 "for having made fundamental contributions to the development of the systems of national accounts and hence greatly improved the basis for empirical economic analysis". [...]

The fundamental contribution of input–output in economics is the transformation of Francois Quesnay's *Tableau Economique* – a descriptive device showing sales and purchases relationships between different producers and consumers in an economy – into an analytical framework which facilitates economic projections and analyses. It assumes that the inputs used in producing a product are related to the industry output by a linear and fixed coefficient production function (at least in the short run). Under this assumption, input and output relationships are transformed into technical relationships, with each column in an input–output coefficient table representing a technique of production (UN 1999, p. 3)."

Source: Handbook of input–output table compilation and analysis, UN (1999), p. 3

Table 3.7 illustrates a simplified input–output accounting framework. The *central matrix F* represents the part of production of a specific year in which the consuming sectors i (e.g., textiles sector) receive inputs from the supplying sectors s (e.g., chemicals sector). Since rows and columns list the same sectors in the same order, F is quadratic. The main diagonal ($i = s$) contains the intra-sectoral provisions, while the other cells present inputs from a supplying sector to a consuming sector (Kalmbach et al. 2005).

Y is the *final demand matrix*, which has the same number of rows as F, but usually a different number of columns as it represents the different components of final demand (private and public consumption, investments, and exports). Adding all columns of F and Y in a row s yields total output X_s. Adding all rows of a consuming sector i results in the intermediate consumption or final use. The

Table 3.7 A simplified input-output accounting framework

	Consuming sectors i	Net final demand	Total output
Supplying sectors s	F	Y	X
Value added (primary inputs)	V		
Total input	X		

Source: own illustration. Modified from: UN (1999), p. 4

Table 3.8 Input-output flow table and accounts

	Sector 1	Sector 2	Sector 3	Net final demand	Total output
Sector 1	10	20	40	30	100
Sector 2	20	10	30	140	200
Sector 3	0	60	20	70	150
Value added	70	110	60		
Total input	100	200	150		

Source: own illustration. Modified from: UN (1999), p. 5

primary inputs matrix has the same amount of columns as F, but another number of rows. V lists different components of value added (e.g., gross operating surplus, compensation of employees, and net taxes on production). Adding the final use and the value added in a consuming sector i finally leads to total inputs X_i (Kalmbach et al. 2005). Table 3.8 illustrates an input–output flow table and the accounts for three sectors. It becomes evident that total inputs of a sector equal its total output.

The following analysis for Germany uses input–output data from the Federal Statistical Office. The inputs of German input–output tables are available in three forms, namely total inputs, imported inputs, and domestically produced inputs. As our study is interested in offshoring, the existence of *import matrices* constitutes a major advantage of German tables over other countries such as the US or the UK. Imports are measured at cost, insurance, freight (cif)-prices, that represent the border-crossing value of the imports and include all costs for insurance and freight, regardless of whether they are generated by a foreign or domestic unit. The German input–output account follows the methodology and concepts of the European SNA 1995.[1] For certain parts, the underlying statistics of the German input–output tables show gaps which are filled by estimates made by the Federal Statistical Office.

Unrevised German input–output tables exist for the period 1991 to 2000, while revised tables are available for the years 1995 through 2004[2]. Unrevised and revised

[1]The only exception is that intra-firm inputs from the same statistical unit are also included in the German input–output tables, unlike the German input–output tables that are published by Eurostat. "The statistical unit for activities or industries recommended by the SNA is the establishment. An operational definition of the establishment unit is a production unit consisting of either "an enterprise, or a part of an enterprise, that is situated in a single location and in which only a single (non-ancillary) productive activity… accounts for most of the value added (SNA, para. 5.21, taken from: UN,1999, p. 41)."

[2]Input–output tables for 2005 were published in August 2008, but were not included in our analyses.

data are not fully comparable due to changes in the classification. The *revision* of the input–output tables integrates, for instance, all the changes of the national accounts revision of 2005 and the new service statistics of the Federal Statistical Office. Major changes include that bank charges are now added to the user of financial services, that intra-firm inputs are now integrated, and that transportation margins are accounted as inputs and no longer as conceptual difference between basic and purchase prices (Braakmann et al. 2005).

German input–output tables originally comprise 71 sectors and due to their symmetry also of 71 inputs. We consider all 36 material inputs plus seven selected service inputs (see Appendix D). Primary inputs (inputs 1–3) and the secondary inputs "mining" and "quarrying" (inputs 4–8) are dropped, as they generally do not represent offshoring sectors. The selection of seven service inputs out of 27 includes tradable *business activities* in the broader sense according to the aggregation of Kalmbach et al. (2005) except for the wholesale sector, which have been defined in Sect. 2.1.2.3.

3.1.3.2 Two Different Measures of Services Offshoring Intensity

We calculate two different measures of offshoring intensity (*a*) and (*b*). The services offshoring intensity $\mathrm{OSS}_{ist}(a)$ represents a more sophisticated measure of services offshoring than import data. It measures the share of service import *s* by sector *i* at time *t* in total non-energy inputs used by sector *i* at time *t* and is calculated as follows:

$$\mathrm{OSS}_{ist}(a) = \frac{(\text{imported input purchases of service } s \text{ by sector } i)_t}{(\text{total non-energy inputs used by sector } i)_t}.$$

The services offshoring intensity $\mathrm{OSS}_{it}(a)$ for sector *i* at time *t* is calculated by taking the sum over all $\mathrm{OSS}_{ist}(a)$:

$$\mathrm{OSS}_{it}(a) = \sum_{s} \mathrm{OSS}_{ist}(a).$$

The denominator contains all 36 non-energy manufacturing inputs plus the seven service sectors selected above. German input–output data differentiates between domestically purchased inputs and imported inputs, whereas sectoral import data are not available for the US and the UK according to Amiti and Wei (2005, 2006). Therefore, they apply the methodology of Feenstra and Hanson (1996)[3] who calculated offshoring intensities of material imports to the US. This second measure of services offshoring intensity $\mathrm{OSS}_{ist}(b)$ for a given sector *i* at time *t* is a *proxy* for

[3]Other studies using this offshoring measure are shown in Table 1.1.

the proportion of imported service input s used in home production. Besides the $OSS_{ist}(a)$ measure, we also calculate the $OSS_{ist}(b)$ measure for Germany to allow for international comparability. The second measure is defined as follows:

$$OSS_{ist}(b) = \left[\frac{(\text{input purchases of service } s \text{ by sector } i)_t}{(\text{total non-energy inputs used by sector } i)_t}\right] \cdot \left[\frac{(\text{imports of service } s)_t}{\text{production}_{st} + \text{imports}_{st} - \text{exports}_{st}}\right]$$

The first bracket calculates the share of the purchased service input s in total non-energy inputs for sector i at time t. However, the first ratio does not distinguish between domestically and foreign purchased service inputs, while services offshoring solely focuses on services from a foreign source. Therefore, the second bracket calculates the share of total imported service s (numerator) in the entire domestic disposability of this service s (denominator), which is composed of home production plus imports minus exports at time t. The data are retrieved from the input–output tables. The services offshoring intensity $OSS_{ist}(b)$ of service s in sector i is calculated by multiplying both ratios. This proxy assumes the same overall import share of service s, regardless of sectoral differences. In Germany, for instance, the overall import share of "other business activities" was 4.5% in 2004. Hence, an import share of 4.5% is assumed for each sector i.

The services offshoring intensity $OSS_{it}(b)$ for sector i at time t is calculated by taking the sum over all $OSS_{ist}(b)$:

$$OSS_{it}(b) = \sum_s OSS_{ist}(b)$$

The sectoral services offshoring intensity OSS_{it} should not be confused with OSS_{st}, which represents the average offshoring intensity of a certain service s across all sectors i. This is calculated by aggregating the respective OSS_{ist}, weighted by total sectoral non-energy inputs INP, which is: $OSS_{st} = \sum_i OSS_{ist} \cdot (INP_{it}/INP_t)$, where $INP_t = \sum_i INP_{it}$.[4]

Summing OSS_{st} over all services s yields the average services offshoring intensity OSS_t at time t across all sectors and services: $OSS_t = \sum OSS_{st}$. Another possibility to calculate OSS_t is: $OSS_t = \Sigma_i OSS_{it} \cdot (INP_{it}/INP_t)$. The materials offshoring intensities OSM_t are calculated analogously.

The definition of the offshoring intensity suffers from three related shortcomings. The first two caveats concern both offshoring intensity measures, whereas the

[4] Amiti and Wei (2005, 2006) use sectoral outputs as weightings. Using total non-energy inputs instead of output results in a more accurate overall offshoring intensity, as it directly refers to the denominator of the offshoring measure.

last one only holds for the $OSS_t(b)$ measure. First, the measures underestimate the actual offshoring values, since import prices are generally lower than the actual purchase prices of these services. Second, the total non-energy inputs only include purchased inputs, but not self-produced inputs used by sector *i*, which might lead to an overestimation problem of the offshoring intensities. Third, the application of the same import share for each sector *s* (in the second bracket) in $OSS_t(b)$ is not accurate, since not every sector uses imports to the same extent. Thus, the offshoring intensity cannot be exactly measured (Amiti and Wei 2005).

Further caveats include first that trade data are mostly reported as gross flows rather than foreign value added, which makes the attribution of offshore destinations difficult. Second, services trade is hard to measure as it "leaves no paper trail" (Grossman and Rossi-Hansberg, 2006, pp. 2–3). Despite these caveats, offshoring intensities, especially $OSS_t(a)$, present a good measure for the proportion of imported service inputs being used in home production at time *t*.

3.1.3.3 Results for Germany

Figure 3.2 plots the development of the *average* $OSS_t(a)$ *and* $OSM_t(a)$ intensities in Germany. The dashed line represents the development between 1991 and 2000 using unrevised input–output data for the calculations, whereas the continuous line illustrates the development between 1995 and 2004 using revised input–output data. *Services offshoring intensities* grew considerably by on average 8.5% per year from 1.2% in 1991 to 2.5% in 2000. Between 1995 and 2004, services offshoring intensities increased from 1.4% in 1995 to 2.9% in 2004 with a CAGR of 8.6%. The higher intensities from 1995 onwards reflect a stronger use of ICTs.

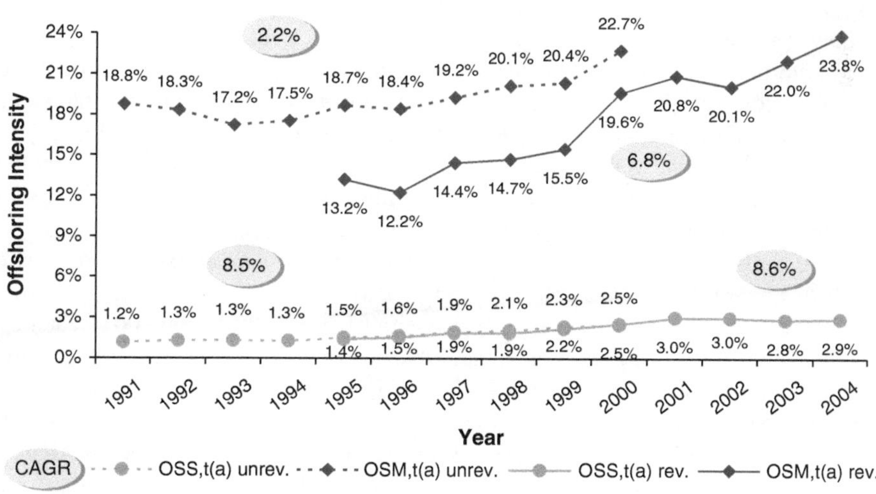

Fig. 3.2 Offshoring intensity of intermediate inputs in Germany
Source: own calculations. Data: Federal Statistical Office Germany, unrevised (1991–2000) and revised (1995–2004) input-output tables

Average *materials offshoring intensities* rose by on average 2.2% per year from 18.8% in 1991 to 22.7% in 2000. Using the revised input–output data, materials offshoring intensities grew from 13.2% in 1995 to 23.8% in 2004, reflecting a CAGR of 6.8%. The stronger growth between 1995 and 2004 can be explained by the fall of the iron curtain and subsequent FDI towards the CEECs, and likewise by the growing significance of Asian markets. Generally, materials offshoring intensities experienced lower growth compared to services offshoring intensities. One explanation would be that the process of materials offshoring, which has already started in the 1980s, might have reached its capacity, while services offshoring has not realized its full potential yet.

3.1.3.4 Comparison with the UK and the US

Finally, an *international comparison* between Germany, the UK, and the US follows. Data for the UK and the US are based on the studies of Amiti and Wei (2005, 2006). Three differences between the German and Anglo-Saxon offshoring measures occur, which we take into account in order to make the offshoring intensities comparable. First, offshoring intensities for the US and the UK are based on the (*b*) measure. Therefore, we also calculated offshoring (*b*) measures for Germany. Second, the US and UK measures use sectoral outputs instead of total non-energy inputs as weightings in order to obtain average offshoring intensities. For comparability reasons, we also weighted sectoral offshoring intensities by sectoral output.

Third, one could object that comparability of OSS_{it} and OSM_{it} is not given, since the respective sectoral classifications differ and are more disaggregated for the Anglo-Saxon countries. However, such differences disappear in OSS_t and OSM_t, as they represent a weighted aggregation of all sectoral offshoring intensities. Comparability of the three countries then requires that similar manufacturing and service sectors are chosen. There should be no problem with manufacturing, since all manufacturing sectors are included in the three studies. Country-specific differences could only arise in the selection of the service inputs. Table 3.9 shows that the selected services are similar with respect to their activities. All services have an equivalent in the other countries, thus allowing for a comparison.

Table 3.10 compares the *average German services and materials offshoring intensities with UK and US intensities* using the available years. Regarding services offshoring, the UK showed the highest intensities between 1992 and 2001, reaching a peak in 2001 (2.60%). This is remarkable, as one would expect services offshoring to be more relevant in the UK due to its former colonial ties and lower linguistic barriers. The US intensities were far below the German levels, but followed an increasing trend. Germany's unrevised data showed the second highest CAGR (6.23%) over the respective period, compared to the UK (7.55%) and the US (5.60%). Using the revised German data, the average annual growth rate (9.13%) was the highest among the three countries, but the overall levels are still lower than the UK data.

Table 3.9 Comparison of selected services in Germany, the UK and the US

Germany	UK	US
Post and telecommunications	Telecommunications	Telecommunications
Financial intermediation, activities related to financial intermediation	Banking and finance, insurance and pension funds, and auxiliary financial services	Insurance, finance
Renting of machinery and equipment	Renting of machinery	Other business services
Computer and related activities	Computer services	Computing and information
Research and development	Research and development	Other business services
Other business activities	Legal activities, accountancy services, market research, and management consultancy	Other business services
Other business activities	Architectural activities and technical consultancy	Other business services
Other business activities	Advertising	Other business services
Other business activities	Other business services	Other business services

Source: German classification: Federal Statistical Office Germany, UK classification: UK National Accounts, US classification: balance of payments statistics
NB: other business services in the US (IMF classification) include merchanting and other trade-related services, operational leasing services and miscellaneous business, professional and technical services

As regards materials offshoring, the UK had the strongest intensities over the entire period with a peak in 1995 (30.7%), followed by Germany and the US, which were close to each other. The US and the revised German intensities grew almost continuously over the considered period. The unrevised German data and the UK data, however, did not follow such a trend. UK measures grew slightly from 1992 until 1995/1996 and then fell back to their initial level. The German unrevised measures started at a very high level in 1991 (18.49%), fell to a low in 1993, before growing steadily until 2000.

3.1.3.5 Offshoring Intensities in OECD Countries

The OECD (2007) calculates the share of imported intermediates in total output for 17 OECD countries on the basis of input–output tables for 1995 and 2000 (see Fig. 3.3). Thereby, the OECD distinguishes between business service inputs and material inputs. Unfortunately, the data source does not concretize which inputs (e.g. business services) are taken into account and thus if comparability to Table 3.10 is given. Moreover, the intensities tend to be lower than the previous measures, since total sectoral output instead of total non-energy inputs are used in the denominator. For the list of country abbreviations see Appendix E.

Table 3.10 Offshoring intensity in Germany, the UK, and the US (%)

Services offshoring intensity				
Year	Germany (*b*) unrevised	Germany (*b*) revised	UK	US
1991	1.01	–	–	–
1992	0.98	–	1.35	0.18
1993	0.98	–	1.58	0.18
1994	0.94	–	1.64	0.20
1995	1.01	0.95	1.62	0.20
1996	1.11	1.07	1.82	0.21
1997	1.33	1.22	1.66	0.23
1998	1.40	1.41	2.00	0.24
1999	1.59	1.70	2.22	0.29
2000	1.74	1.96	2.38	0.29
2001	–	2.26	2.60	–
2002	–	2.21	–	–
2003	–	2.05	–	–
2004	–	2.09	–	–
CAGR	6.2	9.1	7.6	6.1
Materials offshoring intensity				
Year	Germany (*b*) unrevised	Germany (*b*) revised	UK	US
1991	18.49	–	–	–
1992	16.46	–	28.19	11.72
1993	14.93	–	29.49	12.68
1994	16.00	–	29.77	13.41
1995	16.89	12.23	30.70	14.18
1996	16.90	12.23	30.66	14.32
1997	18.32	14.78	29.67	14.55
1998	18.97	14.58	28.00	14.94
1999	19.05	15.43	28.00	15.55
2000	21.51	19.46	28.56	17.33
2001	–	19.88	28.09	–
2002	–	19.69	–	–
2003	–	20.45	–	–
2004	–	23.05	–	–
CAGR	1.7	7.3	0.0	5.0
Service sectors	7	7	9	5
Manufacturing sectors	36	36	69	96

Source: own calculations for Germany. Data: input–output tables, Federal Statistical Office Germany. UK: Amiti and Wei (2005), US: Amiti and Wei (2006). NB: UK data are not directly available, but can be reconstructed thanks to Fig. 2 in Amiti and Wei (2005)

The average *services offshoring intensity* among the 17 countries was 2.2% in 1995 compared to 2.8% in 2000. All countries showed positive growth rates except for Austria and France. Despite the third highest growth rate after Norway and Finland, Germany's services offshoring intensities remained below average. In 1995, Germany showed the third lowest intensity (1.2%) behind the US and

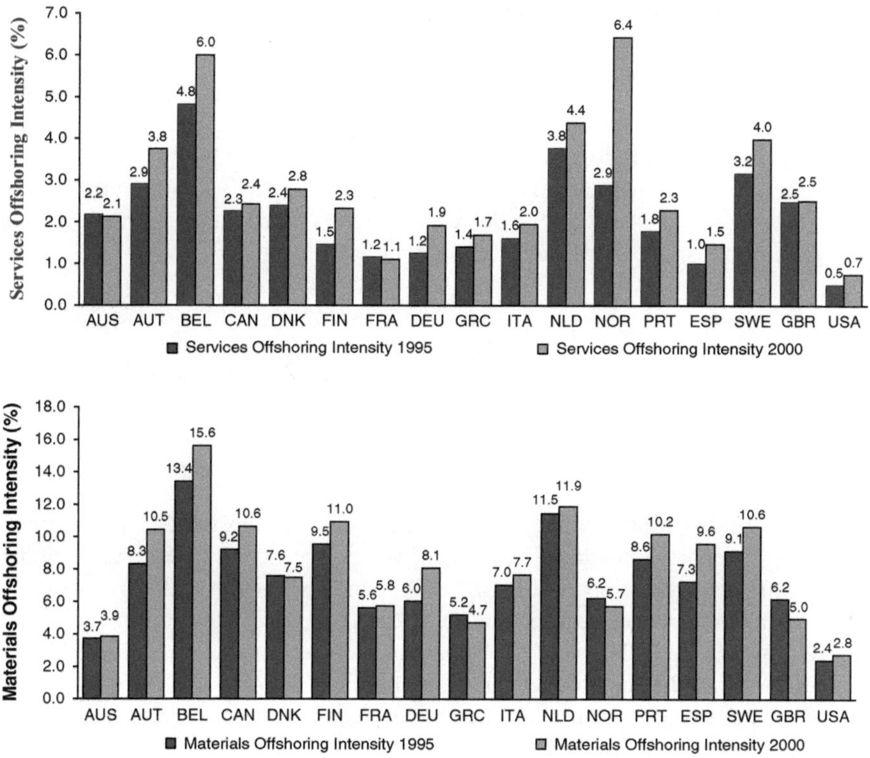

Fig. 3.3 Services and materials offshoring intensities in OECD countries 1995 versus 2000 *Source*: OECD estimates using OECD STAN Input–Output tables. Retrieved from: OECD Employment Outlook 2007, p. 112. 1995 and 1999 for Greece and Portugal; 1997 and 2000 for Canada; and 1997 and 2001 for Norway. NB: Offshoring intensities are measured as percentage of output

Spain, which increased to 1.9% in 2000. In comparison, Norway, Belgium, the Netherlands, and Sweden were the largest services offshorers in 2000.

Concerning materials, the average *materials offshoring intensity* was 7.5% in 1995 and 8.3% in 2000. Again, Germany was below average with intensities of 6.0 and 8.1% in 1995 and 2000, respectively, but at the same time had the highest growth rate among the 17 countries. Materials offshoring intensities in Denmark, Greece, Norway, and the UK decreased, whereas the other 13 countries all experienced positive growth. In 2000, Belgium, the Netherlands, Finland, and Sweden were the countries with the highest materials offshoring intensities.

Nevertheless, the 2000 figures are outdated, and services offshoring might have grown more strongly after 2000. The countries with the highest intensities are mostly smaller economies that have generally a larger trade openness, whereas larger economies, such as France, Germany, the UK and especially the US, mostly showed intensities below average. Since Germany had very high growth rates between 1995 and 2000, one could expect a stronger growth potential in the subsequent years.

3.2 Sectoral Structure of Services Offshoring

Section 3.2.1 identifies the main offshoring sectors as well as the kind of service activities that are most commonly being offshored. First, the global development is discussed (Sect. 3.2.1) before moving on to specific trends in Germany (Sect. 3.2.2). Our global analysis relies on existing studies, while the analysis for Germany uses import data from the Deutsche Bundesbank, which is based on the German Balance of Payments statistics, as well as input–output data.

3.2.1 Sectoral Structure of Global Services Offshoring

3.2.1.1 The Structure of the Offshoring Sectors

Estimations of the global market volume of offshored services vary. Hutzschenreuter et al. (2007) reports an estimated worldwide volume of 32B US$, while Schaaf (2004) estimates a value up to 40B US$. While the bulk of the offshoring market is still undertaken in private sectors, one have to take in mind that it is not exclusively reserved to the latter. Claassen (2006), for instance, reports that the British Department for Work and Pensions, which is the national authority for pensions, unemployment compensation, and child benefits, intends to relocate larger parts of its administrative tasks to India for cost reasons (taken from Hutzschenreuter et al. 2007). Nevertheless, political reasons might hamper a rapid expansion of offshoring within the public sector.

Figure 3.4 presents the *offshore market distribution by sector*. According to this estimation, more than a third (35%) of the offshoring sectors are banking, insurance, and financial services industries. Accordingly, Deutsche Bank was one of the first companies in Germany that offshored services abroad. Its software engineering affiliate Deutsche Software Limited, for instance, has operated in Bangalore since 1992 (Handwerk 2004; taken from Hutzschenreuter et al., 2007). The telecommunications/technology sectors (25%) hold a quarter of the offshoring market, which is followed by manufacturing, retail trade as well as transport and leisure (Schaaf 2004).

The McKinsey Global Institute (2005) analyzes "The Demand for Offshore Talent in Services" with a focus on eight selected manufacturing and service sectors, namely automotive, pharmaceuticals, health care, insurance, IT services, packaged software, retail, and retail banking. The eight sectors are broken down into their functions and occupations in order to determine the sectoral offshoring potential in 2003 (see Fig. 3.5). The study differentiates between sector-specific functions and universal functions.

In the case of *sector-specific functions,* global provision is unlikely due to three possible features. First, the function might require physical proximity (e.g., nursing in health care). Second, certain functions depend on local knowledge (e.g., sales,

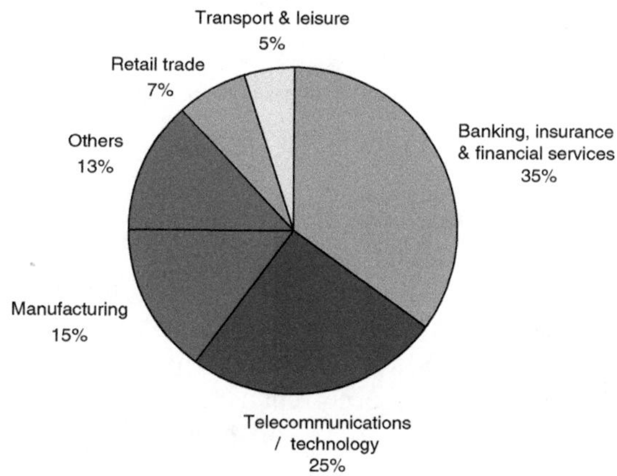

Fig. 3.4 Global offshore market distribution by sector
Source: Deloitte and Touche, 2004, taken from: Schaaf (2004), p. 11

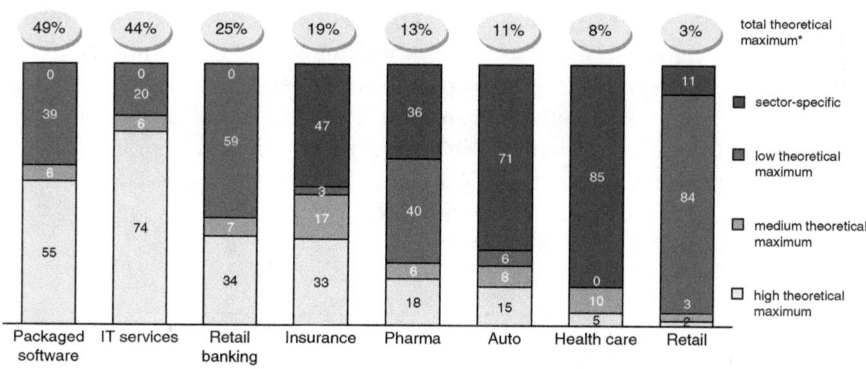

Fig. 3.5 Sectoral employment by services offshoring potential in 2003
Source: own illustration. Data: McKinsey Global Institute (2005), p. 37. NB: high: > 40% average potential; medium: > 20% and < 40% average potential; low: < 20% average potential. Sector-specific functions usually have very low theoretical maxima. (*) The total theoretical maximum corresponds to the share of jobs in the sector that could be relocated

marketing, and legal functions). And third, some occupations require complex interactions (e.g., in management and information coordination). *Universal functions* (e.g., IT and back-office functions), however, have a low, medium, or high theoretical offshoring potential. A high probability is defined as 40% or more, medium describes a potential between 20 and 40%, and a low probability is defined as less than 20%. The *total theoretical maximum* corresponds to the share of jobs in the sector that could be relocated and is determined by a sector's offshoring potential and its size (in terms of employees). The theoretical maximum across all sectors in the global economy[5] averages 11%, but the sectoral shares vary

[5]The study includes a wide range of 36 developed and developing countries.

strongly between 3% in retail and 49% in the packed software sector. The sector IT services shows the second largest share (44%). Thus, Fig. 3.5 confirms the global offshore market distribution, which was shown in Fig. 3.4.

3.2.1.2 The Structure of Offshored Services

The next part focuses on the *structure of offshored services* worldwide. As mentioned in the previous paragraph, three main *kinds of services* are more likely to be relocated: services that do not require physical proximity, that do not require local knowledge, and that are not characterized by complex interactions (McKinsey Global Institute 2005). Besides, offshoring is more likely with services that possess a high explicit information content ("codified knowledge"), that can be transmitted via ICT (ICT-enabled services), that have a high wage-differential with comparable occupations in the destination country, that do not include high set-up barriers, and that do not require high social networking (Bardhan and Kroll 2003).

Table 3.11 categorizes business services according to their *offshoring probability* (high, medium, and low). Sector-independent support services, programming, help-desks and call centers, that usually do not require direct contact with the end-consumer, have a higher offshoring probability. IT infrastructure, data centers (e.g. accounting) or server management have a medium offshoring probability, whereas R&D, network or data backup are less likely offshored (Schaaf 2004).

Table 3.11 The offshoring probability of business services

High
Application development
Programming
Maintenance of old systems
Help-desk
Call centers
Medium
IT infrastructure
Data/computer centers
Network administration
Web hosting
Server management
Low
R&D
System architecture
Network/data backup
Integration of IT and business processes

Source: prism economics, 2004, taken from: Schaaf (2004), p. 10

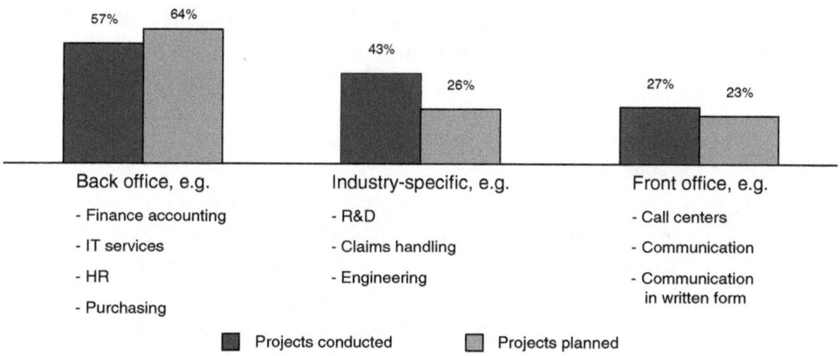

Fig. 3.6 Services offshoring projects by types of service (% of European companies)
Source: UNCTAD and Roland Berger (2004), p. 6. Multiple answers possible. Examples given are ranked by number of mentions

Figure 3.6 reveals that 57% of the UNCTAD and Roland Berger survey (2004) sample, mentioned in Sect. 2.2.2, have relocated *back office services*, of which finance accounting, IT services, HR, and purchasing in this order have been mentioned most often. This share is expected to increase in the future, since almost two-thirds (64%) of the sample indicated that they planned to offshore back office services. *Industry-specific services*, most importantly R&D, claims handling, and engineering, have been relocated by 43% of the respondents, which is expected to fall to 26% for future projects. *Front office services* have been relocated by more than a quarter (27%) of the sample, out of which call centers and communication in written form have been mentioned most often. This share is expected to decrease slightly to 23%. The results confirm that rather sector-independent support services are being offshored (see Table 3.11).

3.2.2 Sectoral Structure of German Services Offshoring

The following subsection analyzes the structure of the offshoring sectors and of the offshored services. We adopt two approaches for the analysis: In a first step, we use services trade data between Germany and non-residents, which is provided by the Deutsche Bundesbank and based on balance of payments statistics. Contrary to the German input–output tables, the Bundesbank data also includes final services. Since final services might also be subject to relocation and thus reflect an offshoring decision, we believe that German service imports – including final and intermediate services – are a good proxy for the sectoral structure of German services offshoring. In a second step, we rely on input–output data which only includes intermediate service imports. Generally, services offshoring involves intermediate services rather than final services. Using the two approaches allows us to obtain a reliable indication of the structure of German services offshoring.

3.2.2.1 The Structure of the Offshoring Sectors

In this paragraph, we evaluate the *structure of the offshoring sectors* to determine the sectors that use imported services most heavily. The Special Statistical Publication 12 of the Deutsche Bundesbank gives insights on the amount of technological service imports per sector of destination. Technological services consist of four services categories, namely patents and licenses, R&D, computer services, and “engineering and other technical services” (see Sect. 2.1.2.3), whereby especially the last three are of particular interest for our study. Table 3.12 shows the import values (M €) of technological services in the different German sectors in 2005. *R&D imports* were mainly absorbed by the manufacturing sectors (68.5%) and more than half of them by the chemical sector (35.2%). The sector “other business activities” received the second largest share (14.6%), followed by the sector “motor vehicles, trailers and semi-trailers” (13.6%).

Computer services imports were mainly used by service sectors, out of which “computer and related activities” obtained the highest share (42.1%). The sectors “financial intermediation” (9.4%) and “other business activities” (8.4%) also received large shares of imported computer services. Among the manufacturing sectors that only imported 25.8% of computer services, the chemical sector (4.8%) absorbed most of the computer services imports. *Imports of engineering and other technical services* were primarily destined for the manufacturing sectors (69.3%), half of them going to the sectors “motor vehicles, trailers and semi-trailers” (21.4%) and “other transport equipment” (13.4%). The third largest share was used by the sector “other business activities” (10.1%). To sum up, computer services imports were mainly absorbed by service sectors, whereas most imports of R&D as well as “engineering and other technical services” went to the manufacturing sectors. The sectors “motor vehicles, trailers and semi-trailers” and “other business activities” were important for the last two services categories, while the chemicals sector played a predominant role for R&D services.

In a second step, *sectoral services offshoring intensities* $OSS_i(a)$ in 1995 and 2004 are plotted for the 35 manufacturing and seven service sectors (Fig. 3.7).[6] The intensities are calculated as described in Sect. 3.1.3.2. Services offshoring intensities are still low in manufacturing, where 26 out of 35 sectors had an intensity level of less than 1% in 2004. Nevertheless, all manufacturing sectors experienced positive growth over the period. The three manufacturing sectors with the highest $OSS_i(a)$ in 2004 were pharmaceuticals (19.65%), tobacco products (3.91%), and publishing (3.02%).

[6]Sectoral services offshoring intensities based on unrevised input-output data and sectoral materials offshoring intensities based on unrevised and revised input-output data are shown in Appendices F–H.

Table 3.12 Service imports per sector in 2005

	Services category					
	Research and development		Computer services		Engineering and other technical services	
	M €	%	M €	%	M €	%
Sector of destination						
All sectors	*4,646*	*100.0*	*6,805*	*100.0*	*5,958*	*100.0*
Manufacturing sectors	*3,182*	*68.5*	*1,753*	*25.8*	*4,121*	*69.2*
Food products, beverages and tobacco	7	0.2	18	0.3	14	0.2
Wood & products of wood and cork; pulp, paper and paper products; printing & publishing	2	0.0	57	0.8	77	1.3
Chemical, rubber, plastics and fuel products	1,635	35.2	325	4.8	300	5.0
Machinery and equipment	34	0.7	56	0.8	330	5.5
Radio, television and communication equip.	50	1.1	83	1.2	320	5.4
Motor vehicles, trailers and semi-trailers	634	13.6	181	2.7	1,277	21.4
Other transport equipment	105	2.3	35	0.5	801	13.4
Wholesale and retail trade; repairs	186	4.0	429	6.3	234	3.9
Transport and storage and communication	8	0.2	323	4.7	132	2.2
Post and telecommunications	3	0.1	274	4.0	101	1.7
Financial intermediation	4	0.1	637	9.4	35	0.6
Real estate, renting and business activities	988	21.3	3,473	51.0	877	14.7
Computer and related activities	5	0.1	2,862	42.1	237	4.0
Research and development	305	6.6	6	0.1	12	0.2
Other business activities	678	14.6	568	8.3	603	10.1
Community, social and personal services	149	3.2	66	1.0	79	*1.3*

Source: own illustration. Data: Deutsche Bundesbank (2006, p. 17), Special Statistical Publication 12 "Technologische Dienstleistungen in der Zahlungsbilanz" (in German only)

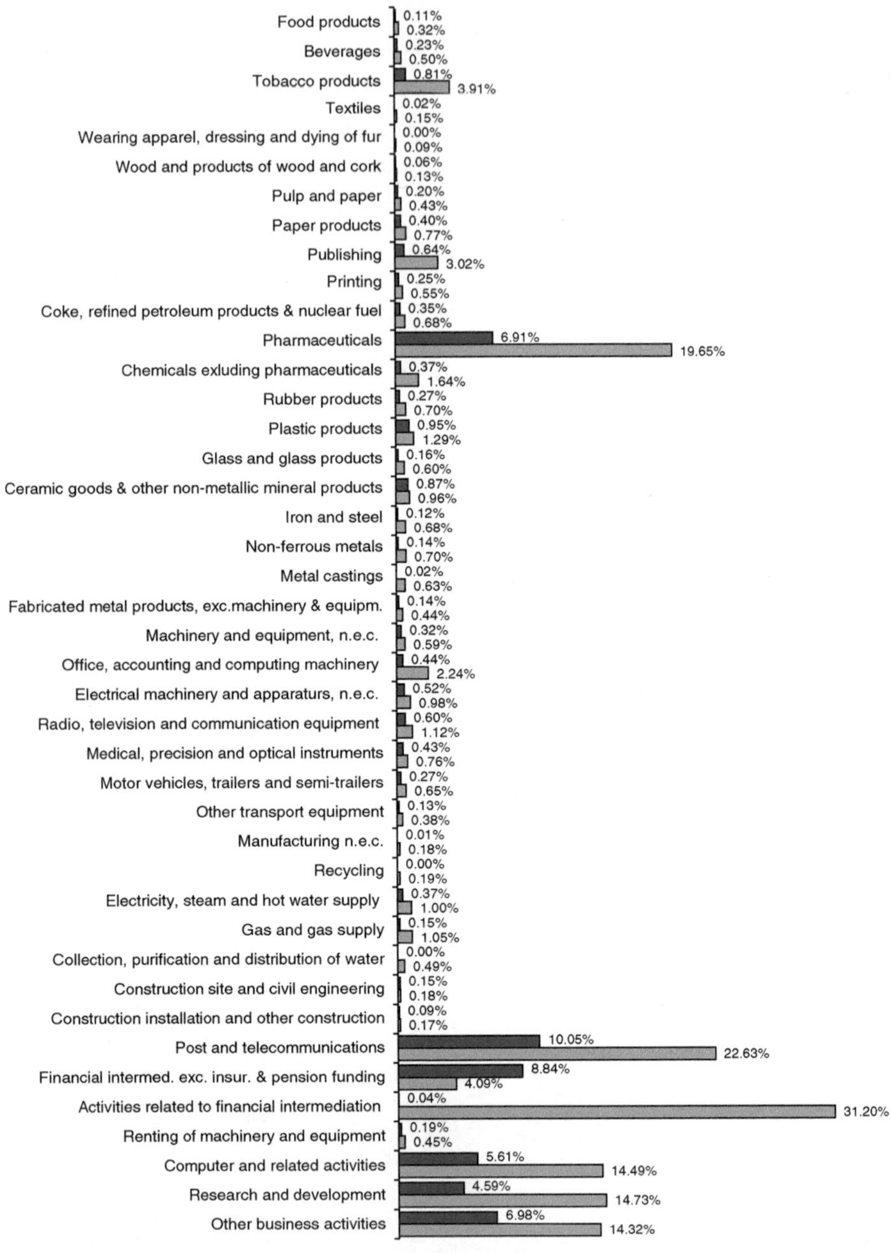

Fig. 3.7 Sectoral services offshoring intensities $OSS_i(a)$ 1995 versus 2004
Source: own illustration. Data: Federal Statistical Office Germany, revised input–output data

Services offshoring intensities in the service sectors are generally higher and exceeded the level of 10% in five of the seven sectors. The highest $OSS_i(a)$ in 2004 were found in the sectors "activities related to financial intermediation" (31.2%) and "post and telecommunications" (22.63%). Interestingly, the three sectors "computer and related activities", R&D, and "other business activities" all imported a similar amount of services in total non-energy inputs, which was around 14.5% in 2004. Only the sector "financial intermediation" experienced negative growth. We conclude that services offshoring still plays a subordinate role in most manufacturing sectors, but services offshoring intensities grew in all manufacturing and service sectors except for "financial intermediation".

3.2.2.2 The Structure of Offshored Services

While the previous sub-subsection focused on the structure of the offshoring sectors, this sub-subsection analyzes the *structure of offshored services*. Following the methodology used above, the first part relies on balance of payments statistics. Table 3.13 presents the sectoral structure of services trade in 2006. *Total services* consist of travel, transport, insurance services, financial services, and "other services". In 2006, total service imports had a value of 176,704M €, out of which other services (38.7%) and travel (33.3%) formed the largest parts. Total service exports were smaller with 138,543M €, out of which other services (46.4%) and transport (26.0%) again formed the largest shares. Thus, German services trade showed a negative balance of −38,161M € in 2006.

The services listed in italic type correspond to the classification of tradable business activities according to Kalmbach et al. (2005). Most of them are found in the category "other services" except for financial services. In 2006, the tradable business activities had an import (offshore) value of 44,679M €, hence a quarter of all service imports represented business activities. The export (onshore) value of business activities was 43,888M €, which represented 31.7% of the total service exports. Thus, the balance was slightly negative with net imports of −791M €. Concerning the structure of the offshored services, commercial services, "engineering and other technical services" as well as computer services showed the highest import values.

Figure 3.8 gives an overview of the *development of the sectoral structure of German services offshoring* for the years 1991, 1996, 2001 and 2006. Only tradable business activities are considered. In 1991, the total sum of imported tradable business activities was 11,479M €, which increased to 17,610M €, 39,496M € and 44,679M € in 1996, 2001 and 2006. The CAGR was strongest between 1996 and 2001 (17.5%). *Financial services imports* had a share of 2.2% in total tradable business activities in 1991 (258M €), which more than quadrupled to 9.6% in 2006 (4,311M €). *R&D imports* had the second largest share of 14.5% (1,665M €) in 1991, which declined to the third smallest share of 10.7% (4,777M €) in 2006. *Imports of engineering and other technical services* had a share of 10% in 1991 (1,141M €), which increased to the third largest share of 16% (7,144M €) in 2006. *Computer services imports* only had the third smallest share of 3.1% (306M €) in

Table 3.13 Sectoral structure of German service imports and exports in 2006

Service activity	Imports (M €)	Share (%)	Exports (M €)	Share (%)	Balance (M €)
Total services	176,704	100.0	138,543	100.0	−38,161
Travel	58,895	33.3	26,091	18.8	−32,804
Transport	31,283	17.7	36,023	26.0	4,740
Insurance services[a]	13,882	7.9	5,522	4.0	−8,360
Financial services	*4,311*	*2.4*	*6,684*	*4.8*	*2,373*
Other services	68,333	38.7	64,223	46.4	−4,110
Other services					
Patents and licences	6,248	3.5	4,685	3.4	−1,563
Research and development	*4,777*	*2.7*	*6,236*	*4.5*	*1,459*
Engineering and other technical services	*7,144*	*4.0*	*8,782*	*6.3*	*1,638*
Computer services	*7,293*	*4.1*	*7,650*	*5.5*	*357*
Construction, assembly work, repairs	5,400	3.1	6,410	4.6	1,011
Overhead expenses	4,895	2.8	2,860	2.1	−2,036
Service transactions	32,576	18.4	27,600	19.9	−4,976
Service transactions					
Communication services	*9,167*	*5.2*	*7,002*	*5.1*	*−2,165*
Advertising and trade fair expenses	4,025	2.3	2,931	2.1	−1,094
Communication services	*5,010*	*2.8*	*3,520*	*2.5*	*−1,490*
Film industry	2,292	1.3	613	0.4	−1,679
Services of self-employed persons	3,417	1.9	1,573	1.1	−1,844
Government services	1,383	0.8	4,925	3.6	3,542
Miscellaneous services	7,282	4.1	7,036	5.1	−246
Miscellaneous services					
Thereof *commissions*	*5,755*	*3.3*	*2,371*	*1.7*	*−3,384*
Thereof *rental and operational leasing*	*1,222*	*0.7*	*1,643*	*1.2*	*421*
Tradable business activities	*44,679*	*25.3*	*43,888*	*31.7*	*−791*

Source: own illustration. Data: Deutsche Bundesbank, Balance of Payments, trade in services with non-residents

[a]Insurance services are calculated as the difference between total services and travel, transport, financial as well as other services

1991, but reached the second largest share of 16.3% (7,293M €) in 2006. This category thus experienced the strongest growth.

Commercial services imports grew from the third largest share of 12.8% (1,479M €) to the largest share (20.5%) in 2006. Communication services *imports* had a share of 11.9% (1,363M €) in 1991, but decreased to the fifth largest share at 11.2% (5,010M €) in 2006. *Expenditures for commissions* had the largest share at 44.4% (5,099M €) in 1991, which dropped to the fourth largest share at 12.9% (5,755M €) in 2006. Imports of rental and operational leasing had the smallest share of 0.8% (94M €) in 1991 compared to 2.7% (1,222M €) in 2006. To sum up, the strongest increase in imported tradable business activities happened between 1996 and 2001, but almost all categories continued to grow in absolute terms

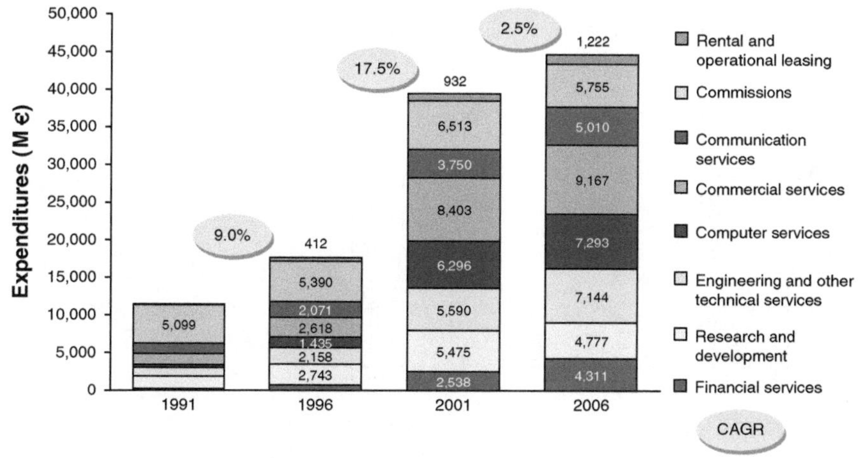

Fig. 3.8 Sectoral structure of German services offshoring (development)
Source: own illustration. Data: Deutsche Bundesbank, Balance of Payments, trade in services with non-residents

between 2001 and 2006 except for commissions and R&D imports. New opportunities due to globalization, trade liberalization, ICT developments, and an increasing amount of well-educated workers in low-income countries lead us to expect continued growth in the years to come.

In a second step, we use input–output data to determine the services that are mostly being offshored. The first column of Table 3.14 presents the *average services offshoring intensities* OSS_{st} (weighted by total non-energy inputs) of the seven selected services s across all 43 sectors i. The average services offshoring intensities OSS_{st} are calculated as described in Sect. 3.1.3.2. This measure tells us the average share of an imported intermediate service s across all 43 sectors. The next two columns show the (unweighted) means and standard deviations. The upper part of the table compares the intensities of 1991 and 2000 using unrevised input–output data, while the lower part uses revised input–output data for the years 1995 and 2004.

We first consider the upper part of the table. At the services level, all service categories except for "renting of machinery and equipment" experienced positive intensity growth. Average intensities of "computer and related activities" inputs grew strongly from 0.02% in 1991 to 0.38% in 2000. R&D offshoring intensities grew from 0.14% in 1991 to 0.34% in 2000. "Other business activities" more than tripled their intensities from 0.23% in 1991 to the largest intensity of 0.73% in 2000. The last three service sectors ("computer and related activities", R&D, and "other business activities"), that are typically associated with services offshoring, formed more than a half (1.45%) of total $\text{OSS}_t(a)$ in 2000. The revised data in the lower part of the table show a similar picture for the years 1995 and 2004. "Computer and related activities" grew strongly from 0.08% in 1995 to 0.39% in 2004. R&D intensities increased from 0.13% in 1995 to 0.35% in 2004. "Other

Table 3.14 Services offshoring intensities per services category in Germany

Unrevised data Service *s*	Rank	OSS_{s1991} (weighted average)	Mean	Std dev	Rank	OSS_{s2000} (weighted average)	Mean	Std dev
Post and telecommunications	2	0.24	0.54	2.92	3	0.46	0.43	2.51
Financial intermediation	7	0.02	0.01	0.02	6	0.05	0.03	0.05
Activities related to financial intermediation	1	0.45	0.18	0.82	2	0.49	0.26	1.21
Renting of machinery and equipment	5	0.07	0.12	0.32	7	0.01	0.00	0.02
Computer and related activities	6	0.02	0.04	0.13	4	0.38	0.72	3.14
Research and development	4	0.14	0.29	1.48	5	0.34	0.65	3.45
Other business activities	3	0.23	0.24	0.37	1	0.73	0.61	1.71
Total $OSS_t(a)$		1.18	1.43	3.31		2.46	2.70	5.68

Revised data Service *s*	Rank	OSS_{s1995} (weighted average)	Mean	Std dev	Rank	OSS_{s2004} (weighted average)	Mean	Std dev
Post and telecommunications	3	0.25	0.25	1.49	2	0.52	0.49	3.04
Financial intermediation	6	0.08	0.06	0.08	6	0.19	0.18	0.10
Activities related to financial intermediation	2	0.31	0.19	1.24	3	0.51	0.80	4.71
Renting of machinery and equipment	7	0.00	0.00	0.00	7	0.00	0.00	0.00
Computer and related activities	5	0.08	0.13	0.62	4	0.39	0.64	2.07
Research and development	4	0.13	0.24	1.00	5	0.35	0.64	2.91
Other business activities	1	0.53	0.35	1.03	1	0.95	0.73	2.06
Total $OSS_t(a)$		1.37	1.23	2.53		2.90	3.48	6.98

Source: own calculations. Data: Federal Statistical Office Germany, unrevised (1991–2000) and revised (1995–2004) input–output tables

business activities" almost doubled their intensities from 0.53% in 1995 to 0.95% in 2004 and thus maintained their lead. The last three service sectors formed more than a half (1.69%) of total OSS_t in 2004.

In both periods almost all services categories increased their average intensities across the 43 sectors, whereby "other business activities", "post and telecommunications" as well as "activities related to financial intermediation" formed the most relevant categories (ranks 1–3). "Computer and related activities" improved their relative position in both periods, while "financial intermediation" and "renting of machinery and equipment" played a smaller role.

3.3 Regional Structure of Services Offshoring

The following section presents the major destination countries from a global and a German perspective. First, we look at the "Destinations of Global Services Offshoring" (Sect. 3.3.1) as presented in existing studies and the IMF Balance of Payments data. We analyze the most relevant offshoring destinations for business services, also focusing on R&D as well as IT and BPO services. In a second step, the "Destinations of German Services Offshoring" (Sect. 3.3.2) are identified relying on import data from the Deutsche Bundesbank.

3.3.1 Destinations of Global Services Offshoring

3.3.1.1 Offshore Destinations for Tradable Services

In the UNCTAD and Roland Berger (2004) study, European companies were surveyed on their offshore destinations. More than a third (37%) of the services offshoring projects has been relocated to Asia, where the main destination country was India (see Fig. 3.9). Western Europe (29%) and Eastern Europe (22%) followed as most attractive services offshoring destinations, while Latin America and other destinations played a subordinate role. The following analysis determines the main global offshore destinations, thereby differentiating between offshoring of IT and BPO services and offshoring of R&D services.

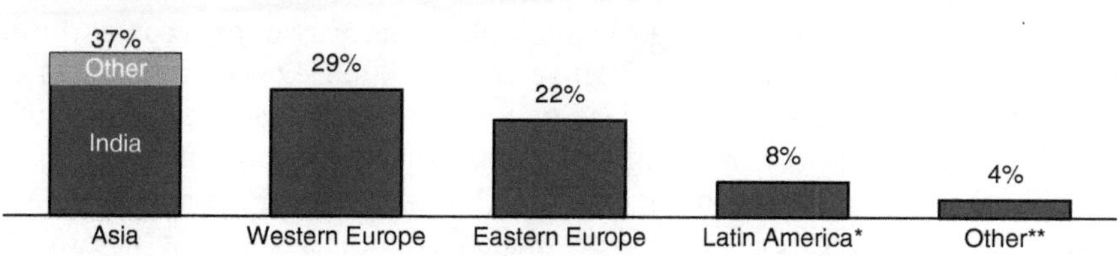

Fig. 3.9 Offshore destinations (% of services offshoring projects)
Source: UNCTAD and Roland Berger (2004), p. 8. (*) Brazil, Caribbean, and Mexico. (**) Middle East, North America, and Africa

The World Investment Report 2004 (UNCTAD 2004) analyzed the most important developing countries that export tradable service activities to developed countries. We selected five subgroups out of nine, namely business services, computer and related services, financial services, internet-related services, and professional services. Business services represent rather low- and medium-skill activities, while professional services form skill-intensive activities that depend on human capital (see Table 3.15). The table confirms the pattern described above. India has taken a leading position in business services and computer and related services.

Another interesting feature is that the production of professional services has extended to less developed or developing countries, such as Singapore, India, and some CEECs. These services had previously been performed largely in developed countries due to a lack of credibility and specialized knowledge in the developing world (UNCTAD 2004). However, India's current economic downturn as a consequence of the financial crisis reveals a deeper concern:

> "India has become the world's front office, handling customer service calls, and its back office, helping to process payments and run accounting and other computer systems. But it has not yet become the head office – making major new products, pioneering marketing techniques or helping to shape corporate strategy (Kahn 2008)."

3.3.1.2 The Largest Onshoring Countries

Table 3.16 examines the *largest services onshoring countries* in 2005 in absolute and relative terms using export data as a proxy for onshoring. Again, our four services categories are taken into account. Most of the top ten countries represent developed economies with a few exceptions. The table also shows that many developing countries are among the top 25 exporting countries. Concerning *computer and information services*, Ireland (18,661M US$), India (11,366M US$), and the UK (10,580M US$) were the largest exporters, but Israel also belongs to the top ten. Remarkably, China was ranked 13th and thus almost reached the top ten. The relative consideration relates service exports to GDP. Ireland clearly showed the highest export share of 9.45%, which was followed by Luxembourg, Israel, and India.

In the next three services categories, the UK and the US always had the first two ranks. Concerning the exports of *other business services*, the front rows were mainly occupied by developed countries, but China and Hong Kong were also ranked among the top ten. Taiwan, Brazil, Saudi Arabia, and Russia represented further important developing countries. At relative consideration, Lebanon (20.68%) was ranked first and thus represented the leading relative importer and exporter of other business services, followed by Hong Kong, Luxembourg, Cyprus, and Austria.

The third column focuses on the exports of *communication services*. While the top ten exporters were exclusively developed countries, the next largest also included some developing countries, such as Kuwait, India, Indonesia, Hong Kong, and Romania. The largest relative offshorers of communication services were Guyana, Luxembourg, Moldova, Cap Verde, and Kuwait. Concerning *financial*

Table 3.15 Selected tradable services from developing countries

Type	Activities	Main exporters
Business services	Various back office processes, customer interaction and technical support. Examples include abstracting and indexing, data entry and processing, electronic publishing, legal transcription, litigation support, mailing list management, remote secretarial services, technical writing, telemarketing, telesupport and web-site design	India is by far the largest developing country exporter of such services, but more and more countries are entering the arena
Computer and related services	Installation of computer hardware, software implementation, data processing, database services, maintenance and repair of office machinery and equipment such as computers, and other computer services	Ireland, India, and Israel account for much of the exports of these services, but there are also many other exporters
Financial services	Insurance and insurance-related services, as well as banking and other financial services. Many developing-country exports of these take the form of joint ventures or affiliates of large financial service TNCs from developed countries. Foreign affiliates provide services not only to the parent company and the local market, but are also involved in exports to third parties, including to other developing country markets	Here, too, India is a major player. In Latin America, reinsurance firms are collaborating with providers of financial services and insurance firms to offer a range of competitive new products
Internet-related services	The supply of the internet itself (telecommunication services), the supply of content, a mix of business services, audiovisual services and computer and related services	Latin American internet companies have expanded to other countries in the region building on the common language base. Hong Kong (China), Lebanon, and Singapore are exporters to their neighbors
Professional services	Various professional services such as legal services, accounting, auditing, taxation, architectural and engineering services, represent some of the most sophisticated areas of services offshoring. This has been a difficult area for developing countries to break into because of high skill requirements and problems in establishing credibility in foreign markets. However, their exports are growing. Commonly offshored processes include bookkeeping for clients, tax co-sourcing solutions, document management, staffing and IT services. Architectural design and other services are also being exported	India, Singapore, and several CEECs are among the exporting countries in this category

Source: own illustration. Based on UNCTAD World Investment Report, 2004, p. 150

Table 3.16 Largest absolute and relative onshoring countries per services category in 2005 (M US$ and % of GDP)

Rank	Country	Computer & information services/GDP	Rank	Country	Other business services/GDP	Rank	Country	Communication services/GDP	Rank	Country	Financial services/GDP
1.	Ireland	18,661	1.	United States	73,038	1.	United Kingdom	5,530	1.	United Kingdom	42,294
2.	India[a]	11,366	2.	United Kingdom	54,536	2.	United States	5,033	2.	United States	29,281
3.	United Kingdom	10,580	3.	Germany	46,406	3.	Netherlands	3,762	3.	Luxembourg	25,170
4.	Germany	8,133	4.	Netherlands	29,069	4.	France	3,480	4.	Switzerland	10,402
5.	United States	6,039	5.	Italy	28,213	5.	Germany	3,426	5.	Germany	6,293
6.	Israel	4,529	6.	Japan	27,279	6.	Belgium	2,209	6.	Ireland	5,812
7.	Netherlands	3,723	7.	France	25,624	7.	Canada	2,192	7.	Japan	5,044
8.	Spain	3,594	8.	China	23,283	8.	Italy	2,190	8.	Hong Kong[b]	4,553
9.	Canada	3,419	9.	Hong Kong[b]	21,798	9.	Sweden	1,435	9.	Singapore	3,695
10.	Sweden	2,673	10.	Austria	19,966	10.	Spain	1,423	10.	Belgium	3,391
13.	China	1,840	16.	Ireland	12,112	11.	Kuwait	1,295	15.	Taiwan	1,517
20.	Singapore	476	17.	Taiwan	11,950	13.	India[a]	1,066	22.	South Africa	534
21.	Malaysia	435	20.	Brazil	6,720	16.	Indonesia	998	23.	Brazil	507
22.	Russia	422	21.	Saudi Arabia	5,916	17.	Hong Kong[b]	852	24.	Czech Republic	424
24.	Hungary	369	22.	Russia	5,309	18.	Romania	674	25.	Russia	390
Rank	**Country**	**Computer & information services/GDP**	**Rank**	**Country**	**Other business services/GDP**	**Rank**	**Country**	**Communication services/GDP**	**Rank**	**Country**	**Financial services/GDP**
1.	Ireland	9.25	1.	Lebanon	20.68	1.	Guyana	3.70	1.	Luxembourg	69.02
2.	Luxembourg	6.39	2.	Hong Kong[b]	12.63	2.	Luxembourg	2.86	2.	Swaziland	5.84
3.	Israel	3.49	3.	Luxembourg	9.21	3.	Moldova	2.04	3.	Vanuatu	4.29

(continued)

Table 3.16 (continued)

Rank	Country	Computer & information services/GDP	Rank	Country	Other business services/GDP	Rank	Country	Communication services/GDP	Rank	Country	Financial services/GDP
4.	India[a]	1.42	4.	Cyprus	8.99	4.	Cape Verde	1.81	4.	Barbados	3.91
5.	Costa Rica	1.29	5.	Austria	6.52	5.	Kuwait	1.74	5.	Singapore	3.16
6.	Cyprus	1.28	21.	United Kingdom	2.48	64.	United Kingdom	0.25	6.	Ireland	2.88
13.	United Kingdom	0.48	30.	Germany	1.66	78.	France	0.16	9.	United Kingdom	1.92
32.	Germany	0.29	40.	France	1.20	82.	India[a]	0.13	32.	United States	0.23
47.	China	0.09	41.	China	1.17	89.	Germany	0.12	33.	Germany	0.23
51.	France	0.08	54.	Russia	0.69	99.	Russia	0.09	50.	Japan	0.11
57.	Russia	0.06	59.	Japan	0.60	109.	United States	0.04	62.	France	0.07
64.	United States	0.05	60.	United States	0.58	113.	China	0.02	73.	Russia	0.05
70.	Japan	0.02	65.	India[a]	0.32	117.	Japan	0.01	74.	India[a]	0.05

Source: own calculations. Data: IMF Balance of Payments, retrieved from: UNCTAD
[a]Most recent available figures for India are for 2003
[b]Most recent available figures for Hong Kong are for 2004

services, we find two developing countries among the top ten, namely the Asian Tigers, Hong Kong and Singapore. Other developing countries among the top ten financial services exporters include Taiwan, South Africa, Brazil, the Czech Republic, and Russia. At relative consideration, Luxembourg had the largest export share, which was more than two-thirds of its GDP (69.02%), followed by Swaziland, Vanuatu, Barbados, and Singapore.

3.3.1.3 Offshore Destinations for Research and Development Services

We now analyze the global offshore destinations for *R&D services*. The World Investment Report 2005 (UNCTAD 2005) focuses on the internationalization of R&D. The 300 leading private R&D spending companies worldwide were surveyed, which were selected from the R&D Scoreboard published by the UK Department of Trade and Industry. The R&D Scoreboard ranks the top 700 R&D spenders, which represented almost half (46%) of total R&D expenditures and more than two-thirds (69%) of business R&D worldwide in 2002. The largest 300 firms were responsible for more than 85% of total R&D expenditures of the top 700 and thus form a very representative sample. Additionally, all firms of the top 700 from developing and emerging markets outside the top 300 were contacted. Only 68 companies out of the 316 selected ones responded to the questionnaire, since many firms consider information on R&D strategically sensitive.

Figure 3.10 shows the *current foreign locations of R&D in 2004*. The US and the UK represented the two most important offshore destinations for R&D. Although the majority of R&D offshore destinations are still developed countries, we also find an important number of developing countries in the sample. China, ranked third, was named by more than a third of the 68 respondents as R&D offshore destination. Besides China, the developing countries India, Singapore, and Brazil represented R&D offshore locations for more than 10% of the respondents, but R&D locations were also found in Russia and Poland.

The respondents were also asked for the *most attractive prospective R&D locations between 2005 and 2009*. We see that 61.8% of the respondents considered China to become their future top R&D destination, which displaced the US to second. The number of prospective R&D locations in developing countries was expected to increase. Among the developing countries, India and Russia were expected to catch up. Asian countries, namely Singapore, Taiwan, Malaysia, South Korea, and Thailand, were also placed among the top 20 R&D destinations, while CEECs, Latin American countries, and African countries were mentioned less often (UNCTAD 2005).

3.3.1.4 Offshore Destinations for IT and BPO Services

Figure 3.11 plots the most relevant services offshoring destinations in 2003 with a focus on BPO and IT services. India (12.2B US$) and Ireland (8.6B US$) produced

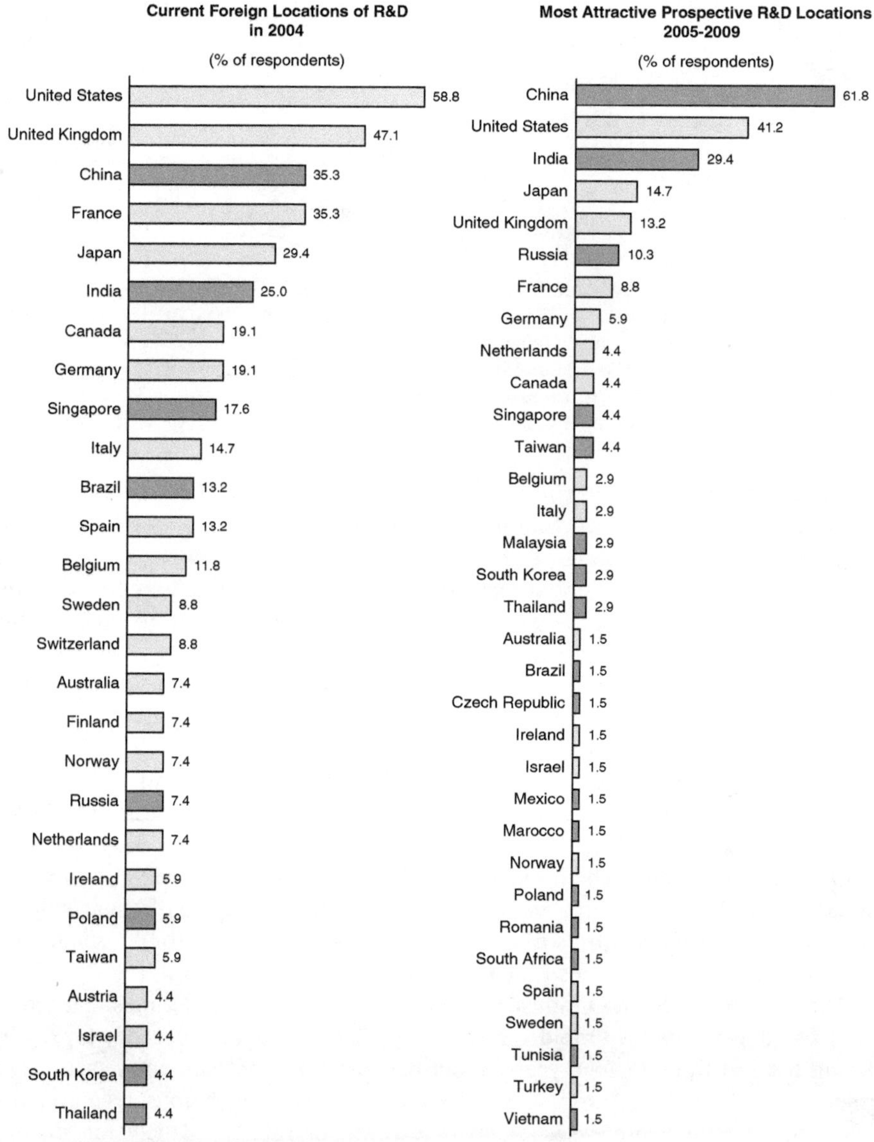

Fig. 3.10 Current and prospective R&D locations
Source: own illustration. Data: UNCTAD World Investment Report (2005), p. 133 and 153

most of these services, followed by Canada, Israel, and China, which all performed a similar output. Ireland represented one of the first offshore destinations, but emerging markets such as India, the Philippines, and other Asian countries quickly followed this trend. Further important offshore destinations are Central and Latin American countries and the CEECs including Russia. Ireland, for instance, specializes in the production of application packages and product development. Canada's

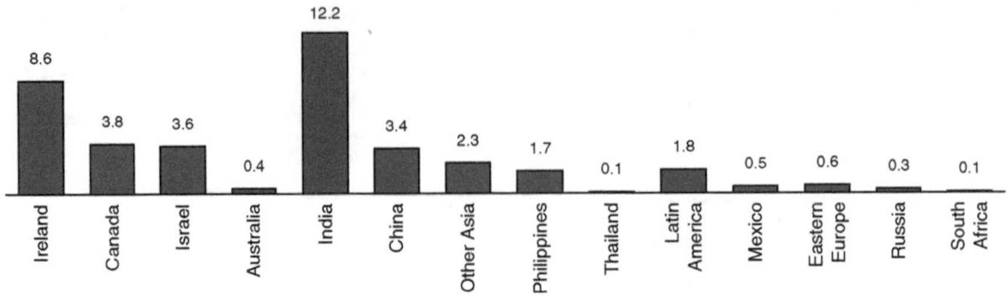

Fig. 3.11 Offshore destinations for IT and BPO services in 2003 (B US$)
Source: own illustration. Data: McKinsey Global Institute analysis (2005), p. 13. NB: Data for China are estimates, based on total Chinese BPO and IT services revenue (7.8%) minus domestic demand for IT services (4.4%). Eastern Europe includes Poland, Romania, Hungary, Ukraine, and Czech Republic. Data for Israel are estimates, based on 2001 market size of 3.0 and assumed growth rate of 20% p.a. Data for Israel and Ireland are primarily composed of MNC captives

service portfolio focuses on application development, BPO, and call centers, which is also performed in Eastern Europe or India (Schaaf 2004). However, using the A.T. Kearney *Global Services Location Attractiveness Index 2007* (see Appendix I) as an indicator for the current attractiveness of offshore destinations for services, Ireland ranks only 50th out of 50 countries, while Canada (rank 35) shows only slightly better results. In contrast, many developing countries occupy the front rows in terms of financial attractiveness, people and skills availability, and business environment (A.T. Kearney 2007). As a result, we emphasize the development of IT and BPO service sectors in emerging markets.

India has become a major exporter of IT-services, BPO, call centers, and application development (see Box 3.2). The Global Services Location Attractiveness Index 2007 ranks India as top offshore destination. Schaaf (2004) quotes a study of Palvia (2003) which claims that North America receives two-thirds of India's software and IT-services. Moreover, India has started to offshore work to lower-income Asian countries like China or the Philippines and to buy small local Western European companies (Schaaf 2004).

The "Indian ITES–BPO Industry: NASSCOM Analysis" underlines that Indian BPO has experienced a "rapid transformation" over the past decade, especially during the last three to four years. India began with basic data entry tasks, then graduated to back-office processes and voice-based services before, recently, also integrating complex processes, such as research or rule-based decision making (NASSCOM 2007b). In July 2007, the NASSCOM published its annual study on the performance of the IT services and BPO sector for the financial year (FY) 2006–2007. The Indian IT–BPO industry including the domestic market exceeded all analysts' expectations achieving revenues of 39.6B US$. Compared to 30.3B US$ in FY 2005–2006. The top "software and service exporters" and "ITES–BPO exporters" in FY 2006–2007 are shown in Table 3.17.

Is China following India's success story and becoming the next major offshore destination for IT and BPO services due to its cost advantages? According to the Global Services Location Attractiveness Index 2007, China is ranked second after

Box 3.2: The case of India

"India's IT export boom can trace its beginnings back to the mid-1980s, when Texas Instruments opened a branch in Bangalore to focus on development, followed a year later by Motorola. Mainly American and West European multinationals from the electronics industry followed suit in the period to the middle of the 1990s; but it was not until the second half of the 1990s that big software houses such as Microsoft, SAP or Adobe opened development centres in India. In a parallel development, the number of Indian companies to which American principals in particular contracted out programming assignments has soared to more than 3,000.

Meanwhile, India's exports of software and services total more than USD 12 bn. If it succeeds in maintaining the momentum of latter years, they will be brushing the USD 38 bn. mark by 2008 [...]. This trend has been encouraged, first, by India's greater opening since 1991 to foreign investment and cooperation agreements. Second, the national industry association NASSCOM's commitment has successfully promoted its members."

Source: Schaaf (2004, p. 8)

Table 3.17 India's top 15 service exporters

Top 15 software & service exporters	Top 15 ITES–BPO exporters
1. Tata Consultancy Services Ltd.	1. Genpact
2. Infosys Technologies Ltd.	2. WNS Global Services
3. Wipro Technologies Ltd.	3. Transworks Information Services
4. Satyam Computer Services Ltd.	4. IBM-Daksh
5. HCL Technlogies Ltd.	5. TCS BPO
6. Tech Mahindra Ltd.	6. Wipro BPO
7. Patni Computer Systems Ltd.	7. Firstsource Solutions
8. I-flex Solutions Ltd.	8. HCL BPO
9. L&T InfoTech Ltd.	9. Infosys BPO
10. Polaris Software Lab Ltd.	10. EXL Service Holdings
11. Hexaware Technologies Ltd.	11. Citigroup Global Services
12. Flextronics Software Systems Ltd. (Aricent)	12. Aegis BPO Services
13. Mphasis BFL Ltd.	13. HTMT Global Solutions
14. Mastek Ltd.	14. 24&7 Customer
15. Siemens Information Systems Ltd.	15. Mphasis BPO

Source: NASSCOM (2007a)

India (Appendix I). The NASSCOM observes the evolution in China's software and service industry since 2001 and released a report in 2002 and in 2007 (NASSCOM 2007d). The 2007 report acknowledges China's potential to develop an important IT–BPO industry due to its numerous well-educated workers, government support to promote the sector (see Box 3.3), and its huge domestic market. China's actual service sector (e.g., data entry tasks or software development) seems to correspond to India's one in its earlier years, but its specialization still lies in embedded services and hardware (NASSCOM 2007c).

Box 3.3: Promoting China's IT software and services development

"To develop China's capabilities as an outsourcing base for IT software and services, the Ministry of Commerce (MOFCOM) has initiated the ten-hundred-thousand program. Through this program China aspires to promote 10 (later increased to 11) cities as key bases for undertaking offshore services outsourcing; attract 100 multinational enterprises to China as an offshore destination and assist the development of at least 1,000 enterprises having the capability and international qualifications to undertake offshore outsourcing with the goal of doubling service exports by 2010.

Key measures identified by MOFCOM towards achieving its targets under the "ten-hundred-thousand" program include:

1. Creating a specific fund for providing specialized training of 300,000–400,000 university students over the next 5 years. This training will include technical qualification and certification, international standards and IPR.
2. Providing incentives and financial support to encourage enterprises to obtain international certification with the target of 700 enterprises obtaining CMM/CMMI Level 3 certifications and 300 enterprises obtaining CMM/CMMI Level 5 certifications.
3. Working with the State Development Bank to provide credit and loans to qualified enterprises to engage in outsourcing.
4. Collaborating with China Export Credit Corporation to provide credit insurance and guarantee services.
5. Working with the Ministry of Information Industry (MII) and other relevant departments to identify and support base cities under the ten-hundred-thousand program, through policy guidance in macroeconomic policy, program designing, human resource training, attracting foreign investment and creating a special fund to support the infrastructure creation required across the base cities.
6. Building a website/portal to provide information to enterprises, universities/colleges, students, research institutions and provide a platform for business transactions.
7. Providing preferential treatment (such as discounted loans) for base cities in the Central and West regions.
8. Formulating a stronger IPR framework and establishing IPR complaint centers in the base cities to take prompt action against any kind of IPR violation."

Source: NASSCOM (2007c)

Mr. Ameet Nivsarkar, then vice president of the NASSCOM, states in the report that "presently the Chinese IT market is hugely skewed towards IT hardware which is 90% of the total market size. The IT software and services sector accounts for just about 0.5% of China's gross domestic product in 2006. While this presents a tremendous opportunity, China has its own set of challenges to overcome such as scalability, global recognition, complex tax and investment incentive systems across different provinces, highly controlled financial systems and regulation of ownership structures, increasing number of "unemployable" resources, pressures of dealing with more evolved (Western) outsourcers and intensifying competition (NASSCOM 2007c)." Together with weaknesses such as the underdeveloped IT infrastructure, unsatisfactory English skills, and the insufficiency of IT specialists, it is unlikely that China will catch up to India over the next three to five years. Nevertheless, one should not underestimate China's potential to provide back office services for companies located in other Asian markets. The evidence of increased partnerships between China and India further contributes to this development (NASSCOM 2007c, d; Schaaf 2004).

The Philippines and other Asian countries have established themselves as new offshore destinations for IT and BPO services, even for India. Being a former colony of Spain and the US, Spanish and English are widely spoken in the Philippines. Since English is an official language, the Philippines are the third largest English-speaking country worldwide. Moreover, its cultural proximity to the West and its young population are advantages that foster the specialization especially in call centers, but also in the BPO of data entry, accounts reporting, accounting, human resources, and transcription as well as animation solutions. IT-based services and programming, however, must still be considered infant-industries (Schaaf 2004). These advantages have contributed to rank the Philippines (rank 8), but also other South East Asian countries such as Malaysia (rank 3), Thailand (rank 4), and Indonesia (rank 6) among the ten most attractive services offshoring destinations in 2007 (A.T. Kearney; see Appendix I).

The NASSCOM Newsline of November 2007 deals with emerging markets and identifies Vietnam as one of the new IT–BPO global destinations listing several reasons. Huge growth rates combined with liberal investment laws, a stable business environment, the improving internet and telecom infrastructure, and a low-cost labor force make Vietnam an attractive offshore destination. As a result, the number of active software companies has gone up to 500 in 2003 compared to only a few in 1998 (NASSCOM 2007e). Despite these advantages, the Global Information Technology Report 2006-2007 of the World Economic Forum ranked Vietnam only 82th on the *Networked Readiness Index* 2006–07 (Appendix A). In comparison, Canada was ranked 11th, Ireland 21st, Malaysia 26th, Thailand 37th, India 44th, China 59th, Indonesia 62nd, and the Philippines 69th (World Economic Forum 2007).

European companies in particular discovered the huge offshore (nearshore) potentials in Eastern Europe and Russia. The main advantages of Eastern Europe over their Asian counterparts are the cultural and geographical proximity to their trading partners, which simplifies personal meetings, and a similar time-zone, which makes telephone calls possible if necessary. Hungary, the Czech Republic, and Poland – the new EU-member countries of the first Eastern enlargement round in 2004 – are characterized by a huge pool of human capital speaking English and German. The Global Services Location Attractiveness Index 2007 ranks Bulgaria,

Estonia, Slovakia, the Czech Republic, Latvia, and Poland among the top 20 service offshore destinations (Appendix I). In terms of the Networked Readiness Index, Hungary and the Czech Republic were ranked 33rd and 34th, respectively, and thus achieved even a better index than India. Bulgaria and Romania – the two EU-member countries of the second Eastern enlargement round in 2007 – dispose of many IT-skilled workers. These countries are specialized in software programming and application development (Schaaf 2004).

Despite its enormous availability of competitive IT talent and its focus on high-end engineering, Russia is not considered a serious global competitor due to the instability of Russia's business environment and technical infrastructure (Schaaf 2004). This is reflected in a worse Global Services Location Attractiveness Index 2007 (rank 37) than most of Russia's Eastern European counterparts (Appendix I). The Networked Readiness Index ranks Russia only 70th (Appendix A). The heterogeneity of Russia's IT providers and their small size has hindered them from becoming international and building up agencies in the West (Schaaf 2004; World Economic Forum 2007).

3.3.2 Destinations of German Services Offshoring

The following subsection identifies the most important services offshoring destinations of German firms, using the previously described Deutsche Bundesbank data, which allocate service imports to their country of origin. We focus on eight services categories, namely financial services, R&D, "engineering and other technical services", computer services, commercial services, communication services, commissions as well as "rental and operational leasing". These eight services categories are selected as they reflect the tradable service activities described above (see Table 3.13).

The countries of origin can roughly be considered German offshore destinations, assuming that the destination countries are to a large extent congruent with Germany's service importers. As indicated in conjunction with the sectoral structure of German services offshoring, service imports include final and intermediate service inputs, while offshoring is rather associated with the relocation of intermediate inputs (see Sect. 3.2.2). Nevertheless final services could also be subject to offshoring decisions. Therefore, we believe that the import data are a good indicator to reflect the regional distribution of the offshore destinations.

Figure 3.12 first identifies the largest regions of destination for German services offshoring by services category for the years 1991, 1996, 2001 and 2006. World imports are subdivided into four main regions of origin: Western Europe (WEU), other industrialized countries (OIN), Central and Eastern Europe (CEE), and developing countries (DEV). All services categories experienced positive and continuous import growth between 1991 and 2006, except for R&D and commissions, where imports declined during the last couple of years. R&D and

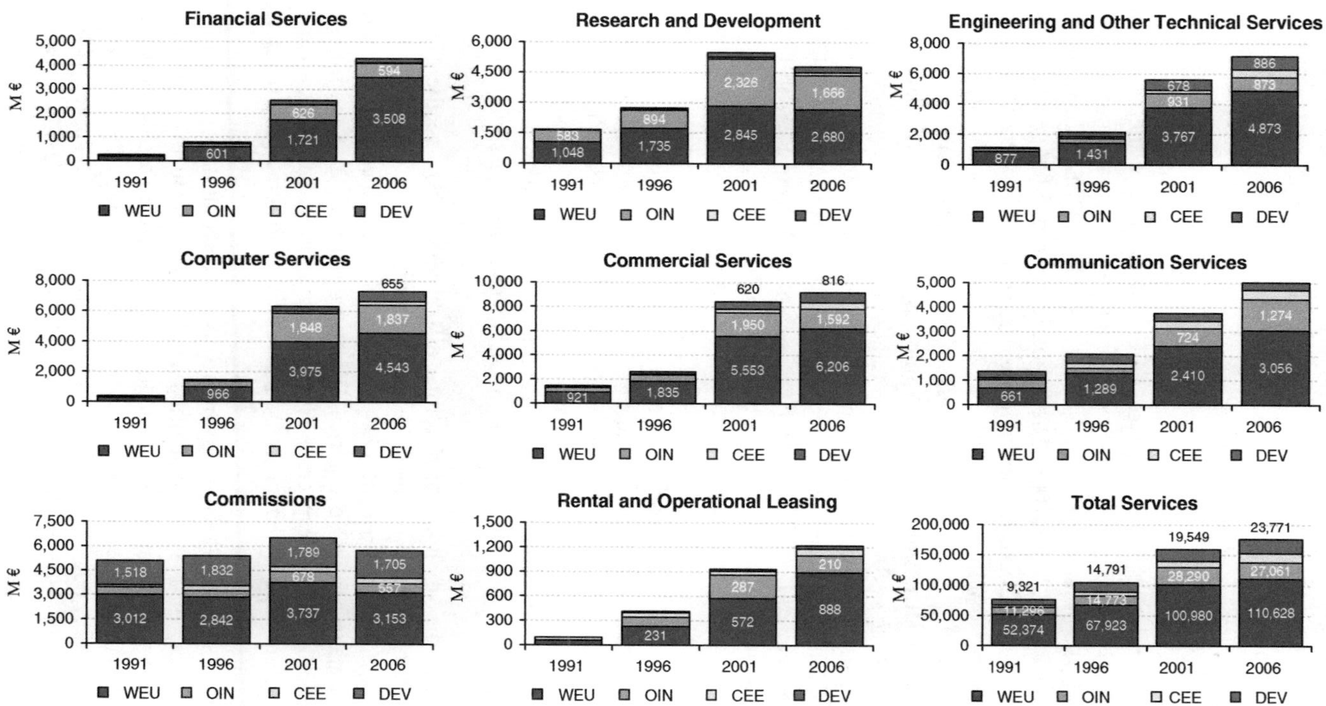

Fig. 3.12 Service imports to Germany by region of origin
Source: own illustration. Data: Deutsche Bundesbank, Balance of Payments, trade in services with non-residents

commissions are also the two categories where imports from WEU do *not* clearly dominate the other regions of origin. R&D imports from developed countries experienced a decline from 98% in 1991 to 91% in 2006, out of which WEU accounted for 56.1% and OIN for 34.9% in 2006. *Commissions* imports were to a large extent originated in WEU, followed by DEV. WEU imported 59.1% in 1991 which dropped to 54.8% in 2006. DEV maintained a share of around 30% in 1991 and 2006.

Besides R&D, the relative importance of CEE and DEV has increased in "engineering and other technical services", computer services, and commercial services. *Engineering and other technical services imports* from CEE had a share of 1.7% in 1991, which rose to 7.2% in 2006. The import share from DEV was 4.9% in 1991 compared to 12.4% in 2006. Regarding *computer services imports*, the share of CEE has grown from 1.6% in 1991 to 3.5% in 2006, but the imports from DEV increased more importantly from 2.4% in 1991 to 9% in 2006. Note that India accounted for a third of all computer services imports from DEV. The share of WEU in *commercial services imports* remained relatively constant over time with around two-thirds, while the share of OIN fell from 25.5% in 1992 to 17.4% in 2006. This loss of OIN was caused by a quadrupling of import shares from CEE between 1992 (1.5%) and 2006 (6%) and by the growth of DEV from 5.2% in 1992 to 8.9% in 2006. The import share of non-developed countries, however, fell in the categories financial services and communication services as well as rental and operational leasing.

Finally, the development of *total* service imports is described as the last category. Note that total services include not only the eight services categories above, but all services listed in Table 3.13. Imports from WEU declined from 68.5% in 1991 to 62.2% in 2006, whereas services from OIN remained relatively constant with shares of 14.8 and 15.3%. Service imports from CEE almost doubled their shares from 4.6% in 1991 to 8.6% in 2006. The share from DEV also increased slightly from 12.2 to 13.5% over the period.

We have seen that the offshore destinations differ with regard to the eight services categories. WEU still constituted the major service importer even though its importance has been reduced over the last years. OIN maintained or increased their import share in many services categories. We also observed a growing importance of non-developed countries, especially CEE, as service importers to Germany. The share of DEV might become larger in the future in view of emerging markets such as China or India.

Hutzschenreuter et al. (2007) analyze the regional distribution of 178 offshoring implementations of 119 German firms. A third (33%) of all offshoring projects are located in Asia, out of which India (15%) and China (8%) are the most important destinations. 26% of the offshoring volumes have been relocated to the CEECs plus Turkey, out of which the Czech Republic (7%), Turkey (4%), Hungary (3%), and Russia (3%) are the most important regions. WEU also shows a share of 26%, with the UK (7%), Spain (4%), and Ireland (3%) being the most relevant countries. Northern and Middle America (NMA) has a share of 12%, which is mainly driven by the US (8%).

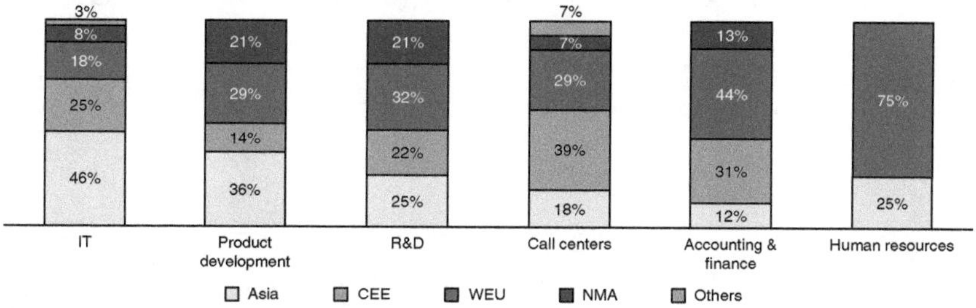

Fig. 3.13 Offshore destinations of German firms
Source: own illustration. Data: Hutzschenreuter et al. (2007), p. 82. Based on 178 offshoring implementations of 119 German firms

A closer look at the different functions is given in Fig. 3.13. The distribution shows that Asia and CEE are very important offshore destinations, especially for IT, call centers, and product development, but also for R&D. WEU and NMA represent important offshore destinations especially for human resources, accounting and finance, R&D, and product development (Hutzschenreuter et al. 2007). The differences from our findings above can be explained by the fact that only 119 firms are represented, while our import data covers the whole German economy. Second, the import data above reflect all previous offshoring decisions, while Fig. 3.13 only considers recent offshoring decisions, thus overestimating low-income countries in Asia and CEE.

Finally, Table 3.18 ranks the ten largest importing countries for each of the eight services categories in 2006 and thus reveals a more detailed picture about the main destinations of German services offshoring. Note that the top ten service importers represent between 55.8% (commissions) and 90.7% (financial services) of total service imports. A larger share might reflect a market structure where fewer countries dominate the market for a specific service. The top ten importers of other services categories not listed here show shares of between 74 and 84%.

Germany's top ten importers of financial services, R&D, and communication services to Germany were exclusively developed countries. The UK and the US as well as Germany's neighbors France, Switzerland, Austria, and the Netherlands belonged to the top ten importers in all eight services categories, while Italy and Belgium can be found in six and five categories, respectively. Regarding developing countries, Singapore was the tenth largest importer of "engineering and other technical services", while India and Israel represented the eighth and ninth largest importers of computer services. China constituted the eighth largest importer of commercial services, while Hong Kong and China were ranked seventh and ninth in commissions. Finally, Russia was the tenth largest importer of "rental and operational leasing".

Despite the fact that there are only a few developing countries among the top ten importers, we have seen previously that the imports from CEE and DEV have gained in importance. The majority of them are not significant enough to be ranked among the top ten. Nonetheless, in 2006, 19.6% of the imported "engineering and

Table 3.18 Germany's top ten importers of selected services in 2006

Financial services				Research and development				Engineering and other technical services				Computer services			
	Country	M €	%		Country	M €	%		Country	M €	%		Country	M €	%
1.	United Kingdom	1,498	34.7	1.	United States	1,279	26.8	1.	United Kingdom	1,431	20.0	1.	United States	1,682	23.1
2.	Luxembourg	831	19.3	2.	France	534	11.2	2.	United States	724	10.1	2.	Ireland	1,446	19.8
3.	United States	465	10.8	3.	Austria	524	11.0	3.	Italy	717	10.0	3.	United Kingdom	798	10.9
4.	Switzerland	405	9.4	4.	United Kingdom	486	10.2	4.	Spain	571	8.0	4.	Switzerland	651	8.9
5.	France	185	4.3	5.	Italy	252	5.3	5.	France	502	7.0	5.	Austria	364	5.0
6.	Austria	131	3.0	6.	Netherlands	217	4.5	6.	Switzerland	414	5.8	6.	France	360	4.9
7.	Japan	114	2.6	7.	Japan	207	4.3	7.	Austria	341	4.8	7.	Netherlands	314	4.3
8.	Belgium	107	2.5	8.	Switzerland	193	4.0	8.	Netherlands	270	3.8	8.	India	219	3.0
9.	Italy	104	2.4	9.	Canada	156	3.3	9.	Belgium	157	2.2	9.	Israel	137	1.9
10.	Netherlands	68	1.6	10.	Sweden	141	3.0	10.	Singapore	137	1.9	10.	Belgium	128	1.8
	Sum top ten	*3,908*	*90.7*		*Sum top ten*	*3,989*	*83.5*		*Sum top ten*	*5,264*	*73.7*		*Sum top ten*	*6,099*	*83.6*
	All countries	*4,311*	*100.0*		*All countries*	*4,777*	*100.0*		*All countries*	*7,144*	*100.0*		*All countries*	*7,293*	*100.0*

Commercial services				Communication services				Commissions				Rental and operational leasing			
	Country	M €	%		Country	M €	%		Country	M €	%		Country	M €	%
1.	United Kingdom	1,848	20.2	1.	United States	1,226	24.5	1.	France	474	8.2	1.	Ireland	239	19.6
2.	United States	1,383	15.1	2.	Austria	429	8.6	2.	United Kingdom	426	7.4	2.	United States	159	13.0
3.	France	986	10.8	3.	United Kingdom	418	8.3	3.	United States	408	7.1	3.	Netherlands	108	8.8
4.	Switzerland	985	10.7	4.	Switzerland	352	7.0	4.	Switzerland	364	6.3	4.	United Kingdom	106	8.7
5.	Netherlands	604	6.6	5.	Netherlands	307	6.1	5.	Italy	346	6.0	5.	Switzerland	100	8.2
6.	Belgium	369	4.0	6.	France	274	5.5	6.	Austria	290	5.0	6.	Austria	85	7.0
7.	Austria	266	2.9	7.	Italy	266	5.3	7.	Hong Kong	271	4.7	7.	Malta	83	6.8
8.	China	227	2.5	8.	Luxembourg	236	4.7	8.	Netherlands	268	4.7	8.	France	54	4.4
9.	Italy	207	2.3	9.	Spain	222	4.4	9.	China	202	3.5	9.	Japan	42	3.4
10.	Ireland	202	2.2	10.	Belgium	154	3.1	10.	Spain	161	2.8	10.	Russia	28	2.3
	Sum top ten	*7,077*	*77.2*		*Sum top ten*	*3,884*	*77.5*		*Sum top ten*	*3,210*	*55.8*		*Sum top ten*	*1,004*	*82.2*
	All countries	*9,167*	*100.0*		*All countries*	*5,010*	*100.0*		*All countries*	*5,755*	*100.0*		*All countries*	*1,222*	*100.0*

Source: own illustration. Data: Deutsche Bundesbank, Balance of Payments, trade in services with non-residents

other technical services" and 12.5% of the imported computer services were originated in CEE and DEV.

References

Amiti M, Wei S-J (2005) Fear of service outsourcing: is it justified? Econ Policy 20(42):308–347

Amiti M, Wei S-J (2006) Service offshoring, productivity and Employment: evidence from the US. CEPR Discussion Paper, No. 5475, February 2006

A.T. Kearney (2007) Global Service Attractiveness Index. http://www.atkearney.com/res/shared/pdf/GSLI_2007.pdf

Bardhan AD, Kroll CA (2003) The new wave of outsourcing. Fisher Center for Real Estate & Urban Economics Report Series, No. 1103, October 2003. University of California, Berkeley

Braakmann A, Hartmann N, Räth N, Strohm W (2005) Revision der Volkswirtschaftlichen Gesamtrechnungen 2005 für den Zeitraum 1991 bis 2004. In: Statistisches Bundesamt (ed), Wirtschaft und Statistik, no 5, pp 425–463

Claassen D (2006) Inder bearbeiten britische Pensionen. The Economist, 27 January 2006

Deutsche Bundesbank (2006) Technologische Dienstleistungen in der Zahlungsbilanz. Special Statistical Publication, No. 12, June 2006

Feenstra RC, Hanson GH (1996) Globalization, outsourcing and wage inequality. Am Econ Rev 86(2):240–245

Grossman GM, Rossi-Hansberg E (2006) The rise of offshoring: it's not wine for cloth anymore. Paper presented at The New Economic Geography: Effects and Policy Implications, Jackson Hole: Federal Reserve Bank of Kansas City, pp 59–102

Handwerk M (2004) Kunden und Auftraggeber rücken näher zusammen. Financial Times Deutschland, 2 November 2004

Hutzschenreuter T, Dressel S, Ressler W (2007) Offshoring von Zentralbereichen, Von den Erfahrungen deutscher und amerikanischer Unternehmen lernen. Springer, Berlin

Kahn J (2008) Recession trickles to India. New York Times, 3 December 2008

Kalmbach P, Franke R, Knottenbauer K, Krämer H (2005) Die Interdependenz von Industrie und Dienstleistungen, Zur Dynamik eines komplexen Beziehungsgeflechts. Berlin

McKinsey Global Institute (2005) The emerging global labor market: part I – the demand for offshore talent in services, June 2005. McKinsey Global Institute

NASSCOM (2007a) Crossing milestones: India's IT–BPO industry comes of age. NASSCOM Newsline, 69. Retrieved from http://www.nasscom.in/Nasscom/templates/NormalPage.aspx?id = 51977

NASSCOM (2007b) Indian ITES-BPO Industry: NASSCOM Analysis. Fact Sheet. Retrieved from http://www.nasscom.org/download/Indian_ITES–BPO_Factsheet.doc

NASSCOM (2007c) NASSCOM releases whitepaper on tracing China's IT software services industry evolution. Press Release. Retrieved from http://www.nasscom.in/Nasscom/templates/NormalPage.aspx?id=52062

NASSCOM (2007d) Tracing China's IT software and services industry evolution. Retrieved from http://www.nasscom.in/Nasscom/templates/NormalPage.aspx?id=52065

NASSCOM (2007e) Vietnam: rapidly emerging on the outsourcing map. NASSCOM Newsline, 73. Retrieved from http://www.nasscom.in/Nasscom/templates/NormalPage.aspx?id=53123

OECD (2007) Offshoring and employment: trends and impact. OECD, Paris

Palvia S (2003) Global outsourcing of IT and IT enabled services: Impact on US and global economy, in: JITCA, Vol. 5, No. 3, pp 9–10

Schaaf J (2004) Offshoring: globalisation wave reaches services sector, digital economy and structural change No. 45, 27-Sep-04: Deutsche Bank Research

UN (1999) Handbook of input–output table compilation and analysis, studies in methods. Handbook of National Accounting, Series F, No. 74, October 1999. United Nations, New York

UNCTAD (2004) The shift towards services, World Investment Report 2004. United Nations, New York and Geneva

UNCTAD (2005) Transnational corporations and the internationalization of R&D, World Investment Report 2005. United Nations, New York and Geneva

UNCTAD & Roland Berger (2004) Service offshoring takes off in Europe – in search of improved competitiveness, service offshoring, June 2004

World Economic Forum (2007) The global information technology report 2006–2007, Connecting to the Networked Economy, 6th ed. Palgrave MacMillan

Chapter 4
Labor Market Effects in (Neo)Classical Models of Offshoring

Abstract This fourth chapter "Labor Market Effects in (Neo)classical Models of Offshoring" evaluates the labor market and national welfare effects in existing classical and neoclassical theories. Section 4.1 studies offshoring of final goods in the Ricardian, Heckscher–Ohlin, and specific-factors model. We first study the welfare gains from trade in Samuelson's (2004) Ricardian model. The model also shows how technological progress in the foreign non-comparative advantage sector erodes all or at least some of the domestic country's previous gains from trade. Second, we evaluate the gains from trade in the basic Heckscher–Ohlin model, before presenting four theorems. Third, we analyze the effects of offshoring in the specific-factors model of Bhagwati et al. (2004). Generally, offshoring leads to social gains, but there are also scenarios where offshoring can generate welfare losses. Section 4.2 focuses on offshoring of intermediate goods. We use the Grossman and Rossi-Hansberg (2006a, b) general equilibrium model, which includes a set of intermediate tasks, to evaluate the wage effects of offshoring. Different scenarios are studied, namely the effects of offshoring low-skill-intensive tasks in a small and a large economy, the labor-supply effect and offshoring of skill-intensive tasks.

4.1 Offshoring of Final Goods

Section 4.1 presents international trade models, while the Sect. 4.2 explicitly models offshoring. International trade can be considered offshoring in a wider sense, if a country switches from autarky equilibrium to trade equilibrium. In autarky, a country must produce all goods itself, but the possibility of international trade leads to efficient specialization among the trading partners. Formerly home-produced goods are then performed by the trading partner, which in the wider sense can be considered offshoring.

D. Winkler, *Services Offshoring and its Impact on the Labor Market*, Contributions to Economics, DOI: 10.1007/978-3-7908-2199-4_4,

More specifically, Sect. 4.1 presents the classical Ricardian trade model of Samuelson (2004), the basic neoclassical Heckscher–Ohlin model, and the neoclassical specific-factors model of Bhagwati et al. (2004). All models are characterized by perfect competition and trade with final goods and constitute simple general equilibrium models, i.e., all markets of an economy are simultaneously characterized by equality of supply and demand.

There are at least three main caveats when using traditional trade models to predict labor market effects of offshoring. First, traditional trade models concentrate on international trade in goods, but do not explicitly model the *possibility of captive-offshoring*, i.e., FDI, which represents preceding capital flows to the destination country. Since we focus on subsequent (re)imports to the domestic market, regardless of the organizational form, traditional trade models capture captive offshoring only in an indirect manner.

Second, neoclassical models presume perfect inter-sectoral labor mobility (of at least one factor in the import-competing sector) and perfect price flexibility, which implies *full employment*. Even in the short-run there is assumed to be no unemployment, since offshoring affects labor markets solely through wage adjustments. If labor supply exceeds labor demand, market equilibrium is reached by an immediate decline in the wage level. Thus, such trade models only consider relative effects (e.g., changes in income distribution or employment structure), but not absolute magnitudes (e.g., number of unemployed). However, assuming labor market rigidities (e.g., minimum wages) that counteract perfect price flexibility, layoffs instead of wage reductions are possible in the short-run.[1] Hence, trade models are suited to make predictions about the losers and winners in the trade process.

Third, traditional trade theories center on *final goods*, whereas services offshoring is about intermediate service inputs. In an economic sense, services and goods trade can be treated equally as we have previously seen. Modeling offshoring of intermediate goods, however, is important and will be taken into account in Sect. 4.2. Offshoring of final goods, on the other hand, is still relevant, as global corporations in the major industrialized countries are not strictly involved in assembly. Much of the import activity in global supply chains is in fully finished goods. In fact, one motive of corporate offshoring, whether at arm's-length or through foreign subsidiaries, is precisely to allow the corporation to focus on its "core competence", while leaving those aspects of product delivery, including production, to others. Many "manufacturing" firms now do no manufacturing at all, but merely provide product and brand design, marketing, supply chain logistics, and financial management services.[2]

[1]For a discussion of unemployment versus relative wages as labor market adjustments to globalization, see, e.g., Eckel (2003).

[2]Parts of this paragraph have been taken from Milberg and Schöller (2008).

4.1.1 *The Ricardian Model*

4.1.1.1 Offshoring in a Two-Goods Model with Autarky

Equilibrium in Autarky

Samuelson's (2004) first part ("Act Ia") models how offshoring benefits countries that are initially in autarky. He considers two countries, one of which has a developed economy (the "domestic" country, e.g., the US), and the other a developing economy (the "foreign" country, e.g., China). As is typical of Ricardian models, the two countries have two sectors (A and B), each of them producing one good. The economy has a single homogeneous factor of production (labor) whose amount is fixed ($\bar{L}$). In Samuelson's (2004) model, the total domestic labor supply is $\bar{L} = 100$, while the total foreign labor supply is $\bar{L}^* = 1,000$. The model presumes perfect goods and factor markets, as well as inter-sectoral labor mobility and international labor immobility. Due to assumed perfect competition and full employment, total labor supply equals the sum of sector-specific labor supply $\bar{L} = L_A + L_B$, where L_A (resp. L_B) designates the labor supply of sector A (resp. B). In Samuelson's example, the sectoral allocation of labor supply in the domestic country is symmetric with $L_A = L_B = 50$, while it is $L_A^* = L_B^* = 500$ in the foreign country.

The two economies have different production technologies, which leads to differences in labor productivity across sectors and countries. Here, *labor productivity* π is defined as the amount of produced output Y per labor input L, and is constant because there are no other factors that could substitute for labor. The domestic labor productivity is $\pi_A = 2$ in sector A and $\pi_B = 1/2$ in sector B, while the foreign labor productivity in sector A is only $\pi_A^* = 1/20$ and $\pi_B^* = 1/5$ in sector B. Note that the foreign productivities are lower in both sectors. The *average productivity* is $\pi = 1/2(\pi_A + \pi_B) = 1.25$ in the home country and $\pi^* = 1/2$ $(\pi_A^* + \pi_B^*) = 0.125$, so the average foreign productivity is only one-tenth of its domestic counterpart ($\pi = 10\pi^*$). This is not the case for sectoral productivities, because the home country's productivity advantage in performing Y_A is greater than one-tenth, whereas the inferiority of the foreign country in performing Y_B is less than one-tenth. As a result, the home country produces a *quantity* of $Y_A = \pi_A L_A = 100$ in sector A and $Y_B = \pi_B L_B = 25$ in sector B, which represents the supply side in autarky equilibrium. The equilibrium outputs of the foreign country are $Y_A^* = \pi_A^* L_A^* = 25$ and $Y_B^* = \pi_B^* L_B^* = 100$. The world outputs are thus $Y_A^W = Y_B^W = 125$.

An alternative presentation of productivity is the reciprocal value, which is the *unit labor requirement* $a = 1/\pi$ and designates the amount of labor which is needed to produce one unit of output. In our numerical example, the domestic sectors' unit labor requirements are $a_A = 1/2$ and $a_B = 2$, while the foreign unit labor requirements are $a_A^* = 20$ and $a_B^* = 5$. The *opportunity costs* for a country to produce one unit of output Y_A measured in units of output Y_B are $a_A/a_B = 1/4$ in the home country and $a_A^*/a_B^* = 4$ in the foreign country. This means that the domestic country has a comparative advantage over the foreign country in producing Y_A, because it needs to remove relatively less labor from its sector B ($a_A/a_B < a_A^*/a_B^*$). However, the foreign country enjoys a comparative advantage over the home country for good Y_B ($a_B^*/a_A^* = 1/4 < a_B/a_A = 4$). A *comparative advantage* is given if the opportunity costs of performing a good in terms of the other good are smaller than in other countries. The *Ricardo theorem of comparative advantage* (1817) states that "[e]ach country exports the good in which it has a comparative labor productivity advantage" (Wong 1995, p. 90).

This concept leads to the idea of trade between the formerly autarkic countries, because both economies could mutually gain from specializing in and exporting the good where they possess a comparative advantage, while importing the good where they have an inferiority.

In a first step, Samuelson (2004) focuses on the equilibrium when both countries are in autarky, so that both must produce both goods and studies how the *domestic supplies* of Y_A and Y_B are determined. As L is the only factor of production, the supply will be determined by movements of L to the sector that pays higher wages. P_A and P_B denote the prices (values) of Y_A and Y_B.

Due to the absence of profits in the Ricardian model, the nominal wages per unit of labor input equal the values of output per unit of labor input, i.e., $w_A = \pi_A P_A = P_A/a_A$ and $w_B = \pi_B P_B = P_B/a_B$. When, e.g., wages of sector A are higher than in sector B, i.e. $P_A/a_A > P_B/a_B$, the total labor supply will be attracted by sector A, so the economy will specialize in the production of Y_A. Since in autarky both goods are produced, this requires that $P_A/a_A = P_B/a_B$ or $P_A/P_B = a_A/a_B$, i.e., the relative goods price of Y_A must equalize the opportunity costs of performing Y_A in terms of Y_B. The same logic applies to the foreign country, too.

Samuelson (2004) follows Mill's assumption where the economy spends half of its income on each of the two goods, which constitutes the demand side. Mill's assumption leads to $D_A = D_B$, where D_A (resp. D_B) designates the demand for Y_A (resp. Y_B). In autarky equilibrium, a good's demand and supply must be equal, which results in $D_A = Y_A = 100$ and $D_B = Y_B = 25$ in the numerical example. The same applies to the foreign economy, where $D_A^* = Y_A^* = 25$ and $D_B^* = Y_B^* = 100$. Note that the above 50–50 labor allocation between the sectors are a consequence of Mill's assumption under perfect competition.

The economy's *utility* can be described with the following Cobb–Douglas function: $U(D_A, D_B) = D_A^{\alpha} D_B^{1-\alpha}$ where $\alpha = 1/2$ describes the demand elasticity of utility. Here, U designates the utility measured in national income terms, which depends on the economy's demand for goods Y_A and Y_B. The choice of $\alpha = 1/2$ shows that the preferences for both goods are the same since $\alpha = 1 - \alpha$. In numerical terms, the economies' real incomes are calculated as follows:

$$U = \sqrt{100 \cdot 25} = 50 \quad \text{and} \quad U^* = \sqrt{25 \cdot 100} = 50.$$

The real per capita income is $U/L = 0.5$ in the home country and $U^*/L^* = 0.05$ in the foreign country.[3] The world's utility is $U^W = \sqrt{125 \cdot 125} = 125$ and designates the real world income, taking both autarkic economies together.

Equilibrium with International Trade

In a next step, the model analyzes how the possibility of international trade changes the autarky equilibrium outcomes. Initially, the opportunity costs in both countries compared to relative world prices are characterized as follows:

$$a_A/a_B = P_A/P_B < P_A^W/P_B^W < a_A^*/a_B^* = P_A^*/P_B^*.$$

Due to comparative advantage, the home country specializes in the production and exports of Y_A and imports the other good, while the foreign economy concentrates on Y_B^* and imports the other good. In numerical terms, the domestic country's total labor supply can produce $Y_A' = \pi_A \bar{L} = \bar{L}/a_A = 200$. The foreign economy can produce $Y_B'^* = \bar{L}^*/a_B^* = 200$. The new world outputs are thus $Y_A'^W = Y_B'^W = 200$ ($Y'^W = 400$), hence the additional output per good is 75 thanks to international trade. Accordingly, the new world's real GDP is $U'^W = \sqrt{200 \cdot 200} = 200$.

Since the model assumes the absence of transport costs, tariffs, and quotas, international trade equalizes the relative prices at home and abroad, so that $P_A/P_B = P_A^*/P_B^* = P_A^W/P_B^W$. The relative price of $Y_A'^W$ corresponds to its relative quantity which is $P_A^W/P_B^W = Y_A'^W/Y_B'^W$.[4] Under Mill's assumption of 50-50 sectoral income distribution, the numerical example results in a relative world price of $P_A^W/P_B^W = 200/200 = 1$. Due to Samuelson's (2004) symmetry assumption, both countries will share equally (not per capita equally) the world's total real outputs. Note that the gains from trade are not necessarily equally distributed among the countries. The new individual real incomes will increase to $U' = \sqrt{100 \cdot 100} = 100$ and

---

[3] The real per capita income can also be obtained by calculating the geometric mean of π_A and π_B, which is $0.5\sqrt{2 \times 1/2} = 0.5$. Since in equilibrium labor productivities correspond to real wages, 0.5 represents the real per capita income. The same holds for the foreign economy.

[4] Since in world equilibrium with total specialization $w_A/P_A = \pi_A$ and $w_B^*/P_B^* = \pi_B^*$, the ratio of domestic to foreign real wages yields: $(w_A/P_A)/(w_B^*/P_B^*) = \pi_A/\pi_B^* = (Y_A/\bar{L})/(Y_B^*/\bar{L}^*)$, which can be written as $P_B^*/P_A = (Y_A/Y_B^*)(\bar{L}^* w_B^*/\bar{L} w_A)$.

Under the assumption of zero profits, the countries' wage-bills equal their incomes, respectively, with $\bar{L} w_A = P_A Y_A$ and $\bar{L}^* w_B^* = P_B^* Y_B^*$. Mill's assumption of equal income shares between both goods in a country has the following results. As the home country does not produce Y_B, it imports Y_B^* from abroad and spends half of its income. Analogously, the foreign country spends half of its income on imported Y_A. Note that the import value must equal the export value of the foreign trading partner. Since the latter constitutes half of the trading partner's own income, the countries' total incomes must be equal. Thus, $\bar{L}^* w_B^* = \bar{L} w_A$ and $P_B^*/P_A = Y_A/Y_B^*$ which corresponds to $P_B^W/P_A^W = Y_A^W/Y_B^W$.

$U'^* = \sqrt{100 \cdot 100} = 100$. The new real per capita income is $U'/\bar{L} = 1$ in the home country and $U'^*/\bar{L}^* = 0.1$ in the foreign country. To sum up, both the home and the foreign country have doubled their total and per-capita real incomes due to free trade.

The gains from trade can also be demonstrated by using the *production possibility frontier* (PPF) in Fig. 4.1. The PPF in the home country is determined by the limits on the economy's resources, which is only labor, defined by the inequality: $a_A Y_A + a_B Y_B \leq \bar{L}$. Equality is attained under efficient production. In that case, the domestic PPF can be graphically illustrated by the line $\overline{Y_A Y_B}$. The PPF can also be formulated as $Y_B = \bar{L}/a_B - (a_A/a_B)Y_A$, which represents the quantity of Y_B that can be produced as a function of the other good Y_A. If Y_A is not produced at all ($Y_A = 0$), the total labor supply will entirely be used for the production of $Y_B = \bar{L}/a_B$. The slope of the PPF is negative with $-(a_A/a_B)$, which designates the above described opportunity costs to produce one unit of Y_A in terms of units of Y_B. In autarky, the country can only consume the amount that it produces, i.e. the consumption possibility frontier (CPF) falls on the PPF.

$\overline{Y_A Y_B}$ describes the equilibrium in autarky, where the home country produces $Y_A = 100$ and $Y_B = 25$. With the possibility of free trade, the slope of the new CPF (dashed line) increases to $-(P_A^W/P_B^W)$. It is evident that the home country's consumption possibilities expand such that $Y_B'^*/2 = 100$, while $Y_A = Y_A'/2 = 100$ remains constant. The foreign country experiences an analogous pattern, only that after trade openness its initial consumption possibilities of good A grow from $Y_A^* = 25$ to $Y_A'/2 = 100$, while the consumption possibilities of good B remain constant with $Y_B^* = Y_B'^*/2 = 100$ (Krugman and Obstfeld 2006; Samuelson 2004).

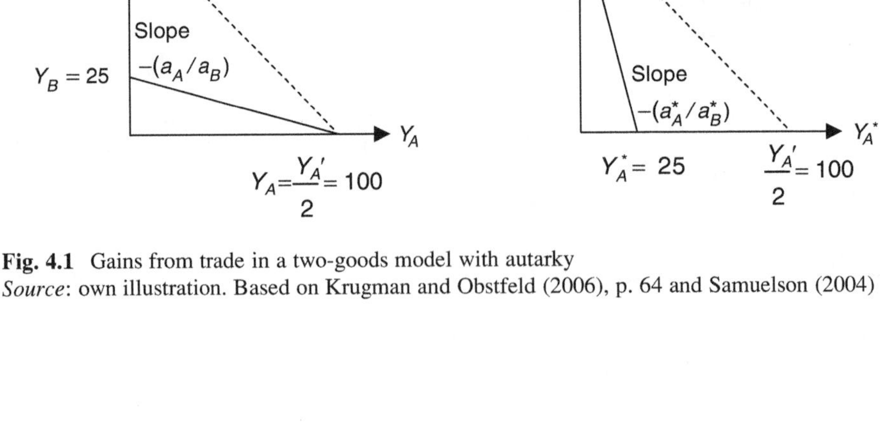

Fig. 4.1 Gains from trade in a two-goods model with autarky
Source: own illustration. Based on Krugman and Obstfeld (2006), p. 64 and Samuelson (2004)

4.1.1.2 Technological Progress in the Two-Goods Model

Technological Progress in the Foreign Export Sector

In the first scenario ("Act Ib"), Samuelson (2004) models the possibility that the foreign country experiences exogenous technological invention in its export sector. This exogenous technological progress raises labor productivity in the foreign sector B^* from initially $\pi_B^* = 1/5$ to $\pi_B^{\prime *} = 4/5$, all other productivities remaining constant, with

$$\left(\pi_A^{\prime}, \pi_B^{\prime}, \pi_A^{\prime *}, \pi_B^{\prime *}\right) = \left(2, \frac{1}{2}, \frac{1}{20}, \frac{4}{5}\right) \quad \text{and} \quad \left(a_A^{\prime}, a_B^{\prime}; a_A^{\prime *}, a_B^{\prime *}\right) = \left(\frac{1}{2}, 2; 20, \frac{5}{4}\right).$$

After the technological progress, the opportunity costs to produce a unit of Y_B^* measured in units of Y_A^* fall to $a_B^{\prime *}/a_A^{\prime *} = 1/16$. Recall that the old and new domestic opportunity costs remain at $a_B^{\prime}/a_A^{\prime} = 4$. Due to comparative advantage, the domestic economy continues to specialize in the production of $Y_A^{\prime} = Y_A^{\prime\prime} = 200$, while the foreign country produces and exports $Y_B^{\prime\prime *} = \pi_B^{\prime *}\bar{L}^* = 4/5 \times 1,000 = 800$ compared to $Y_B^{\prime *} = 200$. Thus, world output rises from its initial level of $Y^{\prime W} = Y_A^{\prime W} + Y_B^{\prime W} = 400$ to a new level, $Y^{\prime\prime W} = Y_A^{\prime\prime W} + Y_B^{\prime\prime W} = 1,000$ due to technological progress in the foreign export sector. The additional output is 600, which yields a new world income of $U^{\prime\prime W} = \sqrt{200 \cdot 800} = 400$.

The domestic economy gains some of the additional income, since the relative prices of the import good decline to $P_B^{\prime W}/P_A^{\prime W} = Y_A^{\prime\prime W}/Y_B^{\prime\prime W} = 1/4$. Thus, domestic income doubles to $U^{\prime\prime} = \sqrt{100 \cdot 400} = 200$ and the new real per capita income doubles to $U^{\prime\prime}/\bar{L} = 2$. The foreign economy gains likewise under assumed Millian 50–50 demand with a double income of $U^{\prime\prime *} = \sqrt{400 \cdot 100} = 200$ and real per-capita income of $U^{\prime\prime *}/\bar{L}^* = 0.2$. However, assuming a more inelastic demand abroad could diminish the foreign country's terms-of-trade such that per-capita income falls, possibly even below its level prior to the technological progress (Samuelson 2004).

Technological Progress in the Foreign Import Sector

In the second scenario ("Act II"), the foreign country enjoys exogenous productivity gains in its import sector B^*. Labor productivity in the foreign sector A^* rises from its initial level, $\pi_A^* = 1/20$ to $\pi^{\prime *}{}_A = 4/5$, assuming all other productivities remaining constant, giving:

$$\left(\pi_A^{\prime}, \pi_B^{\prime}; \pi_A^{\prime *}, \pi_B^{\prime *}\right) = \left(2, \frac{1}{2}; \frac{4}{5}, \frac{1}{5}\right) \quad \text{and} \quad \left(a_A^{\prime}, a_B^{\prime}; a_A^{\prime *}, a_B^{\prime *}\right) = \left(\frac{1}{2}, 2; \ \frac{5}{4}, 5\right).$$

In the foreign economy, the new opportunity costs of producing good A^* in terms of good B^* now fall to $a_A'^*/a_B'^* = 1/4$ from $a_B{}^*/a_A{}^* = 4$. Note that the domestic and foreign opportunity costs are now equal ($a_A'/a_B' = a_A'^*/a_B'^* = 1/4$) and no country has a comparative advantage in producing a certain good. In the new autarky equilibrium and in the absence of specialization, both countries must produce both goods. The countries divide their total labor supply symmetrically between the two sectors with $L_A' = L_B' = 50$ and $L_A'^* = L_B'^* = 500$. As a result, the domestic country produces an output of $Y_A'' = \pi_A' L_A' = 100$ in sector A and $Y_B'' = \pi_B' L_B = 25$ in sector B. The equilibrium outputs of the foreign country are now $Y_A''^* = \pi_A'^* L_A'^* = 400$ and $Y_B''^* = \pi_B'^* L_B'^* = 100$. The world outputs are thus $Y_A''^W = 500$, and $Y_B''^W = 125$, and $Y''^W = 625$. The new world income is $U''^W = \sqrt{500 \cdot 125} = 250$.

The real incomes of the domestic and the foreign country are now $U'' = \sqrt{100 \cdot 25} = 50$ and $U''^* = \sqrt{400 \cdot 100} = 200$. This leads to a per-capita income of $U''/\bar{L} = 0.5$ in the home country and $U''^*/\bar{L}^* = 0.2$ in the foreign country. It is evident that the domestic real per-capita income is cut in half from its income with international trade ($U'/\bar{L} = 1$), while the foreign country doubles its real per-capita income. Recall that both effects are caused by exogenous productivity gains in the foreign import sector. That means that *all* previous gains from international trade have been lost in the home country and the situation is the same as in autarky before free trade. Note that real wages in the home country are still higher than in the foreign country, because the average real wages in equilibrium correspond to the sum of sectoral productivities weighted by their labor shares with $w/P = (L_A/\bar{L})\pi_A' + (L_B/\bar{L})\pi_B' = 1/2(\pi_A' + \pi_B') = 1.25$, whereas the foreign real wage level is $w^*/P^* = (L_A^*/\bar{L}^*)\pi_A'^* + (L_B{}^*/\bar{L}^*)\pi_B'^* = 1/2(\pi_A'^* + \pi_B'^*) = 0.5$ (Samuelson 2004).

Samuelson (2004) also models the second scenario (Act II) within a three-goods framework and trade equilibrium. In this scenario, innovation in the foreign non-comparative advantage sector reduces the domestic country's real GDP as well as its real per-capita income by more than 20%. Compared to the two-goods model, this scenario is more realistic because not all gains from trade are lost as a consequence of foreign innovation (Samuelson 2004). However, since the insights from the three-goods model are basically the same, it will not be presented here.

To sum up, Samuelson (2004) first showed the gains from trade compared to autarky equilibrium. Usually, technological progress in the foreign export sector is beneficial for both countries. However, productivity gains in the foreign non-comparative advantage sector increases only the foreign income, while the home country loses all or at least some of its previous gains from international trade (Samuelson 2004).

In our opinion, the latter point constitutes the most interesting result of the Samuelson (2004) model. Thus, gains from trade can be eroded by innovation in the foreign export sector. Other features of the model, however, are less realistic: only final goods are traded, and there is only one factor of production. Moreover, only offshoring in the wider sense is included, modeled as the transition from autarky to international trade. Hence, the Samuelson (2004) model represents the simplest model of those that we survey.

4.1.2 The Heckscher–Ohlin Model

4.1.2.1 The Basic Model

The traditional Ricardian model can explain specialization of economies thanks to technological differences, but does not consider different factors of production. The *Heckscher–Ohlin–Samuelson-Modell* (Heckscher 1919; Ohlin 1933; Samuelson 1948) addresses this disadvantage allowing for two homogeneous factors of production, e.g., capital K and labor L. K can be interpreted as human capital, whereas L stands for less-skilled labor. Besides the two factors of production, the symmetric model contains two countries – domestic and foreign – each of them producing both final goods, namely the capital-intensive good Y_A and the labor-intensive good Y_B ($2 \times 2 \times 2$ model).

Comparative advantage is the crucial factor for international trade which – contrary to the Ricardian model – is determined by differences in the relative factor endowment in the standard Heckscher–Ohlin model. Both countries have *identical* sectoral technologies with constant returns-to-scale. There is no Ricardian comparative advantage, but the proportions of factors in a country and the proportion of factors used in the production of different goods determine international trade. For this reason, the Heckscher–Ohlin model is also called the factor-proportions model. Another assumptions is perfect factor mobility between the sectors, but international factor immobility and free trade without transport costs, barriers to trade, and restrictions. Beyond that, the demand structure of both countries is characterized by identical homothetic preferences, so the relative demands for a good only depend on its relative prices. As in the classical models, the Heckscher–Ohlin model assumes perfect market competition and perfectly flexible prices, and thus full employment (Marrewijk 2007; Wong 1995).

The *unit factor requirements* are defined as in the Ricardian model (Sect. 4.1.1) and represent the units of factor required for one unit of output. In the domestic economy, they are given by a_{KA}, a_{KB}, a_{LA} and a_{LB}. Note that the PPF as described in Sect. 4.1.1 constitutes a curve and no longer a line, since we have two factors of production. The domestic country is better endowed with (human) capital K and hence has a comparative advantage in the production of the capital-intensive good Y_A, because $K_A/L_A \equiv a_{KA}/a_{LA} < K_B/L_B \equiv a_{KB}/a_{LB}$ where K_i/L_i designates the sectoral capital-to-labor-ratio or capital intensity. The *optimal input amounts* of capital and labor are determined by cost-minimization, where total costs correspond to the wage-bills of capital and labor in sector i for $i = A, B$. The total costs to produce Y_i are given by $rK_i + wL_i$. Hence, the relative input combination K_i/L_i is

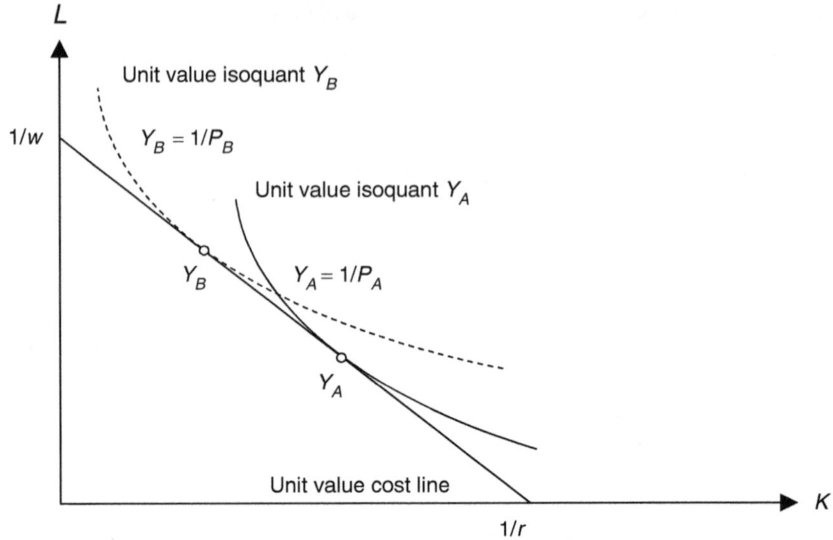

Fig. 4.2 The Lerner diagram (domestic autarky equilibrium)
Source: based on Marrewijk (2007), p. 98

a positive function of w/r with $K_i/L_i = f(w/r)$.[5] The higher w/r, the more capital relative to labor will be used in the production process.

Note that, given the factor prices r and w, one can determine the *unit value isocost line*, which designates all capital–labor input combinations in the economy for which total costs are 1, i.e. $rK + wL = 1$. If only capital is used, then $K = 1/r$, while if only labor is used, then $L = 1/w$. In order to determine the final goods prices P_i, unit value isoquants must be introduced. *Unit value isoquants* are defined as $P_i Y_i = 1$, i.e., they represent all possible output-price combinations in sector i whose products are 1. Given the unit value isocost line, one needs to determine the unit value isoquants $Y_A = 1/P_A$ and $Y_B = 1/P_B$ that are tangent to the unit value isocost line in order to obtain P_A and P_B. This autarky equilibrium is shown in the *Lerner diagram* (Fig. 4.2).

Let us now assume the possibility of *international trade* between the domestic and foreign economy. Given the assumptions above, the domestic country has a better factor endowment with capital and thus specializes in the production and export of the capital-intensive good Y_A, whereas the foreign country is relatively

[5]The unit cost minimization problem is specified by $\min rK_i + wL_i$ s.t. $Y_i = Y(K_i, L_i) = 1$, where Y_i denotes the production function. This minimization problem can be solved using the Lagrange multiplier λ and defining the Lagrangian $\Gamma_i = rK_i + wL_i + \lambda((K_i, L_i) - 1)$. The two first order conditions (FOCs) $\partial\Gamma_i/\partial K_i = \partial\Gamma_i/\partial L_i = 0$ are given by:
$\partial\Gamma_i/\partial K_i = r + \lambda\partial F(K_i, L_i)/\partial K_i = 0$ and $\partial\Gamma_i/\partial L_i = w + \lambda\partial(K_i, L_i)/\partial L_i = 0$.
Thus, the optimal capital-to-labor ratio K_i/L_i can be expressed as a positive function of the wage-rental ratio w/r.

labor-abundant and therefore specializes in the production and exports of the labor-intensive good $Y_B{}^*$. The good which uses the scarce factor more intensively is imported by each country. Note that both countries are not fully specialized.

What are the effects of international trade on the domestic country? Originally (in autarky), we have $K/L > K^*/L^*$. Since under profit maximization the factors are paid their marginal products, the abundant factor is remunerated less than the scarce factor in a country. Hence, the rental–wage ratios of both countries are $r/w < r^*/w^*$. The relative price for capital-intensive goods is thus lower than in the foreign country ($P_A/P_B < P_A{}^*/P_B{}^*$). International trade is advantageous for both countries for the following reasons: increasing foreign demand for the export good Y_A results in a higher product price P_A, a higher demand for the abundant factor K and a higher relative factor price r/w. Therefore, the domestic country augments the production and exports of Y_A. On the other hand, the labor-intensive good Y_B can be imported at a lower price which improves the domestic economy's terms-of-trade.

There are two *income effects* on the scarce factor in the domestic country. First, its purchasing power worsens, since the relative price for the export good P_A/P_B rises. Second, assuming temporary factor immobility, the relative wage of the scarce factor L decreases. When instantaneous wage adjustments are not possible due to labor market rigidities, the second effect could turn into a release of labor. In the long run, inter-sectoral factor mobility leads to a shift from the disadvantaged sector to the export sector, thus equalizing factor prices. As relative prices for goods converge, factor prices tend to equalize between both countries. Thus, free trade leads to an efficient international division of the factors of production (Henneberger et al. 2000; Krugman and Obstfeld 2006; Marrewijk 2007).

The $2 \times 2 \times 2$ framework allows us to study the effects of trade liberalization on different factors of production, which constitutes an improvement compared to the Ricardian models.

4.1.2.2 Free Trade Equilibrium and Four Theorems

Free trade equilibrium in a Heckscher–Ohlin framework is characterized by four theorems:

(1) The *Factor Price Equalization* (*FPE*) *Theorem* states that under free trade internationally equalizing goods prices lead to equalized factor prices (Lerner 1952; Samuelson 1948, 1949).
(2) The *Heckscher–Ohlin Theorem* (Heckscher 1919; Ohlin 1933) states if there are two trading goods and trade is natural, each country exports the good that uses its relatively abundant factor more intensively.
(3) The *Stolper–Samuelson Theorem* (Stolper and Samuelson 1941) is a partial equilibrium result and states that the rise in a good's price increases the real factor price of the factor that is used more intensively in the sector and lowers the real factor price of the other factor.

This theorem can be explained by economic intuition. If the price of Y_A rises (with the price being fixed for Y_B), the production of Y_A will be stimulated and sector A will expand while sector B must shrink. This creates an excess demand for capital and an excess supply of labor in the economy, which raises r, but pushes w down. Moreover, under the zero-profit condition in sector A, a rise in P_A combined with a fall in w means that r must grow more strongly than P_A, so the changes of r and w correspond to real factor price changes.

(4) The *Rybczynski Theorem* (Rybczynski 1955) is also a partial equilibrium result and states that under the assumption of no factor-ratio reversal, diversification of production, and constant goods (and factor) prices, an increase in the amount of a factor raises over-proportionally the output of the sector that uses this factor more intensively, while the output of the other sector declines.

Economic reasoning can be used to explain this theorem. One could assume that the labor endowment grows ($dL > 0$), while the amount of capital is fixed ($dK = 0$). Under the assumption of constant goods and factor prices as well as labor unit requirements, the labor-intensive sector B must expand to absorb the additional labor supply. Sector B must expand at the expense of the capital-intensive sector A, because the production of Y_B also requires additional K, which must be provided from sector A. When sector A contracts, it releases not only K, but also L, which means that the growth rate of labor *employment* and thus the output growth rate is larger in the labor-intensive sector B than the growth rate of labor *endowment* (Baldwin and Robert-Nicoud 2007; Wong 1995).

4.1.3 The Specific-Factors Model

As a quick response to Samuelson's contribution (2004), free trade advocate Bhagwati, in collaboration with Panagariya and Srinivasan (2004), aimed to show with the help of three models that offshoring is generally beneficial to an economy.[6] The models predict a total welfare increase for a country which engages in services offshoring, whereas the exact underlying processes depend on the structure of the economy. However, under certain circumstances welfare losses are also possible. In the following, we present Bhagwati et al.'s (2004) specific-factors model. Specific-factors models designate trade models where some or all factors of production are sector-specific. More specifically, Bhagwati et al.'s (2004) version represents a Ricardo–Viner model, which is characterized by one specific factor in each sector and one mobile factor.

---

[6]The Samuelson (2004) model was published in the *Journal of Economic Perspectives* in Vol. 18, Issue 3, while Bhagwati et al. (2004) responded in Vol. 18, Issue 4, called the "Samuelson–Bhagwati-Debate".

4.1.3.1 Offshoring in a Two-Goods Model

The model integrates trade from the beginning and considers an economy with two sectors *A* and *B* that produce two final goods, Y_A and Y_B, and three factors of production, namely *K*, L_{LS} and L_{HS}. Y_B is the import-competing good that uses the sector-specific factor L_{LS}, while Y_A designates the export good using the sector-specific factor *K*. L_{HS} is used by both sectors. Assuming that the country is already involved in international trade, technological progress now renders offshoring of L_{HS} possible.

Assuming initially constant terms-of-trade, the allocation of L_{HS} between both sectors is shown in Fig. 4.3. The total amount of L_{HS} in the economy is illustrated by the axis O_AO_B, whereby every point on this axis shows the allocation of L_{HS} between the two sectors. The amount of L_{HS} used by the import-competing sector *A* corresponds to the distance O_AL_{HS}, whereas, analogously, the amount of L_{HS} used by the exporting sector corresponds to the distance $L_{HS}O_B$. The marginal product of labor multiplied by the price (value) of one unit of output yields $\text{MPL}_{HSA} \cdot P_A$ and $\text{MPL}_{HSB} \cdot P_B$. If the value of the marginal product is smaller than the nominal wage, firms will always have an incentive to increase their demand for L_{HS} until the value of the marginal product equals marginal costs (wages). L^0_{HS} represents the equilibrium allocation of L_{HS}, which is reached when nominal wages are identical in both sectors with $w_{HS} = w_{HSA} = w_{HSB}$, and graphically when both curves intersect (point *E*). Total welfare is illustrated by the area under both curves up to point that indicates the employment of high-skilled labor L_{HS}.

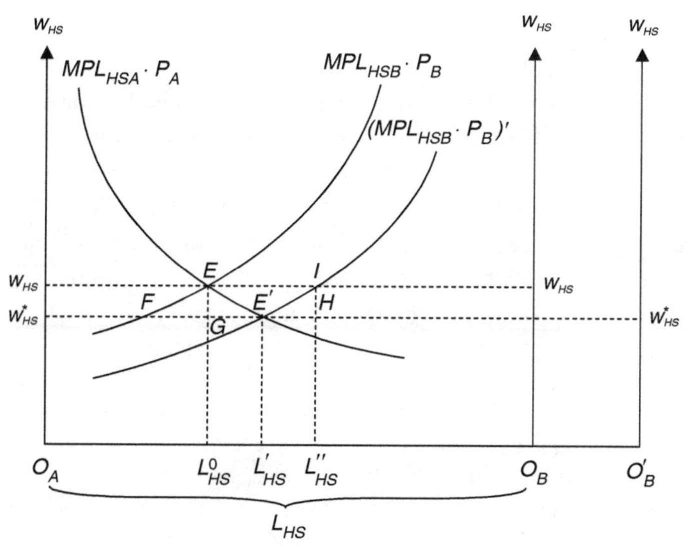

Fig. 4.3 Gains from offshoring in a two-goods model with trade
Source: own illustration. Based on Bhagwati et al. (2004), p. 103

Technological progress now makes offshoring of L_{HS} feasible, so that firms can buy imported services at the foreign wage $w_{HS}{}^{*}$ with $w_{HS}{}^{*} < w_{HS}$. The lower wage abroad results in an excess demand for cheap foreign services of skilled-labor, which is represented by the line $\overline{\mathrm{FE}'}$. This excess demand can be satisfied through offshoring. Offshoring represents an indirect import of foreign high-skilled labor, which is incorporated in the purchased service inputs, and leads to an increased supply of L_{HS} of $\overline{O_B O'_B}$ at foreign wages $w_{HS}{}^{*}$, where $\overline{O_B O'_B} = \overline{\mathrm{FE}'}$. The new equilibrium E' is achieved by shifting the $\mathrm{MPL}_{HSB} \cdot P_B$ curve horizontally to the right by $\overline{O_B O'_B} = \overline{\mathrm{FE}'}$, represented by $(\mathrm{MPL}_{HSB} \cdot P_B)'$.[7] The amount of the horizontal shift is the same at every wage level, and thus $\overline{\mathrm{EI}} = \overline{\mathrm{FE}'}$. As a result of this construction, the import-competing sector A absorbs $\overline{L^0_{HS} L'_{HS}}$, while the exporting sector B employs $\overline{L'_{HS} L''_{HS}}$ of the additional amount of high-skilled labor.

4.1.3.2 The Welfare Effects of Offshoring

In the following, the *welfare effects* of services offshoring are analyzed by comparing the pre- and post-offshoring values of output, starting with the import-competing sector A. Initially, the original output of sector A at $w_{HSA} = w_{HS}$ is reflected by the area under the $\mathrm{MPL}_{HSA} \cdot P_A$ curve up to the amount of L_{HS}, which is $\overline{O_A L^0_{HS}}$. After offshoring, the value of output is illustrated by the area under the $\mathrm{MPL}_{HSA} \cdot P_A$ curve up to the new amount of high-skilled labor employed in sector A, which is $\overline{O_A L'_{HS}}$. Note that not all of the additional output represents a welfare gain, since the foreign labor producing the offshored services needs to be paid, which is the area of the rectangle $L^0_{HS}\mathrm{GE}'L'_{HS}$. Thus, the additional output value is the triangle EGE'.

In the exporting sector B, the extra supply of high-skilled labor has shifted the right-hand axis and the $\mathrm{MPL}_{HSB} \cdot P_B$ curve to the right. Due to this construction, the initial value of output is illustrated both by the area under the $\mathrm{MPL}_{HSB} \cdot P_B$ curve up to $\overline{O_B L^0_{HS}}$ (measuring from right to left) or by the area under the $(\mathrm{MPL}_{HSB} \cdot P_B)'$ curve up to $\overline{O'_B L''_{HS}}$. The feasibility of offshoring leads to a higher output value than before, which is measured by the area under $(\mathrm{MPL}_{HSB} \cdot P_B)'$ up to $\overline{O'_B L'_{HS}}$. Again, the foreign wage bill, represented by the rectangle $L'_{HS}E'HL''_{HS}$, must be subtracted from the welfare gains of sector B, which leads to the remaining gain of the triangle IHE'. Summing the two triangles EGE' and IHE' yields the total social gains.

Under the assumption of diminishing returns to scale for all factors, the increase in the skilled-labor supply at a lower wage level results in a growth of the remaining factor prices, in particular unskilled wages w_{LS}, and the rental rate on capital. Offshoring leads to social gains if the country is small – and thus terms-of-trade

[7] Alternatively, this effect could have been modeled by shifting the $\mathrm{MPL}_{HSA} \cdot P_A$ curve to the left by the same amount.

are fixed – and under the absence of trade distortions. If the country is large – and thus influences its terms-of-trade – offshoring can generate welfare losses in two alternative ways.

First, there might be the case that the supply (output) of the export good rises more strongly than its demand, so that export prices and the terms-of-trade worsen. This *negative terms-of-trade effect* could offset the positive welfare gain from offshoring. However, if the supply of the import-competing good grows, import prices and the terms-of-trade improve and form an additional welfare gain. Second, in the presence of uncorrected distortions, a nation's growth itself could lead to an overall negative welfare effect if the *distortion effect* offsets the positive growth effects. This effect has been studied by Bhagwati (1968) under the term "immiserizing growth". The feasibility of offshoring due to technological progress represents such a growth effect. However, Bhagwati et al. (1998) also found that if a large country does not apply an optimal tariff, the free trade policy itself could act like a distortion and reverse the positive growth effects into overall negative welfare losses.

To sum up, Bhagwati et al. (2004) analyze offshoring of high-skilled labor in a two goods model which integrates trade from the beginning. Under the assumption of diminishing returns to scale for all factors, the increase in the skilled-labor supply at a lower wage level results in a growth of the remaining factor prices. Offshoring leads to social gains if the country is small and in the absence of trade distortions. If the country is large, however, offshoring can generate welfare losses in two alternative ways.

Besides the fact that this model does not include trade in intermediates, one could also object the sector-specificity of less-skilled labor. Thus, less-skilled labor can be considered mobile due to its little sector and firm-specific knowledge. In our opinion, however, the Bhagwati et al. (2004) model allows us to easily study the welfare effects of offshoring despite (or perhaps as a result of) its simplicity.

4.2 Offshoring of Intermediate Goods

One type of intermediate goods model deals with *fragmentation*, where the final good is broken up into a discrete number of components (fragments) that are geographically separable. The final good is produced according to a standard integrated production function using the exogenously-specified fragments. These studies have analyzed how fragmentation influences prices, wages, production, and trade. The model of Jones and Kierzkowski (1990) constitutes one of the most cited fragmentation models which explicitly addresses "the role of services in international production and trade" in a Heckscher–Ohlin setting.[8] This type of model uses verbal description and diagrams where fragmentation (mostly in small countries)

[8]Earlier models integrating trade in intermediates in a Heckscher–Ohlin framework include Batra and Casas (1973), Woodland (1977) and Dixit and Grossman (1982).

happens only in one sector and one direction.[9] Fragmentation is considered as a form of technological progress with complex effects depending on the country's relative endowment of factors, the factor intensity of the sector being fragmented and the factor intensity of the fragment being offshored.

General equilibrium models use mathematical methods to analyze the effects of fragmentation.[10] As offshoring cannot be cost-saving if the FPE theorem holds (see Sect. 4.1.2.2), this type of model is characterized by non-factor price equalization. Therefore, these rather complex models "present a gallery of special cases that firmly establish the ambiguous sign of the general equilibrium price, production, trade and factor price effects" (Baldwin and Robert–Nicoud 2007, p. 3). Most of the studies also assume that fragmentation occurs in only one sector and one direction. Deardorff (2001a, b) uses a Heckscher–Ohlin framework with two countries, two factors, many goods, and Cobb–Douglas technology and preferences. Cost-saving offshoring is modeled by assuming that the countries' endowments lie in different diversification cones. Deardorff (2001a, b) shows that the capital-to-labor-ratios and the domestic weighted average of the goods' factor intensities determine the wage ratio in both countries. Fragmentation changes the factor intensity of the produced goods and can cause converging or diverging relative factor prices. The outcome is determined by the factor intensities of the fragments and of the original technology (Baldwin and Robert-Nicoud 2007).

Fragmentation in the Kohler (2004) model occurs in a specific-factors setting and only in one sector. Cost-saving fragmentation is caused by low foreign wages. The model assumes a small open economy with fixed goods prices and foreign wages and thus avoids the non-FPE discussion. Kohler (2004) addresses both efficiency (welfare) and distributional aspects of fragmentation. The model shows that if international fragmentation occurs without nonconvexity in production technology, it causes an efficiency gain. A larger efficiency gain results in a more moderate redistribution effect. The model also considers a form of nonconvexity where the specific factor used to produce the disintegrated fragment is a fixed input. In such a case, fragmentation might lead to efficiency losses (Kohler 2004).

However, fragmentation models face some problems, as listed by Grossman and Rossi-Hansberg (2006a, b):

> "This research poses apt questions and generates some interesting examples and insights. But, results depend on details about which production process can be disintegrated, whether factor price equalization holds initially, and what are the absolute and relative factor endowments in each country in relation to world demands for the various goods. It is not easy to glean general principles from the cases that have been considered. Nor do the models lend themselves readily to analysis of new issues, because firms in the model make no marginal decisions about how to organize production and there are many different configurations that could characterize an equilibrium. Moreover, the modeling

---

[9]Such models include Jones and Marjit (1992), Arndt (1997–1999), Findlay and Jones (2000, 2001), Jones and Kierzkowski (2001), and Jones et al. (2002).

[10]These studies include Deardorff (2001a, b), Venables (1999), Kohler (2004) and Markusen (2005).

of fragmentation as a discrete choice makes it difficult to study the evolution of task trade over time (Grossman and Rossi-Hansberg 2006b, p. 4)."

Therefore, models have started to focus on trade of a *continuum of inputs*. The production of the inputs can happen in different locations and its organization can vary continuously. Some inputs can be produced offshore and traded, e.g., for cost-reasons, but the offshorability varies and depends on the kind of input. The set of inputs that are produced offshore is the result of an endogenous decision. Ultimately, the cost of the marginal input is equalized across the different locations (Grossman and Rossi-Hansberg 2006a, b). Yi (2003) and Grossman and Rossi-Hansberg (2006a, b) have modeled trade in costly inputs (the former) or tasks (the latter). Feenstra and Hanson (1996) used another approach to determine the set of inputs produced offshore, which in their model depends on the countries' factor endowments. Rodríguez-Clare (2007) includes a continuum of intermediate service inputs using a Ricardian framework, while Yomogida and Zhao (2005) represent one of the rare specific-factors models including trade in intermediates.

In the following, we present the Grossman and Rossi-Hansberg (2006a, b) model[11] which incorporates trade in intermediates ("trade in tasks") to analyze the wage effects of offshoring. This general equilibrium model enjoys a high degree of flexibility over other models for the following reasons: First, it allows not only for a continuum of inputs, but also for two, three, or many factors of production (Sect. 4.2.1.1). Second, offshoring can affect labor through three channels: the productivity effect, the labor-supply effect, and the relative-price effect (Sect. 4.2.1.2). Third, one can analyze the effects in a small economy (Sect. 4.2.2.1) and in a large economy (Sect. 4.2.2.2). Interestingly, this model leads to unambiguous results in the small open economy setting, and allows for the possibility of an anti Stolper–Samuelson effect in the large economy. Fourth, the model is not restricted to offshoring in one sector (see Sect. 4.2.2.4).

4.2.1 The Basic Model

4.2.1.1 Modeling Trade in Tasks

The production process in the Grossman and Rossi-Hansberg (2006a, b) model includes a set of *intermediate tasks* as opposed to the earlier approach of Feenstra and Hanson (1996), who integrate a set of intermediate inputs. Inputs can be distinguished from tasks insofar as the latter require several inputs of some factor of production. There are two countries, home and foreign, and there are two goods, Y_A and Y_B. The domestic country exports one of the two goods (e.g., financial services) and imports the other one (e.g., textiles), but it might also have a second import-substituting sector that produces the other good. Both sectors are assumed to be perfectly competitive.

[11] The final version of this model was published in Grossman and Rossi-Hansberg (2008).

Some tasks can be produced by less-skilled workers L_{LS} (LS-tasks), whereas other tasks must be performed by high-skilled labor L_{HS} (HS-tasks). The model also allows for other tasks that are produced by other factors of production, such as capital or other categories of labor. In addition, the model allows for substitution between the factors, based on the assumption that the sets of LS-tasks and HS-tasks (and any other tasks) can be produced at different intensities. That means that a given output level can be achieved either by using the LS-tasks more frequently than HS-tasks, or vice-versa.[12] The simplest case is when the production of one unit of output requires using each task once.

As in the standard Heckscher–Ohlin model, the two goods have different *factor intensities*, i.e., the production of good Y_A (e.g. financial services) is HS-intensive, while the production of good Y_B (e.g., textiles) is LS-intensive. Note that both goods require both factors of production (and probably other factors, too), but Y_A (e.g., financial services) uses relatively more L_{HS} (performing HS-tasks) than Y_B (e.g., textiles). The authors begin with the scenario that *only LS-tasks can be offshored*, while the remaining tasks must be produced in the home country. Since in both sectors LS-tasks vary in their offshorability (some tasks can be relocated more easily than others), this leads to a variation in the costs of offshoring these tasks.

The authors use an *arbitrary index* $\imath \in [0, 1]$ to identify LS-tasks, where lower indices indicate a higher suitability for offshoring than higher indices. One assumes that a *task* τ, performed in the home country, needs a certain amount of domestic L_{LS}. If the same task τ is performed abroad, it would require $\varphi\tau(\imath) > 1$ units of foreign labor per unit of domestic labor. The tasks τ have been ordered so that $\tau(\imath)$ is an increasing function of $\imath$, i.e. $d\tau(\imath)/d\imath \geq 0$. The parameter φ denotes the *feasibility of offshoring* at a point of time. A higher feasibility of offshoring of LS-tasks, induced by, e.g., developments in ICTs or transportation, would be reflected in a decrease of φ.

A firm's offshoring decision depends on whether the benefits are higher than the costs for certain tasks. The domestic (resp. foreign) wages for less-skilled labor L_{LS} (resp. $L_{LS}{}^*$) are w_{LS} (resp. $w_{LS}{}^*$). LS-tasks with low indexes $\imath$ are offshored if $\varphi\tau(\imath)w_{LS}{}^* < w_{LS}$, while tasks with high indices $\imath$ will be performed in the home country if $\varphi\tau(\imath)w_{LS}{}^* > w_{LS}$. Let I denote the *index of marginal task*, when domestic and foreign costs are equal:

$$w_{LS} = \varphi\tau(I)w_{LS}{}^*. \tag{4.1}$$

Since $\imath \in [0, 1]$, I represents also the share of LS-tasks that are produced abroad.[13]

[12] The authors assume that there is no substitution between LS-tasks or between HS-tasks, so these tasks must be conducted the same number of times.

[13] Here, the authors assume implicitly that each LS-task (HS-task) is conducted the same number of times. The generality of increasing $\tau(\imath)$ is not lost, since each task which is repeated multiple times can be divided into multiple tasks, each of them having different indices. As long as the resulting tasks are characterized by slightly different trade costs, the model has no loss in generality.

The costs c of producing one unit of a good consist of the costs for L_{LS}, the costs for L_{LS}^*, the costs for L_{HS}, as well as the costs for other production factors used. This leads to:

$$c = w_{LS}a_{LS}(1-I) + w_{LS}{}^{*}a_{LS}\varphi T(I) + w_{HS}a_{HS} + \ldots \tag{4.2}$$

where a_{LS} and a_{HS} designate the *factor intensities*, which are the amounts of L_{LS} and L_{HS} used by the sector to produce a typical LS- and HS-task, and w_{HS} is the domestic wage for L_{HS}.[14] $\phi T(I)$ represents the *ratio of foreign labor to domestic labor* that is required to produce all tasks $\tau(\imath)$ with $\imath \le I$ in the offshore location, where $T(I) = \int_0^I \tau(\imath)\mathrm{d}\imath$. $\varphi T(I) > 1$, because extra costs arise when tasks are performed offshore.

The first term on the RHS represents the product of wages and amount of L_{LS} used per unit of output. A unit of output is defined as the product of labor input per task and the share of tasks $(1-I)$ being performed in the home country. Analogously, the second RHS term designates the wages to L_{LS}^* per unit of output. The third term on the RHS is the amount of wages paid to L_{HS} per unit of output. Substituting (4.1) into (4.2) yields the *zero-profit condition*:

$$\begin{aligned} c &= w_{LS}a_{LS}(1-I) + \frac{w_{LS}}{\tau(I)}a_{LS}T(I) + w_{HS}a_{HS} + \ldots \\ &= w_{LS}\left[(1-I) + \frac{T(I)}{\tau(I)}\right]a_{LS} + w_{HS}a_{HS} + \ldots \end{aligned} \tag{4.3}$$

with $\Pi = (1-I) + \frac{T(I)}{\tau(I)} < 1$.[15]

With the possibility of offshoring, the unit cost function in (4.3) shows that the total wage sum of L_{LS} per unit of produced output is a fraction, namely Π, of the situation without offshoring. Note that this holds only before any offshoring-induced changes in factor prices or substitution of factors occur. The authors indicate that in the case when offshoring is *not* feasible, Π in (4.3) could be interpreted as inversely measured *productivity* of L_{LS}, so that a higher productivity would reduce Π and thus lead to direct cost savings. Alternatively, if offshoring becomes cheaper and thus more feasible, i.e. if φ falls, the fraction of the domestic

---

[14] The factor intensities may be fixed due to technical restrictions or simply reflect the firms' optimal choices regarding current factor prices and substitution possibilities. As verbally explained above, sector Y_A is relatively skill-intensive compared to sector Y_B, and thus $a_{HSA}/a_{LSA} > a_{HSB}/a_{LSB}$.

[15] The excess foreign labor requirement for the marginal task $\tau(\mathrm{I})$ is larger than the average excess foreign labor requirement $T(I)/I$, because the tasks with the least costs are relocated first (the marginal task has the highest costs among the offshorable tasks). This yields $T(I)/I < \tau(I)$ or $T(I)/\tau(I) < I$.

wage bill per unit of output Π will decline (because foreign tasks replace domestic ones), which also decreases unit costs. We see that a lower φ is comparable to labor-augmenting technological progress.

Considering the domestic factor markets, the market for L_{LS} clears when the whole domestic labor supply is used in both sectors to perform the tasks at home. Precisely, the fraction $(1-I)$ of LS-tasks is produced at home, and each LS-task in sector A (resp. B) employs a_{LSA} (resp. a_{LSB}) units of labor per output Y_A (resp. Y_B). The *market clearing condition* for L_{LS} is given by

$$(1-I)a_{LSA}Y_A + (1-I)a_{LSB}Y_B = (1-I)L_{LSA} + (1-I)L_{LSB} = L_{LS},$$

or

$$a_{LSA}Y_A + a_{LSB}Y_B = L_{LS}/(1-I). \tag{4.4}$$

Without the possibility of offshoring HS-tasks, the market clearing condition for L_{HS} is

$$a_{HSA}Y_A + a_{HSB}Y_B = L_{HSA} + L_{HSB} = L_{HS}. \tag{4.5}$$

Similarly, the market clearing condition of additional factors is characterized by (4.5).

Concerning the *markets for consumer goods*, consumers are characterized by identical and homothetic preferences (Grossman and Rossi-Hansberg 2006b).

4.2.1.2 The Effects of Falling Offshoring-Costs

Grossman and Rossi-Hansberg (2006a, b) model the *effects of decreasing offshoring costs* (falling φ) in a general equilibrium framework, which allows for 2, 3, or many factors of production. In the neutral case, offshoring possibilities in the two sectors of the economy are equal, i.e. $\tau(\imath)$ and φ hold for both sectors. A decline of φ affects L_{LS} through three channels. First, c will be reduced as described above (*productivity effect*). Second, firms are likely to substitute L_{LS} for $L_{LS}{}^*$, which creates imbalances between labor supply and labor demand (at primary factor prices), output levels and techniques of production (*labor-supply effect*). The effects are equivalent to those of a growing labor supply of L_{LS}. Third, the output might change its composition (at initial prices), since the two sectors of the economy get an incentive to expand. If the country is large, such as the US, it influences world markets at its initial prices leading to a change of the relative good prices (*relative-price effect*).

Assuming that both goods Y_A and Y_B are produced, the *zero-profit conditions* of (4.3) can be formulated for each of them. These two equations combined with the *factor-market clearing conditions* in (4.4) and (4.5) that apply for the number of υ factors, lead to a system of $2 + \upsilon$ equations. Totally differentiating this system, expressed in percentage changes, yields:

$$\hat{w}_{LS} = -\hat{\Pi} - \gamma_1 \hat{P}^{\mathrm{TOT}} - \gamma_2 \frac{\mathrm{d}I}{1-I}, \tag{4.6}$$

where $P^{\mathrm{TOT}} = P_{\mathrm{EX}}/P_{\mathrm{IM}}$ is the terms-of-trade, which is the price of a country's export good relative to the price of its import good.

The first RHS term of (4.6) is the *productivity effect*. Holding all other terms constant, higher offshoring possibilities ($\mathrm{d}\varphi < 0$) lead to a fall of c, which is proportional to the payments for less-skilled labor ($\hat{\Pi} < 0$). The decline in Π increases the demand for L_{LS} and raises w_{LS}. The second RHS term constitutes the *relative-price effect*, which is affected by a fall of φ. If the country's terms-of-trade P^{TOT} increase, w_{LS} are expected to fall, since countries that relocate LS-tasks rather export skill-intensive goods. The third RHS term is the *labor-supply effect*. A falling φ and thus the feasibility to offshore more LS-tasks ($\mathrm{dI} > 0$) makes some of the L_{LS} redundant that previously produced these tasks. This has the same effect as an increase in L_{LS} supply.

Offshoring more LS-tasks also affects the wages of L_{HS}, which consist of two components:

$$\hat{w}_{HS} = \gamma_3 \hat{p} + \gamma_4 \frac{\mathrm{d}I}{1-I}. \tag{4.7}$$

Unlike for w_{LS}, there is no direct productivity effect in (4.7). Equation (4.2) shows that a falling φ has no direct influence on the wage bill of L_{HS}. The relative-price effect will inversely improve w_{HS} when the country exports skill-intensive goods. The labor-supply effect, i.e., an increase in the supply of L_{LS}, also raises w_{HS}. Using this framework, Grossman and Rossi-Hansberg (2006a, b) analyze the effects of offshoring tasks in different scenarios beginning with offshoring in a small Heckscher–Ohlin economy.

4.2.2 Different Scenarios

4.2.2.1 Offshoring in a Small Economy

The Heckscher–Ohlin model is a very appropriate framework to analyze offshoring from a developed to a less-developed country. The $2 \times 2 \times 2$ model includes two countries, two sectors, and two factors of production. The first sector A (e.g., financial services) is relatively high-skill-intensive, while the second sector

B (e.g., textiles) is relatively low-skill-intensive. The factor price effects can be analyzed with (4.6) and (4.7). A small economy (e.g., Belgium) is a country whose economic activities do not affect world prices, i.e. $\hat{P}^{TOT} = 0$. Beyond that, changing factor supplies have no influence on factor prices according to the Heckscher–Ohlin model if both goods are produced in the economy. An excess supply of L_{LS} can be absorbed in the way that the labor-intensive sector B expands, while the skill-intensive sector A shrinks in order to maintain an equal marginal product of L_{LS}. An analogous argument can be made for L_{HS} and the skill-intensive sector A. As explained above, increased offshoring has the same effects as an excess labor supply, i.e. $\gamma_2 = \gamma_4 = 0$.

Including these characteristics of a small economy into (4.6) and (4.7) yields $\hat{w}_{LS} = -\hat{\Pi} > 0$ and $\hat{w}_{HS} = 0$.[16] Interestingly, L_{LS} reaps all the benefits from increased offshoring possibilities in the form of wage increases, whereas L_{HS} remains uninfluenced. The *productivity effect* occurs in stages when the offshoring costs fall. As a first result of increased imports of LS-tasks, the demand for L_{LS} will decline, since $L_{LS}{}^{*}$ performs the tasks that have formerly been produced by L_{LS}. Since both sectors have cost savings from offshoring LS-tasks (c falls when φ falls), both sectors have an incentive to expand, the labor-intensive sector more so than the skill-intensive sector. Recall that this is because a firm's cost savings are proportional to its share of LS-tasks. Thus, due to the *expansion effect*, the initially released workers can be absorbed even at a higher marginal product ($\hat{w}_{LS} > 0$).

Grossman and Rossi-Hansberg (2006b) also evaluate the alternative that offshoring costs *differ* across the two sectors, which have been assumed to be equal until now. First, one can assume the scenario that only the labor-intensive sector B is able to offshore. The consequences are comparable to labor-augmenting technological progress in sector B. The wages of L_{LSB} are expected to grow more strongly than the percentage fall in Π_B ($\hat{w}_{LSB} > 0$), whereas the wages of L_{HSB} will decline ($\hat{w}_{HSB} < 0$). Second, if offshoring of LS-tasks is only feasible in the skill-intensive sector A, labor will be affected inversely with $\hat{w}_{LSA} < 0$ and $\hat{w}_{HSA} > 0$.

[16] The productivity effect can also be derived as follows. Under the assumption that both goods Y_A and Y_B are produced in equilibrium, the zero-profit conditions imply:

$$1 = \Pi w_{LS} a_{LSA}(\Pi w_{LS}/w_{HS}) + w_{HS} a_{HSA}(\Pi w_{LS}/w_{HS}) \text{ and} \quad (4.1)'$$

$$c = \Pi w_{LS} a_{LSB}(\Pi w_{LS}/w_{HS}) + w_{HS} a_{HSB}(\Pi w_{LS}/w_{HS}). \quad (4.2)'$$

It is evident that production technologies depend on the relative average factor costs $\Pi w_{LS}/w_{HS}$ when the profit-maximizing choice of offshoring is applied. Since the factor intensities a_{LSA}, a_{HSA}, a_{LSB} and a_{HSB} are all different, (4.1)' and (4.2)' determine Πw_{LS} and w_{HS} independently of φ. Consequently, as φ falls, $\hat{w}_{LS} = -\hat{\Pi}$ and $\hat{w}_{HS} = 0$.

4.2.2.2 Offshoring in a Large Economy

The following sub-subsection addresses the effects of increased offshoring possibilities on a large economy (e.g., the US) which influences world prices. The effects are analyzed with a Heckscher–Ohlin framework including two large economies – a developed and a less-developed country – that export the good which uses the relatively abundant factor more intensively. Under the assumption that the less-developed economy has inferior productivity in all sectors, it has lower wages than the developed country in both sectors. This has been modeled by assuming a Hicks-neutral productivity inferiority of the less-developed country in both sectors.[17] Initially, offshoring of LS-tasks occurs in both sectors Y_A and Y_B. The authors evaluate the effects of increased offshoring possibilities in both sectors due to technological progress.

Besides the *productivity effect* explained above, which acts in favor of labor in the low-skill-intensive sector B, the authors derive a *relative-price effect*. The expansion of production of labor-intensive goods at their initial prices raises the world prices of skill-intensive goods and increases the developed country's terms-of-trade P^{TOT}. This change in relative prices leads to wage increases of high-skilled labor and to wage decreases of less-skilled labor in both countries, which is comparable to the Stolper–Samuelson-effect (see Sect. 4.1.2.2). We have seen that when offshoring costs fall ($\varphi < 0$), there is a productivity effect ($\hat{\Pi} < 0$) and a relative-price effect ($\hat{P}^{\mathrm{TOT}} > 0$), but there is still *no labor-supply effect* ($\gamma_2 = \gamma_4 = 0$) due to imperfect specialization of both economies.

The net effect on the wages of less-skilled workers in the developed country are ambiguous due to the two opposing effects. The relative-price effect might exceed the productivity effect if supply changes translate into large changes in the terms-of-trade and if these changes translate into wage responses. The first transmission channel is facilitated when demands for the goods are inelastic, while the second channel is supported by similar factor intensities of the export sector A and the import-competing sector B. In such a scenario, less-skilled labor might enjoy wage increases. The alternative scenario, with productivity effects dominating, leads to a "win-win" situation contradicting the Stolper–Samuelson theorem (see Sect.

[17] $T^* > 1$ designates the Hicks-neutral productivity inferiority of foreign firms in both sectors. In other words, if a foreign sector produces all tasks at the same factor intensities as the domestic sector, the output would only be $1/T^*$ as great. The zero-profit conditions for the foreign sectors imply:

$$1 = T^* w_{LS}{}^* a_{LSA}(w_{LS}{}^*/w_{HS}{}^*) + T^* w_{HS} a_{HSA}(w_{LS}{}^*/w_{HS}{}^*) \text{ and} \qquad (4.1)''$$

$$c = T^* w_{LS}{}^* a_{LSB}(w_{LS}{}^*/w_{HS}{}^*) + T^* w_{HS} a_{HSB}(w_{LS}{}^*/w_{HS}{}^*). \qquad (4.2)''$$

If one compares (4.1)'and (4.2)' with (4.1)" and (4.2)", incomplete specialization in both countries implies "adjusted factor price equalization", i.e. $w_{LS}\Pi = w_{LS}{}^*T^*$ and $w_{HS} = w_{HS}{}^*T^*$. The production techniques in the home country are based on the relative average factor costs $w_{LS}\Pi/w_{HS}$, whereas in the foreign economy they are based on factor prices $w_{LS}{}^*/w_{HS}{}^*$.

4.1.2.2). The wages of L_{LS} would increase due to the stronger productivity effect, and wages of L_{HS} would rise due to the relative-price effect.

4.2.2.3 Labor-Supply Effect

Increased offshoring of LS-tasks is expected to *expand the world supply of less-skilled labor*, which should influence domestic wages. In the previous models, there has been no such effect ($\gamma_2 = \gamma_4 = 0$), which is a feature of the Heckscher–Ohlin model with incomplete specialization. The expansion does not affect factor prices, because a factor is absorbed by the composition of output in both countries. If the number of factors exceeds the number of produced goods, the labor-supply effect will dominate, which for instance is the case in the specific-factors model with three factors and two goods.

Grossman and Rossi-Hansberg (2006b) present a simpler Heckscher–Ohlin model with two factors that produce only *one good* Y_A. A *small open economy*, that cannot influence relative prices and takes foreign wages as given, is considered. Falling offshoring costs ($\varphi < 0$) lead to the productivity effect described above ($\hat{\Pi} < 0$), but expand also the total number of less-skilled workers ($L_{LS}+L_{LS}{}^*$), while the supply of high-skilled workers is fixed (as HS-tasks are not offshorable). Equation (4.6) with $\hat{P}^{\mathrm{TOT}} = 0$ yields

$$\hat{w}_{LS} = -\hat{\Pi} - \gamma_2 \frac{\mathrm{d}I}{1-I},$$

where the second term on the RHS is the *labor-supply effect*, which can be decomposed into $\gamma_2 > 0$[18] and $\mathrm{d}I/(1-I) < 0$. The wages of L_{LS} fall ($\hat{w}_{LS} < 0$) if offshoring volumes are small initially, but with growing offshoring this effect could be reversed ($\hat{w}_{LS} > 0$). Recall that the *productivity effect* was positive ($\hat{\Pi} < 0$), which is more likely to dominate the negative labor-supply effect if the following three conditions hold. First, the share of L_{LS} in total costs is large; second, the elasticity of substitution between L_{LS} and L_{HS} is high; and third, there is a sufficiently large decline in costs of offshoring. Recall from (4.7) that the wages of L_{HS} do not include a direct productivity effect ($\hat{\Pi} = 0$), but their marginal product rises, since lower offshoring costs and increased trade in LS-tasks raise the intensity of LS-tasks (Grossman and Rossi-Hansberg 2006a, b).

4.2.2.4 Offshoring of Skill-Intensive Tasks

Given empirical evidence, one could also imagine that skill-intensive tasks (HS-tasks) are offshored to a less-developed country. Wages then are still lower for similar tasks in the developed country due to technology lags. Firms are likely to source HS-tasks from less-developed countries with lower wages if trade costs are

[18] Grossman and Rossi-Hansberg (2006b) derive this effect in detail (pp. 22–23).

low. Offshoring HS-tasks involves the productivity effect, relative-price effect, and the labor-supply effect described above. The *productivity effect* reverses to the benefit of L_{HS}. The *relative-price effect* lowers w_{HS}, since an expansion of the high-skill sector reduces its terms-of-trade ($\hat{P}^{\mathrm{TOT}} < 0$). This leads to rising wages of the relatively scarce factor L_{LS} ($\hat{w}_{LS} > 0$), while wages of L_{HS} fall ($\hat{w}_{HS} < 0$). And last, the *labor-supply effect* leads to an increase in high-skilled labor worldwide ($L_{HS} + L_{HS}{}^{*}$) at a given level of L_{LS} in the domestic country, which may increase the wages of L_{LS} and offset the productivity gains of L_{HS}.

The models considered so far all assume that offshoring is only feasible for one factor of production, namely L_{LS} in the first scenario and L_{HS} in the second. But one could also imagine that offshoring is not linked to skill-levels, so that higher offshoring yields productivity effects for all factors, which would constitute a factor-neutral increase in overall productivity. Hence, there would be neither a relative-price effect, nor a factor-supply effect. As a result, wages of all workers would increase (Grossman and Rossi-Hansberg 2006a, b).

Let us summarize the main results of the Grossman and Rossi-Hansberg model (2006a, b). The production process includes a set of intermediate tasks that can be produced by less-skilled or high-skilled labor. In the first scenario, only LS-tasks can be offshored. A rise of offshorability can affect less-skilled labor through three channels: the productivity effect, the labor-supply effect, and the relative-price effect. Grossman and Rossi-Hansberg (2006a, b) distinguish between offshoring in a small economy and in a large economy. A small economy cannot affect world prices. Moreover, changing factor supplies have no influence on factor prices according to the Heckscher–Ohlin model if both goods are produced in the economy. Thus, only the productivity effect remains. Less-skilled labor reaps all the benefits from increased offshoring possibilities in the form of wage increases, whereas high-skilled labor remains uninfluenced.

In the large economy, the authors derive a productivity effect and a relative-price effect. The expansion of production of labor-intensive goods at their initial prices raises the world prices of skill-intensive goods and increases the developed country's terms-of-trade. This change in relative prices leads to wage increases of high-skilled labor and to wage decreases of less-skilled labor in both countries. There is still no labor-supply effect due to imperfect specialization of both economies. The net effect on the wages of less-skilled workers in the developed country is ambiguous due to the two opposing effects.

The so far absent labor-supply effect can be studied in a *small open economy*, characterized by a simple Heckscher–Ohlin world with two factors that produce only *one good.* Besides the positive productivity effect, the authors derive a negative labor supply effect. The net effect is more likely to be positive if the share of less-skilled labor in total costs is large, if the elasticity of substitution between less- and high-skilled labor is high, and if there is a sufficiently large decline in costs of offshoring. Finally, the authors consider a second scenario, namely offshoring of skill-intensive tasks and also address the possibility that offshoring is not linked to skill-levels.

In our opinion, Grossman and Rossi-Hansberg (2006a, b) present a very realistic and flexible offshoring model. The use of the 2 × 2 × 2 Heckscher–Ohlin framework allows us to study the labor market effects on two factors of production. Note, however, that the model additionally allows for tasks that are produced by other factors of production, such as capital or other categories of labor. Another positive aspect is the feature that LS-tasks vary in their offshorability, i.e., some tasks can be relocated more easily than others, which better reflects reality. Breaking up the net effect on wages into the productivity effect, the labor-supply effect, and the relative-price effect allows for a detailed analysis. The Grossman and Rossi-Hansberg (2006a, b) model is even more flexible, since it is not restricted to the Heckscher–Ohlin framework, and is able to model several other scenarios (e.g. offshoring of skill-intensive tasks).

References

Arndt SW (1997) Globalization and the open economy. N Am J Econ Finance 8(1):71–79

Arndt SW (1998) Super-specialization and the gains from trade. Contemp Econ Policy 16(4):480–485

Arndt SW (1999) Globalization and economic development. J Int Trade Econ Dev 8(3):309–318

Baldwin R, Robert-Nicoud F (2007) Offshoring: general equilibrium effects on wages, production and trade. NBER Working Paper, No. 12991, March 2007

Batra RN, Casas FR (1973) Intermediate products and the pure theory of international trade: A Neo-Heckscher–Ohlin framework. Am Econ Rev 63:297–311

Bhagwati J (1968) Distortions and immiserizing growth: a generalization. Rev Econ Stud 35(4): 481–485

Bhagwati J, Panagariya A, Srinivasan TN (1998) Lectures in trade theory. MIT Press, Cambridge, MA

Bhagwati J, Panagariya A, Srinivasan TN (2004) The muddles over outsourcing. J Econ Perspect 18(4):93–114

Deardorff AV (2001a) Fragmentation across cones. In: Arndt S W, Kierzkowski H (eds) Fragmentation: new production patterns in the world economy. Oxford University Press, New York, pp 35–51

Deardorff AV (2001b) Fragmentation in simple trade models. N Am J Econ Finance 12(2): 121–137

Dixit A, Grossman GM (1982) Trade and protection with multi-stage production. Rev Econ Stud 49(4):583–594

Eckel C (2003) Labor market adjustments to globalization: unemployment versus relative wages. N Am J Econ Finance 14(2):173–188

Feenstra RC, Hanson GH (1996) Globalization, outsourcing and wage inequality. Am Econ Rev 86(2):240–245

Findlay R, Jones RW (2000) Factor bias and technical progress. Econ Lett 68(3):303–308

Findlay R, Jones RW (2001) Input trade and the location of production. Am Econ Rev 91(2):29–33

Grossman GM, Rossi-Hansberg E (2006a) The rise of offshoring: it's not wine for cloth anymore. Paper presented at The New Economic Geography: Effects and Policy Implications. Federal Reserve Bank of Kansas City, Jackson Hole, pp 59–102

Grossman GM, Rossi-Hansberg E (2006b) Trading tasks: a simple theory of offshoring. NBER Working Paper, No. 12721, December 2006

Grossman GM, Rossi-Hansberg E (2008) Trading tasks: A simple theory of offshoring, Am Econ Rev 98(5):1978–1997

Heckscher Eli F (1919) The effect of foreign trade on distribution of income. Ekonomisk Tidskrift pp 497–512, reprinted in Ellis HS, Metzler LA (eds) A.E.A. Readings in the theory of international trade, Philadelphia: Blakiston, 1949, pp 272–300

Henneberger F, Graf S, Vocke M (2000) Globalisierung und Arbeitsmarkt: Auslandsinvestitionen von Dienstleistungsunternehmen und ihre Auswirkungen auf die Beschäftigung, Baden-Baden

Jones RW, Kierzkowski H (1990) The role of services in production and international trade: a theoretical framework. In Jones RW, Krueger A (eds) The political economy of international trade. Basil Blackwell, Oxford, pp 31–48

Jones RW, Kierzkowski H (2001) Globalization and the consequences of international fragmentation. In: Dornbusch R, Calvo G, Obstfeld M (eds) Money, factor mobility and trade: essays in honor of Robert A. Mundell. MIT Press, Cambridge, MA, pp 365–383

Jones RW, Kierzkowski H, Leonard G (2002) Fragmentation and intra-industry trade. In: Lloyd PJ, Lee H-HH (eds) Frontiers of research in intra industry trade. Macmillan, London, pp 67–86

Jones RW, Marjit S (1992) International trade and endogenous production structures. In: Neuefrind W, Riezman R (eds) Economic theory and international trade. Springer, Berlin

Kohler W (2004) Aspects of international fragmentation. Rev Int Econ 12(5):793–816

Krugman PR, Obstfeld M (2006) Internationale Wirtschaft, Theorie und Politik der Außenwirtschaft (7th updated ed.)

Lerner AP (1952) Factor prices and international trade. Economica 19(73):1–15

Markusen J (2005) Modeling the offshoring of white-collar services: from comparative advantage to the new theories of trade and FDI. NBER Working Paper, No. 11827, December 2005

Marrewijk CV (2007) International economics – theory, application, and policy. University Press, Oxford

Milberg W, Schöller D (2008) Globalization, offshoring and economic insecurity in industrialized countries. World Economic and Social Survey 2008 Background Paper. Department of Economic and Social Affairs, New York, United Nations

Ohlin B (1933) Interregional and international trade. Harvard University Press, Cambridge, MA

Rodríguez-Clare A (2007) Offshoring in a Ricardian world. NBER Working Paper, No. 13203, June 2007

Rybczynski TE (1955) Factor endowment and relative commodity prices. Economica 22(88): 336–341

Samuelson PA (1948) International trade and the equalization of factor prices. Econ J 58 (230):163–184

Samuelson PA (1949) International factor-price equalisation once again. Econ J 58(234):181–197

Samuelson PA (2004) Where Ricardo and Mill rebut and confirm arguments of mainstream economists supporting clobalization. J Econ Perspect 18(3):135–146

Stolper WF, Samuelson PA (1941) Protection and real wages. Rev Econ Stud 9:58–73

Venables A (1999) Fragmentation and multinational production. Eur Econ Rev 43(4–6):935–945

Wong KY (1995) International trade in goods and factor mobility. MIT Press, Cambridge, MA

Woodland A (1977) Joint outputs, intermediate inputs and international trade theory. Int Econ Rev 18(3):517–533

Yi KM (2003) Can vertical specialization explain the growth of world trade? J Political Econ 111(1):52–102

Yomogida M, Zhao L (2005) The labor market effects of fragmentation, outsourcing and immigration: two sides of the same story? March 2005. Hitotsubashi University and Kobe University

Chapter 5
Labor Market Effects of Services Offshoring: Empirical Evidence

Abstract This fifth chapter constitutes the major contribution of this work. It comprises a collection of three empirical studies, which estimate the effects of services offshoring on productivity (Sect. 5.1), labor demand (Sect. 5.2), and the relative demand for less-skilled labor (Sect. 5.3) in German manufacturing. The formulation of the hypotheses is based on the underlying theoretical models. Our econometric estimations use both unrevised (1991–2000) and revised (1995–2004) input–output data. We use two different estimation methods for all of our studies, which increases the reliability of our estimation results. Services offshoring had a positive effect on total factor productivity and labor productivity in German manufacturing, while it affected labor demand negatively. Both effects were stronger between 1995 and 2004. The overall results suggest that labor demand decreased, because labor-reducing productivity and substitution effects dominated labor-augmenting scale effects from services offshoring. Moreover, services offshoring significantly reduced the relative demand for less-skilled labor from 1991 to 2000. Interestingly, the results for 1995 to 2004 indicate a relative demand shift away from high-skilled labor, mitigating the declining wage share of less-skilled labor.

Introduction

Trade liberalization is traditionally understood to create winners and losers, and offshoring is no different in this regard, although some of the mechanisms and some of the distributional effects may be new. Figure 5.1 depicts the variety of ways that offshoring impacts productivity and the labor market. Productivity gains from offshoring can occur through various channels, including static efficiency gains, restructuring measures, learning externalities, and variety effects (see Sect. 5.1.1.2). The effects of offshoring on TFP and LP in German manufacturing are measured in Sect. 5.1.

D. Winkler, *Services Offshoring and its Impact on the Labor Market*,
Contributions to Economics, DOI: 10.1007/978-3-7908-2199-4_5,

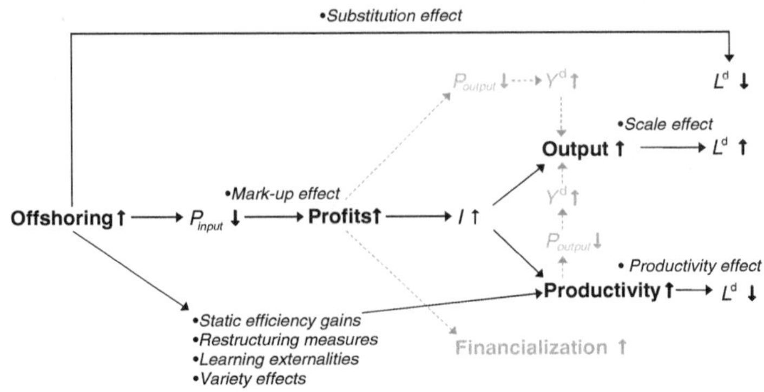

Fig. 5.1 Gains and losses from offshoring
Source: Taken and modified from Milberg and Schöller (2008). NB: Y^{d} = demand for output, I = investments, L^{d} = demand for labor

Labor demand is influenced by at least three mechanisms. Offshoring lowers prices of inputs which should raise profits (*mark-up effect*). If higher profit margins lead to more investment or lower output prices, the demand for inputs and output and thus the demand for labor is expected to increase (*scale effect*). Weakening labor demand results from the direct replacement of domestic by foreign labor (*substitution effect*) and the *productivity effect* which reduces the demand for labor per unit of output. Since the theoretical net effect is not clear in general, the econometric analysis in section 5.2 gives specific insights for the German manufacturing sectors.

Not all of the rise in profits is recycled into investment and labor demand, and this constitutes an important leakage in the system. Corporations may also choose to return their net gains to shareholders, and this has occurred through higher dividend payments and share buybacks. This strategy of *financialization* of the nonfinancial corporate sector also includes the purchase of financial assets and the acquisition of other corporations (M&As). Financialization represents a drain on labor demand and may play an important role in the link between offshoring and labor market effects (Milberg and Schöller 2008).

However, Fig. 5.2 indicates that financialization, measured as interests and dividends in value added as proposed by Stockhammer (2004), shows a rather negative trend in Germany during the last decade. A downward trend can also be observed in Denmark and Japan from the mid 1990s onwards, while financialization of nonfinancial business remained more or less constant in France and the UK in this period. Since German firms did not seem to follow the strategy of financialization from 1995 onwards, we believe that our empirical model in Sect. 5.2 adequately captures the effects of offshoring on labor demand.

Figure 5.1 is a simplification that considers all labor as one type. Thus, in addition to the effect of offshoring on productivity and employment, economic research has also considered the effect of offshoring on different types of labor, e.g., high-skilled and less-skilled labor, through the Stolper–Samuelson effect.

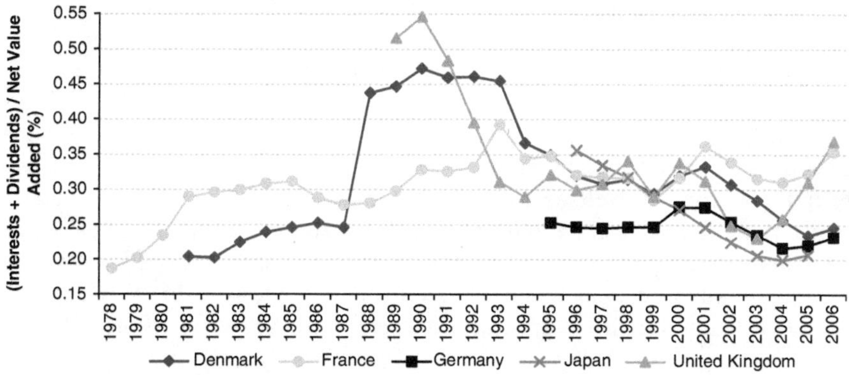

Fig. 5.2 Financialization of nonfinancial businesses
Source: own calculations. Data: OECD National accounts statistics, detailed nonfinancial accounts

This issue is addressed in Sect. 5.3, where we estimate the impact of offshoring on the relative demand for less-skilled labor.

There are four main caveats regarding studies that relate labor market effects to services offshoring. First, long-term effects cannot be predicted yet because of the novelty of the phenomenon. Second, the relationship between offshoring and labor demand is complex as it links foreign trade, domestic production, and gross fixed investment, which can provoke direct and indirect as well as static and dynamic effects (see Fig. 5.1). Hence, the sign and extent of offshoring in existing studies should not be considered universally valid (Tüselmann 1998). Third, the underlying offshoring motives only approximate the labor market effects, since the "real" cause for the domestic employment reduction in the case of cost-oriented motives is not offshoring, but high labor costs. Offshoring then is a symptom of, rather than a reason for, domestic labor market problems (Roling 1999). Fourth, the main driver of services offshoring is not clearly determinate. The increase in services offshoring can be traced back to growing services trade as a consequence of globalization, but also to technological progress (ICTs).

Despite the first caveat, our use of recently published input–output data for the period 1995–2004 strongly improves the predictability of offshoring-induced labor market effects in the (near) future. Compared to many other empirical studies for the 1990s, this period already includes newer developments in ICTs. Concerning the second caveat, we believe we have identified the main channels through which offshoring can affect productivity and labor demand (see Fig. 5.1). Furthermore, part of the potential dynamic effects can be addressed by using newer estimation methods. However, we should bear the third and fourth caveat in mind when discussing possible implications and economic policy recommendations.

All three studies follow the same structure. Each of the studies starts with the "basics of the empirical analysis," which first presents the underlying theoretical model, deduces the empirical model used for our estimations, formulates the hypothesis from the model, and explains the data used in our regressions. Following the basics, the estimations are subdivided into two parts: estimations using unrevised input–output data, which cover the period from 1991 to 2000, and estimations using revised input–output data for the years 1995 through 2004. As mentioned above, the two datasets are not comparable, which makes it essential to differentiate between them. We decided to include both kinds of estimations in order to cover a longer time series as well as to show differences and similarities between the periods. Both kinds of estimations begin with a preliminary analysis of the empirical relationship between services offshoring intensity and the dependent variable productivity, labor demand or the relative demand for less-skilled labor. We then continue with the empirical specification before we move on to the estimation results.

5.1 Services Offshoring and Its Impact on Productivity in Germany

5.1.1 *Basics of the Empirical Analysis*

5.1.1.1 Theoretical and Empirical Model

A firm's linearly homogeneous production function F with constant returns to scale is described as follows:

$$Y = F(L, K, S, M, T), \tag{5.1}$$

$$\frac{\partial F}{\partial x_1} > 0, \quad \frac{\partial^2 F}{\partial x_1^2} < 0, \quad \frac{\partial^2 F}{\partial x_1 \partial x_2} > 0 \text{ with } x_1,\ x_2 = L, K, S, M, T,$$

where labor L, capital K, intermediate services S, intermediate materials M, and technology T are the input factors.[1]

The *technology shifter* $T = T(\mathrm{OSS}, \mathrm{OSM}, \mathrm{DOS}, \mathrm{DOM}, \mathrm{RD}/Y)$ is a function of services and materials offshoring OSS and OSM, domestic services and materials outsourcing DOS and DOM, and R&D-intensity RD/Y. T represents a change of the production function due to international trade (offshoring), domestic outsourcing, and technological progress.

[1]Due to the homogeneity assumption multiplying the inputs with a constant λ ($\lambda = 2, 3, \ldots$) augments production by λ^z where z is constant and positive: $\lambda^z Y = F(\lambda L, \lambda K, \lambda S, \lambda M, \lambda T)$.

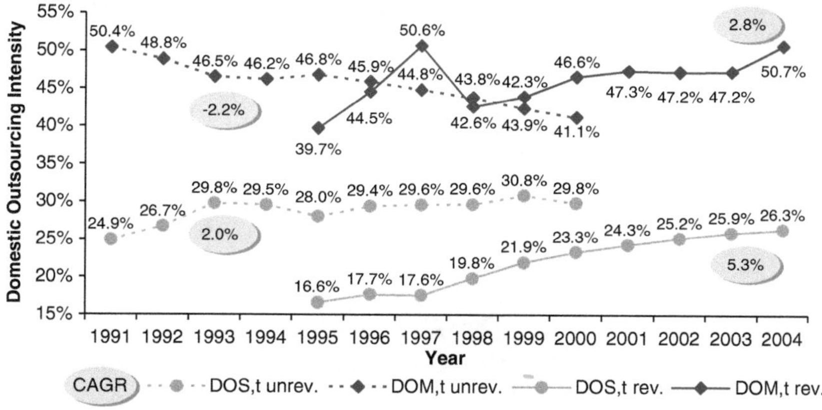

Fig. 5.3 Domestic outsourcing intensity of intermediate inputs in Germany
Source: own calculations. Data: Federal Statistical Office Germany, unrevised (1991–2000) and revised input–output tables (1995–2004)

The domestic services outsourcing intensity DOS is calculated as follows:

$$\mathrm{DOS}_{ist} = \frac{(\text{domestic input purchases of service } s \text{ by sector } i)_t}{(\text{total non-energy inputs used by sector } i)_t}. \quad (5.2)$$

The domestic services outsourcing intensity DOS_{it} for sector i at time t is calculated by taking the sum over all DOS_{ist}: $\mathrm{DOS}_{it} = \Sigma_s \mathrm{DOS}_{ist}$. Summing DOS_{it} over all sectors i, weighted by sectoral total nonenergy inputs INP, yields the average domestic services outsourcing intensity $\mathrm{DOS}_t = \Sigma_i \mathrm{DOS}_{it} \cdot (\mathrm{INP}_{it}/\mathrm{INP}_t)$. The domestic materials outsourcing intensities DOM_t are calculated analogously.

The *development of domestic outsourcing intensities* in Germany is plotted in Fig. 5.3. It is evident that the overall domestic outsourcing intensities are much higher than the offshoring intensities (see Fig. 3.2). The dashed line represents the development between 1991 and 2000 using unrevised input–output data, whereas the continuous line illustrates the development between 1995 and 2004 using revised input–output data. The overall *domestic services outsourcing intensity* increased by on average 2.0% per year from 24.9% in 1991 to 29.8% in 2000. Between 1995 and 2004, domestic services outsourcing grew stronger by on average 5.3% p.a. from 16.6 to 26.3%. The overall *domestic materials outsourcing intensity* fell drastically from 50.4% in 1991 to 41.1% in 2000 with a negative average annual growth rate of −2.2%. Using the revised input–output data, however, shows a growing intensity from 39.7% in 1995 to 50.7% in 2004, which yields a positive CAGR of 2.8%. To conclude, domestic services outsourcing seems to have increased over the last one and a half decades, whereas the trend for domestic materials outsourcing is not clear.

According to the *Solow growth decomposition,* output growth can be attributed the growth rates of the input factors (e.g., L, K, S, and M) and the growth rate of an unexplained residual called *total factor productivity*. Besides the rate of technology, efficiency is considered the most important part of TFP. Both are included in the technology shifter T, since offshoring, outsourcing, and R&D-intensity not only reflect technological progress, but are also expected to increase efficiency.

Equation (5.1) can be written in log-linear form:

$$\begin{aligned}\ln Y_{it} &= \alpha_0 + \alpha_1 \ln L_{it} + \alpha_2 \ln K_{it} + \alpha_3 \ln S_{it} + \alpha_4 \ln M_{it} \\ &+ \beta_1 \ln \mathrm{OSS}_{it} + \beta_2 \ln \mathrm{OSM}_{it} + \beta_3 \ln \mathrm{DOS}_{it} + \beta_4 \ln \mathrm{DOM}_{it} \\ &+ \beta_5 \ln(\mathrm{RD}_{\mathrm{it}}/Y_{it}) + \delta_t D_t + \varepsilon_{it},\end{aligned} \tag{5.3}$$

where i designates the sector dimension, t the time dimension, D_t year fixed effects (such as common shocks influencing all sectors), and ε_{it} a random error term.

As an *alternative* to the model above, we could postulate the following value added equation:

$$(Y - S - M) = \mathrm{VA}/L = G(L, K, T), \tag{5.4}$$

$$\frac{\partial G}{\partial x_1} > 0, \ \frac{\partial^2 G}{\partial x_1^2} < 0, \ \frac{\partial^2 G}{\partial x_1 \partial x_2} > 0 \text{ with } x_1, x_2 = L, K, T,$$

where labor L, capital K, intermediate services S, intermediate materials M, and technology T are the input factors. $\mathrm{VA} = (Y - S - M)$ designates the value added and is the difference between output and service and material inputs. *Labor productivity* is calculated by dividing value added by labor input L. Thus, the modified empirical estimation equation in the log-linear form is:

$$\begin{aligned}\ln(\mathrm{VA}/L)_{it} &= \alpha_0 + \alpha_1 \ln(K/L)_{it} + \beta_1 \ln \mathrm{OSS}_{it} + \beta_2 \ln \mathrm{OSM}_{it} \\ &+ \beta_3 \ln \mathrm{DOS}_{it} + \beta_4 \ln \mathrm{DOM}_{it} + \beta_5 \ln(\mathrm{RD}_{\mathrm{it}}/Y_{it}) + \delta_t D_t + \varepsilon_{it},\end{aligned} \tag{5.5}$$

where K/L denotes capital intensity.

5.1.1.2 Hypothesis

Offshoring and domestic outsourcing are expected to influence *output Y* positively via a rise in T with $\beta_1 > 0$, $\beta_2 > 0$, $\beta_3 > 0$, and $\beta_4 > 0$ in (5.3). Offshoring and domestic outsourcing can increase T through at least four channels. First, a *static efficiency gain* occurs, when firms offshore or outsource less efficient parts of the value chain, which leads to higher productivity of remaining activities. Second, when the firm's offshoring or domestic outsourcing decision is combined with *restructuring measures* expanding its technology frontier, the remaining labor may become more efficient. This might rather be the case for services than for materials. Third, *learning externalities* could arise when purchased services improve the productivity of the workers. This would imply that domestic workers increase productivity due to learning externalities from other firms. And fourth, *variety effects* could raise productivity when various new service and material inputs are used (Amiti and Wei 2006).

A higher R&D-intensity is expected to increase output via an increase in T with $\beta_5 > 0$. Despite the definitional relationship between output and R&D intensity, RD/Y should be included as it controls for the variation in the R&D-intensity of Y, whereas the remaining output variation is controlled by the other exogenous variables. The input factors labor, capital, services, and materials are also expected to influence output positively with $\alpha_1 > 0$, $\alpha_2 > 0$, $\alpha_3 > 0$ and $\alpha_4 > 0$.

Concerning *labor productivity* in (5.5), all coefficients are expected to be positive according to our theoretical predictions. Labor productivity could also be measured as output per labor unit, which would be Y/L. This measure has the disadvantage that offshoring (or domestic outsourcing) necessarily increases labor productivity holding all other variables constant, because less labor is required for the same amount of produced output at time t. Offshoring (or domestic outsourcing) leads to the substitution of domestic labor for purchased service and material inputs (*input substitution effect*), which reflects the substitution of domestic labor for labor in another country or another sector producing these inputs (Houseman 2006). Therefore, value added per labor unit is a more appropriate measure, since the increase in purchased service and material inputs due to offshoring (or domestic outsourcing) will also be reflected in a smaller numerator. Hence, (5.5) only measures productivity effects that go beyond the above-described input substitution effect.

5.1.1.3 Data

Output data Y are often mapped by gross output or value added in the empirical literature. Since the input factors in our production function are not only labor and capital, but also service and material inputs, gross output seems to be a more appropriate measure (for a short discussion, see Strauss-Kahn 2003). Gross output is also derived from the input–output tables. We calculated real output using sectoral producer price indices from the German Federal Statistical Office.[2]

[2]Producer price indices are available at several aggregation levels (28, 107 and 225 sectors). Since some producer prices at the required input–output aggregation level were not available, we used producer prices of more disaggregated sectors (within the same industry) as a proxy, because similar price trends can be expected there. The same procedure was also applied in a few cases where the time series was incomplete.

Labor input L is mapped using sectoral employment data from the input–output tables. The number of employees is preferred to the number of total employment. The latter considers all persons engaged in the domestic production of a country, whereas the former excludes self-employed and unpaid family workers and better reflects the workforce of companies that is exposed to layoffs due to offshoring.

Capital input K is matched using the *sectoral net capital stock* at 2000 prices from the German Federal Statistical office. Net capital stock instead of gross capital stock is chosen, as the latter does not account for depreciation, which in fact, does represent at least two difficulties. First, depreciation reflects physical deterioration and efficiency losses, and second, different rates of depreciation are applied to different types of capital (Hijzen et al. 2005).[3] Some sectors only have data available at a more aggregated level. Therefore, disaggregation is done by weighting the aggregated net capital stock data by the sectoral output shares to fit the input–output aggregation.[4] *Capital intensity K/L* is calculated dividing sectoral capital input *K* by sectoral labor input *L*. Total sectoral *service and material inputs* comprise both domestically produced and imported inputs and are derived from the input–output tables of the German Federal Statistical office. We calculated real service and material inputs using the above-mentioned sectoral producer price indices as deflators.

Input–output data at current prices are used to calculate *offshoring intensities* OSS and OSM as well as *domestic outsourcing intensities* DOS and DOM. Deflation of the numerator and the denominator is not necessary, since ratios are calculated. German input–output tables are disaggregated to 71 sectors following the three-digit and, for some sectors, the four-digit NACE Rev. 1.1 classification (German Federal Statistical Office: unrevised input–output tables 1991–2000 and revised input–output tables 1995–2004, both in current prices; Series 18, No. 2).

Due to the input–output data revision of 2005, our empirical analysis differentiates between the unrevised data from 1991 to 2000 and the revised data between 1995 and 2004. *R&D expenditures* are retrieved from the OECD STAN Industrial Database (ANBERD, R&D Expenditure in Industry (ISIC Rev.3), Vol. 2006 release 01). We cumulated R&D expenditures to obtain R&D stocks and divided R&D stocks by gross output to calculate R&D-intensities.

---

[3]Besides Hijzen et al. (2005), other authors, e.g., Falk and Koebel (2002), Strauss-Kahn (2003) or Geishecker (2006), also used net capital stocks when measuring labor demand equations, whereas the OECD (2007) study uses the gross fixed capital formation due to data limitations. Other studies do not offer further information on the capital used.

[4]For instance, no sectoral data are available for "food products" and "beverages," but only for the aggregated sector "food products and beverages". Since a similar productivity in both sectors can be assumed, we multiplied the net capital stock of the aggregated sector with the respective individual output shares to obtain the net capital stock for each sector. This procedure was done in the following eight sectors, where the net capital stock data of the German national accounts (VGR) have aggregated levels: 1–2, 8–9, 10–11, 15–16, 17–18, 19–21, 32–33, and 35–36.

5.1.2 Estimations with Unrevised Input–Output Data: 1991–2000

5.1.2.1 Preliminary Analysis

Figure 5.4 gives an initial look at the relationship between services offshoring and TFP. The scatter plot shows *German services offshoring intensity versus output growth rates* between 1991 and 2000. All 43 sectors as described in Sect. 3.1.3 in Chap. 3 are taken into account using the $OSS_i(a)$ measures. Thirty-one sectors show a positive output growth ranging from 1.6% (fabricated metal products) to 144% (recycling) from 1991 to 2000. More than half the sectors, namely 23, are placed in the first quadrant and seven in the third quadrant suggesting a positive relationship between services offshoring growth and output growth. Five sectors fall in the second quadrant and eight sectors in the fourth quadrant, as would be characteristic of a negative relationship between both variables.

In a second step, the ten sectors with the strongest services offshoring growth between 1991 and 2000 are ranked in Table 5.1, and their OSS growth rates are compared with output growth rates. Eight of these sectors had positive output growth rates over the respective period. Only tobacco and beverages experienced negative growth. The results indicate a possibly positive relationship between services offshoring and output growth rates.

5.1.2.2 Estimation Results: Total Factor Productivity

The following section measures the impact of services and materials offshoring on TFP and LP in German manufacturing between 1991 and 2000. Since we have both a cross-section and a time-series, we use a panel regression analysis. In the presence

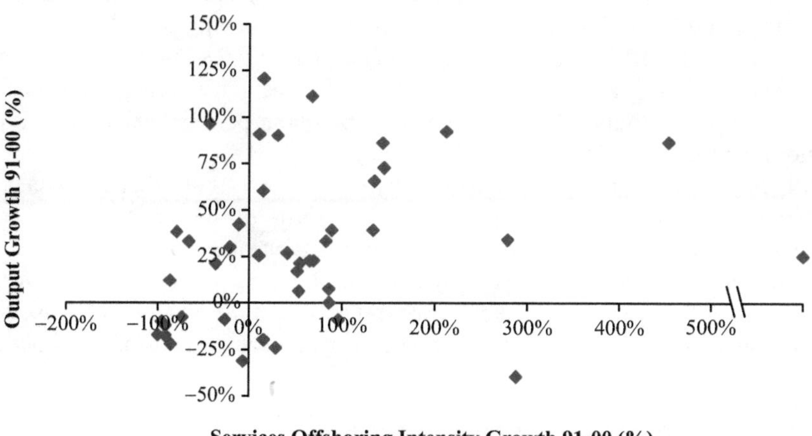

Fig. 5.4 German services offshoring intensity and output growth (1991–2000)
Source: own calculations. Data: Federal Statistical Office Germany

Table 5.1 Ranking of OSS and output growth in Germany (1991–2000)

Ranking of services offshoring growth	Services offshoring intensity growth		Output growth	
Sector	%	Rank	%	Rank
Top Ten				
Computer and related activities	1266.8%	1	44.7%	13
Office, accounting, and computing machinery	453.4%	2	74.6%	9
Tobacco products	288.0%	3	−6.9%	39
Other business activities	278.5%	4	66.9%	10
Research and development	212.3%	5	104.1%	4
Chemicals excluding pharmaceuticals	144.9%	6	85.7%	6
Metal castings	143.3%	7	87.2%	5
Other transport equipment	134.7%	8	23.5%	20
Pharmaceuticals	133.2%	9	32.0%	16
Beverages	96.1%	10	−6.8%	38

Source: own calculations. Data: Federal Statistical Office Germany

of unobserved time-constant sector-specific effects c_i, one considers the following panel data model $y_{it} = \alpha + \beta x_{it} + c_i + \varepsilon_{it}$. If c_i is correlated with some explanatory variables x_{it}, usual pooled OLS regression would be biased and inconsistent. Transforming the pooled OLS using first differences or the fixed effects estimator removes these time-invariant effects c_i. Either method allows for correlation between c_i and some x_{it}, and c_i is estimated as part of the intercept $(\alpha + c_i)$. Therefore, we use the consistent *fixed effects estimator* in the following estimations.[5]

Productivity effects are not always instantaneous. The input factors labor, capital, services, and materials can all affect output and productivity in the subsequent period. This can, for instance, be the case when a project starts in $t = 1$, but only finishes in $t = 2$. If the output of the project enters the balance sheet only in $t = 2$, the inputs used in $t = 1$ influence output in $t = 2$. Therefore, we add *one-period lags* of L, K, S, and M in some of the subsequent specifications. Since technology could also influence productivity in the following period, we add one-period lags of the offshoring, domestic outsourcing, and R&D-intensity variables. This might be the case when the adoption of a new technology translates in measurable productivity effects only in the subsequent period, because employees are not immediately able to use the technology.

All estimations produce standard errors robust to both heteroscedasticity (Huber-White sandwich estimators) and any form of intracluster correlation. Since the clusters are sectors in our case, we correct for intrasector serial correlation and any other correlation provoked by common intrasector shocks. Moreover, all specifications integrate year fixed effects D_t, i.e., time-specific cross-sectoral effects, such as common shocks influencing all sectors at time t. Since the

[5]We dropped the identified outliers "pharmaceuticals" and "office, accounting and computer machinery" due to extremely high services offshoring intensities, which leads to a total of 34 manufacturing sectors.

offshoring variables might be swelled due to other omitted correlated variables, some specifications include the share of total imports in total output as an additional control variable as suggested by Amiti and Wei (2006).

The results of the *fixed effects estimator* are shown in Table 5.2. Columns 1–4 only consider instantaneous productivity effects. Labor, capital, services, and materials all have a positive effect on real output, which is significant in most specifications. To fix ideas, column 1 only considers the offshoring variables OSS and OSM. Services offshoring has a positive effect on real output which narrowly misses the 10% significance level. Materials offshoring shows an insignificantly positive coefficient. Column 2 only considers the domestic outsourcing variables DOS and DOM. Both have a negative effect on real output, which is only significant for domestic services outsourcing. Column 3 includes all technology variables simultaneously. The previous effects remain the same with regard to their coefficient signs except for materials offshoring, which is probably due to the high negative colinearity with DOS averaging around 78%. R&D intensity has a negative impact on real output being highly significant. Column 4 considers the additional control variable import share, which has a negative and almost significant effect. All other technology variables confirm the previous pattern except for materials offshoring, which might be due to the strong positive collinearity with import shares of around 74%. We will also use the following order of specifications for our other estimations in this section.

Columns 5–8 also include one-period lags. Note that even if many individual effects are insignificant in columns 5–8, the F-tests reject the null hypothesis of no joint significance in most cases. The trend described above can be confirmed for all variables except for OSM and DOS. OSM now indicates a negative influence on real output, while DOS has an overall positive effect in columns 6 and 7, which turns negative in column 8. The switching signs could be due to the above-mentioned negative *collinearity* between DOS and OSM. In the case of imperfect collinearity, the estimators are still efficient and unbiased. The problem is that collinearity creates large estimator variances and hence large confidence intervals. In the case of collinearity, the joint influence of the (inter-)correlated independent variables on the dependent variable is given, but the estimation of the individual coefficients is difficult to obtain. This is not due to a misspecification of the model, but due to insufficient information in the data. Note that OSS, OSM, DOM, and R&D-intensity all show a smaller overall coefficient when import shares are included in column 8 compared to column 7.

To sum up, services offshoring shows a significantly positive impact on real output in all specifications, whereas materials offshoring (column 8), domestic services outsourcing (columns 1–4 and 8) and domestic materials outsourcing (columns 6–8), however, have a significantly negative effect on productivity.

The fixed effects estimator is only valid when strict exogeneity of the explanatory variables is assumed. It is plausible that more productive sectors aim at increasing their technology shifter and thus self-select into offshoring (Amiti and Wei 2006), domestic outsourcing, and/or R&D. Similarly, less productive sectors might hope to benefit from offshoring, domestic outsourcing, and/or R&D in order

Table 5.2 TFP – Fixed effects estimator (1991–2000)

Dependent variable: $\ln Y_t$

	Fixed effects estimator: instantaneous effects[a]				Fixed effects estimator: one-period lags[a]			
	(1)	(2)	(3)	(4)	(5)	(6)	(7)	(8)
$\ln L_t$	0.2501***	0.2624**	0.2103**	0.1485**	0.4610***	0.3709**	0.2397***	0.1937***
	(0.010)	(0.015)	(0.017)	(0.037)	(0.009)	(0.022)	(0.006)	(0.001)
$\ln L_{t-1}$					−0.3446**	−0.1532	−0.0693	−0.0182
					(0.022)	(0.284)	(0.439)	(0.770)
$\ln K_t$	0.1425	0.2058**	0.0846	0.0181	0.3592	0.4334*	0.2035	0.2069*
	(0.211)	(0.048)	(0.322)	(0.868)	(0.162)	(0.086)	(0.142)	(0.052)
$\ln K_{t-1}$					−0.1253	−0.1821	0.096	−0.0493
					(0.697)	(0.565)	(0.656)	(0.725)
$\ln S_t$	0.3487**	0.4984***	0.3523*	0.5917***	0.047	0.1173	−0.1813	−0.0003
	(0.027)	(0.002)	(0.055)	(0.000)	(0.756)	(0.542)	(0.296)	(0.997)
$\ln S_{t-1}$					−0.0076	−0.0786	0.0406	0.2492***
					(0.950)	(0.516)	(0.782)	(0.003)
$\ln M_t$	0.1825**	0.0819*	0.1313***	0.0537	0.4861***	0.4834***	0.4683***	0.3255***
	(0.028)	(0.077)	(0.007)	(0.179)	(0.000)	(0.002)	(0.003)	(0.000)
$\ln M_{t-1}$					−0.0589*	−0.0137	0.0701***	0.0385*
					(0.060)	(0.574)	(0.007)	(0.068)
$\ln OSS_t$	0.0171		0.0071	0.009	−0.0016		0.0181*	0.0164*
	(0.102)		(0.537)	(0.343)	(0.867)		(0.077)	(0.084)
$\ln OSS_{t-1}$					0.0210***		0.0070	0.0014
					(0.009)		(0.418)	(0.841)
$\ln OSM_t$	0.036		−0.0918	0.0269	−0.007		−0.1692	−0.0628**
	(0.613)		(0.420)	(0.652)	(0.917)		(0.124)	(0.037)
$\ln OSM_{t-1}$					−0.0502		−0.051	−0.0532*
					(0.511)		(0.272)	(0.078)

(*continued*)

Table 5.2 (continued)

Dependent variable: $\ln Y_t$

	Fixed effects estimator: instantaneous effects[a]				Fixed effects estimator: one-period lags[a]			
	(1)	(2)	(3)	(4)	(5)	(6)	(7)	(8)
$\ln DOS_t$		−0.3834***	−0.3151**	−0.5438***		−0.2178	0.2202	0.0390
		(0.004)	(0.044)	(0.000)		(0.309)	(0.155)	(0.700)
$\ln DOS_{t-1}$						0.2894**	0.0121	−0.1528*
						(0.040)	(0.933)	(0.093)
$\ln DOM_t$		−0.1911	−0.3548	−0.1204		−0.3095**	−0.2783	−0.1242*
		(0.214)	(0.140)	(0.219)		(0.016)	(0.159)	(0.065)
$\ln DOM_{t-1}$						0.1088	−0.2507***	−.1739***
						(0.326)	(0.001)	(0.001)
$\ln(RD/Y)_t$			−0.2227***	−0.1760**			−0.5931***	−0.5122***
			(0.004)	(0.010)			(0.000)	(0.000)
$\ln(RD/Y)_{t-1}$							0.4202***	0.3998***
							(0.000)	(0.000)
$\ln(IM/Y)_t$				−0.0667				−0.0932**
				(0.103)				(0.011)
$\ln(IM/Y)_{t-1}$								0.0756***
								(0.001)
Fixed year effects	Yes	Yes	Yes	Yes	Yes	Yes	Yes	Yes
Joint significance:								
$\ln L_t + \ln L_{t-1} = 0$					$p>F = 0.0326$	$p>F = 0.0443$	$p>F = 0.0063$	$p>F = 0.0000$
$\ln K_t + \ln K_{t-1} = 0$					$p>F = 0.0159$	$p>F = 0.0088$	$p>F = 0.0000$	p>F = 0.0239
$\ln S_t + \ln S_{t-1} = 0$					$p>F = 0.9393$	$p>F = 0.4576$	$p>F = 0.1363$	$p>F = 0.0022$
$\ln M_t + \ln M_{t-1} = 0$					$p>F = 0.0000$	$p>F = 0.0067$	$p>F = 0.0034$	$p>F = 0.0000$
$\ln OSS_t + \ln OSS_{t-1} = 0$					$p>F = 0.0102$		p>F = 0.0810	$p>F = 0.0176$
$\ln OSM_t + \ln OSM_{t-1} = 0$					$p>F = 0.7483$		$p>F = 0.2637$	$p>F = 0.0417$
$\ln DOS_t + \ln DOS_{t-1} = 0$						$p>F = 0.1015$	$p>F = 0.2878$	$p>F = 0.1527$

(*continued*)

Table 5.2 (continued)

Dependent variable: $\ln Y_t$	Fixed effects estimator: instantaneous effects[a]				Fixed effects estimator: one-period lags[a]			
	(1)	(2)	(3)	(4)	(5)	(6)	(7)	(8)
$\ln DOM_t + \ln DOM_{t-1} = 0$						$p > F = 0.0229$	$p > F = 0.0046$	$p > F = 0.0000$
$\ln(RD/Y)_t + \ln(RD/Y)_{t-1} = 0$							$p > F = 0.0000$	$p > F = 0.0000$
$\ln(IM/Y)_t + \ln(IM/Y)_{t-1} = 0$								$p > F = 0.0030$
AIC	−733.6	−795.9	−837.7	−924.3	−705.7	−735.5	−882.5	−1,040.4
Observations	334	340	326	292	300	306	292	261
R-squared (within)	0.61	0.66	0.72	0.85	0.67	0.68	0.83	0.94

Source: own calculations

$p^* < 0.1$, $p^{**} < 0.05$, $p^{***} < 0.001$ (*p* values in parentheses)

[a]All estimations without the outliers "pharmaceuticals" and "office, accounting and computer machinery"

to increase their technology shifter. Therefore, the *instrumental variables* (IV) *two-stage least squares (2SLS) fixed effects estimator* is applied to control for potential endogeneity of $\ln OSS_t$, $\ln OSM_t$, $\ln DOS_t$, $\ln DOM_t$, and $\ln(RD/Y)_t$ using their first three lags as instruments. The results are shown in Table 5.3. Columns 1–4 only include instantaneous effects of the exogenous input factors.

The instantaneous effects of labor, capital, and materials are strongly positive and significant. Services, however, have a negative coefficient sign in columns 1–3, which turns positive in column 4 when import shares are integrated. Services offshoring has a positive effect, which is highly significant in column 1, almost significant in column 3, and insignificant in column 4. Materials offshoring influences productivity negatively, being significant in column 3. Domestic services outsourcing has a positive effect in columns 2 and 3, which turns negative in column 4, possibly due to negative collinearity with import share. Domestic materials outsourcing and R&D-intensity have a significantly negative impact.

Columns 5–8 also add one-period lags. The trends described above can be confirmed. However, the specification in column 5 rejects the null hypothesis that the instruments are valid instruments and that the excluded instruments are correctly excluded (Hansen J statistic), while the estimated covariance matrix of moment conditions are not of full rank in column 8. Columns 5 and 8 should thus be interpreted with caution. The results suggest an overall positive impact of services offshoring and domestic services outsourcing being significant for services offshoring, whereas the overall impact of materials offshoring and domestic materials outsourcing is significantly negative. Again, the effects of OSS, OSM, DOM, and R&D-intensity are smaller when import shares are included.

Before turning to the effects on labor productivity, the significant results of services offshoring should be interpreted. We only consider specifications where all technology variables are included. Services offshoring shows overall positive coefficients of 0.0178 (Table 5.2, column 8) and 0.0436 (Table 5.3, column 7). Services offshoring grew by on average 6.0% p.a. in the manufacturing sectors, from 0.43 to 0.74%. Holding all other variables constant, services offshoring increased real output by on average 0.11 to 0.26% per year and 1.2 and 3.0% over the whole period.

5.1.2.3 Estimation Results: Labor Productivity

We address the potential endogeneity of labor, services, and materials by choosing LP as the dependent variable as postulated in equation (5.5). The results of the *fixed effects estimators* are tabulated in Table 5.4, where columns 1–4 only consider instantaneous effects. Capital intensity has a positive and significant impact on value added per labor. Services offshoring affects LP positively, being significant in columns 1 and 4, whereas materials offshoring shows a positive coefficient in column 1, but a negative one in columns 3 and 4, which again might be due to strong negative collinearity with DOS. Domestic services outsourcing, domestic materials outsourcing, and R&D intensity all show a negative influence on LP being

Table 5.3 TFP – IV 2SLS fixed effects estimator(1991–2000)

	Dependent variable: $\ln Y_t$							
	IV 2SLS fixed effects: instantaneous effects[a]				IV 2SLS fixed effects: one-period lags[a]			
	(1)	(2)	(3)	(4)	(5)	(6)	(7)	(8)
$\ln L_t$	0.2076**	0.4268***	0.3270***	0.2402***	0.5072***	0.4364**	0.3164**	0.2727***
	(0.014)	(0.009)	(0.001)	(0.003)	(0.005)	(0.011)	(0.015)	(0.007)
$\ln L_{t-1}$					−0.4018**	−0.156	−0.126	0.0107
					(0.043)	(0.383)	(0.376)	(0.932)
$\ln K_t$	0.191	0.4418**	0.3164	0.1046	0.3269	0.4469	0.3671*	0.2710
	(0.135)	(0.043)	(0.114)	(0.338)	(0.324)	(0.120)	(0.088)	(0.223)
$\ln K_{t-1}$					−0.1210	−0.1103	−0.1429	−0.3231
					(0.742)	(0.752)	(0.597)	(0.193)
$\ln S_t$	−0.1702	−1.1718	−1.7253**	0.2029	−0.2165	−0.3392	−0.9315*	−0.0538
	(0.314)	(0.160)	(0.024)	(0.410)	(0.123)	(0.405)	(0.052)	(0.760)
$\ln S_{t-1}$					0.1542	0.0878	0.1911**	0.2482***
					(0.336)	(0.568)	(0.047)	(0.001)
$\ln M_t$	0.5549***	1.4687**	1.8237***	0.3442*	0.6933***	0.8084**	1.2568***	0.5252***
	(0.000)	(0.022)	(0.004)	(0.060)	(0.000)	(0.019)	(0.002)	(0.000)
$\ln M_{t-1}$					−0.2528***	−0.1684**	−0.3090**	−0.1313***
					(0.008)	(0.038)	(0.012)	(0.008)
$\ln OSS_t$	0.0530***		0.0622	0.0028	0.0492***		0.0436*	0.0158*
	(0.002)		(0.120)	(0.830)	(0.003)		(0.071)	(0.092)
$\ln OSM_t$	−0.1727		−0.6815***	−0.1043	−0.2811		−0.5385**	−0.2102*
	(0.237)		(0.004)	(0.389)	(0.174)		(0.030)	(0.059)
$\ln DOS_t$		1.2027	1.4424*	−0.3292		0.2763	0.6146	−0.2096
		(0.105)	(0.064)	(0.151)		(0.490)	(0.142)	(0.104)
$\ln DOM_t$		−0.6563**	−1.5952***	−0.5544**		−0.1854	−0.9867***	−0.7470***
		(0.031)	(0.001)	(0.050)		(0.308)	(0.003)	(0.002)

(continued)

Table 5.3 (continued)

	Dependent variable: $\ln Y_t$							
	IV 2SLS fixed effects: instantaneous effects[a]				IV 2SLS fixed effects: one-period lags[a]			
	(1)	(2)	(3)	(4)	(5)	(6)	(7)	(8)
$\ln(RD/Y)_t$			−0.2802**	−0.1924**			−0.2813***	−0.1581***
			(0.013)	(0.013)			(0.004)	(0.007)
$\ln(IM/Y)_t$				−0.1128				−0.1528*
				(0.129)				(0.056)
Fixed year effects	Yes	Yes	Yes	Yes	Yes	Yes	Yes	Yes
Joint significance:								
$\ln L_t + \ln L_{t-1} = 0$					$p>F = 0.0133$	$p>F = 0.0060$	$p>F = 0.0076$	$p>F = 0.0001$
$\ln K_t + \ln K_{t-1} = 0$					$p>F = 0.2472$	$p>F = 0.0586$	$p>F = 0.0156$	$p>F = 0.4279$
$\ln S_t + \ln S_{t-1} = 0$					$p>F = 0.1552$	$p>F = 0.5181$	$p>F = 0.0108$	$p>F = 0.0006$
$\ln M_t + \ln M_{t-1} = 0$					$p>F = 0.0000$	$p>F = 0.0580$	$p>F = 0.0077$	$p>F = 0.0004$
First stage results:								
Shea partial R-squared:								
OSS_t	0.3809		0.2769	0.3938	0.3913		0.3584	0.3779
OSM_t	0.3567		0.2378	0.3258	0.3263		0.4454	0.4404
DOS_t		0.1288	0.1203	0.2531		0.4677	0.4691	0.3019
DOM_t		0.2633	0.185	0.2305		0.3683	0.4848	0.3201
$(RD/Y)_t$			0.4914	0.5817			0.5712	0.6545
$(IM/Y)_t$				0.2063				0.1976
Hansen J statistic[b] p value	$X^2(4) = 0.15$	$X^2(4) = 0.35$	$X^2(10) = 0.22$	$X^2(12) = 0.16$	$X^2(4) = 0.03$	$X^2(4) = 0.11$	$X^2(10) = 0.50$	not reported[c]
AIC	−515.3	−493.2	−509.8	−673.9	−516.2	−560.1	−620.8	−678.3
Observations	231	238	223	199	231	238	223	199
R-squared (within)	0.58	0.49	0.6	0.88	0.59	0.63	0.77	0.88

Source: own calculations

$p^* < 0.1$, $p^{**} < 0.05$, $p^{***} < 0.001$ (p values in parentheses)

[a] All estimations without the outliers "pharmaceuticals" and "office, accounting and computer machinery"

[b] Over-identification test of all instruments

[c] Estimated covariance matrix of moment conditions not of full rank; over-identification statistic not reported, and standard errors and model tests should be interpreted with caution

Table 5.4 Labor productivity – Fixed effects estimator (1991–2000)

	Dependent variable: $\ln(VA/L)_t$							
	Fixed effects estimator: instantaneous effects[a]				Fixed effects estimator: one-period lags[a]			
	(1)	(2)	(3)	(4)	(5)	(6)	(7)	(8)
$\ln(K/L)_t$	0.7030***	0.5991**	0.5902**	0.7390*	0.4388	0.5720*	0.4874**	0.6017***
	(0.008)	(0.026)	(0.036)	(0.050)	(0.170)	(0.054)	(0.020)	(0.002)
$\ln(K/L)_{t-1}$					0.1612	−0.042	0.2034	0.063
					(0.592)	(0.874)	(0.374)	(0.742)
$\ln OSS_t$	0.0631*		0.0477	0.0576*	0.0080		0.0199	0.0177
	(0.085)		(0.157)	(0.053)	(0.656)		(0.328)	(0.364)
$\ln OSS_{t-1}$					0.0286*		0.0050	0.0113
					(0.091)		(0.771)	(0.476)
$\ln OSM_t$	0.1700		−0.1288	−0.0184	0.0826		−0.0978	0.0141
	(0.221)		(0.355)	(0.897)	(0.470)		(0.438)	(0.787)
$\ln OSM_{t-1}$					−0.0378		−0.0776	−0.1112*
					(0.738)		(0.281)	(0.085)
$\ln DOS_t$		−0.2889	−0.4804*	−0.5303		−0.3912**	0.1507	0.1462
		(0.322)	(0.085)	(0.137)		(0.018)	(0.326)	(0.269)
$\ln DOS_{t-1}$						0.2972*	−0.1476	−0.2606*
						(0.091)	(0.370)	(0.071)
$\ln DOM_t$		−0.5078	−0.9837**	−0.7513*		−0.4363**	−0.1791	−0.0411
		(0.209)	(0.019)	(0.054)		(0.014)	(0.515)	(0.830)
$\ln DOM_{t-1}$						0.2009	−0.2486***	−0.2407**
						(0.234)	(0.007)	(0.029)
$\ln(RD/Y)_t$			−0.4118***	−0.4184***			−1.0163***	−0.9326***
			(0.002)	(0.006)			(0.000)	(0.000)
$\ln(RD/Y)_{t-1}$							0.7500***	0.7038***
							(0.000)	(0.000)

(continued)

Table 5.4 (continued)

	Dependent variable: $\ln(VA/L)_t$							
	Fixed effects estimator: instantaneous effects[a]				Fixed effects estimator: one-period lags[a]			
	(1)	(2)	(3)	(4)	(5)	(6)	(7)	(8)
$\ln(IM/Y)_t$				−0.1147				−0.1836**
				(0.374)				(0.034)
$\ln(IM/Y)_{t-1}$								0.1353**
								(0.046)
Fixed year effects	Yes	Yes	Yes	Yes	Yes	Yes	Yes	Yes
Joint significance:								
$\ln(K/L)_t + \ln(K/L)_{t-1} = 0$					$p > F = 0.0000$	$p > F = 0.0000$	$p > F = 0.0000$	$p > F = 0.0000$
$\ln OSS_t + \ln OSS_{t-1} = 0$					$p > F = 0.1475$		$p > F = 0.2592$	$p > F = 0.0811$
$\ln OSM_t + \ln OSM_{t-1} = 0$					$p > F = 0.7510$		$p > F = 0.3715$	$p > F = 0.2093$
$\ln DOS_t + \ln DOS_{t-1} = 0$						$p > F = 0.0508$	$p > F = 0.5436$	$p > F = 0.1852$
$\ln DOM_t + \ln DOM_{t-1} = 0$						$p > F = 0.0265$	$p > F = 0.01026$	$p > F = 0.0640$
$\ln(RD/Y)_t + \ln(RD/Y)_{t-1} = 0$							$p > F = 0.0000$	$p > F = 0.0000$
$\ln(IM/Y)_t + \ln(IM/Y)_{t-1} = 0$								$p > F = 0.0929$
AIC	72.9	68.6	50.7	57.2	−341.2	−357.8	−519.1	−576.2
Observations	332	338	325	291	300	306	292	261
R-squared (within)	0.38	0.38	0.44	0.47	0.48	0.48	0.74	0.84

Source: own calculations

$p^* < 0.1$, $p^{**} < 0.05$, $p^{***} < 0.001$ (*p* values in parentheses)

[a]All estimations without the outliers "pharmaceuticals" and "office, accounting and computer machinery"

significant in columns 3 and 4 except for DOS in column 4. As in the case of TFP, a higher import share affects LP negatively. Columns 5–8 present the estimations including additional one-period lags of the regressors. Almost all variables show similar results compared to columns 1–4 except for domestic services outsourcing in column 7.

For reasons mentioned above, potential *endogeneity* of the technology variables is addressed using the IV 2SLS *fixed effects estimator* in Table 5.5. Again, the first three lags are used as instruments for the potential endogenous variables. Capital spending is subdivided into capital spending on equipment and buildings, as the effects on LP can be different.[6] As a consequence, we see that capital intensity of equipment has a significantly positive overall effect on LP, while capital intensity of buildings has a negative one. The coefficient signs confirm the above-described trends of the technology variables, but almost none is significant. Thus, only services offshoring influences LP positively, while materials offshoring, domestic services outsourcing, domestic materials outsourcing, and R&D-intensity mostly have a negative impact on LP. Only DOM (columns 3, 4, 7 and 8) and R&D-intensity (column 8) show significant results.

In the following, we only interpret the results of the fixed effects estimator (Table 5.4) and focus on specifications that include all technology variables. The coefficients of services offshoring range from 0.0290 (column 8) to 0.0576 (column 4). Between 1991 and 2000, the CAGR of services offshoring was 6.0% for the manufacturing sectors. All other variables being constant, services offshoring increased labor productivity by between 0.18 and 0.35% per year and by between 2.0 and 4.0% over the whole period.

5.1.3 Estimations with Revised Input–Output Data: 1995–2004

5.1.3.1 Preliminary Analysis

A first look at the relationship between services offshoring and TFP is given in Fig. 5.5. The scatter plot shows *German services offshoring intensity versus output growth rates* between 1995 and 2004. Forty-two sectors are taken into account; only the sector "leather, leather products, and footwear" is excluded, since services offshoring intensities are not available. Thirty-one sectors show a positive output growth ranging from 0.4% (wood and products of wood and cork) to 121% (activities related to financial intermediation) over the given period. The majority of the sectors, namely 28, are placed in the first quadrant, suggesting a positive relationship between services offshoring growth and output growth. Only three sectors fall in the second quadrant and eleven sectors in the fourth quadrant, as would be characteristic of a negative relationship between both variables.

[6]Subdividing capital into capital spendings on equipment and buildings did not lead to significant results in the previous estimations.

Table 5.5 Labor productivity – IV 2SLS fixed effects estimator (1991–2000)

	Dependent variable: $\ln(VA/L)_t$							
	IV 2SLS fixed effects: instantaneous effects[a]				IV 2SLS fixed effects: one-period lags[a]			
	(1)	(2)	(3)	(4)	(5)	(6)	(7)	(8)
$\ln(K^{equip}/L)_t$	1.5784***	1.5582***	1.3371***	0.9992***	1.7241***	1.8065***	1.4942***	1.4781***
	(0.000)	(0.000)	(0.004)	(0.008)	(0.000)	(0.000)	(0.000)	(0.001)
$\ln(K^{equip}/L)_{t-1}$					−0.2073	−0.3127	−0.2147	−0.6714**
					(0.724)	(0.505)	(0.670)	(0.047)
$\ln(K^{build}/L)_t$	−0.9756***	−0.9653***	−0.7535**	−0.5164	−1.2403***	−1.2695***	−0.9514***	−0.8658**
	(0.004)	(0.007)	(0.047)	(0.104)	(0.001)	(0.000)	(0.004)	(0.033)
$\ln(K^{build}/L)_{t-1}$					0.3578	0.3844	0.2711	0.4147
					(0.472)	(0.376)	(0.494)	(0.309)
$\ln OSS_t$	0.0258		0.0053	0.02	0.0253		0.0046	0.0225
	(0.237)		(0.850)	(0.370)	(0.250)		(0.865)	(0.280)
$\ln OSM_t$	−0.157		−0.2684	−0.2224	−0.1797		−0.2548	−0.194
	(0.532)		(0.187)	(0.304)	(0.542)		(0.272)	(0.375)
$\ln DOS_t$		−0.0826	−0.2524	−0.2113		−0.0636	−0.2588	−0.2694
		(0.741)	(0.390)	(0.458)		(0.798)	(0.380)	(0.350)
$\ln DOM_t$		−0.018	−0.6207**	−0.9425*		0.0388	−0.5903**	−1.0556*
		(0.953)	(0.031)	(0.097)		(0.908)	(0.035)	(0.072)
$\ln(RD/Y)_t$			−0.152	−0.1743			−0.1632	−0.1898*
			(0.170)	(0.130)			(0.132)	(0.096)
$\ln(IM/Y)_t$				−0.2084				−0.289
				(0.398)				(0.240)
Fixed year effects	Yes	Yes	Yes	Yes	Yes	Yes	Yes	Yes
Joint significance:								
$\ln(K^{equip}/L)_t + \ln(K^{equip}/L)_{t-1} = 0$					$p>F = 0.0000$	$p>F = 0.0000$	$p>F = 0.0009$	$p>F = 0.0042$
$\ln(K^{build}/L)_t + \ln(K^{build}/L)_{t-1} = 0$					$p>F = 0.0008$	$p>F = 0.0008$	$p>F = 0.0164$	$p>F = 0.0901$

(*continued*)

Table 5.5 (continued)

	Dependent variable: $\ln(VA/L)_t$							
	IV 2SLS fixed effects: instantaneous effects[a]				IV 2SLS fixed effects: one-period lags[a]			
	(1)	(2)	(3)	(4)	(5)	(6)	(7)	(8)
First stage results:								
Shea partial *R*-squared:								
OSS_t	0.4233		0.4266	0.4396	0.4226		0.4269	0.4416
OSM_t	0.385		0.4524	0.3972	0.3592		0.4349	0.4051
DOS_t		0.3866	0.4605	0.4565		0.388	0.4554	0.4367
DOM_t		0.3945	0.4143	0.2381		0.3655	0.4041	0.2208
$(RD/Y)_t$			0.4477	0.5868			0.4524	0.5977
$(IM/Y)_t$				0.2442				0.2247
Hansen J statistic[b] *p* value	$X^2(4) = 0.18$	$X^2(4) = 0.13$	$X^2(10) = 0.53$	$X^2(12) = 0.20$	$X^2(4) = 0.12$	$X^2(4) = 0.11$	$X^2(10) = 0.61$	$X^2(12) = 0.12$
AIC	−270.7	−292.1	−290.6	−324.9	−266.7	−287.2	−289.1	−339.6
Observations	231	238	223	199	231	238	223	199
R-squared (within)	0.45	0.47	0.55	0.68	0.45	0.47	0.55	0.71

Source: own calculations

$p^* < 0.1$, $p^{**} < 0.05$, $p^{***} < 0.001$ (*p* values in parentheses)

[a]All estimations without the outliers “pharmaceuticals” and “office, accounting and computer machinery”

[b]Over-identification test of all instruments

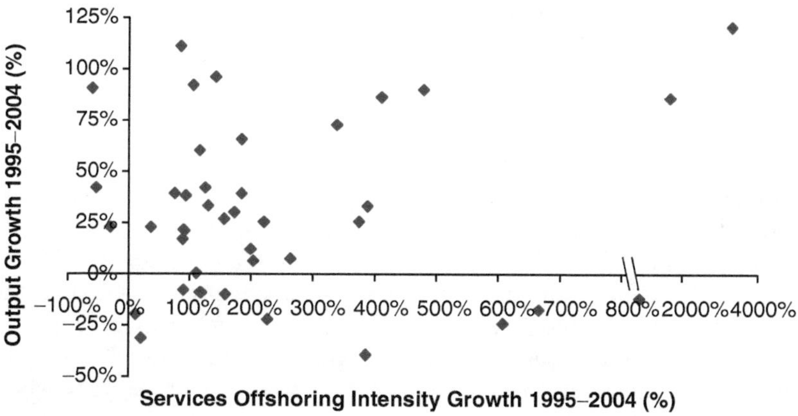

Fig. 5.5 German services offshoring intensity and output growth (1995–2004)
Source: own calculations. Data: Federal Statistical Office Germany. NB: The sector "leather, leather products, and footwear" was dropped, since services offshoring intensities are not available. OSS growth rates for the sectors "wearing apparel, dressing, and dying of fur", "recycling", and "collection, purification, and distribution of water" are calculated for 1996–2004, since OSS is not available for 1995

Table 5.6 Ranking of OSS and output growth in Germany (1995–2004)

Ranking of services offshoring growth	Services offshoring intensity growth		Output growth	
Sector	%	Rank	%	Rank
Top Ten				
Activities related to financial intermediation	81,539.0%	1	120.7%	1
Metal castings	3705.0%	2	86.0%	8
Manufacturing n.e.c.	1567.0%	3	−12.0%	36
Textiles	665.2%	4	−17.4%	37
Gas and gas supply	607.7%	5	−24.1%	40
Iron and steel	478.4%	6	90.1%	6
Office, accounting, and computing machinery	410.6%	7	86.4%	7
Nonferrous metals	388.0%	8	33.1%	18
Tobacco products	385.3%	9	−39.2%	42
Publishing	374.5%	10	25.6%	21

Source: own calculations. Data: Federal Statistical Office Germany. NB: The sector "leather, leather products, and footwear" was dropped, since services offshoring intensities are not available. OSS growth rates for the sectors "wearing apparel, dressing, and dying of fur", "recycling", and "collection, purification, and distribution of water" are calculated for 1996–2004, since OSS is not available for 1995

For further evidence the ten sectors with the strongest services offshoring growth between 1995 and 2004 are shown in Table 5.6, and their OSS growth rates are compared with output growth rates. Six sectors experienced positive output growth over the period, whereas four sectors showed a negative output growth, including three of the top five services offshoring sectors (manufacturing n.e.c., textiles, gas and gas supply). We cannot unambiguously predict a positive relationship between OSS and output growth rates from these results.

5.1.3.2 Estimation Results: Total Factor Productivity

This subsection presents our assessment of the effects of services and materials offshoring on TFP in German manufacturing for the period between 1995 and 2004. The results of the consistent *fixed effects estimator* are shown in Table 5.7.[7] Following the previous estimations, columns 1–4 only consider the instantaneous productivity effects. As predicted, labor, services, and materials have an overall positive impact on real output, which are all significant in columns 2 and 3. Capital spending on equipment also has a significantly positive effect on TFP, while the impact of capital spending on buildings, however, is negative and significant in columns 1 and 2.

Services offshoring affects real output positively, which is highly significant in columns 3 and 4. Materials offshoring shows a positive coefficient in columns 1 and 4, which turns negative in column 3, which could be due to negative collinearity with DOS of more than 40%, but a positive one with import share of around 54%. DOS, DOM, and R&D-intensity show a negative effect on real output which is significant in some specifications. The additional control variable import share in column 4 has a strongly negative effect on TFP. In this specification, all technology variables are smaller compared to the specification in column 3. Columns 5–8 show the results with additional one-period lags of each explanatory variable. The results from columns 1–4 can be confirmed.

In a next step, the explanatory variables should be controlled for potential endogeneity. Table 5.8 presents results using the robust IV 2SLS *fixed effects estimator* including the first three lags of the potentially endogenous variables as instruments for $\ln OSS_t$, $\ln OSM_t$, $\ln DOS_t$, $\ln DOM_t$, and $\ln(RD/Y)_t$. All input factors except for capital spending on buildings seem to influence TFP positively being significant for materials, capital spending on equipment and services (column 2). Again, services offshoring significantly affects real output positively, whereas OSM has no clear trend to show probably due to collinearity with DOS and import share. The remaining technology variables DOS, DOM, and R&D-intensity have a negative impact being significant for most variables in column 3. Adding one-period lags in columns 5–8 yields similar results. However, the specification in column 6 rejects the null hypothesis that the instruments are valid instruments and that the excluded instruments are correctly excluded (Hansen J statistic), while the estimated covariance matrix of moment conditions are not of full rank in column 8. Both specifications should thus be interpreted with caution.

[7] We dropped the identified outliers "pharmaceuticals", due to extremely high services offshoring intensities, and "tobacco", due to very low output figures combined with a high OSS, which leads to a total of 33 manufacturing sectors.

Table 5.7 TFP – Fixed effects estimator (1995–2004)

Dependent variable: $\ln Y_t$	Fixed effects estimator: instantaneous effects[a]				Fixed effects estimator: one-period lags[a]			
	(1)	(2)	(3)	(4)	(5)	(6)	(7)	(8)
$\ln L_t$	0.1881	0.2088*	0.1999*	−0.0035	0.1353	0.1205	0.1309	−0.0657
	(0.139)	(0.073)	(0.072)	(0.958)	(0.393)	(0.406)	(0.262)	(0.340)
$\ln L_{t-1}$					0.0813	0.1547	0.0620	0.0686
					(0.497)	(0.133)	(0.428)	(0.378)
$\ln K^{equip}{}_t$	0.3979*	0.4804**	0.3263*	0.2817***	−0.2254	−0.4669	0.2245	0.2531
	(0.062)	(0.031)	(0.061)	(0.009)	(0.482)	(0.233)	(0.429)	(0.303)
$\ln K^{equip}{}_{t-1}$					0.5991*	0.9559**	0.1243	0.0357
					(0.080)	(0.015)	(0.678)	(0.873)
$\ln K^{build}{}_t$	−0.4063**	−0.4462**	−0.2964	−0.1746	0.4244	0.7714	−0.2804	−0.2623
	(0.039)	(0.029)	(0.118)	(0.148)	(0.314)	(0.138)	(0.378)	(0.277)
$\ln K^{build}{}_{t-1}$					−0.7902**	−1.2394**	0.0068	0.1054
					(0.043)	(0.017)	(0.983)	(0.655)
$\ln S_t$	0.0839	0.3449*	0.2651***	0.3297***	0.172	0.3183**	0.3325***	0.3411**
	(0.707)	(0.059)	(0.006)	(0.004)	(0.243)	(0.021)	(0.001)	(0.024)
$\ln S_{t-1}$					−0.0969	0.0589	−0.0053	0.0649
					(0.366)	(0.713)	(0.944)	(0.468)
$\ln M_t$	0.3248**	0.3361**	0.3831**	0.1540	0.2870***	0.3945***	0.3177***	0.1729**
	(0.048)	(0.034)	(0.022)	(0.117)	(0.009)	(0.005)	(0.007)	(0.050)
$\ln M_{t-1}$					0.0050	−0.1214	0.072	−0.0697
					(0.960)	(0.192)	(0.462)	(0.337)
$\ln OSS_t$	0.0315		0.0476***	0.0404***	0.0425		0.0480**	0.0372**
	(0.131)		(0.009)	(0.002)	(0.189)		(0.043)	(0.046)
$\ln OSS_{t-1}$					−0.0067		0.0217**	0.0181*
					(0.655)		(0.012)	(0.068)
$\ln OSM_t$	0.0721		−0.0417	0.1051*	0.1048*		−0.0729	0.0314

(*continued*)

Table 5.7 (continued)

Dependent variable: $\ln Y_t$	Fixed effects estimator: instantaneous effects[a]				Fixed effects estimator: one-period lags[a]			
	(1)	(2)	(3)	(4)	(5)	(6)	(7)	(8)
	(0.282)		(0.588)	(0.088)	(0.095)		(0.263)	(0.516)
$\ln OSM_{t-1}$					−0.0349		−0.0105	0.0728**
					(0.381)		(0.833)	(0.026)
$\ln DOS_t$		−0.2109	−0.1869	−0.1931**		−0.1022	−0.2293	−0.2355*
		(0.215)	(0.196)	(0.045)		(0.526)	(0.104)	(0.058)
$\ln DOS_{t-1}$						−0.1265	−0.0065	−0.0226
						(0.230)	(0.923)	(0.848)
$\ln DOM_t$		−0.045	−0.1893*	−0.0026		−0.1100	−0.2398***	−0.0968
		(0.679)	(0.078)	(0.971)		(0.191)	(0.007)	(0.195)
$\ln DOM_{t-1}$						0.0785	−0.0233	0.0811
						(0.218)	(0.772)	(0.153)
$\ln(RD/Y)_t$			−0.4277***	−0.3399***			−0.7056***	−0.5803***
			(0.000)	(0.000)			(0.000)	(0.000)
$\ln(RD/Y)_{t-1}$							0.1769***	0.1636***
							(0.001)	(0.001)
$\ln(IM/Y)_t$				−0.1771***				−0.1341***
				(0.000)				(0.001)
$\ln(IM/Y)_{t-1}$								−0.0321
								(0.393)
Fixed year effects	Yes	Yes	Yes	Yes	Yes	Yes	Yes	Yes
Joint significance:								
$\ln L_t + \ln L_{t-1} = 0$					$p>F = 0.3589$	$p>F = 0.0905$	$p>F = 0.1787$	$p>F = 0.5735$
$\ln K^{equip}_t + \ln K^{equip}_{t-1} = 0$					$p>F = 0.1687$	$p>F = 0.0259$	$p>F = 0.1710$	$p>F = 0.0622$
$\ln K^{build}_t + \ln K^{build}_{t-1} = 0$					$p>F = 0.0605$	$p>F = 0.0169$	$p>F = 0.3528$	$p>F = 0.3490$
$\ln S_t + \ln S_{t-1} = 0$					$p>F = 0.0074$	$p>F = 0.0552$	$p>F = 0.0034$	$p>F = 0.0185$

(*continued*)

Table 5.7 (continued)

Dependent variable: $\ln Y_t$	Fixed effects estimator: instantaneous effects[a]				Fixed effects estimator: one-period lags[a]			
	(1)	(2)	(3)	(4)	(5)	(6)	(7)	(8)
$\ln M_t + \ln M_{t-1} = 0$					$p>F = 0.0012$	$p>F = 0.0046$	$p>F = 0.0243$	$p>F = 0.0446$
$\ln OSS_t + \ln OSS_{t-1} = 0$					$p>F = 0.3873$		$p>F = 0.0007$	$p>F = 0.0055$
$\ln OSM_t + \ln OSM_{t-1} = 0$					$p>F = 0.1303$		$p>F = 0.5284$	$p>F = 0.0741$
$\ln DOS_t + \ln DOS_{t-1} = 0$						$p>F = 0.3416$	$p>F = 0.2364$	$p>F = 0.0529$
$\ln DOM_t + \ln DOM_{t-1} = 0$						$p>F = 0.0973$	$p>F = 0.0236$	$p>F = 0.1793$
$\ln(RD/Y)_t + \ln(RD/Y)_{t-1} = 0$							$p>F = 0.0000$	$p>F = 0.0000$
$\ln(IM/Y)_t + \ln(IM/Y)_{t-1} = 0$								$p>F = 0.0001$
AIC	−612.7	−633.1	−806.7	−918.2	−562.6	−577.9	−804.9	−915.5
Observations	327	340	327	299	294	306	294	269
R-squared (within)	0.64	0.63	0.81	0.89	0.63	0.62	0.84	0.92

Source: own calculations
$p^* < 0.1$, $p^{**} < 0.05$, $p^{***} < 0.001$ (*p* values in parentheses)
[a]All estimations without the outliers "pharmaceuticals" and "tobacco"

Table 5.8 TFP– IV 2SLS fixed effects estimator (1995–2004)

Dependent variable: $\ln Y_t$

	IV 2SLS fixed effects: instantaneous effects[a]				IV 2SLS fixed effects: one-period lags[a]			
	(1)	(2)	(3)	(4)	(5)	(6)	(7)	(8)
$\ln L_t$	0.0091	0.0949	0.1007	0.0410	−0.0053	−0.0053	0.0776	0.0200
	(0.929)	(0.331)	(0.188)	(0.582)	(0.957)	(0.958)	(0.285)	(0.768)
$\ln L_{t-1}$					0.0769	0.1021*	0.0525	0.0160
					(0.266)	(0.075)	(0.343)	(0.772)
$\ln K^{equip}_t$	0.2229	0.3610*	0.2875**	0.3025**	0.2200	−0.2291	0.2010	0.7180***
	(0.208)	(0.096)	(0.037)	(0.012)	(0.564)	(0.418)	(0.374)	(0.000)
$\ln K^{equip}_{t-1}$					0.2044	0.6298**	0.1988	−0.3756*
					(0.605)	(0.039)	(0.511)	(0.073)
$\ln K^{build}_t$	−0.0868	−0.2107	−0.2148	−0.1869	−0.1598	0.3156	−0.2540	−0.7013***
	(0.764)	(0.366)	(0.243)	(0.213)	(0.704)	(0.454)	(0.325)	(0.008)
$\ln K^{build}_{t-1}$					−0.1029	−0.5207	−0.0232	0.5450*
					(0.802)	(0.189)	(0.940)	(0.053)
$\ln S_t$	−0.0491	0.3323*	0.1253	−0.011	0.0142	0.0827	0.0925	−0.1490
	(0.706)	(0.062)	(0.388)	(0.914)	(0.896)	(0.600)	(0.532)	(0.274)
$\ln S_{t-1}$					−0.1059	−0.0564	−0.0073	−0.0269
					(0.188)	(0.577)	(0.845)	(0.537)
$\ln M_t$	0.6429***	0.5400***	0.5105***	0.3621***	0.6497***	0.6744***	0.6169***	0.4814***
	(0.000)	(0.005)	(0.000)	(0.002)	(0.000)	(0.000)	(0.000)	(0.001)
$\ln M_{t-1}$					−0.2119*	−0.2057	−0.1373***	−0.1029**
					(0.052)	(0.115)	(0.003)	(0.018)
$\ln OSS_t$	0.0570*		0.0857***	0.0483**	0.0364		0.0780***	0.0429**
	(0.092)		(0.000)	(0.013)	(0.236)		(0.000)	(0.016)
$\ln OSM_t$	−0.041		−0.1348**	0.0522	0.0717		−0.1112	0.0693
	(0.666)		(0.026)	(0.484)	(0.442)		(0.100)	(0.345)
$\ln DOS_t$		−0.4656	−0.1182	−0.0826		−0.0231	−0.0912	0.0506
		(0.115)	(0.526)	(0.502)		(0.899)	(0.608)	(0.681)

(*continued*)

Table 5.8 (continued)

Dependent variable: $\ln Y_t$	IV 2SLS fixed effects: instantaneous effects[a]				IV 2SLS fixed effects: one-period lags[a]			
	(1)	(2)	(3)	(4)	(5)	(6)	(7)	(8)
$\ln DOM_t$		0.0280	−0.2929***	−0.1869**		0.0377	−0.3254***	−0.2410***
		(0.846)	(0.001)	(0.022)		(0.778)	(0.000)	(0.007)
$\ln(RD/Y)_t$			−0.6032***	−0.4271***			−0.5649***	−0.4137***
			(0.000)	(0.000)			(0.000)	(0.000)
$\ln(IM/Y)_t$				−0.1936***				−0.1953***
				(0.000)				(0.000)
Fixed year effects	Yes	Yes	Yes	Yes	Yes	Yes	Yes	Yes
Joint significance:								
$\ln L_t + \ln L_{t-1} = 0$					$p>F = 0.5069$	$p>F = 0.2005$	$p>F = 0.2903$	$p>F = 0.8739$
$\ln K^{equip}_t + \ln K^{equip}_{t-1} = 0$					$p>F = 0.1032$	$p>F = 0.0635$	$p>F = 0.0028$	$p>F = 0.0001$
$\ln K^{build}_t + \ln K^{build}_{t-1} = 0$					$p>F = 0.4756$	$p>F = 0.3122$	$p>F = 0.1623$	$p>F = 0.0228$
$\ln S_t + \ln S_{t-1} = 0$					$p>F = 0.3346$	$p>F = 0.7063$	$p>F = 0.7780$	$p>F = 0.5128$
$\ln M_t + \ln M_{t-1} = 0$					$p>F = 0.0000$	$p>F = 0.0007$	$p>F = 0.0000$	$p>F = 0.0036$
First stage results:								
Shea partial R-squared:								
OSS_t	0.4889		0.4352	0.4071	0.4638		0.4917	0.4546
OSM_t	0.2988		0.2677	0.2599	0.2690		0.4185	0.3634
DOS_t		0.1894	0.3378	0.2464		0.3125	0.3959	0.3534
DOM_t		0.2262	0.2111	0.3007		0.2723	0.3097	0.3478
$(RD/Y)_t$			0.5161	0.4454			0.5974	0.5398
$(IM/Y)_t$				0.4384				0.4696
Hansen J statistic[b] p-value	$X^2(4) = 0.89$	$X^2(4) = 0.27$	$X^2(10) = 0.20$	$X^2(12) = 0.39$	$X^2(4) = 0.89$	$X^2(4) = 0.06$	$X^2(10) = 0.23$	not reported[c]
AIC	−534.9	−519.2	−715.3	−771.8	−571.5	−570.0	−737.4	−754.9
Observations	228	238	228	209	228	238	228	209
R-squared (within)	0.62	0.56	0.83	0.9	0.69	0.66	0.85	0.9

Source: own calculations

$p^* < 0.1$, $p^{**} < 0.05$, $p^{***} < 0.001$ (p values in parentheses)

[a]All estimations without the outliers "pharmaceuticals" and "tobacco"

[b]Over-identification test of all instruments

[c]Estimated covariance matrix of moment conditions not of full rank; over-identification statistic not reported, and standard errors and model tests should be interpreted with caution

The results show that services offshoring had an overall positive effect on TFP in the German manufacturing sectors from 1995 to 2004. For the following interpretation, we only focus on specifications that include all technology variables and show significant results. The overall coefficients of the fixed effects estimations vary between 0.0404 (Table 5.7, column 4) and 0.0857 (Table 5.8, column 3). Between 1995 and 2004, services offshoring grew with an annual rate of 11.6% in the manufacturing sectors, from 0.38 to 1.02%. Holding all other variables constant, services offshoring increased real output by on average 0.47–0.99% per year and by 4.1–8.6% over the period.

5.1.3.3 Estimation Results: Labor Productivity

In the following, the effect of services offshoring on LP, defined as value added per labor unit, is estimated as specified in (5.5). The results using the *fixed effects estimator* are shown in Table 5.9. Columns 1–4 only consider instantaneous effects on LP. Capital intensity is the only input factor besides technology, but has no clear trend to show.[8] Services offshoring has a significantly positive effect on LP, while materials offshoring shows positive and negative signs probably due to the above-mentioned negative collinearity with DOS. The influence of domestic services outsourcing on LP is positive, but insignificant, whereas the effects of domestic materials outsourcing and R&D-intensity are significantly negative. The specifications in columns 5–8 with additional one-period lags confirm the described trends.

Table 5.10 uses the IV 2SLS *fixed effects estimator* to control for potential endogeneity of offshoring, domestic outsourcing, and R&D-intensity. Capital intensity still shows an insignificant positive effect on LP. The results show that services offshoring has a significantly positive effect, whereas materials offshoring, domestic services outsourcing, domestic materials outsourcing, and R&D-intensity seem to have a negative impact. They are significant in some specifications.

In a next step, we discuss the significant results of services offshoring for LP focusing on specifications that include all technology variables. The coefficients vary between 0.2288 (Table 5.9, column 3) and 0.3696 (Table 5.9, column 8). Between 1995 and 2004, the CAGR of services offshoring was 11.6% for the manufacturing sector. All other variables being constant, services offshoring increased LP by on average 2.65–4.28% per year and 21.5–32.5% between 1995 and 2004.

[8]Capital spending on equipment and buildings is aggregated, since disaggregation yields no significant results for both variables.

Table 5.9 Labor productivity – Fixed effects estimator (1995–2004)

Dependent variable: $\ln(VA/L)_t$	Fixed effects estimator: instantaneous effects[a]				Fixed effects estimator: one-period lags[a]			
	(1)	(2)	(3)	(4)	(5)	(6)	(7)	(8)
$\ln(K/L)_t$	−0.0203	0.0055	−0.0149	0.3991	0.2263	0.3451	0.2416	0.6631
	(0.946)	(0.988)	(0.958)	(0.291)	(0.609)	(0.501)	(0.557)	(0.222)
$\ln(K/L)_{t-1}$					−0.3849	−0.5105	−0.275	−0.2909
					(0.320)	(0.277)	(0.461)	(0.438)
lnOSS_t	0.1763*		0.2288***	0.2522**	0.1809		0.2338**	0.2611**
	(0.055)		(0.008)	(0.019)	(0.161)		(0.023)	(0.036)
lnOSS_{t-1}					0.0573		0.1086**	0.1085*
					(0.485)		(0.044)	(0.066)
lnOSM_t	0.0794		−0.1599	−0.1071	0.2082		−0.2362	−0.2207
	(0.617)		(0.242)	(0.556)	(0.252)		(0.138)	(0.147)
lnOSM_{t-1}					−0.1795*		−0.0521	−0.0899
					(0.056)		(0.601)	(0.553)
lnDOS_t		0.1403	0.2107	0.2975		0.3089	0.0273	0.0029
		(0.706)	(0.502)	(0.330)		(0.393)	(0.929)	(0.993)
lnDOS_{t-1}						−0.2829	0.1660	0.3645
						(0.148)	(0.403)	(0.262)
lnDOM_t		−0.3522	−0.8014**	−0.9092**		−0.5460	−1.1252***	−1.2084**
		(0.255)	(0.029)	(0.035)		(0.131)	(0.009)	(0.012)
lnDOM_{t-1}						0.2344**	0.1304	0.0345
						(0.048)	(0.440)	(0.830)
$\ln(\text{RD}/Y)_t$			−1.0450***	−1.1315***			−1.8696***	−1.9896***
			(0.001)	(0.002)			(0.000)	(0.000)
$\ln(\text{RD}/Y)_{t-1}$							0.4551**	0.4258*
							(0.036)	(0.077)

(continued)

Table 5.9 (continued)

Dependent variable: $\ln(VA/L)_t$	Fixed effects estimator: instantaneous effects[a]				Fixed effects estimator: one-period lags[a]			
	(1)	(2)	(3)	(4)	(5)	(6)	(7)	(8)
$\ln(\text{IM}/Y)_t$				−0.1665				0.0401
				(0.412)				(0.755)
$\ln(\text{IM}/Y)_{t-1}$								−0.06
								(0.817)
Fixed year effects	Yes	Yes	Yes	Yes	Yes	Yes	Yes	Yes
Joint significance:								
$\ln(K/L)_t + \ln(K/L)_{t-1} = 0$					$p>F = 0.5902$	$p>F = 0.5490$	$p>F = 0.7570$	$p>F = 0.4634$
$\ln\text{OSS}_t + \ln\text{OSS}_{t-1} = 0$					$p>F = 0.0815$		$p>F = 0.0055$	$p>F = 0.0297$
$\ln\text{OSM}_t + \ln\text{OSM}_{t-1} = 0$					$p>F = 0.1544$		$p>F = 0.1360$	$p>F = 0.3420$
$\ln\text{DOS}_t + \ln\text{DOS}_{t-1} = 0$						$p>F = 0.3142$	$p>F = 0.6738$	$p>F = 0.4809$
$\ln\text{DOM}_t + \ln\text{DOM}_{t-1} = 0$						$p>F = 0.0976$	$p>F = 0.0316$	$p>F = 0.0382$
$\ln(\text{RD}/Y)_t + \ln(\text{RD}/Y)_{t-1} = 0$							$p>F = 0.0006$	$p>F = 0.0001$
$\ln(\text{IM}/Y)_t + \ln(\text{IM}/Y)_{t-1} = 0$								$p>F = 0.9366$
AIC	264.7	275.4	219.3	208.0	275.4	251.2	181.6	178.8
Observations	314	327	314	286	283	295	283	258
R-squared (within)	0.25	0.23	0.37	0.41	0.28	0.23	0.43	0.46

Source: own calculations
$p^* < 0.1$, $p^{**} < 0.05$, $p^{***} < 0.001$ (p values in parentheses)
[a]All estimations without the outliers “pharmaceuticals” and “tobacco”

Table 5.10 Labor productivity – IV 2SLS fixed effects estimator (1995–2004)

Dependent variable: $\ln(VA/L)_t$	IV 2SLS fixed effects: instantaneous effects[a]				IV 2SLS fixed effects: one-period lags[a]			
	(1)	(2)	(3)	(4)	(5)	(6)	(7)	(8)
$\ln(K/L)_t$	0.2090	0.1870	0.1950	0.2394	0.2217	0.2673	0.1727	0.2569
	(0.498)	(0.599)	(0.460)	(0.464)	(0.539)	(0.474)	(0.576)	(0.549)
$\ln(K/L)_{t-1}$					−0.0179	−0.1186	0.0386	−0.0271
					(0.938)	(0.595)	(0.862)	(0.919)
$\ln OSS_t$	0.1506*		0.2585***	0.2409***	0.1507*		0.2580***	0.2405***
	(0.074)		(0.001)	(0.003)	(0.076)		(0.001)	(0.002)
$\ln OSM_t$	−0.0254		−0.2633**	−0.1395	−0.027		−0.2654***	−0.1384
	(0.850)		(0.011)	(0.335)	(0.840)		(0.010)	(0.339)
$\ln DOS_t$		−0.2753	−0.1230	−0.3306		−0.2937	−0.1164	−0.3361
		(0.176)	(0.563)	(0.228)		(0.149)	(0.573)	(0.201)
$\ln DOM_t$		0.0807	−0.6212	−0.7789**		0.0726	−0.6019	−0.7806**
		(0.795)	(0.108)	(0.018)		(0.812)	(0.119)	(0.018)
$\ln(RD/Y)_t$			−1.2424***	−1.2784***			−1.2363***	−1.2780***
			(0.001)	(0.000)			(0.001)	(0.000)
$\ln(IM/Y)_t$				−0.2800**				−0.2822**
				(0.021)				(0.016)
Fixed year effects	Yes	Yes	Yes	Yes	Yes	Yes	Yes	Yes
Joint significance:								
$\ln(K/L)_t + \ln(K/L)_{t-1} = 0$					$p>F = 0.7941$	$p>F = 0.7365$	$p>F = 0.7398$	$p>F = 0.7416$
First stage results:								
Shea Partial R-squared:								
OSS_t	0.5117		0.4442	0.3913	0.5104		0.4456	0.3886
OSM_t	0.3425		0.4058	0.2399	0.3430		0.4068	0.2391
DOS_t		0.4483	0.4607	0.3481		0.4392	0.4563	0.3528
DOM_t		0.2225	0.2030	0.1845		0.2193	0.2032	0.1851

(continued)

Table 5.10 (continued)

Dependent variable: $\ln(VA/L)_t$

	IV 2SLS fixed effects: instantaneous effects[a]				IV 2SLS fixed effects: one-period lags[a]			
	(1)	(2)	(3)	(4)	(5)	(6)	(7)	(8)
$(RD/Y)_t$			0.3726	0.3214			0.3736	0.3208
$(IM/Y)_t$				0.3555				0.3587
Hansen J statistic[b] p value	$X^2(4) = 0.46$	$X^2(4) = 0.35$	$X^2(10) = 0.55$	$X^2(12) = 0.67$	$X^2(4) = 0.45$	$X^2(4) = 0.38$	$X^2(10) = 0.54$	$X^2(12) = 0.69$
AIC	−133.9	−123.6	−215.1	−225.5	−131.7	−121.4	−212.9	−223.5
Observations	224	234	224	205	224	234	224	205
R-squared (within)	0.33	0.26	0.55	0.63	0.33	0.26	0.55	0.63

Source: own calculations

$p^* < 0.1$, $p^{**} < 0.05$, $p^{***} < 0.001$ (p values in parentheses)

[a]All estimations without the outlier "pharmaceuticals" and "tobacco"

[b]Over-identification test of all instruments

5.2 Services Offshoring and Its Impact on Labor Demand in Germany

5.2.1 Basics of the Empirical Analysis

5.2.1.1 Theoretical and Empirical Model

Theoretical Model

A firm's linearly homogeneous production function F with constant returns to scale is described as follows:

$$Y = F(L, \Omega), \frac{\partial F}{\partial x_1} > 0, \frac{\partial^2 F}{\partial x_1^2} < 0, \frac{\partial^2 F}{\partial x_1 \partial x_2} > 0 \text{ with } x_1, x_2 = L, \Omega, \quad (5.6)$$

where Y is the output, L is the homogeneous labor input, Ω is a vector of homogeneous other inputs.

The corresponding linearly homogeneous cost function is assumed:

$$C = C(Y, w, \omega), \frac{\partial C}{\partial c_1} > 0, \ \frac{\partial^2 C}{\partial c_1 \partial c_2} > 0 \text{ with } c_1, c_2 = w, \omega. \quad (5.7)$$

The labor demand function is based on the *cost minimization* of a firm conditional on output Y. Total costs are calculated summing up the products of optimal factor demands and their respective factor prices. Note that optimal factor demand refers to *profit-maximizing amounts*. Factor demand depends on wages w, the vector of other input prices ω, and output Y. Using *Shephard's Lemma*[9], the following factor demand functions can be derived:[10]

$$L^* = C_w = \frac{\partial C(Y, w, \omega)}{\partial w} \text{ and } \Omega^* = C_\omega = \frac{(Y, w, \omega)}{\partial w}. \quad (5.8)$$

The ratio $\frac{L^*}{\Omega^*} = \frac{C_w}{C_\omega}$ implies that cost-minimization results in an input use that equals the ratio of the marginal effects on costs. The *conditional labor demand function*, holding output Y constant, can be specified as follows:

$$L^* = L^{\mathrm{d}}(Y, w, \omega). \quad (5.9)$$

---

[9]According to Shephard's Lemma (1953) factor demand is determined by the first partial derivative of the cost function with respect to the corresponding factor price, regardless of the kind of production function.

[10]Note that a * as a superscript in this section refers to the equilibrium amount.

Under the assumption that Y is linearly homogeneous and therefore $C(w, \omega, Y) = YC(w, \omega, 1)$, the *elasticity of substitution* σ between other inputs Ω and labor L results in

$$\sigma = \frac{CC_{w\omega}}{C_w C_\omega}, \tag{5.10}$$

which is shown by Uzawa (1962). The following *factor demand elasticities* given a constant output Y can be computed:

$$\eta_L = -(1-m)\sigma < 0 \tag{5.11}$$

and

$$\eta_\Omega = (1-m)\sigma > 0, \tag{5.11$'$}$$

where η_L is the price elasticity of labor demand, η_Ω is the cross-elasticity of demand for labor due to a change in other input prices and m is the share of labor in total costs. A larger m for a given σ yields a smaller η_L, since there are less substitution possibilities for labor when wages increase. Equations (5.11) and (5.11)$'$ are standard results from the theory of factor demand. An increase in the wage w is expected to reduce domestic labor demand L, whereas the growth of other input prices ω (such as purchased inputs) is likely to augment domestic labor demand, as companies will substitute inputs for labor (Hamermesh 1993).

Empirical Model

The firm's production function (5.6) is assumed as specified in (5.1):

$$Y = F(L, K, S, M, T).$$

The corresponding linearly homogeneous cost function, conditional on the level of output Y, is the following:

$$C = C(Y, w, r, p^{\mathrm{S}}, p^{\mathrm{M}}, p^{\mathrm{T}}) \tag{5.12}$$

$$\frac{\partial C}{\partial c_1} > 0, \ \frac{\partial\, C}{\partial c_1 \partial c_2} > 0 \text{ with } c_1, c_2 = w, r, p^{\mathrm{S}}, p^{\mathrm{M}}, p^{\mathrm{T}}$$

where w designates wages, r the rental rate on capital, p^{S}, p^{M}, and p^{T} the prices for service, material and technology inputs, and Y the constant output.

Using *Shephard's Lemma*, the conditional labor demand function L^{d} is derived as follows:

$$L^* = L^d(Y, w, r, p^S, p^M, p^T). \tag{5.13}$$

The following section measures the impact of services and materials offshoring on labor demand in the manufacturing sector including the 36 material and seven service inputs in a panel regression analysis. The conditional labor demand function (5.13) can be written in *log-linear* form as:

$$\ln L_{it} = \alpha_0 + \eta_Y \ln Y_{it} + \eta_L \ln w_{it} + \eta_K \ln r_{it} + \eta_S \ln p^S_{it} + \eta_M \ln p^M_{it} + \eta_T \ln p^T_{it}. \tag{5.14}$$

In this form, the equation results in the employment–output elasticity η_Y, the price elasticity of demand for labor η_L, the cross-elasticity of demand for labor due to a change in the rental rate on capital η_K, the cross-elasticities of demand for labor due to a change in input prices for services, materials, and technology η_S, η_M and η_Y.

Besides wages, the other input prices need to be concretized as follows. The *rental rate on capital r* is expected to be the same for all companies and a function of time $r = f(t)$. r is not directly included in the estimation model, but will be captured by adding year fixed dummies. The *input prices for service and material inputs* p^S *and* p^M can be subdivided into foreign input prices and domestic input prices. As for *foreign input prices*, foreign wages could serve as a proxy. This is, however, only applicable to employment in foreign affiliates. In the case of offshore outsourcing, companies are more interested in import prices than foreign wages. Furthermore, fixing an adequate income level becomes difficult for certain countries. Therefore, Amiti and Wei (2005) decided to use offshoring intensities as inverse proxies for import prices of services as well as materials. The lower the input prices of services or materials, the higher should be their intensities. Therefore, we use the OSS and OSM measures which have been calculated in the previous chapter.

Concerning *domestic input prices*, the prices of domestically purchased material and service inputs should be taken into account. As it is difficult to determine the adequate price level for each sector, we use domestic outsourcing intensities DOS and DOM as inverse proxies for domestically purchased services and materials. Finally, *the input prices* p^T of the technology shifter T need to be determined. As adequate measures for p^T are not available, we use OSS, OSM, DOS, DOM, and RD/Y as inverse proxies for p^T. Falling prices of technology inputs p^T would thus be reflected in a higher offshoring, outsourcing, or R&D-intensity.

The specification of (5.14) in log-linear form thus specializes to:

$$\begin{aligned}\ln L_{it} = {} & \alpha_0 + \eta_Y \ln Y_{it} + \eta_L \ln w_{it} + \eta_{\text{OSS}} \ln \text{OSS}_{it} + \eta_{\text{OSM}} \ln \text{OSM}_{it} \\ & + \eta_{\text{DOS}} \ln \text{DOS}_{it} + \eta_{\text{DOM}} \ln \text{DOM}_{it} + \eta_{\text{RD}} \ln(\text{RD}/Y)_{it} + \delta_t D_t + \varepsilon_{it},\end{aligned} \tag{5.15}$$

where D_t designates year fixed effects, such as common shocks influencing all sectors, and ε_{it} the idiosyncratic error term.

The conditional labor demand function in (5.15) only considers the productivity and substitution effect. Scale effects are taken into account, when the output price is substituted for the quantity of output (Amiti and Wei 2006). The output price $P=P(w, r, p^S, p^M, p^T)$ is a function of all input prices and thus an inverse function of offshoring, domestic outsourcing and R&D-intensity. Allowing for scale effects, the *unconditional labor demand equation* is described as follows:

$$\begin{aligned}\ln L_{it} = {} & \alpha_0 + \eta_L \ln w_{it} + \eta_{\mathrm{OSS}} \ln \mathrm{OSS}_{it} + \eta_{\mathrm{OSM}} \ln \mathrm{OSM}_{it} \\ & + \eta_{\mathrm{DOS}} \ln \mathrm{DOS}_{it} + \eta_{\mathrm{DOM}} \ln \mathrm{DOM}_{it} + \eta_{\mathrm{RD}} \ln(\mathrm{RD}/Y)_{it} + \delta_t D_t + \varepsilon_{it}.\end{aligned} \tag{5.16}$$

Note that OSS, OSM, DOS and DOM have two functions in (5.15) and (5.16). First, they are used as inverse proxies for other input prices, and second, they are used as inverse proxies for the prices of the technology shifter T. Equation (5.16) is characterized by a third function, as offshoring and domestic outsourcing represent inverse proxies for the output price.

5.2.1.2 Hypothesis

Rising output is expected to influence labor demand positively with $\eta_Y > 0$, whereas increasing wages are expected to have a negative impact with $\eta_L > 0$. Concerning OSS and OSM, their net effect is not unambiguously predictable (Amiti and Wei 2006). Offshoring, domestic outsourcing, and R&D-intensity can have a threefold negative effect on employment. (1) If input prices p^S and p^M fall, i.e., if OSS, OSM, DOS, and DOM increase, imported and domestically purchased inputs are likely to be substitutes for labor (*input substitution effect*). (2) If input prices p^T decrease, i.e., if OSS, OSM, DOS, DOM, and RD/Y rise, technology is likely to substitute for labor (*technology substitution effect*). (3) Offshoring, domestic outsourcing, and R&D-intensity could augment productivity via T so that less labor is needed for the same amount of output (*productivity effect*). The substitution effect influences labor demand in a direct manner, whereas the productivity effect is indirect. The previous chapter showed empirical evidence that services offshoring has a significantly positive impact on TFP and labor productivity. Thus, a productivity-induced decrease in labor demand is expected.

Opposing these three negative effects, *scale effects* could influence labor demand positively. If productivity effects lead to lower prices, this could result in higher competitiveness of firms and foster the demand for goods and labor. Thus, the net effect of offshoring, domestic outsourcing, and R&D-intensity is not clear. If the negative substitution and/or productivity effects are larger than the positive scale effects for all variables, then $\eta_{\mathrm{OSS}} < 0$, $\eta_{\mathrm{OSM}} < 0$, $\eta_{\mathrm{DOS}} < 0$, $\eta_{\mathrm{DOM}} < 0$, and $\eta_{\mathrm{RD}} < 0$. Conversely, if the scale effects dominate the other effects, one expects $\eta_{\mathrm{OSS}} > 0$, $\eta_{\mathrm{OSM}} > 0$, $\eta_{\mathrm{DOS}} > 0$, $\eta_{\mathrm{DOM}} > 0$, and $\eta_{\mathrm{RD}} > 0$. Numerous other scenarios are conceivable.

5.2.1.3 Data

Labor demand and *output* is mapped using sectoral employment data and gross output data from the input–output tables as described in Sect. 5.1.1.3. Again, real output was calculated using sectoral producer price indices from the German Federal Statistical Office as deflators. Offshoring intensities OSS and OSM, domestic outsourcing intensities DOS and DOM, and R&D-intensity are calculated as described in Sect. 5.1.1.3.

Sector-specific labor compensation of employees is used as a measure for disaggregated *wages w* and is retrieved from the OECD STAN Industrial Database based on Federal Statistical Office data. Labor compensation consists of annual wages and salaries of employees at a sectoral level paid by producers, as well as supplements such as contributions to social security, private pensions, health insurance, life insurance, and similar schemes. Labor compensation instead of gross wages and salaries is chosen, since labor demand is largely driven by a firm's entire labor costs.

Some sectors only have wage data available at a more aggregated level. Therefore, disaggregation is accomplished weighting the wage data by their sectoral output share.[11] The data are divided by the respective sectoral employment to calculate average annual labor compensation per employee. As labor demand depends on *real wages*, an appropriate price index is needed. Therefore, sectoral producer price indices from the German Federal Statistical Office are used, since producer prices rather than consumer prices matter.

5.2.2 Estimations with Unrevised Input–Output Data: 1991–2000

5.2.2.1 Preliminary Analysis

Following the structure of Sect. 5.1, this subsection gives a preliminary analysis of the empirical linkage between services offshoring and employment. Figure 5.6 maps a scatter plot of the *German services offshoring intensity and employment growth* from 1991 to 2000. All 43 sectors as selected in Sect. 3.1.3 in Chap. 3 are taken into account using the $OSS_i(a)$ measures. Thirty-four sectors denote a negative employment growth, which ranges from -1% (motor vehicles, trailers, and semi-trailers) to -66% (office, accounting, and computing machinery). Twenty-one

[11]Thus, for instance, wage data are only available for the aggregated sector "food products and beverages". The wages of the aggregated sector are weighted with the respective output shares of the individual sectors "food products" and "beverages" in order to achieve disaggregated sectoral wages. This procedure was done eight times in the following sectors: 1–2, 8–9, 10–11, 15–16, 17–18, 19–21, 32–33, and 35–36.

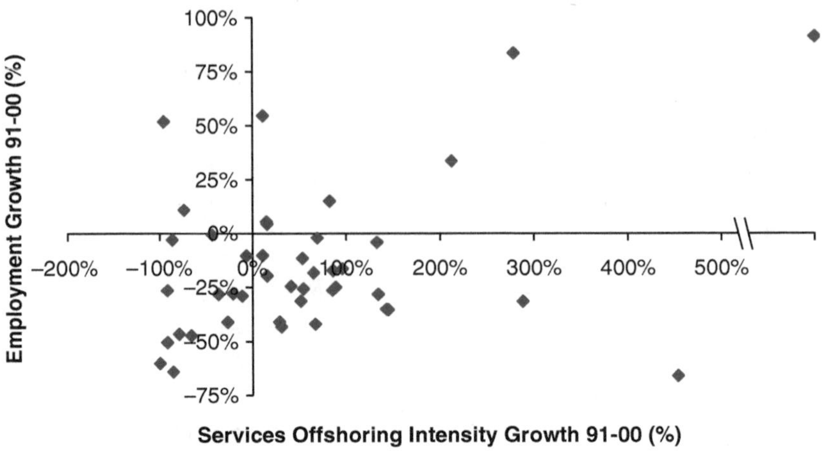

Fig. 5.6 German services offshoring intensity and employment growth (1991–2000)
Source: own calculations. Data: Federal Statistical Office Germany, STAN Industrial Database OECD

sectors are placed in the fourth quadrant plus two sectors in the second quadrant, implying a possible negative relationship between services offshoring growth and employment growth. Since seven sectors are situated in the first quadrant and 13 sectors in the third quadrant, this suggests a possible positive relationship between both variables.

For further indications, the ten sectors with the strongest services offshoring growth between 1991 and 2000 are ranked in Table 5.11 in order to check whether these sectors are more likely to show negative employment growth. The three highlighted service sectors "computer and related activities" (1,267%), "other business activities" (279%) as well as research and development (212%) have positive employment growth rates. Note that computer and related activities display the largest growth rates in both services offshoring and employment (91%). Five of the seven service sectors are situated in the first quadrant of Fig. 5.6. However, the remaining seven manufacturing sectors out of the top ten all have negative employment growth rates. As a first indication, one could presume a positive relationship between services offshoring and employment growth in the service sectors but a rather negative one in the manufacturing sectors.

5.2.2.2 Estimation Results

The following section measures the impact of services and materials offshoring on labor demand in 34 manufacturing sectors using the unrevised input–output data between 1991 and 2000.[12] Following section 5.1, we apply the consistent *fixed*

[12]As in Sect. 5.1.2, the two outliers "pharmaceuticals" and "office, accounting and computer machinery" are dropped due to extremely high services offshoring intensities.

Table 5.11 Ranking of OSS and employment growth in Germany (1991–2000)

Ranking of services offshoring growth	Services offshoring intensity growth		Employment growth	
Sector	%	Rank	%	Rank
Top Ten				
Computer and related activities	1,266.8%	1	91.4%	1
Office, accounting and computing machinery	453.4%	2	−65.9%	43
Tobacco products	288.0%	3	−31.6%	31
Other business activities	278.5%	4	83.5%	2
Research and development	212.3%	5	33.7%	5
Chemicals excluding pharmaceuticals	144.9%	6	−35.4%	33
Metal castings	143.3%	7	−35.1%	32
Other transport equipment	134.7%	8	−28.4%	28
Pharmaceuticals	133.2%	9	−4.1%	13
Beverages	96.1%	10	−16.4%	17

Source: own calculations. Data: Federal Statistical Office Germany, STAN Industrial Database OECD

effects estimator producing robust standard errors. We also integrate year fixed effects D_t in all specifications as well as the additional control variable import shares in some specifications.

Employment effects are not always instantaneous. Y is expected to affect employment in the subsequent period, because companies adapt their investment and other decisions (such as labor demand) to their expected output, which is mostly calculated on the basis of preceding years' results. Assuming labor market rigidities wage changes are also likely to influence labor demand in the next period. Hence, one-period lags $\ln Y_{t-1}$ and $\ln w_{t-1}$ should be included in the model. Finally, technology could also influence labor demand in the following period; we thus add one-period lags of the offshoring, domestic outsourcing, and R&D-intensity variables.

The estimation results of the conditional labor demand functions are shown in Table 5.12. As predicted in the theory, real output influences labor demand positively over all specifications, whereas real wages are responsible for employment losses, both at a highly significant level. However, the specifications show no clear trend about which effect is stronger. Columns 1–4 only consider instantaneous labor demand effects. Regarding the different specifications, column 1 focuses on offshoring, column two on domestic outsourcing, and column three on all prices. Column 4 additionally includes import shares as further control variable. Services offshoring has a positive instantaneous, but insignificant effect on employment. Materials offshoring influences labor demand negatively, which is only significant in column one. Domestic services and materials outsourcing show a positive effect on employment being highly significant. R&D intensity and import share show positive, but insignificant coefficients.

Columns 5–8 include one-period lags of each regressor. The significant effects of output and wages can be confirmed. Services offshoring seems to have a slightly positive, but insignificant effect on labor demand. Materials offshoring shows a significantly negative effect when only offshoring is considered (column 5), which

Table 5.12 Labor demand – Fixed effects estimator (1991–2000)

	Dependent variable: $\ln L_t$							
	Fixed effects estimator: instantaneous effects[a]				Fixed effects estimator: one-period lags[a]			
	(1)	(2)	(3)	(4)	(5)	(6)	(7)	(8)
$\ln Y_t$	0.4494***	0.4892***	0.4787***	0.4418***	0.1844***	0.1919***	0.3139**	0.4258**
	(0.000)	(0.000)	(0.000)	(0.000)	(0.004)	(0.003)	(0.031)	(0.013)
$\ln Y_{t-1}$					0.4037***	0.3998***	0.2602**	0.1587
					(0.000)	(0.000)	(0.036)	(0.270)
$\ln w_t$	−0.6348***	−0.5782***	−0.5728***	−0.6124***	−0.3746***	−0.3638***	−0.3892***	−0.4131***
	(0.000)	(0.000)	(0.000)	(0.000)	(0.000)	(0.000)	(0.001)	(0.001)
$\ln w_{t-1}$					−0.2740**	−0.2167*	−0.1451	−0.2179**
					(0.021)	(0.076)	(0.189)	(0.035)
$\ln \text{OSS}_t$	0.0059		0.0065	0.0096	−0.0043		−0.0044	−0.0018
	(0.686)		(0.660)	(0.501)	(0.648)		(0.645)	(0.845)
$\ln \text{OSS}_{t-1}$					0.0044		0.0049	0.0050
					(0.638)		(0.639)	(0.622)
$\ln \text{OSM}_t$	−0.2021**		−0.0405	−0.0413	−0.1027*		−0.0305	0.0075
	(0.047)		(0.640)	(0.655)	(0.086)		(0.491)	(0.873)
$\ln \text{OSM}_{t-1}$					0.0177		0.0878	0.0632
					(0.802)		(0.365)	(0.524)
$\ln \text{DOS}_t$		0.1991***	0.1625*	0.1814*		0.0402	0.0320	0.0398
		(0.010)	(0.076)	(0.055)		(0.505)	(0.684)	(0.633)
$\ln \text{DOS}_{t-1}$						0.0632	0.0768	0.0633
						(0.404)	(0.339)	(0.416)
$\ln \text{DOM}_t$		0.4221***	0.4007**	0.3991**		0.1854**	0.1733**	0.1912**
		(0.000)	(0.011)	(0.011)		(0.019)	(0.039)	(0.039)
$\ln \text{DOM}_{t-1}$						0.0879	0.2239	0.2233
						(0.213)	(0.145)	(0.115)

(*continued*)

Table 5.12 (continued)

	Dependent variable: $\ln L_t$							
	Fixed effects estimator: instantaneous effects[a]				Fixed effects estimator: one-period lags[a]			
	(1)	(2)	(3)	(4)	(5)	(6)	(7)	(8)
$\ln(\mathrm{RD}/Y)_t$			0.0905	0.0511			0.1473	0.2134
			(0.127)	(0.361)			(0.225)	(0.121)
$\ln(\mathrm{RD}/Y)_{t-1}$							−0.0597	−0.1421
								(0.464)
$\ln(\mathrm{IM}/Y)_t$				0.0267				0.0672
				(0.624)				(0.158)
$\ln(\mathrm{IM}/Y)_{t-1}$								−0.0258
								(0.518)
Year fixed effects	Yes	Yes	Yes	Yes	Yes	Yes	Yes	Yes
Joint significance tests:								
$\ln Y_t + \ln Y_{t-1} = 0$					$p>F = 0.0000$	$p>F = 0.0000$	$p>F = 0.0000$	$p>F = 0.0000$
$\ln w_t + \ln w_{t-1} = 0$					$p>F = 0.0004$	$p>F = 0.0008$	$p>F = 0.0010$	$p>F = 0.0001$
$\ln \mathrm{OSS}_t + \ln \mathrm{OSS}_{t-1} = 0$					$p>F = 0.7770$		$p>F = 0.7482$	$p>F = 0.8293$
$\ln \mathrm{OSM}_t + \ln \mathrm{OSM}_{t-1} = 0$					$p>F = 0.0775$		$p>F = 0.5103$	$p>F = 0.8126$
$\ln \mathrm{DOS}_t + \ln \mathrm{DOS}_{t-1} = 0$						$p>F = 0.4345$	$p>F = 0.5668$	$p>F = 0.6229$
$\ln \mathrm{DOM}_t + \ln \mathrm{DOM}_{t-1} = 0$						$p>F = 0.0284$	$p>F = 0.0676$	$p>F = 0.0701$
$\ln(\mathrm{RD}/Y)_t + \ln(\mathrm{RD}/Y)_{t-1} = 0$							$p>F = 0.3030$	$p>F = 0.2938$
$\ln(\mathrm{IM}/Y)_t + \ln(\mathrm{IM}/Y)_{t-1} = 0$								$p>F = 0.2621$
AIC	−824.3	−855.6	−873.5	−818.3	−829.8	−858.6	−866.0	−809.3
Observations	334	340	326	302	300	306	292	270
R-squared	0.76	0.79	0.81	0.82	0.75	0.77	0.79	0.81

Source: own calculations

$p^* < 0.1$, $p^{**} < 0.05$, $p^{***} < 0.001$ (*p* values in parentheses)

[a]All estimations without the outliers "pharmaceuticals" and "office, accounting and computer machinery"

turns insignificantly positive in the other specifications, probably due to strongly negative collinearity with DOS of around 74%. Domestic services and materials outsourcing still influence labor demand positively, which is only significant for DOM. Likewise, the overall effect of R&D intensities and import shares remain positive, but insignificant. Note that the AIC suggests to prefer the specifications without import shares (columns 3 and 7) to columns 4 and 8.

The unsatisfactory results raise the question of whether the model is correctly specified with regard to our dataset. Imagine that a company has closed a contract with an external service or material provider, who is supposed to deliver in $t=2$. It might be possible that in some cases offshoring or outsourcing in $t=2$ already leads to layoffs in the precedent period $t=1$. One explanation would be that firms anticipate the layoffs and prepone part of the layoffs to $t=1$ e.g., for political reasons. The novelty of services offshoring in the 1990s might have led firms to act like this. Statistically, this would also capture cases where a firms intends to purchase service inputs at the beginning of $t=2$ (e.g., in January), but already releases workers at the end of $t=1$ (e.g., in December).

One could object that it is impossible for a company to maintain a given level of output with fewer inputs. Concerning material inputs, it is imaginable that companies still rely on their resources to bridge the transition period. Concerning service inputs, many services might not be needed immediately in the current production process (e.g., web page development or design). To test these assumptions, one-period leads $\ln OSS_{t+1}$, $\ln OSM_{t+1}$, $\ln DOS_{t+1}$ and $\ln DOM_{t+1}$ instead of one-period lags should be included.

The results of the *fixed effects estimations with leads* are shown in columns 1–4 of Table 5.13. The leads of services offshoring are all negative and significant in columns 1, 3 and 4. The net effect is weakly negative, too, and significant except for column 1. The lead of materials offshoring is also negative and significant in column 1. The insignificant results of materials offshoring in columns 3 and 4 might be caused by the collinearity problem with DOS. The leads of domestic materials outsourcing are significantly positive in all specifications, while domestic services outsourcing shows no clear trend. Again, the AIC suggests to prefer the specification of column 3. To sum up, services offshoring seems to have had a weakly negative net impact on the conditional labor demand in the 1990s.

The results so far only considered the productivity and substitution effects of offshoring (5.15). In the following, we estimate the unconditional labor demand function (5.16), which also takes scale effects into account. The results are shown in columns 5–8 of Table 5.13. Columns 5 and 6 only consider instantaneous effects, while columns 7 and 8 also include one-period leads of the offshoring and domestic outsourcing variables. Services offshoring shows an insignificantly positive influence on employment, whereas materials offshoring affects the unconditional labor demand negatively being highly significant. Domestic services and materials outsourcing still have a positive impact, which is only significant for DOM. R&D intensity affects employment negatively, being insignificant. The results suggest that services offshoring has a negative effect when we consider only productivity and substitution effects, while the overall effect turns (insignificantly) positive,

Table 5.13 Labor demand – Fixed effects estimator: Leads and scale effects (1991–2000)

Dependent variable: $\ln L_t$

	Fixed effects estimator: one-period leads[a]				Fixed effects estimator: scale effects[a]			
	(1)	(2)	(3)	(4)	(5)	(6)	(7)	(8)
$\ln Y_t$	0.2487***	0.2778***	0.3647**	0.4526***				
	(0.004)	(0.000)	(0.030)	(0.004)				
$\ln Y_{t-1}$	0.3079***	0.3083***	0.1729	0.1172				
	(0.000)	(0.001)	(0.111)	(0.287)				
$\ln w_t$	−0.3687***	−0.3835***	−0.3959***	−0.4408***	−0.4954***	−0.3439***	−0.3349**	−0.2292**
	(0.001)	(0.000)	(0.001)	(0.000)	(0.001)	(0.005)	(0.010)	(0.048)
$\ln w_{t-1}$	−0.2780***	−0.2185*	−0.1304	−0.2133***			−0.1565*	−0.0487
	(0.007)	(0.089)	(0.138)	(0.003)			(0.090)	(0.641)
$\ln OSS_t$	0.0069		0.0099	0.0113	0.0234	0.0128	0.019	0.0179
	(0.458)		(0.312)	(0.250)	(0.257)	(0.538)	(0.137)	(0.146)
$\ln OSS_{t+1}$	−0.0116*		−0.0122*	−0.0117*			−0.0010	−0.0099
	(0.086)		(0.088)	(0.096)			(0.905)	(0.290)
$\ln OSM_t$	−0.0622		0.0064	0.0103	−0.2993**	−0.1385**	−0.1319*	−0.0207
	(0.224)		(0.928)	(0.882)	(0.016)	(0.033)	(0.074)	(0.771)
$\ln OSM_{t+1}$	−0.1075*		−0.0467	−0.0095			−0.2111***	−0.1442***
	(0.051)		(0.257)	(0.805)			(0.001)	(0.006)
$\ln DOS_t$		0.1085	0.0799	0.0734		0.1361		0.0276
		(0.132)	(0.328)	(0.419)		(0.224)		(0.797)
$\ln DOS_{t+1}$		−0.0371	0.0069	−0.0048				0.0654
		(0.557)	(0.931)	(0.950)				(0.259)
$\ln DOM_t$		0.1571***	0.2024	0.2293*		0.3368**		0.2037
		(0.009)	(0.103)	(0.057)		(0.044)		(0.169)
$\ln DOM_{t+1}$		0.1496**	0.1406**	0.1624**				0.1522*
		(0.044)	(0.034)	(0.027)				(0.088)

(continued)

Table 5.13 (continued)

Dependent variable: $\ln L_t$	Fixed effects estimator: one-period leads[a]				Fixed effects estimator: scale effects[a]			
	(1)	(2)	(3)	(4)	(5)	(6)	(7)	(8)
$\ln(RD/Y)_t$			0.1414	0.1728		−0.0846		−0.0254
			(0.302)	(0.212)		(0.126)		(0.705)
$\ln(RD/Y)_{t-1}$			−0.0534	−0.0995				−0.0414
			(0.565)	(0.295)				(0.472)
$\ln(IM/Y)_t$				0.0049				
				(0.890)				
$\ln(IM/Y)_{t+1}$				0.0609				
				(0.299)				
Year fixed effects	Yes	Yes	Yes	Yes	Yes	Yes	Yes	Yes
Joint significance tests:								
$\ln Y_t + \ln Y_{t-1} = 0$	$p>F = 0.0002$	$p>F = 0.0000$	$p>F = 0.0000$	$p>F = 0.0000$				
$\ln w_t + \ln w_{t-1} = 0$	$p>F = 0.0031$	$p>F = 0.0019$	$p>F = 0.0038$	$p>F = 0.0001$			$p>F = 0.0349$	$p>F = 0.1272$
$\ln OSS_t + \ln OSS_{t+1} = 0$	$p>F = 0.1388$		$p>F = 0.0357$	$p>F = 0.0498$			$p>F = 0.2923$	$p>F = 0.0796$
$\ln OSM_t + \ln OSM_{t+1} = 0$	$p>F = 0.1427$		$p>F = 0.5142$	$p>F = 0.9389$			$p>F = 0.0057$	$p>F = 0.0069$
$\ln DOS_t + \ln DOS_{t+1} = 0$		$p>F = 0.2075$	$p>F = 0.6065$	$p>F = 0.6968$				$p>F = 0.4845$
$\ln DOM_t + \ln DOM_{t+1} = 0$		$p>F = 0.0089$	$p>F = 0.0532$	$p>F = 0.0478$				$p>F = 0.0907$
$\ln(RD/Y)_t + \ln(RD/Y)_{t-1} = 0$			$p>F = 0.2710$	$p>F = 0.4193$				$p>F = 0.4260$
$\ln(IM/Y)_t + \ln(IM/Y)_{t+1} = 0$				$p>F = 0.5655$				
AIC	−785.1	−805.9	−810.5	−763.2	−703.0	−774.0	−684.0	−743.1
Observations	266	272	258	239	334	336	266	258
R-squared	0.77	0.79	0.81	0.83	0.66	0.73	0.66	0.75

Source: own calculations
$p^* < 0.1$, $p^{**} < 0.05$, $p^{***} < 0.001$ (*p* values in parentheses)
[a]All estimations without the outliers "pharmaceuticals" and "office, accounting and computer machinery"

when we also control for scale effects. Interestingly, the significantly negative effect of materials offshoring strongly increases when we also consider scale effects.

In a next step, the explanatory variables should be controlled for potential endogeneity. It is plausible that sectors with relatively low employment compared to other inputs, i.e., a smaller L/Ω, aim to increase their output and self-select into offshoring, domestic outsourcing, and/or spending more on R&D. On the other hand, sectors that employ much labor relative to other inputs might hope to increase their output by substituting labor for purchased inputs. Hence, Table 5.14 applies the IV 2SLS *fixed effects estimator*. Columns 1–4 use the first three lags of the potentially endogenous variables as instruments for $\ln OSS_t$, $\ln OSM_t$, $\ln DOS_t$, $\ln DOM_t$, and $\ln(RD/Y)_t$. Output and wages show the expected coefficient signs and are highly significant. All endogenously-treated variables show insignificant results except for DOS in column 2. When we control for scale effects in column 4, the overall trends only change for OSM and R&D intensity, both remaining insignificant.

Instead of the first three lags, the first two leads are used as instruments in columns 5–8. Interestingly, $\ln OSS_t$ and $\ln OSM_t$ always show a negative and mostly significant impact on labor demand. Nevertheless, the negative influence of services offshoring seems to be much smaller than the one of materials offshoring. DOM shows significantly positive coefficients, whereas the positive effect of DOS is insignificant. Estimating the unconditional labor demand function in column 8 mostly confirms the trend of column 7. The negative effect of services offshoring, however, misses the 10% significance level. To sum up, using leads instead of lags yields more significant results for the period 1991–2000. Accordingly, services and materials offshoring had a significantly negative impact on conditional labor demand in German manufacturing. Controlling for scale effects, only materials offshoring has a significantly and even stronger negative impact, while the negative effect of services offshoring becomes insignificant.

The significant results using the *conditional labor demand function* should be interpreted. The coefficients of services offshoring vary between −0.0004 (Table 5.13, column 4) and −0.0245 (Table 5.14, column 7). Between 1991 and 2000, services offshoring grew by on average 6.0% p.a. in the manufacturing sectors, from 0.43 to 0.74%. Thus, services offshoring led to an average employment reduction of between 0.00 and −0.15% p.a. and between −0.02 and −1.3% over the entire period. Controlling for potential scale effects in the *unconditional labor demand function*, the results become ambiguous. On the one hand, the overall coefficient of the fixed effects estimator is 0.008 (Table 5.13, column 8), which reflects an average employment increase of 0.05% per year or of 0.4% over the whole period. On the other hand, the coefficient of the IV 2SLS fixed effects estimator is −0.0216 (Table 5.14, column 8), but narrowly misses the 10% significance level. This would reflect an average employment reduction of −0.13% p.a. or of −1.2% over the whole period. We conclude that the impact of services offshoring on labor demand seems to be weakly negative or even slightly positive depending on the specification and estimation methodology. Since the potential of

Table 5.14 Labor demand – IV 2SLS fixed effects estimator (1991–2000)

Dependent variable: $\ln L_t$	IV 2SLS fixed effects estimator[a] with lags[b]				IV 2SLS fixed effects estimator[a] with leads[c]			
	(1)	(2)	(3)	(4)	(5)	(6)	(7)	(8)
$\ln Y_t$	0.2014***	0.2391***	0.2745***		0.3066***	0.2284***	0.3251***	
	(0.000)	(0.000)	(0.001)		(0.008)	(0.006)	(0.001)	
$\ln Y_{t-1}$	0.3378***	0.3317***	0.2790***		0.1449	0.2972***	0.2212***	
	(0.000)	(0.000)	(0.001)		(0.305)	(0.000)	(0.005)	
$\ln w_t$	−0.3818***	−0.4068***	−0.4800***	−0.3089***	−0.3143**	−0.3718***	−0.3372***	−0.1916
	(0.000)	(0.000)	(0.000)	(0.001)	(0.026)	(0.006)	(0.007)	(0.127)
$\ln w_{t-1}$	−0.2256*	−0.1872	−0.0430	0.0950	−0.2159*	−0.2551***	−0.2066**	−0.0806
	(0.098)	(0.195)	(0.724)	(0.402)	(0.063)	(0.008)	(0.038)	(0.435)
$\ln OSS_t$	0.0060		0.0036	0.0106	−0.0329**		−0.0245*	−0.0216
	(0.730)		(0.832)	(0.679)	(0.042)		(0.054)	(0.185)
$\ln OSM_t$	−0.0413		0.0843	−0.0425	−0.6449**		−0.1778*	−0.3496**
	(0.765)		(0.515)	(0.713)	(0.026)		(0.078)	(0.039)
$\ln DOS_t$		0.1756*	0.1736	0.0898		0.0513	0.0819	0.0681
		(0.082)	(0.182)	(0.553)		(0.642)	(0.540)	(0.707)
$\ln DOM_t$		0.1552	0.2829	0.242		0.3873***	0.3884**	0.4874**
		(0.207)	(0.162)	(0.194)		(0.003)	(0.017)	(0.040)
$\ln(RD/Y)_t$			0.0712	−0.1496			0.1168*	0.0026
			(0.353)	(0.119)			(0.096)	(0.965)
Fixed year effects	Yes	Yes	Yes	Yes	Yes	Yes	Yes	Yes
Joint significance:								
$\ln Y_t + \ln Y_{t-1} = 0$	$p>F = 0.0000$	$p>F = 0.0000$	$p>F = 0.0000$		$p>F = 0.0022$	$p>F = 0.0000$	$p>F = 0.0000$	
$\ln w_t + \ln w_{t-1} = 0$	$p>F = 0.0000$	$p>F = 0.0000$	$p>F = 0.0000$	$p>F = 0.0033$	$p>F = 0.0324$	$p>F = 0.0027$	$p>F = 0.0017$	$p>F = 0.1791$

(continued)

Table 5.14 (continued)

Dependent variable: $\ln L_t$

	IV 2SLS fixed effects estimator[a] with lags[b]				IV 2SLS fixed effects estimator[a] with leads[c]			
	(1)	(2)	(3)	(4)	(5)	(6)	(7)	(8)
First stage results:								
Shea partial *R*-squared:								
OSS_t	0.4007		0.4441	0.4322	0.2931		0.4445	0.4464
OSM_t	0.3638		0.4262	0.4548	0.067		0.2797	0.3041
DOS_t		0.4357	0.5475	0.5328		0.5429	0.4382	0.4563
DOM_t		0.3914	0.4355	0.4335		0.3768	0.3762	0.3704
$(RD/Y)_t$			0.7603	0.5026			0.5656	0.5981
Hansen J statistic[d] *p* value	$X^2(4) = 0.44$	$X^2(4) = 0.16$	$X^2(10) = 0.52$	$X^2(10) = 0.62$	$X^2(3) = 0.21$	$X^2(2) = 0.07$	$X^2(5) = 0.23$	$X^2(5) = 0.18$
AIC	−699.8	−724.9	−718.2	−666.8	−566.5	−754.0	−725.4	−629.8
Observations	231	238	223	223	198	238	225	225
R-squared (within)	0.61	0.64	0.67	0.57	0.68	0.80	0.80	0.69

Source: own calculations

$p^* < 0.1$, $p^{**} < 0.05$, $p^{***} < 0.001$ (*p* values in parentheses)

[a]All estimations without the outliers "pharmaceuticals" and "office, accounting and computer machinery"

[b]The first three lags are used as instruments

[c]The first two leads are used as instruments

[d]Over-identification test of all instruments

services offshoring has not fully been exploited yet, future negative employment effects could be stronger. The employment effects of services offshoring for the period 1995 to 2004 are thus estimated in the next step.

5.2.3 Estimations with Revised Input–Output Data: 1995–2004

5.2.3.1 Preliminary Analysis

A first look at the relationship between services offshoring and employment is given in Fig. 5.7. The scatter plot shows *German services offshoring intensity versus employment growth rates* between 1995 and 2004. The sector "leather, leather products, and footwear" has been dropped, since services offshoring intensities are not available. Therefore, 42 sectors have been taken into account. 33 sectors show a negative employment growth ranging from −3% (medical, precision, and optical instruments) to −55% (wearing apparel, dressing, and dying of fur) over the period. The majority of the sectors, namely 22 are placed in the fourth quadrant, implying a possible negative relationship between services offshoring growth and employment growth. Only eight sectors are located in the first quadrant and two sectors in the third quadrant, where one would expect a possible positive relationship between both variables.

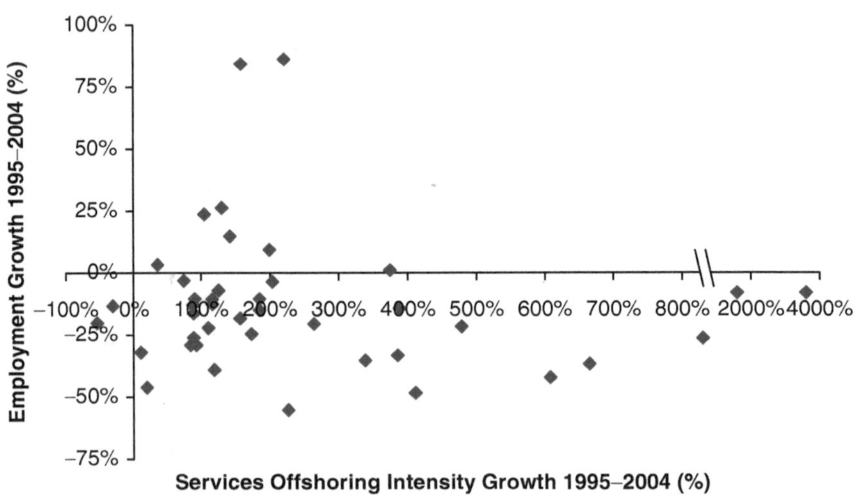

Fig. 5.7 German services offshoring intensity and employment growth (1995–2004)
Source: own calculations. Data: Federal Statistical Office Germany, STAN Industrial Database OECD.
NB: The sector "leather, leather products, and footwear" was dropped, since services offshoring intensities are not available. OSS growth rates for the sectors "wearing apparel, dressing, and dying of fur", "recycling", and "collection, purification, and distribution of water" are calculated for 1996–2004, since OSS is not available for 1995

Table 5.15 Ranking of OSS and employment growth in Germany (1995–2004)

Ranking of services offshoring growth	Services offshoring intensity growth		Employment growth	
Sector	%	Rank	%	Rank
Top Ten				
Activities related to financial intermediation	81,539.0%	1	−8.0%	14
Metal castings	3,705.0%	2	−8.0%	13
Manufacturing n.e.c.	1,567.0%	3	−26.3%	31
Textiles	665.2%	4	−36.7%	37
Gas and gas supply	607.7%	5	−42.2%	39
Iron and steel	478.4%	6	−21.5%	27
Office, accounting, and computing machinery	410.6%	7	−48.3%	41
Nonferrous metals	388.0%	8	−14.3%	21
Tobacco products	385.3%	9	−33.3%	35
Publishing	374.5%	10	1.2%	9

Source: own calculations. Data: Federal Statistical Office Germany, STAN Industrial Database OECD

NB: The sector "leather, leather products, and footwear" was dropped, since services offshoring intensities are not available. OSS growth rates for the sectors "wearing apparel, dressing, and dying of fur", "recycling", and "collection, purification, and distribution of water" are calculated for 1996–2004, since OSS is not available for 1995

For further insights, the ten sectors with the strongest services offshoring growth between 1995 and 2004 are ranked in Table 5.15 and compared to employment growth rates. It is evident that all these sectors have experienced negative employment growth over the respective period except for the sector "publishing". Even the service sector "activities related to financial intermediation" with the highest OSS growth shows a negative, but relatively small employment reduction. As four of the seven service sectors fall in the first quadrant of Fig. 5.7, one might presume a negative relationship between services offshoring and employment, especially for the manufacturing sectors.

5.2.3.2 Estimation Results

In the following subsection, we estimate the impact of services and materials offshoring on labor demand in the German manufacturing sectors for the period 1995 to 2004.[13] The estimation results using the consistent *fixed effects estimators* are shown in Table 5.16. All specifications use robust standard errors and include fixed year effects. Columns 1–4 only consider instantaneous effects on conditional labor demand, while columns 5–8 also include one-period lags, for reasons described above. As expected, real output has a significantly positive effect on labor demand, whereas real wages have a significantly negative influence on labor demand in all specifications.

[13]The outlier "pharmaceuticals" is excluded from the cross-section due to its extremely high services offshoring intensities, which leads to a total of 34 manufacturing sectors.

Table 5.16 Labor demand – Fixed effects estimator (1995–2004)

Dependent variable: $\ln L_t$

	Fixed effects estimator: instantaneous effects[a]				Fixed effects estimator: one-period lags[a]			
	(1)	(2)	(3)	(4)	(5)	(6)	(7)	(8)
$\ln Y_t$	0.3547***	0.3259***	0.4517***	0.3237**	0.1297**	0.1264**	0.3002**	0.5054***
	(0.001)	(0.003)	(0.000)	(0.018)	(0.018)	(0.022)	(0.048)	(0.001)
$\ln Y_{t-1}$					0.2530***	0.2209**	0.2224	−0.1904
					(0.009)	(0.012)	(0.162)	(0.261)
$\ln w_t$	−0.5627***	−0.5533***	−0.5770***	−0.5312***	−0.4770***	−0.4651***	−0.4985***	−0.4613***
	(0.000)	(0.000)	(0.000)	(0.000)	(0.000)	(0.000)	(0.000)	(0.000)
$\ln w_{t-1}$					−0.1090*	−0.1125*	−0.1178**	−0.1144**
					(0.067)	(0.098)	(0.032)	(0.014)
$\ln \text{OSS}_t$	−0.0397*		−0.0446***	−0.0233*	−0.0097		−0.0157	0.0036
	(0.056)		(0.005)	(0.056)	(0.641)		(0.319)	(0.851)
$\ln \text{OSS}_{t-1}$					−0.0398**		−0.0460***	−0.0295***
					(0.013)		(0.003)	(0.004)
$\ln \text{OSM}_t$	0.0065		−0.0015	−0.0015	−0.0040		0.0073	0.0196
	(0.788)		(0.945)	(0.961)	(0.825)		(0.740)	(0.479)
$\ln \text{OSM}_{t-1}$					0.0039		−0.0076	0.0128
					(0.882)		(0.704)	(0.620)
$\ln \text{DOS}_t$		0.1389*	0.1145*	0.1474*		0.0911*	0.1052**	0.1029**
		(0.072)	(0.055)	(0.068)		(0.062)	(0.012)	(0.043)
$\ln \text{DOS}_{t-1}$						0.0424	0.0148	0.0434
						(0.372)	(0.686)	(0.277)
$\ln \text{DOM}_t$		0.0178	0.0109	0.0006		0.0233	0.0529**	0.0593***
		(0.766)	(0.786)	(0.989)		(0.518)	(0.026)	(0.008)
$\ln \text{DOM}_{t-1}$						−0.0066	−0.0337	−0.0411
						(0.890)	(0.454)	(0.321)
$\ln(\text{RD}/Y)_t$			0.1572***	0.0931			0.2190	0.3903***
			(0.009)	(0.139)			(0.114)	(0.001)
$\ln(\text{RD}/Y)_{t-1}$							−0.0113	−0.2544**
							(0.924)	(0.017)

(continued)

Table 5.16 (continued)

Dependent variable: $\ln L_t$

	Fixed effects estimator: instantaneous effects[a]				Fixed effects estimator: one-period lags[a]			
	(1)	(2)	(3)	(4)	(5)	(6)	(7)	(8)
$\ln(\mathrm{IM}/Y)_t$				0.0512				0.0568**
				(0.169)				(0.028)
$\ln(\mathrm{IM}/Y)_{t-1}$								−0.0258
								(0.502)
Year fixed effects	Yes	Yes	Yes	Yes	Yes	Yes	Yes	Yes
Joint significance tests:								
$\ln Y_t + \ln Y_{t-1} = 0$					$p>F = 0.0047$	$p>F = 0.0121$	$p>F = 0.0002$	$p>F = 0.0022$
$\ln w_t + \ln w_{t-1} = 0$					$p>F = 0.0000$	$p>F = 0.0000$	$p>F = 0.0000$	$p>F = 0.0000$
$\ln \mathrm{OSS}_t + \ln \mathrm{OSS}_{t-1} = 0$					$p>F = 0.0398$		$p>F = 0.0029$	$p>F = 0.0134$
$\ln \mathrm{OSM}_t + \ln \mathrm{OSM}_{t-1} = 0$					$p>F = 0.9643$		$p>F = 0.8828$	$p>F = 0.7646$
$\ln \mathrm{DOS}_t + \ln \mathrm{DOS}_{t-1} = 0$						$p>F = 0.0907$	$p>F = 0.0050$	$p>F = 0.1015$
$\ln \mathrm{DOM}_t + \ln \mathrm{DOM}_{t-1} = 0$						$p>F = 0.6675$	$p>F = 0.0769$	$p>F = 0.0123$
$\ln(\mathrm{RD}/Y)_t + \ln(\mathrm{RD}/Y)_{t-1} = 0$							$p>F = 0.0080$	$p>F = 0.0051$
$\ln(\mathrm{IM}/Y)_t + \ln(\mathrm{IM}/Y)_{t-1} = 0$								$p>F = 0.0752$
AIC	−836.7	−830.4	−874.9	−860.4	−803.3	−809.0	−841.9	−825.5
Observations	337	350	337	309	303	315	303	278
R-squared (within)	0.65	0.65	0.7	0.71	0.66	0.66	0.71	0.72

Source: own calculations

$p^* < 0.1$, $p^{**} < 0.05$, $p^{***} < 0.001$ (p values in parentheses)

[a]All estimations without the outlier "pharmaceuticals"

The negative influence of OSS is significant in all specifications, while materials offshoring shows no clear trend, possibly due to negative collinearity with DOS. Domestic services and materials outsourcing as well as R&D intensity influence employment positively, which is significant for DOS and for R&D intensity in column 3. Including the additional control variable import share in column 4 reduces the negative effect of services offshoring. However, the AIC suggests to prefer column 3 to column 4. Integrating one-period lags of each explanatory variable in columns 5–8 confirms these results. Now, the overall effects of all variables except for OSM become significant in columns 7 and 8.

In a next step, we control for scale effects estimating the unconditional labor demand function (5.16). The results are shown in columns 1–4 of Table 5.17. Columns 1 and 3 include all variables, while columns 2 and 4 additionally control for import shares. The wage effects on the unconditional demand for labor are significantly negative. Services offshoring has a negative influence on unconditional labor demand, being significant when one-period lags are included (columns 3 and 4). Again, the negative effect becomes smaller when import shares are added (columns 2 and 4). Materials offshoring as well as domestic services and materials outsourcing all have a positive effect on employment controlling for scale effects. R&D intensity and import shares seem to show a weakly negative impact on unconditional labor demand, which is almost always insignificant (except for R&D intensity in column 4).

Finally, the explanatory variables should be controlled for potential endogeneity. The specifications in columns 5–8 of Table 5.17 use the IV 2SLS *fixed effects estimator*. All specifications use the first three lags of the potentially endogenous variables as instruments for $\ln OSS_t$, $\ln OSM_t$, $\ln DOS_t$, $\ln DOM_t$, $\ln(RD/Y)_t$, and $\ln(IM/Y)_t$. Output and wages influence labor demand as expected. Services offshoring has a negative impact on labor demand, which becomes significant in column 7. Materials offshoring shows negative coefficients estimating the conditional labor demand function, but a positive one estimating the unconditional labor demand equation, all being insignificant. Domestic services outsourcing affects labor demand positively, which is significant in columns 6 and 7 and narrowly misses the 10% level when we control for scale effects (column 8). Domestic materials outsourcing seems to influence labor demand negatively, but the results are not significant. R&D-intensities show a significantly positive coefficient in column 7, which turns insignificantly negative in column 8. To sum up, services offshoring seems to affect conditional and unconditional labor demand negatively. Controlling for endogeneity, however, only shows significant results for the conditional labor demand function.

The results show consistently and significantly that real output influences labor demand positively, whereas real wages have a negative effect. In the following, the results should be interpreted in terms of job losses or job creation due to services offshoring, using the largest and smallest significant coefficients of those specifications that control for scale effects and include at least all offshoring and domestic outsourcing variables simultaneously. The coefficients of services offshoring range between −0.0163 (Table 5.17, column 4) and −0.0371 (Table 5.17, column 3).

Table 5.17 Labor demand – FE and IV 2SLS FE estimator (1995–2004)

Dependent variable: ln L_t

	Fixed effects estimator: scale effects[a]				IV 2SLS fixed effects estimator[a]			
	(1)	(2)	(3)	(4)	(5)	(6)	(7)	(8)
$\ln Y_t$					0.1439*	0.1608	0.3539**	
					(0.059)	(0.129)	(0.017)	
$\ln Y_{t-1}$					0.2361***	0.1606**	0.1769**	
					(0.006)	(0.031)	(0.014)	
$\ln w_t$	−0.4763***	−0.4725***	−0.4548***	−0.3776***	−0.4573***	−0.5439***	−0.5184***	−0.4589***
	(0.000)	(0.000)	(0.000)	(0.000)	(0.000)	(0.000)	(0.000)	(0.000)
$\ln w_{t-1}$			−0.0500	−0.1501***	−0.1078*	−0.1001	−0.1077**	−0.0862
			(0.679)	(0.005)	(0.073)	(0.132)	(0.027)	(0.354)
$\ln OSS_t$	−0.0316	−0.0140	0.0099	0.0099	−0.0402		−0.0550***	−0.0218
	(0.177)	(0.304)	(0.679)	(0.599)	(0.161)		(0.010)	(0.536)
$\ln OSS_{t-1}$			−0.0470**	−0.0262**				
			(0.015)	(0.011)				
$\ln OSM_t$	0.0535**	0.0611*	0.0396	0.0513*	−0.0238		−0.0352	0.0053
	(0.030)	(0.075)	(0.193)	(0.063)	(0.627)		(0.617)	(0.935)
$\ln OSM_{t-1}$			0.0201	0.0293				
			(0.547)	(0.223)				
$\ln DOS_t$	0.1399	0.1821**	0.0960	0.1231**		0.3400*	0.2736*	0.3352
	(0.156)	(0.032)	(0.156)	(0.028)		(0.082)	(0.071)	(0.114)
$\ln DOS_{t-1}$			0.0361	0.0676				
			(0.593)	(0.110)				
$\ln DOM_t$	0.0786	0.0522	0.0587*	0.0689**		−0.1421	−0.0484	−0.0867
	(0.166)	(0.335)	(0.070)	(0.026)		(0.280)	(0.709)	(0.624)
$\ln DOM_{t-1}$			0.0335	−0.0070				
			(0.519)	(0.861)				

(*continued*)

Table 5.17 (continued)

Dependent variable: ln L_t	Fixed effects estimator: scale effects[a]				IV 2SLS fixed effects estimator[a]			
	(1)	(2)	(3)	(4)	(5)	(6)	(7)	(8)
$\ln(RD/Y)_t$	−0.0221	−0.0132	0.0709	0.0822			0.2063**	−0.1379
	(0.571)	(0.774)	(0.470)	(0.171)			(0.037)	(0.153)
$\ln(RD/Y)_{t-1}$			−0.0942	−0.0893*				
			(0.265)	(0.081)				
$\ln(IM/Y)_t$		−0.005		−0.0072				
		(0.898)		(0.822)				
$\ln(IM/Y)_{t-1}$				−0.0069				
				(0.846)				
Fixed year effects	Yes	Yes	Yes	Yes	Yes	Yes	Yes	Yes
Joint significance:								
$\ln Y_t + \ln Y_{t-1} = 0$					$p>F = 0.0128$	$p>F = 0.0324$	$p>F = 0.0005$	
$\ln w_t + \ln w_{t-1} = 0$			$p>F = 0.0000$	$p>F = 0.0000$	$p>F = 0.0000$	$p>F = 0.0000$	$p>F = 0.0000$	$p>F = 0.0000$
$\ln OSS_t + \ln OSS_{t-1} = 0$			$p>F = 0.0392$	$p>F = 0.0378$				
$\ln OSM_t + \ln OSM_{t-1} = 0$			$p>F = 0.1214$	$p>F = 0.1398$				
$\ln DOS_t + \ln DOS_{t-1} = 0$			$p>F = 0.1537$	$p>F = 0.0854$				
$\ln DOM_t + \ln DOM_{t-1} = 0$			$p>F = 0.1856$	$p>F = 0.0386$				
$\ln(RD/Y)_t + \ln(RD/Y)_{t-1} = 0$			$p>F = 0.4542$	$p>F = 0.2000$				
$\ln(IM/Y)_t + \ln(IM/Y)_{t-1} = 0$				$p>F = 0.9395$				
First stage results:								
Shea Partial R-squared:								
OSS_t					0.5066		0.4936	0.5223
OSM_t					0.3173		0.3705	0.3605
DOS_t						0.3014	0.2904	0.2839
DOM_t						0.1861	0.2571	0.2578

(continued)

Table 5.17 (continued)

Dependent variable: ln L_t								
	Fixed effects estimator: scale effects[a]				IV 2SLS fixed effects estimator[a]			
	(1)	(2)	(3)	(4)	(5)	(6)	(7)	(8)
$(RD/Y)_t$							0.6569	0.4974
Hansen J statistic[b] p value					$X^2(4) = 0.42$	$X^2(4) = 0.83$	$X^2(10) = 0.26$	$X^2(10) = 0.44$
AIC	−770.1	−831.8	−727.7	−796.2	−666.8	−639.3	−670.8	−589.7
Observations	337	309	303	278	235	245	235	235
R-squared (within)	0.58	0.68	0.58	0.69	0.63	0.57	0.64	0.48

Source: own calculations
$p^* < 0.1$, $p^{**} < 0.05$, $p^{***} < 0.001$ (p values in parentheses)
[a]All estimations without the outlier "pharmaceuticals"
[b]Over-identification test of all instruments

Between 1995 and 2004, the CAGR of services offshoring was 11.6% for the manufacturing sectors, growing from 0.38 to 1.02%. Thus, services offshoring led to an average employment reduction of between −0.19 and −0.43% p.a., which represents a reduction of between −1.7 and −3.9% over the entire period, holding all other variables constant. Having a total of 10,917,000 employees in the manufacturing sector in 1995, this would imply an employment reduction of between 187,000 and 429,000 employees.

Since services offshoring has a negative effect for Germany, but a positive one for the UK and the US (Amiti and Wei 2005, 2006), we draw the following conclusion. Companies in Germany that offshore services do not create new jobs despite efficiency gains, and thus, layoffs are not compensated for. This hypothesis is supported by a study of the McKinsey Global Institute saying that the US gained 1.14–1.17 for every dollar being invested in the Indian service sector. Germany, on the other hand, obtains only 0.74 € per euro that has been invested in Indian and Eastern European service jobs indicating an overall economic loss of 26%. According to this study, the principal reason is the higher re-employment chance of released labor in more productive activities in the US due to the more flexible labor market as well as the disposability of more productive jobs in the high-tech sector (McKinsey Global Institute 2005; Farrel 2004).

5.3 Services Offshoring and Its Impact on the Relative Demand for Less-Skilled Labor in Germany

5.3.1 Basics of the Empirical Analysis

5.3.1.1 Theoretical and Empirical Model

Theoretical Model

A linearly homogeneous production function F with constant returns to scale is described as follows:

$$Y = \tilde{F}(X_1, ..., X_n), \tag{5.17}$$

$$F_j = \frac{\partial F}{\partial X_j} > 0, \; F_{jj} = \frac{\partial^2 F}{\partial X_j^2} < 0, \; F_{jk} = \frac{\partial^2 F}{\partial X_j \partial X_k} > 0 \text{ for all } j, \; k = 1, \ldots, n$$

where Y is the output and X is a vector of homogeneous inputs j. Due to the homogeneity assumption, multiplying the inputs with a constant λ ($\lambda = 2, 3, ...$) augments production by λ^z, where z is constant and positive: $\lambda^z Y = F(\lambda X)$.

The labor demand functions are based on the cost minimization of a firm. On the assumption that a firm maximizes its profits and the production function has convex isoquants, total costs are calculated by summing up the products of optimal input demands and their respective factor prices. The *total cost function* dual to (5.17) can be described as follows:

$$\mathrm{CT} = \tilde{G}(Y, P_1, P_2, P_n) \tag{5.18}$$

where P_j is the input price of X_j, n is the total number of inputs, and $\mathrm{CT} = \sum_{j=1}^{n} P_j X_j$ is total cost conditional on the level of output Y.

Using *Shephard's Lemma*[14], the *conditional input demand function*, holding output Y constant, can be derived:

$$X_j^* = X_j^d(Y, P_j) = \frac{\partial \mathrm{CT}(Y, P_j)}{\partial P_j} \tag{5.19}$$

Under the assumption that Y is linearly homogeneous and therefore $\mathrm{CT}(P_j, Y) = Y\mathrm{CT}(P_j, 1)$, the elasticity of substitution σ_{jk} between input factor X_j and input factor X_k is obtained by the partial derivatives of the total cost function as shown by Uzawa (1962). Thus, the *static equilibrium elasticity of substitution* is as follows:

$$\sigma_{jk} = \frac{\mathrm{CT}\,\mathrm{CT}_{jk}}{\mathrm{CT}_j\,\mathrm{CT}_k} \tag{5.20}$$

where $\mathrm{CT}_j = \partial \mathrm{CT}/\partial P_j$ and $\mathrm{CT}_{jk} = \partial \mathrm{CT}_j/\partial P_k$.

If one considers a *partial state equilibrium* as introduced by Brown and Christensen (1981), only the variable factor inputs are in the state equilibrium, and the remaining inputs Z are fixed or quasi-fixed. The introduction of quasi-fixed input factors relaxes the assumption of full static equilibrium. Then, the following *variable unit cost function* CV, conditional on Y and the remaining inputs Z, is assumed:

$$\mathrm{CV} = \tilde{H}(Y, P_1, \ldots, P_l, Z_1, \ldots, Z_m), \tag{5.21}$$

where Z_j is considered a subset of X_j which is not necessarily at a static equilibrium level,

$$l + m = n \text{ and } \mathrm{CV} = \sum_{j=1}^{l} P_j X_j.$$

[14] According to Shephard's Lemma (1953), the factor demand X_j^* is determined by the first partial derivative of the cost function with respect to the corresponding factor price P_j, regardless of the kind of production function. Note that a * as a superscript in this section refers to the equilibrium amount.

The *partial static equilibrium elasticity of substitution* conditional on the level of output Y and the levels of fixed factors Z is derived from the variable cost function:

$$\sigma_{jk}^{P} = \frac{\mathrm{CV}\,\mathrm{CV}_{jk}}{\mathrm{CV}_j\,\mathrm{CV}_k}, \tag{5.22}$$

where $\mathrm{CV}_j = \partial \mathrm{CV}/\partial P_j$ and $\mathrm{CV}_{jk} = \partial \mathrm{CV}_j/\partial P_k$. σ_{jk}^{P} represents the elasticity of substitution only between the variable factor inputs, but not between the fixed and variable factors or among the fixed factor inputs.

Empirical Model

A *variable unit cost function* CV is specified following Geishecker (2002, 2006):

$$\mathrm{CV} = \mathrm{CV}(Y, w_{HS}, w_{LS}, K/Y, T) \tag{5.23}$$

where Y denotes the output and w_{HS} and w_{LS} are the exogenous wages for the *variable input factors* high skilled labor L_{HS} and less-skilled labor L_{LS}. Capital is considered a *quasi-fixed input factor* in the form of the capital coefficient K/Y. The *technology shifter* $T = T(\mathrm{OSS}, \mathrm{OSM}, \mathrm{DOS}, \mathrm{DOM}, \mathrm{RD}/Y)$ is defined as in the previous study. The following *transcendental logarithmic(translog) form*[15] of a variable unit short-run cost function as introduced by Brown and Christensen (1981) is used, allowing for l variable input factors $(P_j : j = 1, \ldots, l)$ and m quasi-fixed input factors $(Z_j : j = 1, \ldots, m)$:

$$\begin{aligned}
\ln \mathrm{CV} = {} & \alpha_0 + \alpha_Y \ln Y + \sum_{j=1}^{l} \alpha_j \ln P_j + \sum_{j=1}^{m} \beta_j \ln Z_j \\
& + \frac{1}{2}\gamma_{YY}(\ln Y)^2 + \frac{1}{2}\sum_{j=1}^{l}\sum_{k=1}^{l} \gamma_{jk} \ln P_j \ln P_k + \frac{1}{2}\sum_{j=1}^{m}\sum_{k=1}^{m} \delta_{jk} \ln Z_j \ln Z_k \\
& + \sum_{j=1}^{l} \zeta_{Yj} \ln Y \ln P_j + \sum_{j=1}^{l}\sum_{k=1}^{m} \zeta_{jk} \ln P_j \ln Z_k + \sum_{j=1}^{m} \eta_{Yj} \ln Y \ln Z_j \\
& + \theta_T T + \frac{1}{2}\theta_{TT} T^2 + \theta_{TY} T \ln Y + \sum_{j=1}^{l} \theta_{Tj} T \ln P_j + \sum_{j=1}^{m} \rho_{Tj} T \ln Z_j
\end{aligned} \tag{5.24}$$

[15]The translog cost function in the empirical work on trade and the demand for heterogeneous labor was first introduced by Berman et al. (1994) and applied by e.g., Feenstra and Hanson (1996), Geishecker (2002, 2006), Strauss-Kahn (2003), Hijzen et al. (2005), and Ekholm and Hakkala (2006).

In this partial static equilibrium framework, there are two variable input factors, $l = 2$, namely $P_1 = w_{HS}$ and $P_2 = w_{LS}$. We denote the corresponding coefficients by α_{HS} and α_{LS}. Also, there is only one quasi-fixed input factor, $m = 1$, namely $Z_1 = K/Y$. Now (5.24) specializes to:

$$\begin{aligned}
\ln \mathrm{CV} &= \alpha_0 + \alpha_Y \ln Y + \alpha_{HS} \ln w_{HS} + \alpha_{LS} \ln w_{LS} + \beta_K \ln \frac{K}{Y} + \frac{1}{2}\gamma_{YY}(\ln Y)^2 \\
&+ \frac{1}{2}\gamma_{HSLS} \ln w_{HS} \ln w_{LS} + \frac{1}{2}\gamma_{HSHS}(\ln w_{HS})^2 + \frac{1}{2}\gamma_{LSHS} \ln w_{LS} \ln w_{HS} \\
&+ \frac{1}{2}\gamma_{LSLS}(\ln w_{LS})^2 + \frac{1}{2}\delta_{KK}(\ln \frac{K}{Y})^2 + \zeta_{YHS} \ln Y \ln w_{HS} + \zeta_{YLS} \ln Y \ln w_{LS} \\
&+ \zeta_{HSK} \ln w_{HS} \ln \frac{K}{Y} + \zeta_{LSK} \ln w_{LS} \ln \frac{K}{Y} + \eta_{YK} \ln Y \ln \frac{K}{Y} \\
&+ \theta_T T + \frac{1}{2}\theta_{TT} T^2 + \theta_{TY} T \ln Y \\
&+ \theta_{\mathrm{OSS}HS} \mathrm{OSS} \ln w_{HS} + \theta_{\mathrm{OSS}LS} \mathrm{OSS} \ln w_{LS} \\
&+ \theta_{\mathrm{OSM}HS} \mathrm{OSM} \ln w_{HS} + \theta_{\mathrm{OSM}LS} \mathrm{OSM} \ln w_{LS} \\
&+ \theta_{\mathrm{DOS}HS} \mathrm{DOS} \ln w_{HS} + \theta_{\mathrm{DOS}LS} \mathrm{DOS} \ln w_{LS} \\
&+ \theta_{\mathrm{DOM}HS} \mathrm{DOM} \ln w_{HS} + \theta_{\mathrm{DOM}LS} \mathrm{DOM} \ln w_{LS} \\
&+ \theta_{\mathrm{RD}HS} \frac{RD}{Y} \ln w_{HS} + \theta_{\mathrm{RD}LS} \frac{RD}{Y} \ln w_{LS} + \rho_{TK} T \ln \frac{K}{Y}. \qquad (5.25)
\end{aligned}$$

For symmetry reasons, the following parameter restrictions are imposed:

$$\gamma_{jk} = \gamma_{kj} \text{ and } \delta_{jk} = \delta_{kj}.$$

In order for homogeneity of degree one in input prices to hold, the following linear restrictions are required:

$$\sum_j^l \alpha_j = 1,$$

$$\sum_j^l \gamma_{jk} = \sum_j^l \gamma_{kj} = \sum_j^l \zeta_{jk} = 0 \text{ for all } k, \text{ and}$$

$$\sum_j^l \zeta_{Yj} = \sum_j^l \theta_{Tj} = 0$$

Applying Shephard's Lemma yields the respective factor demand which is the *factor's share in total variable costs* as the cost function is in logarithmic form:

$$\frac{\partial \ln \mathrm{CV}}{\partial \ln w_{HS}} = \frac{\partial \mathrm{CV}/\mathrm{CV}}{\partial w_{HS}/w_{HS}} = \frac{w_{HS}}{\mathrm{CV}} \frac{\partial \mathrm{CV}}{\partial w_{HS}} = \frac{w_{HS} L_{HS}}{\mathrm{CV}} = S_{HS}, \qquad (5.26)$$

$$\frac{\partial \ln \mathrm{CV}}{\partial \ln w_{LS}} = \frac{\partial \mathrm{CV}/\mathrm{CV}}{\partial w_{LS}/w_{LS}} = \frac{w_{LS}}{\mathrm{CV}}\frac{\partial \mathrm{CV}}{\partial w_{LS}} = \frac{w_{LS}L_{LS}}{\mathrm{CV}} = S_{LS}, \tag{5.27}$$

where L_{HS} and L_{LS} is the demand for high-skilled and less-skilled labor with $L_{HS} = \partial \mathrm{CV}/\partial w_{HS}$ and $L_{LS} = \partial \mathrm{CV}/\partial w_{LS}$. S_{HS} and S_{LS} is the cost share of L_{HS} and L_{LS} in variable costs CV. Since in (5.26) and (5.27) w_{HS} and w_{LS} are the only variable costs, CV is determined by the sum of the products of the variable factor costs with their respective factors: $\mathrm{CV} = w_{HS}L_{HS} + w_{LS}L_{LS} = wL$, where w designates the average wage per labor L, regardless of the qualification. Thus, S_{HS} and S_{LS} can be determined as follows:

$$S_{HS} = \frac{w_{HS}L_{HS}}{w_{LS}L_{LS} + w_{HS}L_{HS}} = \frac{w_{HS}L_{HS}}{wL}, \tag{5.26'}$$

$$S_{LS} = \frac{w_{LS}L_{LS}}{w_{LS}L_{LS} + w_{HS}L_{HS}} = \frac{w_{LS}L_{LS}}{wL}. \tag{5.27'}$$

Since L_{HS} and L_{LS} are the only variable inputs, and thus $S_{HS} + S_{LS} = 1$, only one cost share is linearly independent. The first partial derivative of (5.25) with respect to $\ln w_{LS}$ yields the *conditional demand for less-skilled labor*:

$$\begin{aligned} S_{LS} = {} & \alpha_{LS} + \zeta_{YLS} \ln Y + 1/2\gamma_{HSLS} \ln w_{HS} + 1/2\gamma_{LSHS} \ln w_{HS} + \gamma_{LSLS} \ln w_{LS} \\ & + \zeta_{LSK} \ln(K/Y) + \theta_{\mathrm{OSS}LS}\mathrm{OSS} + \theta_{\mathrm{OSM}LS}\mathrm{OSM} \\ & + \theta_{\mathrm{DOS}LS}\mathrm{DOS} + \theta_{\mathrm{DOM}LS}\mathrm{DOM} + \theta_{\mathrm{RD}LS}(\mathrm{RD}/Y). \end{aligned} \tag{5.28}$$

According to (5.27)' a decrease of S_{LS} can reflect both a fall in L_{LS} and/or a fall in w_{LS} which implies according to (5.26)' a rise in S_{HS} and thus an increase in L_{HS} and/or in w_{HS}. Hence, the composite term S_{LS} can be considered as the relative demand for less-skilled labor. Due to symmetry and homogeneity, we have $\gamma_w = \gamma_{HSLS} = \gamma_{LSLS} = -\gamma_{LSLS} = -\gamma_{HSHS}$. Thus, (5.28) leads to the following model:[16]

$$\begin{aligned} S_{LS,it} = {} & \alpha + \zeta_Y \ln Y_{it} + \gamma_w \ln \frac{w_{HS,it}}{w_{LS,it}} + \zeta_K \ln(K/Y)_{it} + \theta_{\mathrm{OSS}}\mathrm{OSS}_{it} + \theta_{\mathrm{OSM}}\mathrm{OSM}_{it} \\ & + \theta_{\mathrm{DOS}}\mathrm{DOS}_{it} + \theta_{\mathrm{DOM}}\mathrm{DOM}_{it} + \theta_{\mathrm{RD}}(\mathrm{RD}/Y)_{it} + D_t + \varepsilon_{it}. \end{aligned} \tag{5.29}$$

5.3.1.2 Hypothesis

The sign of the coefficient ζ_Y of output Y is not unambiguously predictable. An increase in Y normally leads to a higher overall wage bill and hence to larger CV. If the cost increase is equally distributed among less-skilled and high-skilled labor, there should be no influence on S_{LS}. If the wage bill of high-skilled labor increases

[16] We dropped the subscripts LS in the coefficients of (5.29).

more than proportionally, e.g., due to better bargaining power, this results in a higher L_{HS} and/or w_{HS} and S_{LS} is expected to fall ($\zeta_Y < 0$).

One expects a lower S_{LS} and thus a lower cost share of L_{LS} in variable costs CV when relative wages for high-skilled labor as part of CV rise ($\gamma_w < 0$). The composite term S_{LS} is correlated with (w_{HS}/w_{LS}), since $S_{LS} = (w_{LS}L_{LS}/wL)$. Despite the definitional relationship between S_{LS} and relative wages, the relative wage variable should be included as it controls for the variation in the relative wages of S_{LS}, whereas the variation in relative employment of S_{LS} is controlled by the other exogenous variables (see Geishecker 2002, 2006).

An increase in the capital coefficient is predicted to reduce S_{LS}, since capital can be considered as a substitute for less-skilled labor ($\zeta_K < 0$). The influence of OSS, OSM, DOS, DOM, and RD/*Y* on S_{LS} is not easily predictable, as all variables could be substitutes for less-skilled ($\theta_{\text{OSS}} < 0$, $\theta_{\text{OSM}} < 0$, $\theta_{\text{DOS}} < 0$, $\theta_{\text{DOM}} < 0$ and $\theta_{\text{RD}} < 0$) or for high-skilled labor ($\theta_{\text{OSS}} > 0$, $\theta_{\text{OSM}} > 0$, $\theta_{\text{DOS}} > 0$, $\theta_{\text{DOM}} > 0$ and $\theta_{\text{RD}} > 0$). One might rather expect a demand shift away from less-skilled labor.

5.3.1.3 Data

Skill-specific data are needed to calculate both S_{LS} and *relative wages*. Employment data at a sectoral level are divided into the two occupational groups, production workers and nonproduction employees. We assume that production workers rather represent less-skilled labor, whereas nonproduction employees represent high-skilled labor. As S_{LS} corresponds to the share of less-skilled labor in the total *wage bill of companies*, the numerator of (5.27)' consists of total sectoral wages for less-skilled labor, while the denominator includes the sum of total sectoral wages and salaries for all workers and employees. Sectoral wages are calculated by dividing total sectoral gross wages and salaries by the number of workers and employees, respectively. As relative wages are calculated, wage data do not need to be deflated by a price index. The data are retrieved from the second STATIS-Archive-CD (2004) of the German Federal Statistical Office (*Monatsbericht für Unternehmen und Betriebe im Bergbau und im verarbeitenden Gewerbe/Betriebsergebnisse: Lohn- und Gehaltssummen an Arbeiter/innen und Angestellte*).

The *capital coefficient* is obtained by dividing *capital K* by *gross output Y*. Both variables as well as the technology variables OSS, OSM, DOS, DOM, and R&D-intensity are calculated as described in Sect. 5.1.1.3. In the study with unrevised input–output data (1991–2000), the 36 manufacturing sectors of the input–output classification are aggregated to 28 sectors in order to match the available wage and employment data.[17] The regression with revised input–output data (1995–2004) disposes of disaggregated wage and employment data.

[17]The following sectors have been aggregated: 1–2, 8–9, 13–14, 15–16, 17–18, 19–21, and 35–36.

5.3.2 *Estimations with Unrevised Input–Output Data: 1991–2000*

5.3.2.1 Preliminary Analysis

Following 5.1 and 5.2, Fig. 5.8 gives preliminary indications on the relationship between services offshoring and the relative demand for less-skilled labor. Accordingly, German services offshoring intensity versus S_{LS} growth rates between 1991 and 2000 are plotted. Note that only 28 manufacturing sectors are taken into account due to missing occupational wage and employment data for the service sectors and some disaggregated manufacturing sectors. The scatter plot reveals that 27 out of the 28 manufacturing sectors experienced negative S_{LS} growth over the period, ranging from −0.7% (printing) to −39% (publishing). The outlier in the first quadrant is the sector "office, accounting and computing machinery". Services offshoring intensity growth rates were positive in 17 sectors and negative in the remaining eleven sectors. Thus, 16 sectors in the second quadrant suggest a negative relationship between OSS and S_{LS} growth. However, the remaining 11 sectors in the third sector and the outlier in the first sector rather propose a positive relationship.

The ten sectors with the strongest services offshoring growth between 1991 and 2000 are ranked in Table 5.18 and compared with their corresponding S_{LS} growth rates. Except for the outlier "office, accounting and computing machinery", all sectors experienced a shrinking relative demand for less-skilled labor over the respective period. Thus, Table 5.18 suggests a negative relationship between services offshoring and S_{LS} for the manufacturing sectors.

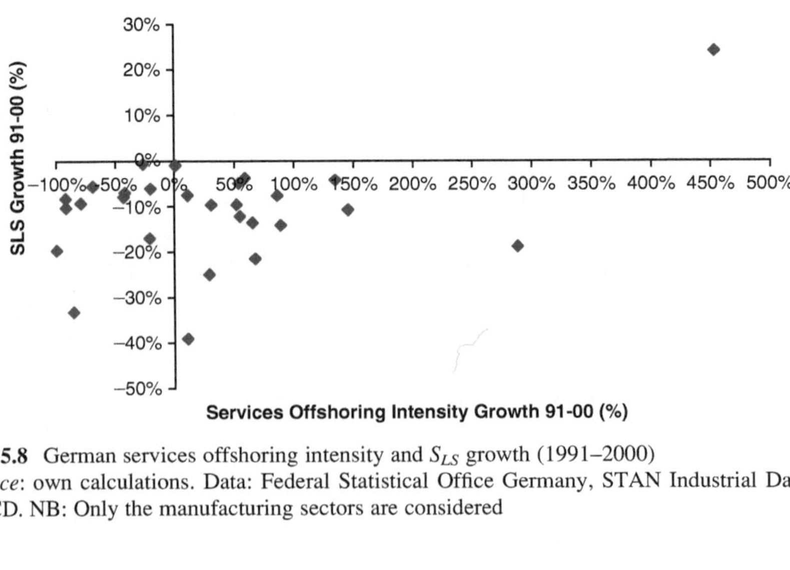

Fig. 5.8 German services offshoring intensity and S_{LS} growth (1991–2000)
Source: own calculations. Data: Federal Statistical Office Germany, STAN Industrial Database OECD. NB: Only the manufacturing sectors are considered

Table 5.18 Ranking of OSS and S_{LS} Growth in Germany (1991–2000)

Ranking of services offshoring growth	Services offshoring intensity growth		S_{LS} growth	
Sector	%	Rank	%	Rank
Top Ten				
Office, accounting, and computing machinery	453.4%	1	24.0%	1
Tobacco products	288.0%	2	−18.9%	23
Chemicals (including pharmaceuticals)	145.1%	3	−10.9%	18
Other transport equipment	134.7%	4	−4.3%	5
Medical, precision, and optical instruments	88.9%	5	−14.2%	21
Wood and products of wood and cork	86.1%	6	−7.7%	11
Radio, television, and communication equipment	67.5%	7	−21.5%	25
Collection, purification, and distribution of water	65.4%	8	−13.6%	20
Rubber products and plastic products	59.1%	9	−3.8%	4
Electrical machinery and apparatus, n.e.c.	54.6%	10	−12.3%	19

Source: own calculations. Data: Federal Statistical Office Germany, STAN Industrial Database OECD. NB: Only the manufacturing sectors are considered

5.3.2.2 Estimation Results

This sub-subsection measures the impact of services and materials offshoring on the relative demand for less-skilled labor German manufacturing using the unrevised input–output data from 1991 to 2000.[18] Following the previous analyses, we apply the consistent *fixed effects estimator* and correct the standard errors for heteroscedasticity and autocorrelation. We control for fixed year effects in all estimations and include import shares as additional control variable in some specifications.

Employment effects are not always instantaneous, which also accounts for the case of heterogeneous labor. We have already discussed in Sect. 5.2.2.2 that output, wages, and technology can influence the demand for labor in the subsequent period. Capital can affect labor demand in the following period for the following reasoning. Imagine that a firm increases its capital stock and buys a labor-substituting machine in $t = 1$. In order to avoid productivity losses, a firm will not release its workers unless the machine can perfectly substitute for the workers, e.g., in $t = 2$. Hence, there might be a transitional period, where both the machine and the workers are used in the production process. If this is the case, the purchase of a machine leads to layoffs in the following period. Therefore, one-period lags of all independent variables are included in some of the subsequent specifications.

The *results* of the *fixed effects estimator* are shown in Table 5.19. Column 1 only focuses on the effects of offshoring, column 2 on domestic outsourcing, while

[18]The two outliers "office, accounting and computer machinery" and chemicals (including pharmaceuticals) are dropped due to their high services offshoring intensities, leading to a total of 26 manufacturing sectors.

Table 5.19 Relative demand for less-skilled labor – Fixed effects estimator (1991–2000)

Dependent variable: $S_{LS,t}$

	Fixed effects estimator: instantaneous effects[a]				Fixed effects estimator: one-period lags[a]			
	(1)	(2)	(3)	(4)	(5)	(6)	(7)	(8)
$\ln Y_t$	0.0063	0.0034	−0.0025	−0.0447	−0.0338	−0.0283	0.0214	−0.0389
	(0.863)	(0.927)	(0.932)	(0.112)	(0.463)	(0.575)	(0.598)	(0.541)
$\ln Y_{t-1}$					0.0089	−0.0009	−0.0492	−0.0125
					(0.847)	(0.986)	(0.220)	(0.831)
$\ln(w_{HS}/w_{LS})_t$	−0.1855***	−0.1769***	−0.1738***	−0.1611***	−0.3168***	−0.3254***	−0.2819***	−0.1889***
	(0.002)	(0.001)	(0.002)	(0.005)	(0.000)	(0.000)	(0.000)	(0.001)
$\ln(w_{HS}/w_{LS})_{t-1}$					0.1087**	0.1276**	0.0624	0.0611*
					(0.010)	(0.015)	(0.104)	(0.088)
$\ln(K^{\text{equip}}/Y)_t$	0.0602*	0.0548	0.0556*	0.0177	0.0325	0.0209	0.0125	0.0147
	(0.091)	(0.127)	(0.082)	(0.622)	(0.529)	(0.712)	(0.808)	(0.778)
$\ln(K^{\text{equip}}/Y)_{t-1}$					−0.0014	0.0005	0.0233	−0.0299
					(0.969)	(0.988)	(0.546)	(0.509)
$\ln(K^{\text{build}}/Y)_t$	−0.0815**	−0.0814**	−0.0802**	−0.0713*	−0.0872*	−0.0718	−0.0349	−0.0673
	(0.040)	(0.033)	(0.044)	(0.051)	(0.054)	(0.207)	(0.477)	(0.249)
$\ln(K^{\text{build}}/Y)_{t-1}$					0.0083	−0.0056	−0.0565	−0.0045
					(0.857)	(0.911)	(0.243)	(0.931)
OSS_t	−1.0716		−2.1769	−1.9611*	−1.1600		−1.9484*	−1.6483
	(0.432)		(0.105)	(0.072)	(0.200)		(0.063)	(0.103)
OSS_{t-1}					−0.0230		−0.5272	−0.4553
					(0.974)		(0.545)	(0.575)
OSM_t	−0.1620		−0.7974**	−0.3346	−0.0125		−0.8018***	−0.2537
	(0.294)		(0.011)	(0.246)	(0.878)		(0.003)	(0.282)
OSM_{t-1}					−0.2261**		−0.2259	−0.1780
					(0.019)		(0.349)	(0.483)

(continued)

Table 5.19 (continued)

Dependent variable: $S_{LS,t}$

	Fixed effects estimator: instantaneous effects[a]				Fixed effects estimator: one-period lags[a]			
	(1)	(2)	(3)	(4)	(5)	(6)	(7)	(8)
DOS_t		0.1842	−0.5684*	−0.4779		0.0052	−0.7428***	−0.3057
		(0.302)	(0.096)	(0.141)		(0.944)	(0.005)	(0.217)
DOS_{t-1}						0.2520**	−0.0097	−0.355
						(0.050)	(0.967)	(0.190)
DOM_t		0.1442	−0.6348*	−0.4468		−0.0033	−0.7968***	−0.3307
		(0.369)	(0.074)	(0.183)		(0.970)	(0.006)	(0.208)
DOM_{t-1}						0.2211**	−0.0283	−0.2819
						(0.029)	(0.910)	(0.325)
$(RD/Y)_t$			0.035	0.0511***			0.1878***	0.1363***
			(0.312)	(0.000)			(0.000)	(0.010)
$(RD/Y)_{t-1}$							−0.1382***	−0.0775*
							(0.007)	(0.094)
$(IM/Y)_t$				−0.1642***				−0.0990***
				(0.000)				(0.002)
$(IM/Y)_{t-1}$								−0.0811***
								(0.000)
Fixed year effects	Yes	Yes	Yes	Yes	Yes	Yes	Yes	Yes
Joint significance:								
$\ln Y_t + \ln Y_{t-1} = 0$					$p>F = 0.7112$	$p>F = 0.7220$	$p>F = 0.4371$	$p>F = 0.2564$
$\ln(w_{HS}/w_{LS})_t + \ln(w_{HS}/w_{LS})_{t-1} = 0$					$p>F = 0.0001$	$p>F = 0.0004$	$p>F = 0.0001$	$p>F = 0.0021$
$\ln(K^{equip}/Y)_t + \ln(K^{equip}/Y)_{t-1} = 0$					$p>F = 0.7473$	$p>F = 0.8914$	$p>F = 0.4856$	$p>F = 0.7891$
$\ln(K^{build}/Y)_t + \ln(K^{build}/Y)_{t-1} = 0$					$p>F = 0.0861$	$p>F = 0.1660$	$p>F = 0.0837$	$p>F = 0.1885$
$OSS_t + OSS_{t-1} = 0$					$p>F = 0.3434$		$p>F = 0.1597$	$p>F = 0.1546$
$OSM_t + OSM_{t-1} = 0$					$p>F = 0.0140$		$p>F = 0.0102$	$p>F = 0.3869$

(*continued*)

Table 5.19 (continued)

Dependent variable: $S_{LS,t}$

	Fixed effects estimator: instantaneous effects[a]				Fixed effects estimator: one-period lags[a]			
	(1)	(2)	(3)	(4)	(5)	(6)	(7)	(8)
$DOS_t + DOS_{t-1} = 0$						$p > F = 0.0607$	$p > F = 0.0174$	$p > F = 0.1737$
$DOM_t + DOM_{t-1} = 0$						$p > F = 0.0190$	$p > F = 0.0215$	$p > F = 0.2284$
$(RD/Y)_t + (RD/Y)_{t-1} = 0$							$p > F = 0.0000$	$p > F = 0.0013$
$(IM/Y)_t + (IM/Y)_{t-1} = 0$								$p > F = 0.0000$
AIC	−1,497.3	−1,492.7	−1,506.4	−1,451.9	−1,411.4	−1,404.0	−1,431.7	−1,378.3
Observations	260	260	260	230	234	234	234	207
R-squared (within)	0.72	0.72	0.74	0.85	0.74	0.73	0.77	0.86

Source: own calculations

$p^* < 0.1$, $p^{**} < 0.05$, $p^{***} < 0.001$ (p values in parentheses)

[a]All estimations without the outliers "chemicals" and "office, accounting and computer machinery"

column 3 also includes R&D-intensity. Column 4 additionally controls for import shares. Real output shows no clear results. Relative wages have a significantly negative effect on S_{LS}. Capital spending on equipment has an overall positive effect on the relative demand for less-skilled labor, while capital spending on buildings shows a negative impact, both being significant in most specifications. Services and materials offshoring affect S_{LS} negatively which is significant for OSS in column 4 and for OSM in column 3. Domestic services and materials outsourcing show insignificantly positive coefficients when only domestic outsourcing is included (column 2), which turn significantly negative when all variables are integrated (column 3). This could be due to negative collinearity with OSM of 67% for DOS and 53% for DOM. R&D-intensity affects the relative demand for less-skilled labor positively, which is significant in column 4, while import share has a significantly negative influence. Adding one-period lags in columns 5–8 confirms these trends. Thus, services and materials offshoring both influence the relative demand for less-skilled labor negatively, while a higher R&D intensity positively affects S_{LS}.

The fixed effects estimator is only valid when strict exogeneity of the explanatory variables is assumed. It is plausible that sectors with a relatively low share of L_{LS} compared to other inputs want to increase their output and self-select into offshoring, domestic outsourcing, and/or spending more on R&D. On the other side, sectors that employ a high share of L_{LS} relative to other inputs might hope to increase their output by substituting L_{LS} for purchased inputs. Therefore, the IV 2SLS *fixed effects estimator* is used to control for potential endogeneity of offshoring, domestic outsourcing, and R&D-intensity. We use the first three lags of the potentially endogenous variables as instruments for OSS_t, OSM_t, DOS_t, DOM_t, and $(RD/Y)_t$. The results are shown in Table 5.20. Columns 1–4 only consider instantaneous effects, while columns 5–8 also include one-period lags of the strictly exogenous variables. Beyond that, columns 4 and 8 allow for scale effects, since we substitute the output price for the profit-maximizing quantity of output (see Sect. 5.2.1.1).

Output has an overall positive but insignificant effect on S_{LS}, whereas relative wages show a significantly negative effect. Services and materials offshoring both affect the relative demand for less-skilled labor negatively, which is significant when all variables are included (columns 3 and 4). Note that the coefficient of OSS is higher than OSM. Considering only domestic services and materials outsourcing in column 2, both variables influence S_{LS} positively which is almost significant for DOM. However, when all variables are included in columns 3 and 4, the positive coefficient signs turn significantly negative, possibly due to the above-mentioned negative collinearity problem with materials offshoring. R&D-intensity always presents positive coefficient signs, but none of the variables is significant. Allowing for scale effects in column 4 confirms the significant results of column 3 with slightly larger coefficients of the offshoring and domestic outsourcing variables. The specifications in columns 5–8 confirm this trend. Columns 7 and 8 should be interpreted with caution since the estimated covariance matrix of moment conditions is not of full rank.

Table 5.20 Relative demand for less-skilled labor – IV 2SLS estimator (1991–2000)

	Dependent variable: $S_{LS,t}$							
	IV 2SLS fixed effects: instantaneous effects[a]					IV 2SLS fixed effects: one-period lags[a]		
	(1)	(2)	(3)	(4)	(5)	(6)	(7)	(8)
$\ln Y_t$	0.0212	0.0210	0.0187		0.0239	0.0237	0.0292	
	(0.243)	(0.304)	(0.335)		(0.292)	(0.291)	(0.209)	
$\ln Y_{t-1}$					−0.0045	−0.0004	−0.0159	
					(0.826)	(0.980)	(0.469)	
$\ln(w_{HS}/w_{LS})_t$	−0.2197***	−0.2183***	−0.1996***	−0.2061***	−0.2193***	−0.2259***	−0.2105***	−0.2227***
	(0.004)	(0.001)	(0.002)	(0.002)	(0.004)	(0.002)	(0.006)	(0.006)
$\ln(w_{HS}/w_{LS})_{t-1}$					−0.0033	0.0141	0.0082	0.0228
					(0.967)	(0.870)	(0.931)	(0.822)
$\ln(K^{equip}/Y)_t$	0.0132	0.0147	0.0022	0.0156	0.0481	0.0461	0.0204	0.0260
	(0.763)	(0.750)	(0.959)	(0.692)	(0.284)	(0.359)	(0.704)	(0.637)
$\ln(K^{equip}/Y)_{t-1}$					−0.0470	−0.0471	−0.0283	−0.0235
					(0.379)	(0.404)	(0.578)	(0.669)
$\ln(K^{build}/Y)_t$	−0.0661	−0.0609	−0.0694*	−0.0770*	−0.0268	−0.0276	0.0041	−0.0104
	(0.130)	(0.147)	(0.078)	(0.057)	(0.482)	(0.546)	(0.940)	(0.840)
$\ln(K^{build}/Y)_{t-1}$					−0.0272	−0.0243	−0.0628	−0.0632
					(0.616)	(0.677)	(0.309)	(0.319)
OSS_t	−1.5037		−3.6898**	−3.7908**	−1.4012		−3.9243**	−4.1780**
	(0.346)		(0.039)	(0.031)	(0.374)		(0.026)	(0.021)
OSM_t	−0.3092		−1.2239**	−1.3555**	−0.2997		−1.2036**	−1.4869**
	(0.137)		(0.041)	(0.027)	(0.153)		(0.034)	(0.022)
DOS_t		0.2389	−0.8759*	−1.0095**		0.2839	−0.7957*	−1.0832**
		(0.294)	(0.064)	(0.035)		(0.254)	(0.082)	(0.034)
DOM_t		0.2816	−0.9408*	−1.0494**		0.2859	−0.9079*	−1.1706**
		(0.139)	(0.067)	(0.044)		(0.122)	(0.064)	(0.034)
$(RD/Y)_t$			0.0390	0.0549			0.0436	0.0635
			(0.532)	(0.442)			(0.495)	(0.400)
Fixed year effects	Yes	Yes	Yes	Yes	Yes	Yes	Yes	Yes

(*continued*)

Table 5.20 (continued)

	Dependent variable: $S_{LS,t}$							
	IV 2SLS fixed effects: instantaneous effects[a]					IV 2SLS fixed effects: one-period lags[a]		
	(1)	(2)	(3)	(4)	(5)	(6)	(7)	(8)
Joint significance:								
$\ln Y_t + \ln Y_{t-1} = 0$					$p>F = 0.5343$	$p>F = 0.5554$	$p>F = 0.5730$	
$\ln(w_{HS}/w_{LS})_t + \ln(w_{HS}/w_{LS})_{t-1} = 0$					$p>F = 0.0083$	$p>F = 0.0036$	$p>F = 0.0030$	$p>F = 0.0060$
$\ln(K^{equip}/Y)_t + \ln(K^{equip}/Y)_{t-1} = 0$					$p>F = 0.5235$	$p>F = 0.6024$	$p>F = 0.1241$	$p>F = 0.8876$
$\ln(K^{build}/Y)_t + \ln(K^{build}/Y)_{t-1} = 0$					$p>F = 0.4845$	$p>F = 0.5244$		$p>F = 0.2661$
First stage results:								
Shea partial R-squared:								
OSS_t	0.5576		0.4013	0.3989	0.5501		0.4050	0.4015
OSM_t	0.3393		0.3536	0.3461	0.3378		0.3581	0.3414
DOS_t		0.4286	0.3891	0.3843		0.4342	0.3994	0.3783
DOM_t		0.3486	0.3745	0.3665		0.3297	0.3845	0.3600
$(RD/Y)_t$			0.6565	0.6417			0.6333	0.6448
Hansen J statistic[b] p value	$X^2(4) = 0.65$	$X^2(4) = 0.38$	$X^2(10) = 0.62$	$X^2(10) = 0.47$	$X^2(4) = 0.58$	$X^2(4) = 0.30$	not reported[c]	not reported[c]
AIC	−1,118.0	−1,117.4	−1,123.4	−1,116.8	−1,115.7	−1,107.6	−1,114.9	−1,107.6
Observations	182	182	182	182	182	182	182	182
R-squared (within)	0.52	0.52	0.55	0.53	0.54	0.52	0.55	0.52

Source: own calculations
$p^* < 0.1$, $p^{**} < 0.05$, $p^{***} < 0.001$ (p values in parentheses)
[a]All estimations without the outliers "chemicals" and "office, accounting and computer machinery"
[b]Over-identification test of all instruments
[c]Estimated covariance matrix of moment conditions not of full rank; over-identification statistic not reported, and standard errors and model tests should be interpreted with caution

The results show that services offshoring had an overall negative effect on the relative demand for less-skilled labor in the German manufacturing sectors between 1991 and 2000. In the following, the significant results of services offshoring are interpreted focusing on specifications where all variables are included. The overall coefficient of services offshoring varies between −1.9611 (Table 5.19, column 4) and −3.7908 (Table 5.20, column 4). Between 1991 and 2000, services offshoring increased by 0.3 percentage points in the manufacturing sector from 0.43 to 0.74%. Holding all other variables constant, this implies that services offshoring reduced the relative demand for less-skilled labor by between −0.59 and −1.14 percentage points over the period. The wage share of less-skilled labor fell by 4.9 percentage points, from 56.2% in 1991 to 51.3% in 2000. Thus, services offshoring can account for between 11.9 and 23.1% of the decline in the wage share of less-skilled labor.

5.3.3 *Estimations with Revised Input–Output Data: 1995–2004*

5.3.3.1 Preliminary Analysis

First indications on the relationship between German services offshoring intensity and S_{LS} growth rates over the period 1995–2004 are given in Fig. 5.9. Thirty-four out of the 35 manufacturing sectors are taken into account, since services offshoring intensities for the sector "leather, leather products, and footwear" are not available.

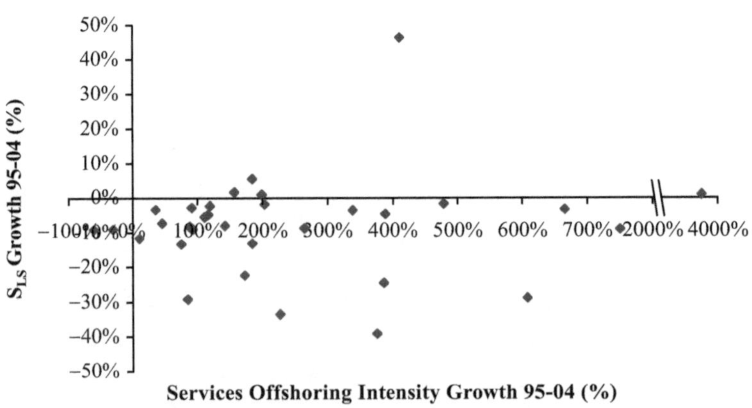

Fig. 5.9 German services offshoring intensity and S_{LS} Growth (1995–2004)
Source: own calculations. Data: Federal Statistical Office Germany. NB: Only the manufacturing sectors are considered. The sector "leather, leather products, and footwear" was dropped, since services offshoring intensities are not available. OSS growth rates for the sectors "wearing apparel, dressing, and dying of fur", "recycling", and "collection, purification, and distribution of water" are calculated for 1996–2004, since OSS is not available for 1995

Table 5.21 Ranking of OSS and S_{LS} growth in Germany (1995–2004)

Ranking of services offshoring growth	Services offshoring intensity growth		S_{LS} growth	
Sector	%	Rank	%	Rank
Top Ten				
Metal castings	3,705.3%	1	0.9%	5
Manufacturing n.e.c.	1,566.6%	2	−9.0%	22
Textiles	665.2%	3	−3.3%	10
Gas and gas supply	607.7%	4	−28.9%	31
Iron and steel	478.4%	5	−1.7%	6
Office, accounting, and computing machinery	410.6%	6	46.2%	1
Nonferrous metals	388.0%	7	−4.6%	13
Tobacco products	385.3%	8	−24.6%	30
Publishing	374.5%	9	−39.2%	34
Chemicals	338.1%	10	−3.5%	12

Source: own calculations. Data: Federal Statistical Office Germany.
NB: Only the manufacturing sectors are considered. The sector "leather, leather products, and footwear" was dropped, since services offshoring intensities are not available. OSS growth rates for the sectors "wearing apparel, dressing, and dying of fur", "recycling", and "collection, purification, and distribution of water" are calculated for 1996–2004, since OSS is not available for 1995

Thirty of the 35 manufacturing sectors show negative S_{LS} growth rates ranging from −1.7% (iron and steel) and −39.2% (publishing). In 32 sectors, services offshoring intensity grew positively between 1995 and 2004. Twenty-eight manufacturing sectors are situated in the second quadrant, suggesting a negative relationship between services offshoring growth and S_{LS} growth.

As a further indication, the ten sectors with the strongest services offshoring growth between 1995 and 2004 and their corresponding S_{LS} growth rates are shown in Table 5.21. All sectors except for the outlier "metal castings" and "office, accounting and computing machinery" have experienced a falling relative demand for less-skilled labor over the respective period. Therefore, Table 5.21 confirms the assumed negative relationship between services offshoring and S_{LS} growth in the German manufacturing sectors.

5.3.3.2 Estimation Results

In this sub-subsection, we measure the effects of services and materials offshoring on the relative demand for less skilled labor in the German manufacturing sectors between 1995 and 2004.[19] As discussed in Sect. 5.3.2.2, we include one-period lags of all independent variables in some specifications, since employment effects are

[19]The outlier "pharmaceuticals" is excluded due to extremely high services offshoring intensities, which leads to a total of 33 manufacturing sectors.

not always instantaneous. All estimations are robust to heteroscedasticity and autocorrelation and integrate year fixed effects D_t. Some specifications include the additional control variable import share.

Table 5.22 shows the results of the *fixed effects estimator*. Columns 1–4 only consider instantaneous effects. As in the previous specifications, column 1 only considers offshoring, column 2 only domestic outsourcing, while column 3 includes all variables simultaneously. Column 4 additionally controls for import share. As in subsection 5.3.2, real output influences the relative demand for less-skilled labor positively, which is now significant. As expected, relative wages have a negative impact on S_{LS}, which is significant (columns 3 and 4) or misses the 10% level only narrowly (columns 1 and 2). As in subsection 5.3.2, capital spending on equipment affects S_{LS} negatively, which is only significant in column 1, while capital spending on buildings shows a positive but insignificant impact on S_{LS}.

Services and materials offshoring show positive but insignificant coefficients in columns 1–4, while domestic services and materials outsourcing affect the relative demand for less-skilled labor positively, also being insignificant. R&D intensity and import share also have a negative but insignificant influence on S_{LS}. Adding one-period lags of each regressor in columns 5–8 yields more significant results. Thus, services offshoring shows a significantly positive overall impact, whereas the negative overall effects of domestic services and materials outsourcing also turn significant in columns 7 and 8. The positive overall impact of materials offshoring is only significant in column 5, which could refer to negative collinearity with DOS of around 43%.

Applying the IV 2SLS *fixed effects estimators* yields positive, but insignificant effects for services offshoring in all specifications. Therefore, we will not report the results of the IV 2SLS estimators.

We have seen that columns 5, 7, and 8 of Table 5.22 showed a positive effect of services offshoring on the relative demand for less-skilled labor. The (overall) coefficients of services offshoring range from 0.3745 (Table 5.22, column 7) to 0.5197 (Table 5.22, column 8). Services offshoring in the manufacturing sectors grew by 0.64 percentage points between 1995 and 2004, from 0.38 to 1.02%. Holding all other variables constant, this implies that services offshoring led to an *increase* in the relative demand for less-skilled labor of between 0.24 and 0.33 percentage points. As the average wage share of less-skilled labor in manufacturing fell by 3.7 percentage points, from 52.9% in 1995 to 49.2% in 2004, the results suggest that services offshoring has mitigated the decline of the relative demand for less-skilled labor. Without services offshoring, the wage share of less-skilled labor would have fallen by between 3.94 and 4.03 percentage points.

Since L_{HS} and L_{LS} are the only variable inputs, and thus $S_{HS} + S_{LS} = 1$, only one cost share is linearly independent (see Sect. 5.3.1.1). Therefore, a significantly positive overall effect on S_{LS} implies a significantly negative effect on the demand for high-skilled labor S_{HS}. Analogously, the results indicate that services offshoring led to a decline of the relative demand for high-skilled labor of between 0.24 and 0.33 percentage points. As the average wage share of high-skilled labor in manufacturing rose by 3.7 percentage points, from 47.1% in 1995 to 50.8% in 2004,

Table 5.22 Relative demand for less-skilled labor – Fixed effects estimator (1995–2004)

	Dependent variable: $S_{LS,t}$							
	Fixed effects estimator: instantaneous effects[a]				Fixed effects estimator: one-period lags[a]			
	(1)	(2)	(3)	(4)	(5)	(6)	(7)	(8)
$\ln Y_t$	0.0529***	0.0592***	0.0561***	0.0525**	0.0241*	0.0366**	0.0356**	0.0335**
	(0.008)	(0.005)	(0.009)	(0.025)	(0.066)	(0.029)	(0.028)	(0.047)
$\ln Y_{t-1}$					0.0284**	0.0228*	0.0177	0.0107
					(0.044)	(0.052)	(0.177)	(0.413)
$\ln(w_{HS}/w_{LS})_t$	−0.1092	−0.1163	−0.1359*	−0.1412*	−0.0834	−0.0841	−0.1091	−0.1133
	(0.131)	(0.132)	(0.062)	(0.075)	(0.222)	(0.251)	(0.118)	(0.128)
$\ln(w_{HS}/w_{LS})_{t-1}$					−0.0045	−0.0121	−0.0196	−0.0227
					(0.939)	(0.830)	(0.718)	(0.668)
$\ln(K^{equip}/Y)_t$	−0.0835*	−0.077	−0.0627	−0.0693	−0.0564	−0.0241	−0.0117	0.0124
	(0.079)	(0.110)	(0.236)	(0.167)	(0.302)	(0.672)	(0.819)	(0.834)
$\ln(K^{equip}/Y)_{t-1}$					−0.0331	−0.0747	−0.0374	−0.0698
					(0.676)	(0.358)	(0.597)	(0.373)
$\ln(K^{build}/Y)_t$	0.0385	0.0383	0.0279	0.0274	0.0322	0.0131	−0.0024	−0.0271
	(0.344)	(0.349)	(0.516)	(0.528)	(0.627)	(0.845)	(0.967)	(0.659)
$\ln(K^{build}/Y)_{t-1}$					0.0158	0.0504	0.0276	0.0478
					(0.842)	(0.523)	(0.696)	(0.519)
OSS_t	0.1362		0.3128	0.3922	−0.9522		−1.2173*	−1.4955*
	(0.839)		(0.592)	(0.523)	(0.167)		(0.078)	(0.057)
OSS_{t-1}					1.0203*		1.5918***	2.0152**
					(0.086)		(0.009)	(0.015)
OSM_t	0.0159		0.0082	0.0088	0.035		0.0207	0.0252
	(0.619)		(0.823)	(0.809)	(0.236)		(0.536)	(0.459)
OSM_{t-1}					−0.027		−0.0156	−0.012
					(0.125)		(0.423)	(0.570)

(*continued*)

Table 5.22 (continued)

	Dependent variable: $S_{LS,t}$							
	Fixed effects estimator: instantaneous effects[a]				Fixed effects estimator: one-period lags[a]			
	(1)	(2)	(3)	(4)	(5)	(6)	(7)	(8)
DOS_t		−0.0427	−0.0488	−0.0543		−0.0485	−0.0657*	−0.0772**
		(0.369)	(0.254)	(0.192)		(0.246)	(0.085)	(0.048)
DOS_{t-1}						−0.007	0	−0.0087
						(0.843)	(0.999)	(0.775)
DOM_t		−0.0184	−0.0165	−0.015		−0.0253***	−0.0234**	−0.0240**
		(0.126)	(0.279)	(0.330)		(0.006)	(0.041)	(0.043)
DOM_{t-1}						0.0075	0.0046	0.01
						(0.587)	(0.765)	(0.510)
$(RD/Y)_t$			−0.038	−0.0194			−0.0257	−0.0264
			(0.309)	(0.611)			(0.272)	(0.399)
$(RD/Y)_{t-1}$							−0.0541**	−0.0244
							(0.022)	(0.513)
$(IM/Y)_t$				−0.0236				−0.0206
				(0.618)				(0.322)
$(IM/Y)_{t-1}$								−0.0315
								(0.359)
Fixed year effects	Yes	Yes	Yes	Yes	Yes	Yes	Yes	Yes
Joint significance:								
$\ln Y_t + \ln Y_{t-1} = 0$					$p > F = 0.0373$	$p > F = 0.0230$	$p > F = 0.0502$	$p > F = 0.1204$
$\ln(w_{HS}/w_{LS})_t + \ln(w_{HS}/w_{LS})_{t-1} = 0$					$p > F = 0.4494$	$p > F = 0.4831$	$p > F = 0.2167$	$p > F = 0.2674$
$\ln(K^{equip}/Y)_t + \ln(K^{equip}/Y)_{t-1} = 0$					$p > F = 0.0958$	$p > F = 0.1712$	$p > F = 0.6165$	$p > F = 0.5145$
$\ln(K^{build}/Y)_t + \ln(K^{build}/Y)_{t-1} = 0$					$p > F = 0.5346$	$p > F = 0.4101$	$p > F = 0.8703$	$p > F = 0.8087$
$OSS_t + OSS_{t-1} = 0$					$p > F = 0.1195$		$p > F = 0.0289$	$p > F = 0.0462$
$OSM_t + OSM_{t-1} = 0$					$p > F = 0.0594$		$p > F = 0.2625$	$p > F = 0.3181$

(continued)

Table 5.22 (continued)

	Dependent variable: $S_{LS,t}$							
	Fixed effects estimator: instantaneous effects[a]				Fixed effects estimator: one-period lags[a]			
	(1)	(2)	(3)	(4)	(5)	(6)	(7)	(8)
$\text{DOS}_t + \text{DOS}_{t-1} = 0$						$p>F = 0.2500$	$p>F = 0.0128$	$p>F = 0.0101$
$\text{DOM}_t + \text{DOM}_{t-1} = 0$						$p>F = 0.0172$	$p>F = 0.0850$	$p>F = 0.0473$
$(\text{RD}/Y)_t + (\text{RD}/Y)_{t-1} = 0$							$p>F = 0.0531$	$p>F = 0.3827$
$(\text{IM}/Y)_t + (\text{IM}/Y)_{t-1} = 0$								$p>F = 0.5673$
AIC	−1,897	−1,903.5	−1,903.6	−1,905.3	−1,748	−1,749.5	−1,762.9	−1,771.9
Observations	340	340	340	340	306	306	306	306
R-squared (within)	0.57	0.58	0.58	0.59	0.57	0.57	0.61	0.62

Source: own calculations

$p^{*}<0.1$, $p^{**}<0.05$, $p^{***}<0.001$ (*p* values in parentheses)

[a]All estimations without the outlier pharmaceuticals

the results suggest that services offshoring has counteracted the increase in the relative demand for high-skilled labor.

This fifth chapter presented our analysis of the effects of services offshoring on productivity, labor demand, and the relative demand for less-skilled labor in German manufacturing. Our econometric estimations used both unrevised (1991–2000) and revised (1995–2004) input–output data. Services offshoring had a positive effect on total factor productivity and labor productivity in German manufacturing, while it affected labor demand negatively. Both effects were stronger between 1995 and 2004. The overall results suggest that labor demand decreased because labor-reducing productivity and substitution effects dominated labor-augmenting scale effects from services offshoring. Moreover, services offshoring significantly reduced the relative demand for less-skilled labor from 1991 to 2000. Interestingly, the results for 1995 to 2004 indicated a relative demand shift away from high-skilled labor, mitigating the declining wage share of less-skilled labor.

References

Amiti M, Wei S-J (2005) Fear of service outsourcing: is it justified? Econ Policy 20(42):308–347

Amiti M, Wei S-J (2006) Service offshoring, productivity and employment: evidence from the US. CEPR Discussion Paper, No. 5475, February 2006

Berman E, Bound J, Griliches Z (1994) Changes in the demand for skilled labor within U.S. manufacturing: evidence from the annual survey of manufacturers. Q J Econ 109(2):367–397

Brown RS, Christensen LR (1981) Estimating elasticities of substitution in a model of partial static equilibrium: an application to U.S. agriculture, 1947–1974. In Berndt ER, Field BC (eds) Modeling and measuring natural resource substitution. MIT, Cambridge, MA, pp 209–229

Ekholm K, Hakkala K (2006) The effect of offshoring on labour demand: evidence from Sweden. CEPR Discussion Paper, No. 5648, April 2006

Falk M, Koebel BM (2002) Outsourcing, imports and labour demand. Scand J Econ 104(4): 567–586

Farrel D (2004) Can Germany win from offshoring. July 2004. McKinsey Global Institute

Feenstra RC, Hanson GH (1996) Globalization, outsourcing and wage inequality. Am Econ Rev 86(2):240–245

Geishecker I (2002) Outsourcing and the demand for low-skilled labour in german manufacturing: new evidence. DIW Discussion Paper, No. 313, November 2002

Geishecker I (2006) Does outsourcing to central and eastern europe really threaten manual workers' jobs in Germany? World Econ 29(5):559–583

Hamermesh D (1993) Labor demand. Princeton University Press, Princeton, NJ

Hijzen A, Görg H, Hine RC (2005) International outsourcing and the skill structure of labour demand in the United Kingdom. Econ J 115(506):860–878

Houseman S (2006) Outsourcing, offshoring, and productivity measurement in U.S. Manufacturing. Upjohn Institute Staff Working Paper, No. 06–130, June 2006

McKinsey Global Institute (2005) How offshoring of services could benefit France. June 2005, McKinsey Global Institute

Milberg W, Schöller D (2008) Globalization, offshoring and economic insecurity in industrialized countries. World Economic and Social Survey 2008 Background Paper. Department of Economic and Social Affairs, United Nations, New York

Milberg W, v Arnim R, Mahoney M, Schneider M (2007) Dynamic gains from U.S. services offshoring: a critical view. In: Paus E (ed) Global capitalism unbound: winners and losers from offshore outsourcing. Palgrave Macmillan, London

OECD (2007) Offshoring and employment: trends and impact. OECD, Paris

Roling J (1999) Bedeuten deutsche Direktinvestitionen im Ausland einen Export' deutscher Arbeitsplätze? Zeitschrift für Wirtschaftspolitik 48(2):147–167

Shephard RW (1953) Cost and Production Functions. Princeton University Press, Princeton

Stockhammer E (2004) Financialisation and the slowdown of accumulation. Camb J Econ 28 (5):719–741

Strauss-Kahn V (2003) The role of globalization in the within-industry shift away from unskilled workers in France. NBER Working Paper, No. 9716, May 2003

Tüselmann H-J (1998) Deutsche Auslandsinvestitionen in den neunziger Jahren: Abwanderung der deutschen Industrie und Abbau von Arbeitsplätzen? WSI Mitteilungen 5:292–303

Uzawa H (1962) Production functions with constant elasticity of substitution. Rev Econ Stud 29 (4):291–299

Chapter 6
Conclusion

Abstract This sixth and concluding chapter summarizes the main findings of our study in Sect. 6.1. Section 6.2 discusses some implications and economic policy recommendations for Germany. Our own results combined with the literature survey indicate that, besides Germany, other developed countries have also experienced negative labor market effects due to offshoring. Considering labor market insecurity as one of the most important implications of offshoring, we show indicators of labor market insecurity in selected OECD countries. We then identify different country models with respect to labor market security and flexibility, and analyze several measures and reforms to promote "flexicurity" in Germany, by continuing high levels of labor support and raising labor market flexibility above current levels. Finally, we address possibilities to counteract the shortage of skilled labor in Germany. If political factors require limits on offshoring and migration as the only short-term solutions, a medium- or long-term option would be an effective education policy to produce enough talent at home. We describe the measures that have been taken in recent years to reduce the shortage of workers with the use of vocational education. We also show that fewer measures have been taken to face the shortage of workers with tertiary education.

6.1 Summary of Results

Since the new tradability of services has made services vulnerable to relocation, the public awareness of services offshoring and its potential labor market effects has increased considerably. One of the main objectives of this study was to evaluate if and to what extent growing productivity levels, increasing unemployment rates, and the widening gap between high- and low-skilled unemployment rates in Germany can be related to services offshoring from the 1990s onwards. To frame our investigation, we built a "Framework of Services Offshoring" in Chap. 2, comprising its classification and drivers. We analyzed the "Structure of Services Offshoring" with

D. Winkler, *Services Offshoring and its Impact on the Labor Market*,
Contributions to Economics, DOI: 10.1007/978-3-7908-2199-4_6,

a focus on Germany in Chap. 3. Chapter 4 evaluated the "Labor Market Effects in (Neo)classical Models of Offshoring" distinguishing between offshoring of final and intermediate goods. In Chap. 5, we presented three empirical studies, where we measured the impact of services offshoring on productivity, labor demand, and the relative demand for less-skilled labor in German manufacturing.

Our "Classification of Services Offshoring" (Sect. 2.1) provided a "Definition of Services Offshoring" (Sect. 2.1.1), distinguishing outsourcing from offshoring. The former (outsourcing) considers the "source" of production (inside or outside the firm), whereas the latter (offshoring) asks for the "shore" of production (at home or abroad). While our general working definition of services offshoring comprises all kinds of foreign service activities, our special working definition designates the provision of foreign service inputs for cost reasons that are re-imported to the home country.

In "Services and their Tradability" (Sect. 2.1.2), we first showed that services are of particular interest, since their significance has grown in terms of both quantity and quality. In quantitative terms, services dominate, e.g., the structural distribution of German outward FDI stocks and the foreign employment of German MNCs. In qualitative terms, services have undergone a tremendous change. One decade ago, most services were considered non-tradable, but the emergence and development of new ICTs has contributed to overcoming geographical distance. This development has started to break down the prior universality of the uno-actu-principle. Since the physical proximity between the provider and the user became inessential, disembodied services appeared. We also showed that differentiating services from goods is sometimes difficult, since the former possess many characteristics of goods and vice versa. This ambiguity made it difficult to provide a general definition of services.

In a next step, we showed that services trade can be classified according to the geographical location of agents and according to the modes of service supply in the GATS. Recall that there are four modes of supply, namely cross-border supply of services, consumption abroad, commercial presence, and the presence of natural persons. Since, according to our definition of services offshoring, the consumers are situated in the country of origin, we only focus on the cross-border supply of services (mode 1). As a clear definition of services does not exist, we used the "pragmatic approach" and compared several classifications of service activities. We defined "other business activities" according to Kalmbach et al. (2005), and used this definition for our empirical analysis. We saw that "other commercial services" go beyond the definition of "other business activities", whereas "technological services" and "IT and BPO services" comprise fewer services.

Section 2.1.3 addressed the two generic organizational forms of offshoring, theoretically discussed as the make-or-buy decision. Firms thus decide endogenously whether to "make" certain levels of the value chain (in-house production) or to "buy" them from an external firm (outsourcing), which implies a vertical view of the value chain. "Efficiency-Based Motives for Outsourcing" were used to explain why firms buy inputs externally via the market. External procurement is hence chosen to save labor costs, to raise flexibility, or to gain specialization advantages.

In resource-based theories of the firm, outsourcing helps strongly diversified firms to focus on their core competencies and resources, e.g., knowledge, and thus to reduce the number of mistakes. Finally, in-house production in TAC-based theories is advantageous, when TACs are high, e.g., in the case of uncertainties, market failure, imperfect contracts, and information asymmetries.

The changes of the international trading environment reflect technological, political, and economic developments that have together encouraged services offshoring. The section "Drivers of Services Offshoring" (Sect. 2.2) was thus subdivided into global developments, services offshoring motives of firms, and developments in the destination countries. One of the most important "Global Developments" (Sect. 2.2.1) was found in "Developments in ICTs". First, the age of information and telecommunications and its implications were discussed. Recent developments in ICTs have made it possible to uncouple information from its physical storage, rendering the transfer of huge amounts of data possible in a matter of seconds ("disembodied services"). Thus, the prior universality of the uno-actu-principle has been called into question. Second, we showed that LDCs seem to catch up in terms of ICT penetration and interregional internet bandwidth, but there is still a long way to go for the poorest among them. Besides developments in ICTs, multilateral and regional liberalization of trade in services were listed among the main global developments. The GATS constitutes the first and only set of multilateral agreements covering international trade in services. Besides the GATS, the liberalization of trade in services is also fostered by endeavors of RTAs. Here, the EU shows the deepest regional initiative. Finally, we discussed arguments in favor of the multilateral or regional form of trade liberalization.

"Services Offshoring Motives of Firms" (Sect. 2.2.2), the second main driver of services offshoring, comprise market-oriented, cost-oriented, and procurement-oriented motives. Market-oriented motives aim at building up, maintaining, or increasing a company's market share abroad. Cost-oriented motives aim at exploiting lower costs abroad, such as lower prices as well as production-, location-, and scale effect-oriented advantages. Procurement-oriented motives aim at securing the provision of inputs that are rare or unavailable in the home country. More recent motives, such as the procurement of agglomeration advantages and human capital, were also discussed. We evaluated the expected employment effects for all offshoring motives according to the substitutionality, complementarity, and neutrality hypothesis, which depends on the relationship between domestic and foreign production. Thus, mainly cost-oriented offshoring is expected to create negative employment effects.

"Developments in the Destination Countries" (Sect. 2.2.3) constitute the third main driver. We started with the "Availability of Human Capital in Less-Developed Countries". Besides the high absolute number of qualified labor, India's advantages include the young demographic profile, its vast network of academic infrastructure, its English-speaking workforce, but also the quality of Indian suppliers with most CMM Level 5 certifications worldwide. Besides India, other countries are also experiencing a success story, such as Ireland, Israel, and China. Investments in human resources seem to have fostered the increase in talent pool in these countries, but the excess supply of human capital and the "diaspora" to industrialized countries were also identified as main drivers. Besides human capital, the development and growth of domestic software industries was also fostered by the "Presence of Multinational Companies" due to an increased competition and demand effect. Finally, the "Liberalization of Service Sectors", especially constant privatization, competition, and independent regulation, enabled the transformation from protectionist to open market economies in the last one to two decades. We studied the liberalization of the telecommunication services markets with a focus on the success stories of India and China. While public policy focused rather on privatization in India, China's success was predominantly caused by a public policy of competition.

Chapter 3 analyzed the "Structure of Services Offshoring", beginning with "German Services Offshoring in an International Comparison" (Sect. 3.1). We identified the largest services offshoring countries in a worldwide comparison (Sect. 3.1.1), using import data of computer and information services, other business services, communication services, and financial services as proxies for services offshoring. We found, for instance, that, besides the US, Germany was the largest absolute offshorer in 2005. The balance revealed that Germany had the third largest deficit in 2004, whereas the UK and the US represented the largest surplus countries. We studied the "Development of Services Offshoring in Selected OECD Countries" (Sect. 3.1.2) between 1991 and 2006, focusing on France, Germany, Japan, the UK, and the US. From the mid-1990s on, Germany and the US have become the leading overall offshoring countries. The data also revealed that the Anglo-Saxon countries increased their net surpluses, whereas Germany and Japan managed to reduce their net deficits. Finally, the "Calculation of Services Offshoring Intensities" (Sect. 3.1.3) yields a more sophisticated measure of services offshoring than import data. Services offshoring intensities measure the share of service imports in total non-energy inputs per sector. The overall services offshoring intensity has grown from 1.2% in 1991 to 2.5% in 2000 using unrevised input–output data, while it has increased from 1.4% in 1995 to 2.9% in 2004 using revised data. German services offshoring intensities have a lower level than the UK, but a higher one than the US. We expected that, unlike materials offshoring, services offshoring in Germany has not yet realized its full potential.

The "Sectoral Structure of Services Offshoring" (Sect. 3.2) evaluated the "Sectoral Structure of Global Services Offshoring" (Sect. 3.2.1) in a first step. Banking, insurance and finance, and telecommunications constitute the largest offshoring sectors, as they comprise many universal functions with a high theoretical offshoring potential. The structure of the offshored services revealed that services that do not require physical proximity or local knowledge and that are not characterized by complex interactions are more likely to be relocated. Other criteria that determine a higher offshoring probability were also mentioned. In a next step, we used both services trade data based on the balance of payments statistics, including intermediate and final services, and input–output data, including only intermediate services, to obtain a reliable indication of the "Sectoral Structure of German Services Offshoring" (Sect. 3.2.2). The services trade data showed that computer services imports were mainly absorbed by service sectors, whereas most imports of

R&D as well as "engineering and other technical services" went to the manufacturing sectors. Focusing on imports of intermediate services (input–output data), services offshoring still plays a subordinate role in most manufacturing sectors, but services offshoring intensities grew in all manufacturing and service sectors except for "financial intermediation". Relying on balance of payments trade data, the structure of the offshored services revealed that commercial services, "engineering and other technical services" as well as computer services showed the highest import values. Using input–output data, we saw for the periods 1991–2000 and 1995–2004 that almost all services categories increased their average intensities, whereby "other business activities", "post and telecommunications" as well as "activities related to financial intermediation" formed the most relevant categories. "Computer and related activities" improved their relative position in both periods.

Section 3.3 focused on the "Regional Structure of Services Offshoring". Following the previous structure, we began with the "Destinations of Global Services Offshoring" (Sect. 3.3.1). We detected the main offshore destinations for tradable services using existing studies and balance of payments statistics data. Among the top 25 service exporters, we found many developing countries, especially India and China, but also other Asian and Eastern European countries. These countries have become important offshore destinations for R&D as well as IT and BPO services. In a last step, we identified the major "Destinations of German Services Offshoring" (Sect. 3.3.2) focusing on eight services categories. The offshore destinations differed with regard to the eight services categories. WEU still constitutes the major service importer, even though its importance has been reduced over the last years. OIN maintained or increased their import shares in many services categories. We also observed a growing importance of non-developed countries, especially CEE, as service importers to Germany. The share of developing countries might become larger in the future in view of emerging markets such as China or India. At a country level, the UK and the US as well as Germany's neighbors, France, Switzerland, Austria and the Netherlands, belong to the top ten service importers in all eight services categories. There are only a few developing countries among the top ten importers, since the majority of them are not significant enough. That said, in 2006, 19.6% of the imported "engineering and other technical services" and 12.5% of the imported computer services were originated in CEE and developing countries.

Chapter 4 evaluated the "Labor Market Effects in (Neo)classical Models of Offshoring", differentiating between "Offshoring of Final Goods" (Sect. 4.1) and "Offshoring of Intermediate Goods" (Sect. 4.2). The first section presents the Ricardian, Heckscher–Ohlin, and Specific-Factors models. We began with the Ricardian model of Samuelson (2004) in Sect. 4.1.1. Samuelson (2004) first showed the welfare gains from trade compared to autarky equilibrium. Usually, productivity gains in the foreign export sector are beneficial for both countries. However, technological progress in the foreign non-comparative advantage sector increases only the foreign income, while the home country loses all or at least some of its previous gains from international trade (Samuelson 2004). Section 4.1.2 presented the Heckscher–Ohlin ($2 \times 2 \times 2$) model. We showed that, compared to autarky, international trade leads to increasing foreign demand for a country's export goods, which raises its product prices, and leads to a higher demand for the abundant factor, which increases its relative factor price. The other goods can be imported at a lower price which improves the economy's terms-of-trade. We then presented four theorems of the traditional Hecker–Ohlin model: the Factor Price Equalization theorem, the Heckscher–Ohlin theorem, the Samuelson theorem, and the Rybczynski theorem. Finally, Sect. 4.1.3 presented the effects of offshoring in the Specific-Factors model. Bhagwati et al. (2004) analyze offshoring of high-skilled labor in a two goods model which integrates trade from the beginning. Under the assumption of diminishing returns to scale for all factors, the increase in the skilled-labor supply at a lower wage level results in a growth of the remaining factor prices. Offshoring leads to social gains if the country is small and under the absence of trade distortions. If the country is large, however, offshoring can generate welfare losses in two alternative ways.

The second section models "Offshoring of Intermediate Goods" (Sect. 4.2) using the Grossman and Rossi-Hansberg (2006a, b) general equilibrium model, which includes a set of intermediate tasks that can be produced by less-skilled or high-skilled labor (Sect. 4.2.1). The authors capture the effects of offshoring studying different scenarios (Sect. 4.2.2). In the first scenarios only less-skilled tasks can be offshored. "Offshoring in a Small Economy" with a Heckscher–Ohlin framework only allows for productivity effects. Thus, offshoring results in wage increases of less-skilled labor, whereas high-skilled labor remains uninfluenced. "Offshoring in a Large Economy" with a Heckscher–Ohlin framework leads to a productivity and relative-price effect, but there is still no labor-supply effect due to imperfect specialization of both economies. The net effect on the wages of less-skilled workers is ambiguous due to the two opposing effects. Other scenarios such as the labor-supply effect or offshoring skill-intensive tasks were also addressed.

The major contribution of this work was presented in Chap. 5, entitled "Labor Market Effects of Services Offshoring – Empirical Evidence". We related services offshoring to productivity, employment, and employment structure in German manufacturing. In the first study, we analyzed "Services Offshoring and its Impact on Productivity in Germany" (Sect. 5.1). Based on the theoretical model, we hypothesized that services offshoring affects TFP and LP positively. The results for 1991–2000 showed that services offshoring increased real output by on average 0.11–0.26% per year and 1.2–3.0% over the whole period, while labor productivity rose by between 0.18 and 0.35% per year and by between 2.0 and 4.0% over the whole period due to services offshoring. The estimations for the period from 1995 to 2004 indicated that services offshoring increased real output by on average 0.47–0.99% per year and 4.1–8.6% over the period. LP grew by on average 2.65–4.28% per year and 21.5–32.5% between 1995 and 2004 due to services offshoring. Hence, the positive productivity effects of services offshoring were stronger between 1995 and 2004. Both estimations confirmed our prior hypothesis.

The second study focused on "Services Offshoring and its Impact on Labor Demand in Germany" (Sect. 5.2). A clear hypothesis could not be drawn from the theoretical model, but several indications led to the conjecture that services offshoring affects labor demand negatively. Using the unrevised input–output data for 1991 to 2000, we found that services offshoring led to an average employment reduction of up to −1.3% over the entire period, using the conditional labor demand function. Using the unconditional labor demand function, however, the results were ambiguous. The negative impact was unambiguous and larger when revised input–output data for 1995–2004 were used. Here, services offshoring reduced employment by on average between −0.19 and −0.43% p.a., which represents a reduction of between −1.7 and −3.9% over the entire period. As in the previous study, the effects were stronger between 1995 and 2004. The results indicated that positive scale effects are dominated by negative substitution and productivity effects.

While labor has been treated as a homogenous input in the previous study, the third study "Services Offshoring and its Impact on the Relative Demand for Less-Skilled Labor in Germany" (Sect. 5.3) considered labor as heterogeneous factor. Precisely, we included high-skilled and less-skilled labor in our estimations. Again, we could not derive a clear hypothesis from the theoretical model. Thus, our conjecture was based on several indications suggesting that services offshoring leads to a demand shift away from less-skilled labor. We estimated the effect of services offshoring on the relative demand for less-skilled labor and found for 1991–2000 that services offshoring reduced the relative demand for *less-skilled labor* by between −0.59 and −1.14 percentage points over the period. The estimations for 1995 to 2004 revealed that services offshoring led to an average decline of the relative demand for *high-skilled labor* of −0.24 to −0.33 percentage points over the period. Our results suggest that services offshoring has counteracted the decline of (resp. increase in) the relative demand for less-skilled (resp. high-skilled) labor between 1995 and 2004.

6.2 Implications and Economic Policy Recommendations

Based on the insights of the previous chapters, we here venture a number of economic policy recommendations. Chapter 5 revealed that services offshoring has led to negative labor market effects in German manufacturing. The literature survey in Table 1.1 indicated that, besides Germany, other developed countries have also experienced negative labor market effects due to offshoring. Considering labor market insecurity as one of the most important implications of offshoring, Sect. 6.2.1 shows indicators of perceived (Sect. 6.2.1.1) and actual (Sect. 6.2.1.2) labor market insecurity in Germany, Denmark, France, Japan, the United Kingdom, and the United States. Section 6.2.2 addresses two aspects of labor markets, namely security and flexibility. Different country models are identified with respect to labor support and labor market flexibility (Sect. 6.2.2.1). We then analyze the measures and reforms to promote "flexicurity" in Germany, a situation with high labor support and low to medium labor market flexibility (Sect. 6.2.2.2).

Finally, we address possibilities to counteract the shortage of skilled labor in Germany (see Sect. 2.2.2.3). If political reasons constrain offshoring and migration as the only short-term solutions, a remaining medium- or long-term option would be an effective education policy to produce enough talent at home. Thus, Sect. 6.2.3 addresses the necessity of an effective education policy to counteract the shortage of human capital in Germany. We first describe the measures that have been implemented in the last years to reduce the shortage of workers with vocational education (Sect. 6.2.3.1). We also show that fewer initiatives have been taken to increase the proportion of tertiary educated in the population (Sect. 6.2.3.2).

6.2.1 Labor Market Insecurity in Selected OECD Countries

In the following subsection, we compare the perceived and actual labor market insecurity in Germany to the four large developed countries, France, Japan, the United Kingdom, and the United States, previously considered in Sect. 3.1.2.[1] Since Denmark is characterized by a mix of labor market flexibility, ample social protection, and active labor market policies – so-called "flexicurity" –, we add Denmark to the country sample. These countries represent a broad spectrum of the advanced industrialized world, and although all have expanded their exposure to offshoring and international trade (see Sect. 3.1 and Appendix J), they have not all experienced the same degree of unemployment and wage inequality.

6.2.1.1 Perceptions of Labor Market Insecurity

Popular perceptions of labor market insecurity do not necessarily reflect the objective indicators in a precise way, but we find a generally high level of fear of globalization among our sample countries, especially in the US and France. According to the German Marshall Fund (2007), 34% of Americans and 38% of Europeans had a negative view of globalization. About half of Americans and Europeans think that "freer trade" results in more job loss than job creation, although between 2005 and 2007 American sentiment turned against freer trade, while European sentiment became less skeptical of the employment benefits of trade liberalization. Half of Americans and a slightly higher percentage of Europeans saw the growth of China's economy as a threat.

At the country level, the survey revealed that the US and especially France show the most skepticism towards international trade and investment (see Fig. 6.1). Of all countries surveyed, these two had the highest percentage of respondents who "did not favor freer trade" with 63% of French and 40% of Americans. In both countries, more than half of the respondents agreed that "trade costs more jobs than it creates" with 59% of French and 57% of Americans. France also shows the highest

[1]This subsection is taken and slightly modified from Milberg and Schöller (2008).

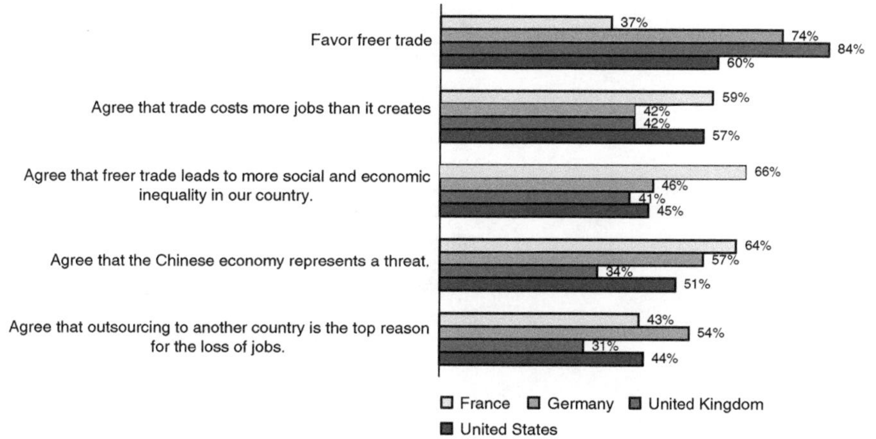

Fig. 6.1 Concerns about free trade (% of respondents)
Source: own illustration. Data: German Marshall Fund (2007)

agreement that "freer trade leads to more social and economic inequality" (66%) and that "the Chinese economy represents a threat" (64%). In Germany, more than half (54%) of the respondents agreed that "outsourcing to another country is the top reason for the loss of jobs".

The contrast between perceptions of globalization in France and Denmark is clear from a recent survey of the European Commission that asked "what comes first to mind when you hear the word 'globalization'?". 75% of French respondents said that the word "globalization" evoked the "relocation of some companies to countries where labor is cheaper". Among Danes, 47% responded that the word "globalization" evoked "opportunities for national companies in terms of new outlets". Germany is situated between the two countries, since a large fraction of the respondents (46%) name relocation to low-income countries as their first thought, but almost a third first thinks of "opportunities for domestic companies" (Fig. 6.2).

6.2.1.2 Unemployment, Inequality, and the Burden of Risk

Unemployment and Inequality

We now turn to actual indicators of labor market insecurity, namely unemployment and inequality. Table 6.1 plots the development of unemployment and wage inequality for our country sample between 1991 and 2006. The average *rate of unemployment* in percentage of the civilian labor force (on a standardized basis) has been reduced in the US, and even more strongly in the UK and Denmark, while Japan's and notably Germany's unemployment rates almost doubled. The rate of unemployment remained more or less constant in France. The incidence of *long-term unemployment* (i.e., unemployment duration greater than one year) also rose in

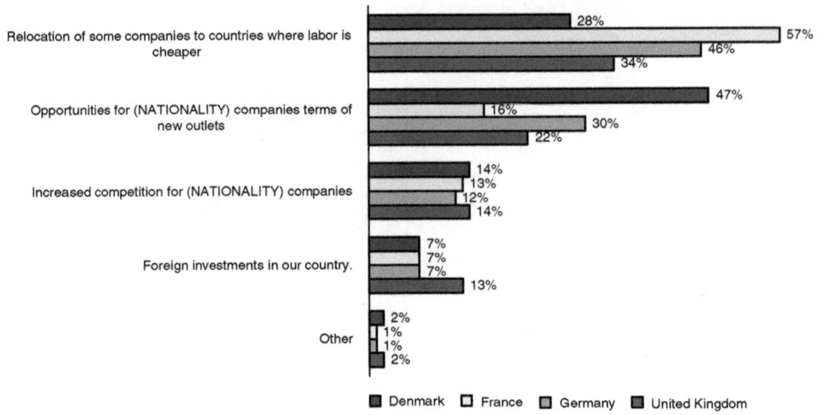

Fig. 6.2 The perception of globalization (% of respondents)
Question: "There are multiple consequences of the globalisation of trade. When you hear the world 'globalisation', what comes first to mind?"
Source: own illustration. Data: EU(2007), Eurobarometer 67, Fieldwork April–May 2007

Table 6.1 Unemployment (1991 vs. 2005/2006)

		Denmark	France	Germany	Japan	UK	US
Unemployment rate in civilian labor force (%)	1991	9.2	9.5	5.6	2.1	8.4	6.8
	2006	4.1	9.1	10.4	4.1	5.4	4.6
Share of long-term unemployed (>1 year) in total unemployed (%)	1991	31.4	34.2	31.5	17.5	28.5	6.3
	2006	20.3	42.9	56.6	33.0	22.1	10.0
Share of involuntary part-time workers in total employment (%)	1991	2.2	2.9[a]	0.6	0.9	1.5	n.a.
	2006	2.3	3.8	4.2	4.4	1.8	n.a.
Unemployment rate by skill group[b]							
Below upper secondary education (%)	1991	14.2	10.6	7.4	4.3[c]	10.4	12.3
	2005	6.8	12.4	20.2	6.7[d]	6.6	9.0
Upper and post secondary education (%)	1991	9.1	6.6	4.7	3.3[c]	6.5	6.5
	2005	4.0	7.3	11.0	4.9	3.2	5.1
Tertiary education (%)	1991	4.9	3.7	3.2	2.6[c]	3.3	2.9
	2005	3.7	6.0	5.5	3.1	2.0	2.6

Source: own illustration. Data: OECD Labor Force Statistics and OECD Education at a Glance (2007a), pp. 138–139
[a]1992 data for France
[b]Number of 25- to 64-year-olds in unemployment as a percentage of the labor force aged 25–64, by level of educational attainment
[c]1993 data for Japan
[d]2003 data for Japan

Table 6.2 Inequality (1991–2005)

		Denmark	France	Germany	Japan	UK	US
Inequality of unemployment rates							
Below upper secondary-to-	1991	2.9	2.9	2.3	1.7	3.2	4.2
tertiary education-ratio	2005	1.8	2.1	3.7	2.2	3.3	3.5
Upper and post-secondary-to-	1991	1.9	1.8	1.5	1.3	2.0	2.2
tertiary education-ratio	2005	1.1	1.2	2.0	1.6	1.6	2.0
Wage inequality	1991	2.2	3.3	2.8	3.1	3.4	4.3
(90 percentile-to-							
10 percentile-ratio)[a]	2005	2.6	2.9	3.3	3.1	3.6	4.9

Source: own illustration. Data: OECD Labor Force Statistics and OECD Education at a Glance (2007a), pp. 138–139

[a]Wage per full-time employee. Wages only for West Germany. 1990 data for Denmark, 2004 data for France

Germany, France, Japan, and surprisingly also in the US between 1991 and 2006. Denmark and the UK saw a decline in long-term unemployment.

Concerning the share of *involuntary part-time employment* in total employment, Germany and Japan showed the largest increase between 1991 and 2006. France and the UK saw a small increase and in Denmark the share remained effectively constant. Comparable data on this variable for the US were unavailable. Finally, Table 6.1 plots the *unemployment rate by level of educational attainment* on a standardized basis for 1991 and 2005. The unemployment rates of all three skill groups rose in Japan, France, and most sharply in Germany. The UK, the US, and most obviously Denmark managed to reduce their unemployment rates.

The deterioration in an economy's labor market performance is not only reflected in higher rates of unemployment, but also in the *rise in inequality*. Table 6.2 plots the ratio of unemployment rates of less-skilled relative to high-skilled workers. The unemployment rates of "below upper secondary educated" relative to tertiary educated increased in Germany and Japan, fell in Denmark, France, and the US, and remained constant in the UK. The unemployment rates of "upper and post secondary educated" relative to tertiary educated were reduced in Denmark, France, the UK and slightly in the US, whereas this ratio grew in Germany and Japan. Finally, the ratio of wages in the top decile of the wage distribution to those in the bottom decile is shown for 1991 and 2005. US inequality has been far above the others, and the compression of incomes is much greater in Denmark than in all the other countries. Between 1991 and 2005 heightened inequality has been most pronounced in the US and Germany, with smaller increases in earnings dispersion in Denmark and the UK. Inequality in Japan remained constant over the entire period, while France experienced a decline in wage inequality from the fourth largest ratio to the second smallest after Denmark.

To sum up, Germany constitutes the only country where all unemployment and inequality indicators deteriorated between 1991 and 2005/06. Moreover, Germany's current unemployment rates and inequality ratios were mostly higher than in the other five countries. Note that Japan experienced a similar development. Denmark and the

Table 6.3 Labor market policy indicators

		Denmark	France	Germany	Japan	UK	US
Gross unemployment replacement rate (%)	1981	54.2	31.3	29.3	8.8	24.2	14.6
	1991	51.9	37.6	28.8	9.9	17.8	11.1
	2001	50.9	43.5	29.4	9.1	16.6	13.5
	2005	48.9	39.0	24.2	7.7	15.6	13.5
Public expenditures for active labor market programs (% of GDP)	1980	0.4	n.a.	n.a.	n.a.	0.6	0.2
	1990	1.1	0.8	1.0	0.3	0.6	0.2
	2000	1.6	1.3	1.1	0.2	0.4	0.1
	2003	1.6	1.1	1.1	0.3	0.5	0.1

Source: own illustration. Data: OECD Social Expenditures and OECD Tax-Benefit Models. Gross unemployment replacement rate: the OECD summary measure is defined as the average of the gross unemployment benefit replacement rates for two earnings levels, three family situations, and three durations of unemployment

UK were the best performing countries and managed to reduce unemployment as well as part of their inequality.

The Burden of Risk

There are public and private responses to rising labor market insecurity. *Government responses* to labor market insecurity vary greatly as shown in Table 6.3. All countries except for France experienced a decline in their unemployment benefit replacement rates since 1981, and this rate declined in France after 2001. Moreover, among our sample of countries, only Denmark and France increased spending on active labor market programs as a percentage of GDP since 1990, with France again showing a decline after 2000. Germany's spending share remained stable and constituted the second largest share in 2003 (1.1%).

On the *private side*, households may borrow in order to insulate their spending patterns from earnings volatility, and the rise in home equity loans in the US and consumer credit in the UK was partly for this reason.[2] Thus, household saving rates out of disposable income fell over the 1990s for most of the countries in our sample (Germany and France being the exceptions), indicating the need for households to limit saving in order to maintain economic security and to incur debt for the same purpose (OECD 2007b).

Finally, there has been a different pattern of change in terms of *employment protection legislation* (EPL). The term EPL as used by the OECD refers to all types of employment protection measures, whether grounded primarily in legislation,

[2]Barbosa-Filho et al. (2005), e.g., find that the deterioration in the US current account between 1995 and 2003 closely tracks the rise in health care spending by Americans. The authors take this as an indicator that Americans were not so obviously on a whimsical buying spree, but instead were trying to retain spending in the face of stagnant real wages and rapidly rising costs of health care.

Table 6.4 Strictness of employment protection legislation

	1990	1998	2003
Denmark	2.32	1.42	1.42
France	2.70	2.98	3.05
Germany	3.17	2.46	2.21
Japan	2.10	2.03	1.84
United Kingdom	0.60	0.60	0.75
United States	0.21	0.21	0.21

Source: own illustration. Data: OECD Labor Statistics. NB: higher values indicate stricter regulation on hiring and firing

court rulings, collectively bargained conditions of employment or customary practice.[3] Employment protection refers both to regulations concerning hiring (e.g., rules favoring disadvantaged groups, conditions for using temporary or fixed-term contracts, training requirements) and firing (e.g., redundancy procedures, mandated prenotification periods and severance payments, special requirements for collective dismissals and short-time work schemes).[4] The data reveal that EPL in Denmark, Germany, and Japan was becoming less strict, while France and to some extent the UK adopted stricter legislation on hiring and firing (see Table 6.4).

6.2.2 *Security and Flexibility: The "Flexicurity" Model*

The following subsection identifies different country models with respect to labor market security and flexibility (Sect. 6.2.2.1).[5] We pay special attention to the "flexicurity" model, a situation with high labor support and low to medium labor market flexibility. We then analyze several measures and reforms to promote "flexicurity" in Germany (Sect. 6.2.2.2).

6.2.2.1 Different Country Models

We have seen differences across countries in terms of the degree of labor market flexibility, the level of unemployment benefits, and spending on active labor market programs (see Sect. 6.2.1.2). Labor market insecurity is higher where the state provision of protection is lower or, alternatively, where social protection is more closely tied to employment. By looking at these three variables – strictness of EPL, gross unemployment replacement rate and public expenditures on active labor market programs – all at once and across the OECD, we detect some clear patterns

[3]See http://stats.oecd.org/glossary/detail.asp?ID=3535.

[4]See http://stats.oecd.org/glossary/detail.asp?ID=3534.

[5]This sub-subsection was taken and slightly modified from Milberg and Schöller (2008).

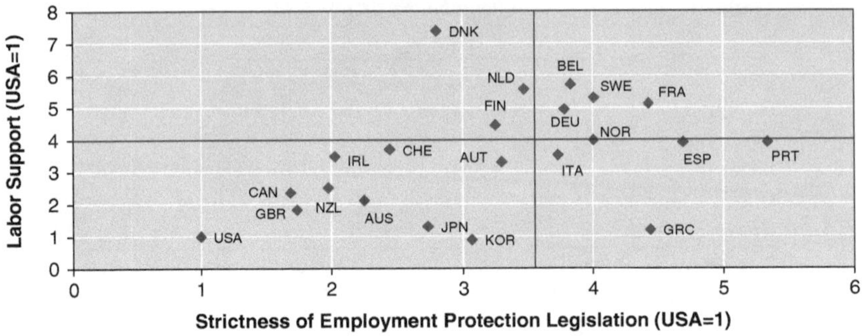

Fig. 6.3 Strictness of EPL vs. labor support in OECD countries in 2003
Source: own calculations. Data: OECD Employment Outlook 2004, OECD Social Expenditures and OECD Tax-Benefit Models. NB: The Strictness of Employment Protection Legislation Index has been calculated indexing the USA = 1, i.e. dividing the values of all other countries by the US value. Higher values indicate stricter regulation on hiring and firing. Labor support is an index (using equal weights) composed of the indexed (USA = 1) Active Labor Market Expenditures (as % of GDP) as well as the indexed (USA = 1) Gross Unemployment Replacement Rate. Higher values indicate a higher security level. Gross Unemployment Replacement Rate: The OECD summary measure is defined as the average of the gross unemployment benefit replacement rates for two earnings levels, three family situations and three durations of unemployment

in the government response to economic insecurity. We calculated an index of the strictness of EPL by setting the US level of EPL equal to one and recalculating the relative levels for the other countries. The year 2003 had to be used, since more recent data on the strictness of EPL are unavailable. We constructed an index of labor support by again setting US levels of gross unemployment replacement rates and public expenditures on active labor market programs equal to one and (with equal weights on each variable) combining them into a single index. A scatter plot of these two indexes is shown in Fig. 6.3. For a list of country abbreviations, see Appendix E.

Five distinct "models" emerge and they follow closely the groupings presented in Boeri (2002). On the lower left, we can identify an *Anglo-Saxon model* with low levels of regulation on hiring and firing and low levels of worker support. Here, we find the US, the UK, Canada, Australia, Ireland, and New Zealand. Countries on the lower right follow the *Mediterranean model* that combines relatively strict employment legislation and low levels of worker support. This group includes Greece, Portugal, Spain, Italy and, to a lesser extent, Norway. Countries on the upper right of the scatter plot – the *Rhineland model* – combine relatively strict EPL and high levels of worker support. Here, we find France, Sweden, Belgium, and Germany. On the upper left are countries with relatively flexible labor markets and high levels of worker support. We call this the *'flexicurity' model*, and its followers include Denmark, Finland, and the Netherlands.

Japan has always been difficult to categorize in such schemes because although the state supports only low levels of labor market and social protection, the private sector has traditionally supported long-term employment security. We would propose an *East Asian model* including Japan and Korea, who both have greater employment protection than those in the Anglo-Saxon group in Fig. 6.3. It would seem that the traditional role for the private sector in Japan has given way to a great extent, as seen by the increase to European levels of Japanese long-term unemployment and involuntary part-time employment.

The "flexicurity" model has attracted a lot of attention because of a superior Danish performance in trade and employment and the unusual combination of policies, with flexibility in terms of hiring and firing and strong social protection for those seeking employment, including a high level of unemployment benefits and considerable levels of spending on active labor market programs.[6] This system of "flexicurity" is in part the reason for Denmark's attainment of a high level of economic security.

6.2.2.2 Promoting "Flexicurity" in Germany

Industrialized countries have implemented very different sets of policies, and we have identified five "models". On one extreme are the US and other Anglo-Saxon economies with lax hiring and firing regulations, low unemployment benefits, and very limited spending on active labor market policies. On the other extreme is the Rhineland model including France and Germany, who have relatively high levels of employment protection, large unemployment benefits, and significant spending on active labor market programs. Denmark (and a few other countries) seem to have found an effective combination of the two, with its model of "flexicurity", comprising labor market flexibility with high replacement income programs for the unemployed and extensive active labor market programs. France and Germany have moved towards "flexicurity", but were still quite a distance from a Danish-type system in 2003 (Milberg and Schöller 2008).

While Germany already belongs to the OECD countries with the highest levels of labor support (see Fig. 6.3), it is still lower than in the Netherlands, Finland, and especially Denmark. Thus, Germany should at least maintain its current level of labor support. Also, Germany already represented the most flexible country of the Rhineland model countries in terms of strictness of EPL in 2003. This implies that fewer efforts will be necessary to reduce EPL, compared, e.g., to France. In the following paragraph, we present important reforms of EPL that have taken place in Germany in recent years, many of them after 2003.

Reforms of Employment Protection Legislation

Strict EPL is likely to increase the duration of unemployment for less-skilled labor and marginal groups. It "constitutes a cost to firing workers, which entails disincentives to hiring in the first place. Thus, EPL can be expected to reduce both

[6]See, for example, Clasen 2007.

inflows to and outflows from unemployment, implying that its expected impact on the unemployment rate is ambiguous" (Brandt et al. 2005, p. 34). Restrictive EPL might result in higher unemployment for the following reasons. First, insufficiently flexible wages that cannot compensate for high dismissal costs, e.g., due to minimum wages, have a negative impact on the job prospects of low-wage workers. Second, there might be more long-term unemployed under strict EPL. Third, the OECD (2004) finds that the job prospects of workers that are relatively weakly attached to the labor market, such as women and young workers, worsen. A related fourth argument is that the effectiveness of active labor market policies (e.g., public employment service) to reintegrate the unemployed might be impeded due to restrictive EPL (Brandt et al. 2005).

A moderate degree of EPL, on the other hand, can counteract implicit contracts between workers and firms in sectors with seasonal employment fluctuations. If EPL was very low, workers would have an incentive to draw unemployment benefits in off-peak seasons and to be re-employed by the same firm in peak seasons, which effectively represents a continuous employment relationship (Brandt et al. 2005). We have seen that Germany has reduced its strictness of EPL between 1990 and 2003 from the highest level among the six countries to the second highest level after France (see Table 6.4). Compared to Denmark, however, employment protection is still high and remains in need of reform for the reasons mentioned above. We expect that the strictness of EPL has further fallen since 2003 due to several reforms, which are described in the following.

Initiatives to ease EPL in Germany focused on regulatory changes and financial support for *non-regular forms of employment* (see Brandt et al. 2005). As a consequence, atypical contracts, such as employment in "mini-jobs" – a special sort of part-time jobs – or via a temporary work agency (TWA), strongly increased during the last years, as they raise a firm's flexibility. Since April 2003, "mini-jobs", which are more important in terms of numbers, are subject to new regulations in Germany.[7] There are two sorts of "mini-jobs": 400 €-"mini-jobs" and short-term "mini-jobs". *400 €-"mini-jobs"* pay a salary which is limited to 400 € per month, but the previously limited weekly working time of 15 hours no longer applies. *Short-term "mini-jobs"* limit the working time to two months or 50 working days per year. Both kinds of "mini-jobs" exempt workers from paying social charges and have a reduced taxation. Employers of 400 €-"mini-jobs" must pay pension and health insurance charges (but workers have no health insurance coverage), while short-term "mini-jobs" exempt employers from paying these charges.[8] The reform in April 2003 rendered "mini-jobs" very attractive, especially as a supplement to a worker's main occupation.

The development of temporary work in Germany is outlined by Boss et al. (2007). According to a regulation of 1972, temporary workers were given an unlimited work

---

[7] See http://www.minijob-zentrale.de.

[8] Employers paid 12% for pension insurance, 11% for health insurance, and 2% for the state. Since July 2006, the overall charges have increased from 25 to 30% (15 + 13 + 2).

contract, which constituted the "prohibition of limitation" (*Befristungsverbot*). The maximum subcontracting period in the borrowing firm was limited to three months. The "prohibition of synchronization" (*Synchronisationsverbot*) required that the contract period between the TWA and the worker had to exceed the subcontracting period between the worker and the first borrowing firm.[9] The "prohibition of reemployment" (*Wiedereinstellungsverbot*) stated that the TWA was not allowed to dismiss and reemploy the worker within three months (Boss et al. 2007).

Several regulatory reforms have come into effect since then. Since 2002, temporary workers were allowed to stay within the same borrowing firm for up to 24 months (instead of then twelve). From the thirteenth month onwards, employees on loan were subject to the "principle of equal treatment" (*Gleichbehandlungsgrundsatz*), i.e. they must be treated as equal as regular employees in terms of wages and employment conditions. As part of the Agenda 2010, the "prohibition of limitation", the "prohibition of synchronization", and the "prohibition of reemployment" were abolished in January 2004, and the limited stay of temporary workers in the borrowing firm became unlimited. In return, the "principle of equal treatment" now holds from the beginning. However, TWAs can deviate from this principle if the working conditions are regulated by collective bargaining. As a consequence, the compensation of temporary workers often differs from the compensation of the regular workforce (Boss et al. 2007).

The total number of employees in Germany subject to social insurance contribution increased by 176,000 between June 2005 and June 2006. The number of temporary workers rose by 145,000 over the same period, which constitutes 82% of the former group. This indicates a growing relevance of temporary workers in absolute and relative terms and reflects the positive influence of the reforms. Temporary workers allow for more flexible labor force adjustments, since the *fluctuation rates* in this sector are much higher with 1.7 in 2005 compared to the overall German fluctuation rate of employees that are subject to social insurance contribution of 0.24 in 2005.[10] The IAB regional file 1975–2001 indicates a continuously growing *wage differential*. In 2001, the average gross daily wage of temporary workers relative to regular employed persons had fallen to 50%. The "principle of equal treatment", however, reduced this wage differential somewhat. Thus, the ratio increased by between 7 and 27% as shown by Alewell (2006) (taken from Boss et al. 2007).

In Germany, the stricter EPL for regular employment relative to non-regular employment contains the risk of creating a *dual labor market* with a growing fraction of atypical employment forms. While "mini-jobs" or TWAs might help reintegrate unemployed persons into regular employment, some disadvantages occur when strict EPL for regular employment is combined with deregulated temporary employment. First, these temporary and "mini-jobs" are less-stable or marginal.

---

[9]This implied that TWAs continued to pay the worker for another three months if he could not be placed in another borrowing firm after his first assignment (Wurzel 2006).
[10]Fluctuation rate = 0.5 (inflows + outflows)/average annual stock.

Second, only employers of 400 €-"mini-jobs" need to pay social charges, which lowers the revenue of the social insurance system, and might lead to higher labor taxation (Wurzel 2006).

Further disadvantages are listed by Brandt et al. (2005). Thus, Bentolila and Dolado (1994) found that trade unions, which focus mainly on the interests of regular workers ("insiders"), increase their wage pressures with low risk of job loss, since the negative effects will be absorbed mainly by temporary workers ("outsiders"). Beyond that, the higher turnover in the segment of temporary workers might imply disincentives to train these workers and does not lead to permanent employment as outlined by Blanchard and Landier (2002). Finally, an increasing number of firms tend to substitute temporary workers for their regular workforce. In particular, firms release employees and borrow them back from TWAs in order to benefit from lower wages and higher flexibility (Boss et al. 2007).

Therefore, further reforms of EPL should address *regular employment* in order to avoid the disadvantages of a dual labor market. The Agenda 2010 also included the reform of the "dismissal protection act" (*Kündigungsschutzgesetz*), which became law in January 2004. The reform of dismissal protection legislation was intended "to create more transparency and legal security for companies in the event of dismissals for operational reasons and to reduce restrictions on new hires" (Ubber 2004, pp. 135–136). In particular, the high number of court cases related to dismissals was supposed to be reduced.

The reform introduced the following changes. First, the *dismissal protection* act now only applies to firms with more than ten employees, while the threshold was five before. However, protection continues for employees in small businesses who were entitled to protection prior to 2004. Second, the *social criteria* for dismissals due to operational reasons were formulated. Traditionally, job tenure, age, and maintenance obligations represented important factors, while other social criteria depended on the individual situation of the employee (e.g., state of health, income of spouse). The new reform reduced the number of social criteria to four, namely job tenure, age, maintenance obligations plus severe disability. Moreover, the reform included two exemptions: employees who dispose of special skills, expertise, and abilities, and who secure the existing structure of the staff are no longer subject to the social criteria test.

Third, the *rights of compensation*, which less-skilled workers were not legally entitled to before, are now regulated by law and harmonized for all employees. Three conditions are to be fulfilled: employees must be released for *operational* reasons, the employer must refer to the rights of compensation in his letter of cancellation, and the amount of compensation must equal 0.5 × monthly income × job tenure. Fourth, the period for filing suit is now limited to three weeks, while it was not regulated by law before. And fifth, entrepreneurs who *founded a new business* no more than four years ago are allowed to limit their work contracts to up to four years. Shorter periods are also possible, because work contracts can be extended several times thereafter (Funke 2004; Ubber 2004).

To sum up, EPL has eased in Germany since 2003, especially for non-regular forms of employment. Since more recent EPL data should reflect these efforts, we expect that Germany will shift closer to the "flexicurity" countries in Fig. 6.3. The reforms in dismissal protection legislation are first steps towards a higher flexibility in regular employment. Compared to the regulatory changes in temporary employment, however, more effort should be put into raising the flexibility and transparency of regular employment forms. Some reforms showed that the move towards higher flexibility is combined with higher security (e.g., temporary workers are protected by the "principle of equal treatment" from the beginning, and less-skilled workers have the right of compensation by law). In our opinion, Germany has taken the right steps towards more "flexicurity".

Flexibility in (Setting) Work Conditions and Wages

Flexibility in Germany has increased not only in EPL, but also in work conditions, wage setting, and wages over recent years. Since the early 1990s, the *determination of wages and work conditions has become more decentralized.* According to Wurzel (2006), "[t]o a large degree this reflects a response to steep increases in collectively bargained wages after reunification" (Wurzel 2006, p. 20). A rising share of collective agreements between the unions and employers' associations include *opening clauses* from multi-firm collective contracts, single-firm collective agreements, or individual contracts. Opening clauses allow for some firm-level agreements between the management and the work council, which often need to be approved by the collective bargaining partners.[11] Furthermore, the share of firms that are not covered by collective agreements as well as the share of firms with firm-specific agreements between management and a union rose during the last one and a half decades.

Firm-level agreements, in particular, led to higher flexibility in work conditions and wages. Wurzel (2006) refers to an enterprise survey of the DIHK (2004), according to which only 15% of the firms had introduced *more flexible working time arrangements* compared to two-thirds in 2004.[12] Working time flexibility seems to be relatively high compared to the EU average.[13] The implementation of working time accounts in many firms allows workers to compensate periods of overtime by working fewer hours in other periods, which is possible up to several years after the periods of overtime. As cited by Wurzel (2006), Hübler (2005) found empirical evidence that arrangements on working time flexibility and working time prolongation affect job creation positively, while agreements on employment guarantees have a negative impact. This study only considered firms with firm-specific agreements on wages and work conditions.

---

[11]See, e.g, Bispinck and WSI-Tarifarchiv (2005b) for an overview of opening clauses by sector and bargaining area (Wurzel 2006).

[12]See, e.g., Bispinck and WSI-Tarifarchiv (2005a) for an overview of different types of working time regulations across collective bargaining areas (Wurzel 2006).

[13]Wurzel (2006) quotes a study of Spitznagel and Wanger (2004) who refer to a study of the European Commission in 1999.

Although the wage inequality among full-time employees in Germany started to increase from the mid-1990s on, which according to Wurzel (2006) reflects mainly reduced entry wages of new hires, some studies find important wage rigidities across skills.[14] Other studies showed that local unemployment rates weakly influence real wages in Germany, indicating *wage rigidities*.[15] Several explanations for higher wage rigidity in Germany are given. First, Pfeiffer (2004) shows that wage rigidities can have positive effects on firms, as the former increase efficiency and maintain productivity. Parts of the German wage rigidities reflect the firms' rational behavior. Firms might intend to protect early investments, to keep a contract, or to maintain employee morale through nominal efficiency wage contracts (see Sect. 2.1.3.1).

Second, his analysis also shows that part of German wage rigidity is based on the collective bargaining power of the employees. These additional rigidities have reached a level which induces negative employment effects in Germany. In a hypothetical country without any wage rigidities, the unemployment rates would clearly be lower (Pfeiffer 2004). Gerlach and Stephan (2005) found a higher wage compression for Germany in sectors with collective contracts establishments, compared to establishments with firm-level contracts and uncovered establishments. Thus, high sectoral union density is more likely to result in more wage compression (Wurzel 2006).

Third, some authors explain wage rigidities with deficiencies in the benefit and placement system (Wurzel 2006). They blame the welfare state and social assistance for creating a fixed wage floor in the collective agreement system. High wage replacement benefits, however, discourage the unemployed from working at lower wage levels. According to this reasoning, firms will not employ workers in the low-wage sector if the wages are higher than the added value created. Hence, policy suggestions include offering wage supplements instead of wage compensation in order to re-activate the unemployed and to guarantee a sufficient income, known as active welfare (*Aktivierende Sozialhilfe*) (see, e.g., Sinn et al. 2002).

We conclude that, during recent years, Germany has moved towards more flexibility in setting wages and work conditions. However, recent discussions to introduce an economy-wide legal *minimum wage* seem to counteract these efforts. The demand for minimum wages is fostered by growing international competition on labor and product markets, especially the possibility of offshoring, which puts a downward pressure on wages. Minimum wages benefit the "insiders" of the labor market, while the "outsiders" (i.e., the unemployed) are less likely to be re-employed. Likewise, minimum wages might worsen the competitiveness of smaller firms that have less weight in bargaining outcomes (Wurzel 2006).[16]

---

[14]Investigations on the evolution of wage inequality includes, e.g., the studies of Fitzenberger and Franz (2001), Pfeiffer (2004), Möller (2005), Fitzenberger and Garloff (2005), Gernand and Pfeiffer (2005), Kohn (2006), and Fitzenberger and Kohn (2006).

[15]Wurzel (2006) refers to De Galdeano and Turunen (2005) or Montuenga et al. (2003).

[16]Wurzel (2006) refers to Kohaut and Schnabel (2003) who showed that the larger and older a firm, the higher the probability that the firm is subject to multi-firm collective agreements.

Further negative consequences could include the rationalization of production via substitution of labor by capital, the increase of final goods prices for the customer, the refuge into a shadow economy, or the "escape" into self-employment since minimum wages only apply to employees (Ragnitz and Thum 2007). The study of Lechthaler and Snower (2006) indicates that a rise in the minimum wage leads to less training for low-skilled workers and more training for high-skilled workers, creating a "low-skill trap". The case of France has shown that if minimum wages are combined with a reduction in working hours (e.g., 35 h per week), this puts upward pressure on minimum wages in order to prevent a fall in real income as a result of working fewer hours and increases the risk of labor market exclusion (OECD 2005). Finally, regional labor market adjustments to supply and demand shocks are hampered due to a lower "responsiveness of wages at the low end of the wage distribution" (Wurzel 2006, p. 22).

On the other hand, setting minimum wages does not seem to have reduced employment in the UK or the US, which is mainly explained by *monopsony power*. Thus, minimum wages can increase employment if employers have monopsony power, i.e., they can determine wages without the influence of employees, if there is quasi-full employment, so that new employees can only be attracted by wage increases, and if employers do not have much possibility for substituting capital and foreign labor for less-skilled labor at home. Given these three conditions, positive employment effects of minimum wages are rather unlikely in Germany, in contrast to the UK and the US with quasi-full employment and a higher bargaining power of employers (Snower 2006).

Therefore, future reforms should aim to eliminate remaining wage rigidities in Germany and not to increase them. The higher flexibility in setting wages and work conditions combined with the ease of EPL has brought Germany towards more "flexicurity". However, "flexicurity" as a way of managing state–market relations in a globalized economy is likely not sufficient over the longer term to maintain high levels of economic security. For this, the macroeconomic effects of offshoring must be rechanneled away from finance and towards the domestic reinvestment of efficiency gains from offshoring. Tighter labor markets driven not by unsustainable consumer debt but by productivity-enhancing private investment is the long-term key to "sharing the gains" from globalization. A second long-term key to maintaining the high share of high- and medium-skilled activities in Germany lies in an effective education policy as described in the next subsection.

6.2.3 Effective Education Policy

We have seen in Sect. 2.2.2.3 that the procurement of human capital through *offshoring* (indirect provision) can counteract the shortage of skilled labor in Germany, at least in the short term. A second alternative would be the direct provision through *immigration of skilled labor*. The recently published "Report on Germany's Technological Performance" of the Federal Ministry of Education and Research (*Bundesministerium für Bildung und Forschung, BMBF*) also expressed concern about the shortage of skilled labor in Germany. Immigration as a short-term measure can fall into two main categories:

First, the proportion of foreign students leaving Germany after graduation should be lowered. Currently, between 80 and 95% of the foreign students must leave the country due to temporary residence permits. Many of these students were enrolled in technically oriented fields; a quarter of the foreign students (2,500 in 2005) obtained degrees in engineering sciences, especially mechanical and electrical engineering. Many foreign students have lived and studied in Germany for some years, which makes further integration relatively easier. Second, the barriers to skill-oriented immigration to Germany should be reduced. If firms in Germany struggle to fill vacancies with foreign workers in the short-term, their only alternative is to look for skilled workers abroad (offshoring) (BMBF 2007).

Since the shortage is not restricted to specifically qualified workers, but affects many sectors and professions, the "minimum income limit" (*Mindestverdienstgrenze*) should be reduced. The minimum annual income limit for foreign talent to obtain unlimited residence permits in Germany was set as high as 86,400 €, and corresponded to the double of the contribution assessment ceiling of statutory health insurance. The new "labor migration regulation law" (*Arbeitsmigrationssteuerungsgesetz*), which has become effective on 1 January, 2009, reduced the "minimum income limit" to currently 63,600 €, which now corresponds to the contribution assessment ceiling of statutory pension insurance.[17]

If political considerations limit the possibility of offshoring or immigration, a medium- to long-term option would be an *effective education policy* to produce enough talent at home. The shortage of human capital reflects "much scope for significant improvements in Germany's education system, ranging from preschooling over secondary education and vocational training to the university system" (Wurzel 2006, p. 24). In the following, we distinguish between the shortage of workers with vocational education (Sect. 6.2.3.1) and the shortage of workers with tertiary education (Sect. 6.2.3.2).

6.2.3.1 Shortage of Workers with Vocational Education

As mentioned in Sect. 2.2.2.3, the DIHK (2007) survey reported on the shortage of human capital in Germany, especially of technically skilled labor. Firms had more difficulties in finding workers with vocational training and further education than college or university graduates. Of all firms with difficulties in filling their job vacancies, 43% could not find adequate workers with vocational training. Every sixth manufacturing firm in Germany was affected. The problems were greater in small- and medium-sized firms: more than 45% of the firms with difficulties in filling their vacancies were mainly lacking workers with dual vocational training (DIHK 2007).

[17]The "labor migration regulation law" implements the regulations of an action program formulated by the German government to secure the skilled-labor supply via migration.

As part of the Lisbon strategy[18], the European social partners adopted a *framework of actions for the lifelong development of competences and qualifications* in March 2002. Four key priorities have been outlined: namely, to identify and anticipate competences and qualifications needed; to recognize and validate competences and qualifications; to inform, support, and provide guidance; and to mobilize resources. Some instruments at the national, sectoral, and company level have been developed and improved in recent years with respect to these four priorities. In the following, we focus on the first and the fourth priority.

The first priority, to *identify and anticipate competences* in Germany, includes measures enabling workers to fit the firms' needs, given that 25% of all school leavers do not have the necessary basic skills to enter into a regular apprenticeship. Thus, Germany's Federal Institute for Vocational Education and Training (*Bundesinstitut für Berufliche Bildung*), for instance, grants a yearly award to firms for innovative further education and training (European Commission 2006). At the sectoral level, the German social partners adapted professions to business and technological developments. Their measures included the elaboration and restructuring of 107 training regulations (*Ausbildungsordnungen*), 26 federal and numerous regional training regulations for job advancement (*Fortbildungsregelungen*), and various master craftsman's regulations. The social partners also created 23 new job profiles. Moreover, the social partners completed several collective agreements including issues such as initial training. In the chemical industry, for instance, the social partners within the collective agreement "future with initial vocational training" (*Zukunft durch Ausbildung*) agreed to offer 7% more apprenticeship places between 2003 and 2007. At the company level, several projects were promoted by employers and unions to further develop skills acquisition and consultancy, including the implementation of special units in larger companies (European Commission 2006).

The fourth priority to *mobilize resources* was also addressed by several instruments at the national, sectoral, and company level. The completion of the National Pact on Vocational Training and Young Apprentice Development (*Nationaler Pakt für Ausbildung und Fachkräftenachwuchs in Deutschland*) by the German Federal Government and the main organizations representing German business[19] in June 2004 was probably the most important measure at the national level. The goal was to offer a vocational training opportunity, e.g., an apprenticeship contract with a firm, for every capable and willing young person over the next three years. Special pre-training measures are taken for people with limited prospects to prepare them for regular vocational training. The pact was extended in March 2007 for a further

[18]The Lisbon strategy, set out by the EU leaders at the Lisbon summit in March 2000, aims to make the EU "the most dynamic and competitive knowledge-based economy in the world capable of sustainable economic growth with more and better jobs and greater social cohesion, and respect for the environment by 2010" (http://ec.europa.eu).

[19]Bundesvereinigung der Deutschen Arbeitgeberverbände (BDA), Bundesverband der Deutschen Industrie e.V. (BDI), Deutscher Industrie- und Handelskammertag (DIHK), and Zentralverband des Deutschen Handwerks (ZDH).

three years. According to the new target[20], 60,000 new apprenticeship places and 40,000 new traineeship places (for pre-training measures) should be offered per year, compared to 30,000 and 25,000, respectively, in the first three years (http://www.ilo.org). The DIHK (2008) reports that 2007 was the most successful year in the pact's history: 89,000 new apprenticeship places and 43,000 traineeship places were offered and 54,000 (instead of the promised 30,000) firms offered apprenticeship places for the first time.

The Confederation of German Trade Unions (*Deutscher Gewerkschaftsbund, DGB*) (2007), however, criticizes the East–West differential, in that almost all new apprenticeship places were created in Western Germany. Beyond that, 595,000 out of 760,000 graduates, or 78.2%, found an apprenticeship place in 1992, while this ratio dropped to 625,000 out of 946,200, or 66%, in 2007. Finally, the number of old job candidates who previously applied for an apprenticeship place (*Altbewerber*) is still very high and estimated to exceed 300,000 (DGB 2007). The new Qualification Initiative (*Qualifizierungsinitiative*) from January 2008 addresses this problem. Bonuses of up to 6,000 € should support repeat job candidates to successfully terminate a vocational training. During the next three years, 100,000 repeat job candidates should be considered (BMBF 2008).

Other instruments at the national level include financial support for workers attending a school for master craftsmen (*Meister-BAFöG*) and financial support for vocational training (*Berufsausbildungsbeihilfe*). At the sectoral level, collective agreements, e.g., in the textiles and clothing sector, were made to promote (further) education and training. At the company level, measures have been taken to increase the number of trainee-jobs, e.g., in private and public banks, and apprenticeship grants have been reduced in order to increase the number of apprentices in the company, e.g., at Volkswagen AG. Concerning *further education*, the evaluation report however criticized that there were few improvements in Germany between 2002 and 2006 (European Commission 2006).

6.2.3.2 Shortage of Workers with Tertiary Education

Besides the shortage of workers with vocational education, the DIHK (2007) survey also showed that especially *innovative sectors* are lacking qualified employees. We have seen in Sect. 2.2.3.1 that at 22.5% in 2006, the share of tertiary educated in the economically active population (Fig. 2.9) was generally lower in Germany than in many other large developed countries. The DIHK (2007) survey reported that of all firms having problems filling vacancies, 36% did not find adequate candidates with a bachelor's degree (including *Fachhochschulabschluss*). This share was 45% in manufacturing, 64% in IT, and 62% in the electrical engineering. Especially, vacancies in IT and natural sciences could not be filled. The shortage of graduates with a master's degree (including university degrees) is smaller: only 25% of the firms could not fill their vacancies.

[20]See http://www.bmwi.de for details.

Large firms with more than 1,000 employees, in particular, did not find adequate candidates with tertiary education. Thus, 60% (resp. 57%) of the large firms with difficulties in finding job candidates could not find adequate graduates with a bachelor's (resp. master's) degree. In quantitative terms, one should therefore not underestimate the shortage of graduates with tertiary education. Almost three-quarters of the firms that are lacking natural scientists complain about a shortage of candidates with a master's degree; the share is 90% in R&D firms. The lack of qualified researchers in Germany is expected to hamper the innovation capability and the future growth potential of the firms (DIHK 2007).

The extent of *economic losses* due to involuntary job vacancies with tertiary education requirements has been estimated by a recent survey of the Institute for the German Economy (*Institut der Deutschen Wirtschaft*). Tertiary education refers to employees with a university or college (Fachhochschule) degree, technicians, and master craftsmen. The survey included data of 3,070 manufacturing and service firms, which were classified into eight broad sectors. These data were extrapolated to obtain the basic population, using the broad sector classification and the size of the firms as weightings. According to the results, more than 165,000 job vacancies could not be filled with tertiary educated candidates, and almost 65,000 job vacancies only with delay. MINT-qualifications and technicians made up more than three quarters of the shortage. These involuntary job vacancies were multiplied by their respective average sectoral value added per capita in 2006. The logistics sector, for instance, had an average value added of 58,000 €, while the per capita value added in other business services was 91,000 €. The total *loss of value added* in 2006 due to involuntary job vacancies was estimated to reach 18.5B €, which corresponds to 0.8% of GDP (Koppel 2008).

The *reasons for involuntary job vacancies* requiring a tertiary education are numerous. First, the number of graduates in MINT in Germany is very low by international standards, reflecting lower *enrollment numbers* (see Fig. 6.4). For a list of country abbreviations, see Appendix E. In 2005, the number of graduates in MINT per 1,000 workers in OECD countries ranged from 1.7 in Austria to 5.3 in Poland. Germany ranked 20th out of 23 countries with only 1.9 graduates. Scandinavian countries, such as Finland and Sweden, faced similar problems at the beginning of the 1990s due to a growing demand for highly qualified engineers and natural

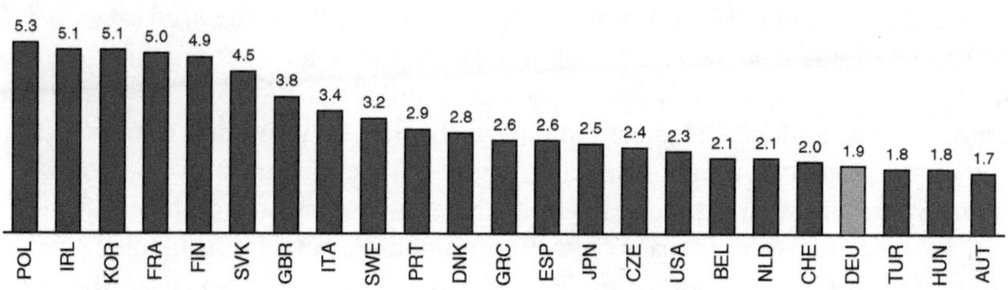

Fig. 6.4 Number of graduates in MINT in OECD countries 2005 (per 1,000 workers)
Source: own illustration. Data: OECD, taken from: Institut der Deutschen Wirtschaft. NB: MINT = Mathematics, Informatics, Natural Sciences, and Technical Engineering

scientists. At this time, both countries were ranked behind Germany, but investments in their national education system significantly improved their number of graduates in MINT. In Germany, however, we observe a shift towards studies in law, economics and business administration, social sciences, linguistics, and cultural sciences (Koppel 2007). The BMBF report (2007) confirmed the decline in the enrollment numbers in MINT. Between 1996 and 2001, the enrollment numbers in natural and engineering sciences dropped by 27 and 30%, respectively (BMBF 2007).

Second, the *proportion of women* is still very low in MINT. Koppel (2007) refers to data from the German Federal Statistical Office (Statistisches Bundesamt 2006), according to which the proportion of women enrolled in arts went up to 80%, while this share only reached 22% in engineering in 2005. The proportion of women is approximately 10% in electrical engineering, 20% in informatics, and 25% in civil engineering. Currently, the proportion of female engineers among all engineers that are subject to social security contribution is only 10% – we can thus expect a slight increase in the medium term. However, a large proportion of the employment potential is not yet used (Koppel 2007). The BMBF report (2007) reveals that the number of female graduates in MINT per 1,000 female workers between the age of 25 and 34 years increased only slightly from 3.2 in 1998 to 4.3 in 2003. Australia (11.7), Finland (11.4), the UK (11.1), Sweden (8.7), Spain (7.1), Italy (6.1), and the US (5.9) showed higher numbers in 2003. The performance of the Scandinavian countries also holds for the proportion of women. Thus, Finland experienced the strongest increase, having only 2.1 female graduates in MINT in 1998, followed by Sweden and the UK with only 4.9 and 7.8, respectively (BMBF 2007).

Third, the *drop-out rate* of students in engineering sciences in Germany is above average. Currently, about one-third of first-year university students do not obtain a degree in engineering or another field of study. The figures look slightly better with college (Fachhochschule) students, but even here the drop-out rate in electrical engineering reaches 32%, compared to 22% in other engineering sciences (Koppel 2007). Reducing the drop-out rates by one-third would yield an additional 7,000–8,000 graduates in natural and engineering sciences per year (BMBF 2007).

These problems at the labor supply side call for adequate *education policy measures*, which can meet the shortage of human capital only in the mid- and long-term. Besides immigration as a short-term measure, the BMBF report (2007) addresses three main fields of improvement. In the mid-term, the *high drop-out rate of students should generally be lowered* by improvements in teaching, a better student-support ratio, and individual support in order to better use the performance potential of the students. This can be financed either by providing more additional funds (e.g., additional public financing, study fees, cooperation with firms) or by creating more efficient structures within the universities and colleges. A second measure in the mid-term focuses on the recruitment of potential students in order to *increase the number of enrollments*. The improvements in teaching described above could increase the attractiveness of studying. According to the BMBF report (2007), barriers to studying, such as high local numeri clausi or specific qualifying exams, should be reconsidered, since limiting the number of students is unacceptable from a macroeconomic perspective. Teaching *and* research should become equally important. Considerations to complement the "excellence initiative" (*Exzellenzi-Exzellenzinitiative*)[21], focusing on excellent research, with a promotion of teaching, go into the right direction (BMBF 2007).

In the long-term, a *higher proportion of students should be enabled to obtain a higher education entrance qualification*. This requires a reform of the German education system from a selective to a supportive philosophy. The main focus should not be put on selecting "the appropriate" student who enters the next level of education, but on maximizing individual support in order to fully exploit a student's intellectual potential. Education at all levels ranging from pre-schooling to the tertiary education system should be afforded greater attention (BMBF 2007).

Expenditures for education should generally be increased. German public and private expenditures on educational institutions relative to GDP were 5.2% in 2004, while the OECD average reached 5.7%. Iceland (8.0%), the US (7.4%), South Korea (7.2%), and Denmark (7.2%) exceeded Germany's share by more than two percentage points. Across all OECD countries with available data, Germany was only ranked 17th. Finland ranked tenth with an expenditure share of 6.1% (OECD 2007a). The PISA study of the OECD, however, graded Finland's education system very good. This indicates that not only expenditures for education, but also *more efficient structures* contribute to a better education system. The BMBF (2007) report, for instance, blames the current system of decentralized competences as a major cause for the inefficiencies in the German education system. National educational targets take a subordinate role, since the federal system complicates a collective agreement on specific targets and their cooperative realization (BMBF 2007).

We have seen that many measures have been taken in recent years to reduce the shortage of workers with vocational education. Likewise, measures should be taken to increase the proportion of tertiary educated in the population. We have discussed mid-term targets that aim to increase the number of enrollments and the proportion of women, and to reduce the drop-out rate of students. Additionally, more efficient structures should be created and expenditures for education should be increased. If Germany wants to raise the skill-intensity of national value added in the future, it should act now.

References

Alewell D (2006) Zeitarbeit und Interimsmanagement in Deutschland – Ein empirischer und institutioneller Vergleich. Schmalenbachs Zeitschrift für betriebswirtschaftliche Forschung 58:990–1012

[21]The excellence initiative of the BMBF grants financial funds to promote leading research at German universities. Graduate schools, excellence clusters, and "future concepts to strengthen leading research at universities" represent the three kinds of funded projects (see http://www.bmbf.de).

Barbosa-Filho NH, Rada C, Taylor L, Zamparelli L (2005) US macro imbalances: trends, cycles, and policy implications. SCEPA Policy Note, December 2005
Bentolila S, Dolado JJ (1994) Labour flexibility and wages: lessons from Spain. Econ Policy 9(18): 55–99
Bhagwati J, Panagariya A, Srinivasan TN (2004) The muddles over outsourcing. J Econ Perspect 18(4):93–114
Bispinck R, WSI-Tarifarchiv (2005a) Immer flexibler – und immer länger? Tarifliche Regelungen zur Arbeitszeit und ihrer Gestaltung – Eine Analyse von 24 Tarifbereichen, Informationen zur Tarifpolitik, Elemente qualitativer Tarifpolitik, *57*: Hans Böckler Stiftung.
Bispinck R, WSI-Tarifarchiv (2005b) Wie flexibel sind Tarifverträge? – Eine Untersuchung von Tarifverträgen in über 20 Wirtschaftszweigen und Tarifvbereichen, Informationen zur Tarifpolitik, Elemente qualitativer Tarifpolitik, *60*: Hans Böckler Stiftung
Blanchard O, Landier A (2002) The perverse effects of partial labour market reform: fixed-term contracts in France. Econ J 112(480):214–244
BMBF (2007) Bericht zur technologischen Leistungsfähigkeit Deutschlands 2007. Bonn, Berlin. BMBF
BMBF (2008) 100.000 Altbewerber sollen Ausbildungsplätze erhalten. Press Release 001/2008. Retrieved from http://www.bmbf.de/press/2211.php
Boeri T (2002) Making Social Europe(s) Compete. Mimeo. Milan: Università Bocconi and Fondazione Rodolfo Debenedetti
Boss A, Dovern J, Meier C-P, Oskamp F, Scheide J (2007) Verbessertes Arbeitsmarktumfeld stärkt Wachstum des Produktionspotentials in Deutschland. Kieler Diskussionsbeitrag, No. 441/442, April 2007. Kiel Institute for the World Economy
Brandt N, Burniaux J-M, Duval R (2005) Assessing the OECD jobs strategy: past developments and reforms. OECD Economics Department Working Paper, No. 429, May 2005
Clasen J (2007) Flexicurity – a new Buzzword in EU Labour Market Policy. Mimeo, November 2007. University of Edinburgh School of Social and Political Studies
De Galdeano AS, Turunen J (2005) Real wages and local unemployment in the Euro Area. European Central Bank Working Paper Series, No. 471, April 2005
DGB (2007) Sehrbrock: Angebot an Ausbildungsplätzen weiter unzureichend. Press Release PM 204: Deutscher Gewerkschaftsbund (DGB). Retrieved from http://www.dgb.de/presse/pressemeldungen/pmdb/pressemeldung_single?pmid=3112
DIHK (2004) Individuell und flexibel . Wettbewerbsfaktor Arbeitszeitgestaltung, Ergebnisse einer DIHK-Unternehmensbefragung Herbst 2004, Berlin
DIHK (2007) Kluge Köpfe – vergeblich gesucht! Fachkräftemangel in der deutschen Wirtschaft, Ergebnisse einer DIHK-Unternehmensbefragung. Fall 2007
DIHK (2008) Paktjahr 2007 – Ein Jahr der Rekorde! Press Release, 31 January 2008. Retrieved from http://bildungsklick.de/pm/58159/paktjahr-2007-ein-jahr-der-rekorde
EU (2007) Fieldwork April–November 2007. Eurobarometer 67, Public Opinion in the EU, May 2007
European Commission (2006) Framework of actions for the lifelong development of competencies and qualifications, Evaluation Report 2006, January 2006: European Commission
Fitzenberger B, Franz W (2001) Jobs. Jobs? Jobs! Orientierungshilfen auf dem Weg zu mehr Beschäftigung. In: Franz W, Hesse H, Ramser H, Stadler M (eds) Wirtschaftspolitische Herausforderungen an der Jahrhundertwende: Mohr Siebeck
Fitzenberger B, Garloff A (2005) Labour market transitions, and residual wage dispersion. ZEW Discussion Paper, No. 05–04
Fitzenberger B, Kohn K (2006) Gleicher Lohn für gleiche Arbeit? – Zum Zusammenhang zwischen Gewerkschaftsmitgliedschaft und Lohnstruktur in Westdeutschland 1985–1997. ZEW Discussion Paper, No. 06–06
Funke S (2004) Kündigungsschutz seit 1.1.2004. Retrieved from http://www.123recht.net/printarticle.asp?a=7739

Gerlach K, Stephan G (2005) Wage distributions by wage-setting regimes. IAB Discussion Paper, No. 9/2005

German Marshall Fund (2007) Trade and poverty reduction survey, Topline Data October 2007. Retrieved from http://www.gmfus.org/economics/tpsurvey/Trade_survey_2007_Topline_Data.pdf

Gernandt J, Pfeiffer F (2005) Einstiegslöhne bei unvollkommenen Arbeitsmärkten. ZEW Discussion Paper, No. 05–26

Grossman GM, Rossi-Hansberg E (2006a) The rise of offshoring: it's not wine for cloth anymore. Paper presented at The New Economic Geography: Effects and Policy Implications, Jackson Hole: Federal Reserve Bank of Kansas City, pp 59–102

Grossman GM, Rossi-Hansberg E (2006b) Trading tasks: a simple theory of offshoring. NBER Working Paper, No. 12721, December 2006

Hübler O (2005) Sind betriebliche Bündnisse für Arbeit erfolgreich? Jahrbücher für Nationalökonomie und Statistik. 225(6):630–652

Kalmbach P, Franke R, Knottenbauer K, Krämer H (2005) Die Interdependenz von Industrie und Dienstleistungen, Zur Dynamik eines komplexen Beziehungsgeflechts, Berlin

Kohaut S, Schnabel C (2003) Tarifverträge. nein danke!? Ausmass und Einflussfaktoren der Tarifbindung west- und ostdeutscher Betriebe. Jahrbücher für Nationalökonomie und Statistik 223(3):312–331

Kohn K (2006) Rising wage dispersion, after all! The German wage structure at the turn of the century. IZA Discussion Paper, No. 2098

Koppel O (2007) Ingenieurmangel in Deutschland – Ausmaβ und gesamtwirtschaftliche Konsequenzen. IW-Trends – Vierteljahresschrift zur empirischen Wirtschaftsforschung aus dem Institut der deutschen Wirtschaft Köln, No. 2/2007, May 2007. Köln

Koppel O (2008) Nicht besetzbare Stellen für beruflich Hochqualifizierte in Deutschland – Ausmaβ und Wertschöpfungsverluste. IW-Trends – Vierteljahresschrift zur empirischen Wirtschaftsforschung aus dem Institut der deutschen Wirtschaft Köln, No. 1/2008, January 2008

Lechthaler W, Snower DJ (2006) Minimum wages and firm training. Kiel Working Paper, No. 1298, September 2006. The Kiel Institute for the World Economy

Milberg W, Schöller D (2008) Globalization, offshoring and economic insecurity in industrialized countries. World Economic and Social Survey 2008 Background Paper. Department of Economic and Social Affairs, New York, United Nations

Möller J (2005) Die Entwicklung der Lohnspreizung in West- und Ostdeutschland. In: Bellmann L, Hübler O, Meyer W, Stephan G (eds) Institutionen, Löhne und Beschäftigung, Beiträge zur Arbeitsmarkt- und Berufsforschung, Vol 294. Nürnberg

Montuenga V, Garcia I, Fernandez M (2003) Wage flexibility: evidence from five EU countries based on the wage curve. Econ Lett 78(2):169–174

OECD (2004) Employment protection legislation and labour market performance, OECD employment outlook, Chapter 4, June 2004. OECD, Paris

OECD (2005) OECD economic surveys: France. OECD, Paris

OECD (2007a) Education at a Glance 2007, OECD Indicators, September 2007. OECD, Paris

OECD (2007b) Offshoring and employment: trends and impact. OECD, Paris

Pfeiffer F (2004) Ausmaβ und Konsequenzen von Lohnrigiditäten. ZEW Discussion Paper, No. 04–13

Ragnitz J, Thum M (2007) The empirical relevance of minimum wages for the low-wage sector in Germany. CESifo Forum. 8:35–37

Samuelson PA (2004) Where Ricardo and Mill rebut and confirm arguments of mainstream economists supporting globalization. J Econ Perspect 18(3):135–146

Sinn H-W, Holzner C, Meister W, Ochel W, Werding M (2002) Aktivierende Sozialhilfe: Ein Weg zu mehr Beschäftigung und Wachstum. ifo Schnelldienst 55(9):3–52

Snower DJ (2006) Ein Mindestlohn in Deutschland schadet mehr als er nützt. IfW-Fokus, No. 25. Kiel Institute for the World Economy

Spitznagel E, Wanger S (2004) Mit längeren Arbeitszeiten aus der Beschäftigungskrise? IAB Kurzbericht 10/2004: IAB. Retrieved from http://doku.iab.de/kurzber/2004/kb1004.pdf
Statistisches Bundesamt (2006) Bildung und Kultur, Fachserie 11, Reihe 4.3.1, Nichtmonetäre hochschulstatistische Kennzahlen. https://www-ec.destatis.de
Ubber T (2004) Agenda 2010: reform of German labour law: impact on hiring and firing staff. German Law J 5(2):135–141
Wurzel E (2006) Labour market reform in Germany: how to improve effectiveness. Economics Department Working Papers, No. 512, September 2006

Appendices

A: The Networked Readiness Index 2006–2007 Rankings

Rank 2006/2007	Country	Score 2006/2007	Rank 2005/2006
1	Denmark	5.71	3
2	Sweden	5.66	8
3	Singapore	5.60	2
4	Finland	5.59	5
5	Switzerland	5.58	9
6	Netherlands	5.54	12
7	United States	5.54	1
8	Iceland	5.50	4
9	United Kingdom	5.45	10
10	Norway	5.42	13
11	Canada	5.35	6
12	Hong Kong SAR	5.35	11
13	Taiwan, China	5.28	7
14	Japan	5.27	16
15	Australia	5.24	15
16	Germany	5.22	17
17	Austria	5.17	18
18	Israel	5.14	19
19	Korea, Rep.	5.14	14
20	Estonia	5.02	23
21	Ireland	5.01	20
22	New Zealand	5.01	21
23	France	4.99	22
24	Belgium	4.93	25
25	Luxembourg	4.90	26
26	Malaysia	4.74	24
27	Malta	4.52	30
28	Portugal	4.48	27

(*continued*)

(continued)

Rank 2006/2007	Country	Score 2006/2007	Rank 2005/2006
29	United Arab Emirates	4.42	28
30	Slovenia	4.41	35
31	Chile	4.36	29
32	Spain	4.35	31
33	Hungary	4.33	38
34	Czech Republic	4.28	32
35	Tunisia	4.24	36
36	Qatar	4.21	39
37	Thailand	4.21	34
38	Italy	4.19	42
39	Lithuania	4.18	44
40	Barbados	4.18	n/a
41	Slovak Republic	4.15	41
42	Latvia	4.13	51
43	Cyprus	4.12	33
44	India	4.06	40
45	Jamaica	4.05	54
46	Croatia	4.00	57
47	South Africa	4.00	37
48	Greece	3.98	43
49	Mexico	3.91	55
50	Bahrain	3.89	49
51	Mauritius	3.87	45
52	Turkey	3.86	48
53	Brazil	3.84	52
54	Kuwait	3.80	46
55	Romania	3.80	58
56	Costa Rica	3.77	69
57	Jordan	3.74	47
58	Poland	3.69	53
59	China	3.68	50
60	Uruguay	3.67	65
61	El Salvador	3.66	59
62	Indonesia	3.59	68
63	Argentina	3.59	71
64	Colombia	3.59	62
65	Panama	3.58	66
66	Dominican Republic	3.56	89
67	Botswana	3.56	56
68	Trinidad and Tobago	3.55	74
69	Philippines	3.55	70
70	Russian Federation	3.54	72
71	Azerbaijan	3.53	73
72	Bulgaria	3.53	64
73	Kazakhstan	3.52	60
74	Serbia and Montenegro	3.48	80
75	Ukraine	3.46	76
76	Morocco	3.45	77

(continued)

(continued)

Rank 2006/2007	Country	Score 2006/2007	Rank 2005/2006
77	Egypt	3.44	63
78	Peru	3.43	85
79	Guatemala	3.41	98
80	Algeria	3.41	87
81	Macedonia, FYR	3.41	82
82	Vietnam	3.40	75
83	Venezuela	3.32	81
84	Pakistan	3.31	67
85	Namibia	3.28	78
86	Sri Lanka	3.27	83
87	Mauritania	3.25	n/a
88	Nigeria	3.23	90
89	Bosnia and Herzegovina	3.2	97
90	Mongolia	3.18	92
91	Tanzania	3.13	84
92	Moldova	3.13	94
93	Georgia	3.12	96
94	Honduras	3.09	100
95	Kenya	3.07	91
96	Armenia	3.07	86
97	Ecuador	3.05	107
98	Guyana	3.01	111
99	Burkina Faso	2.97	n/a
100	Uganda	2.97	79
101	Mali	2.96	95
102	Madagascar	2.95	102
103	Nicaragua	2.95	112
104	Bolivia	2.93	109
105	Kyrgyz Republic	2.9	103
106	Cambodia	2.88	104
107	Albania	2.87	106
108	Nepal	2.83	n/a
109	Benin	2.83	108
110	Suriname	2.82	n/a
111	Malawi	2.79	n/a
112	Zambia	2.75	n/a
113	Cameroon	2.74	99
114	Paraguay	2.69	113
115	Mozambique	2.64	101
116	Lesotho	2.61	n/a
117	Zimbabwe	2.6	105
118	Bangladesh	2.55	110
119	Ethiopia	2.55	115
120	Angola	2.42	n/a
121	Burundi	2.4	n/a
122	Chad	2.16	114

Source: World Economic Forum (2007), The Global Information Technology Report 2006–2007

B: Absolute Onshoring Development per Services Category (M US$)

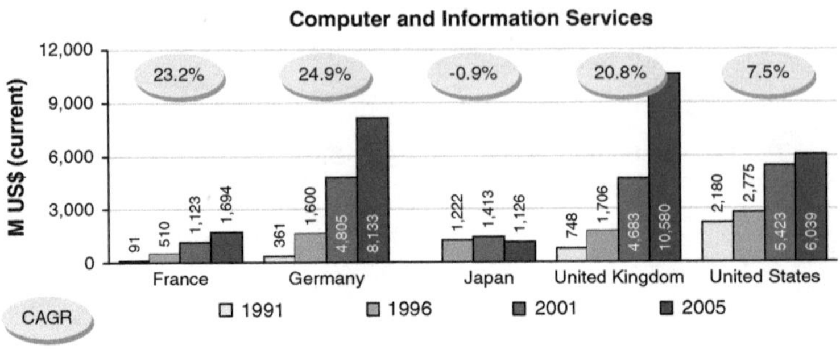

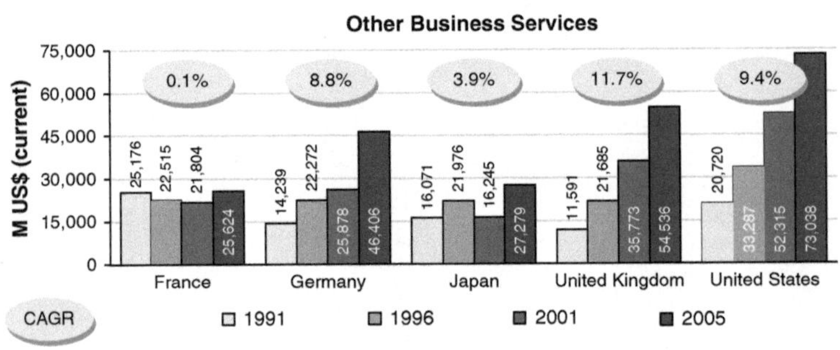

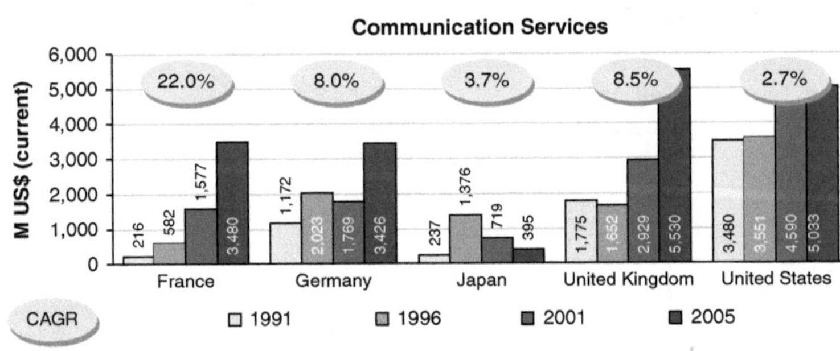

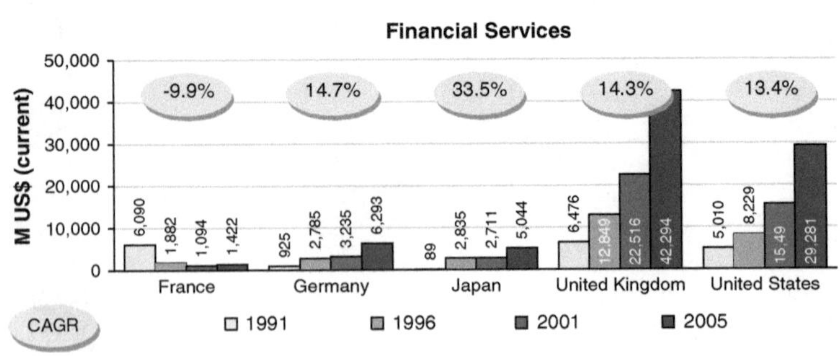

Source: own calculations. Data: IMF Balance of Payments, retrieved from: UNCTAD

C: Relative Onshoring Development per Services Category (% of Other Services)

		1991	1996	2001	2005
Computer and information services	France	0.2	1.5	3.3	3.6
	Germany	1.1	3.5	9.6	9.3
	Japan	n.a.	2.9	3.8	1.8
	United Kingdom	2.6	3.3	5.6	7.6
	United States	3.2	2.5	3.7	2.9
Other business services	France	60.3	64.3	64.4	54.9
	Germany	42.0	48.3	51.7	52.9
	Japan	67.4	52.3	43.7	44.0
	United Kingdom	39.9	41.6	42.7	39.1
	United States	30.7	30.5	35.4	34.5
Communication services	France	0.5	1.7	4.7	7.5
	Germany	3.5	4.4	3.5	3.9
	Japan	1.0	3.3	1.9	0.6
	United Kingdom	6.1	3.2	3.5	4.0
	United States	5.2	3.2	3.1	2.4
Financial services	France	14.6	5.4	3.2	3.0
	Germany	2.7	6.0	6.5	7.2
	Japan	0.4	6.7	7.3	8.1
	United Kingdom	22.3	24.6	26.9	30.3
	United States	7.4	7.5	10.5	13.8

Source: own calculations. Data: IMF Balance of Payments, retrieved from: UNCTAD. Other services correspond to total services minus transportation and travel

D: Material and Service Inputs

Material inputs (36)	
1	Food products
2	Beverages
3	Tobacco products
4	Textiles
5	Wearing apparel, dressing and dying of fur
6	Leather, leather products and footwear
7	Wood and products of wood and cork
8	Pulp and paper
9	Paper products
10	Publishing
11	Printing
12	Coke, refined petroleum products and nuclear fuel
13	Pharmaceuticals
14	Chemicals excluding pharmaceuticals
15	Rubber products
16	Plastic products

(*continued*)

(continued)

Material inputs (36)	
17	Glass and glass products
18	Ceramic goods and other non-metallic mineral products
19	Iron and steel
20	Non-ferrous
21	Metal castings
22	Fabricated metal products, except machinery and equipment
23	Machinery and equipment, n.e.c.
24	Office, accounting and computing machinery
25	Electrical machinery and apparatus, n.e.c.
26	Radio, television and communication equipment
27	Medical, precision and optical instruments
28	Motor vehicles, trailers and semi-trailers
29	Other transport equipment
30	Manufacturing n.e.c.
31	Recycling
32	Electricity, steam and hot water supply
33	Gas and gas supply
34	Collection, purification and distribution of water
35	Contruction site and civil engineering
36	Contruction installation and other construction
Service inputs (7)	
37	Post and telecommunications
38	Financial intermediation except insurance and pension funding
39	Activities related to financial intermediation
40	Renting of machinery and equipment
41	Computer and related activities
42	Research and development
43	Other business activities

Source: input–output tables, Federal Statistical Office Germany

E: List of Country Abbreviations

Abbreviation	Country
AUS	Australia
AUT	Austria
BEL	Belgium
CAN	Canada
CZE	Czech Republic
DNK	Denmark
FIN	Finland
FRA	France
DEU	Germany

(*continued*)

(continued)

Abbreviation	Country
GRC	Greece
HUN	Hungary
IRL	Ireland
ITA	Italy
JPN	Japan
KOR	South Korea
NLD	Netherlands
NZL	New Zealand
NOR	Norway
POL	Poland
PRT	Portugal
ESP	Spain
SVK	Slovak Republic
SWE	Sweden
CHE	Switzerland
GBR	UK
USA	USA
TUR	Turkey

F: Sectoral Services Offshoring Intensities $OSS_i(a)$ 1991 versus 2000

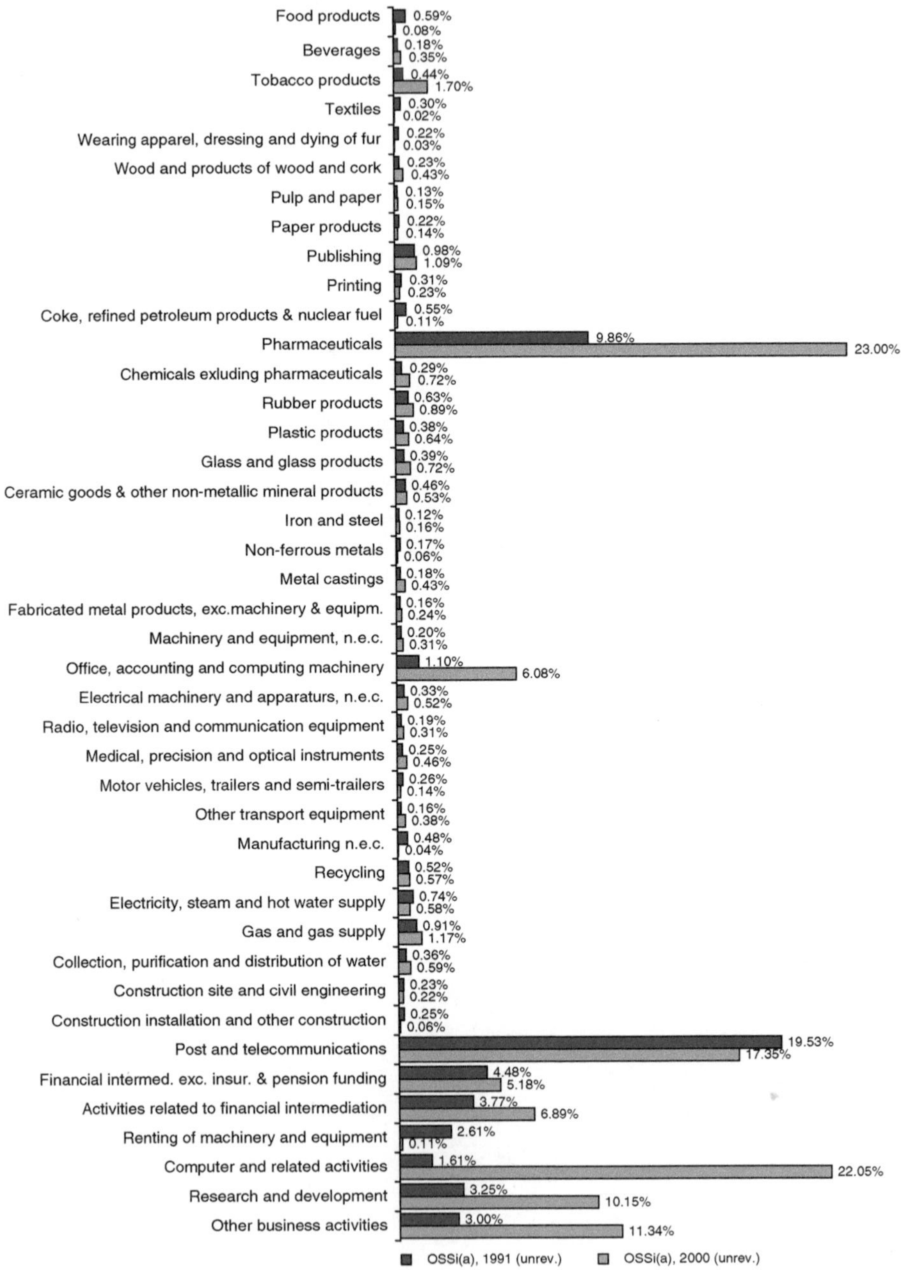

Source: own illustration. Data: Federal Statistical Office Germany, unrevised input–output tables

G: Sectoral Materials Offshoring Intensities OSM$_i$(a) 1991 versus 2000

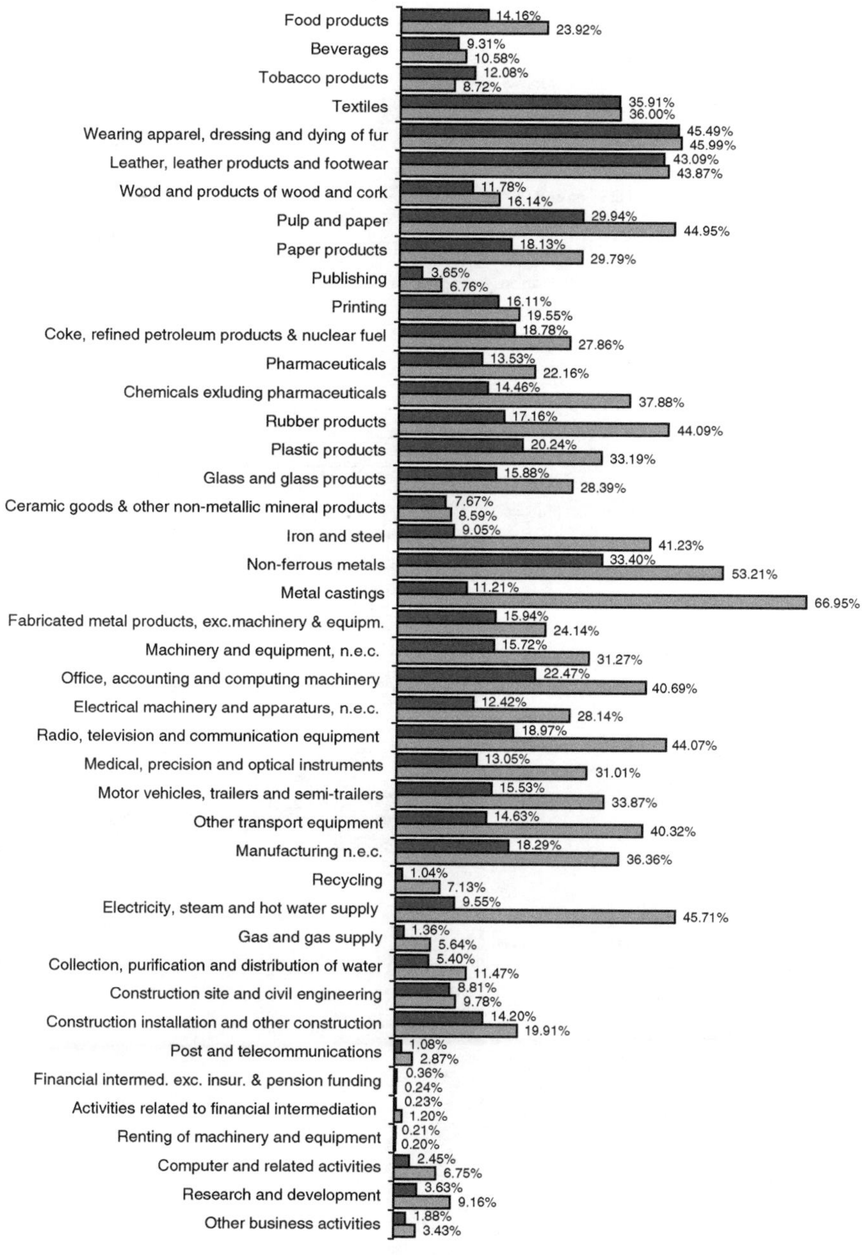

Source: own illustration. Data: Federal Statistical Office Germany, unrevised input–output tables

H: Sectoral Materials Offshoring Intensities $OSM_i(a)$ 1995 versus 2004

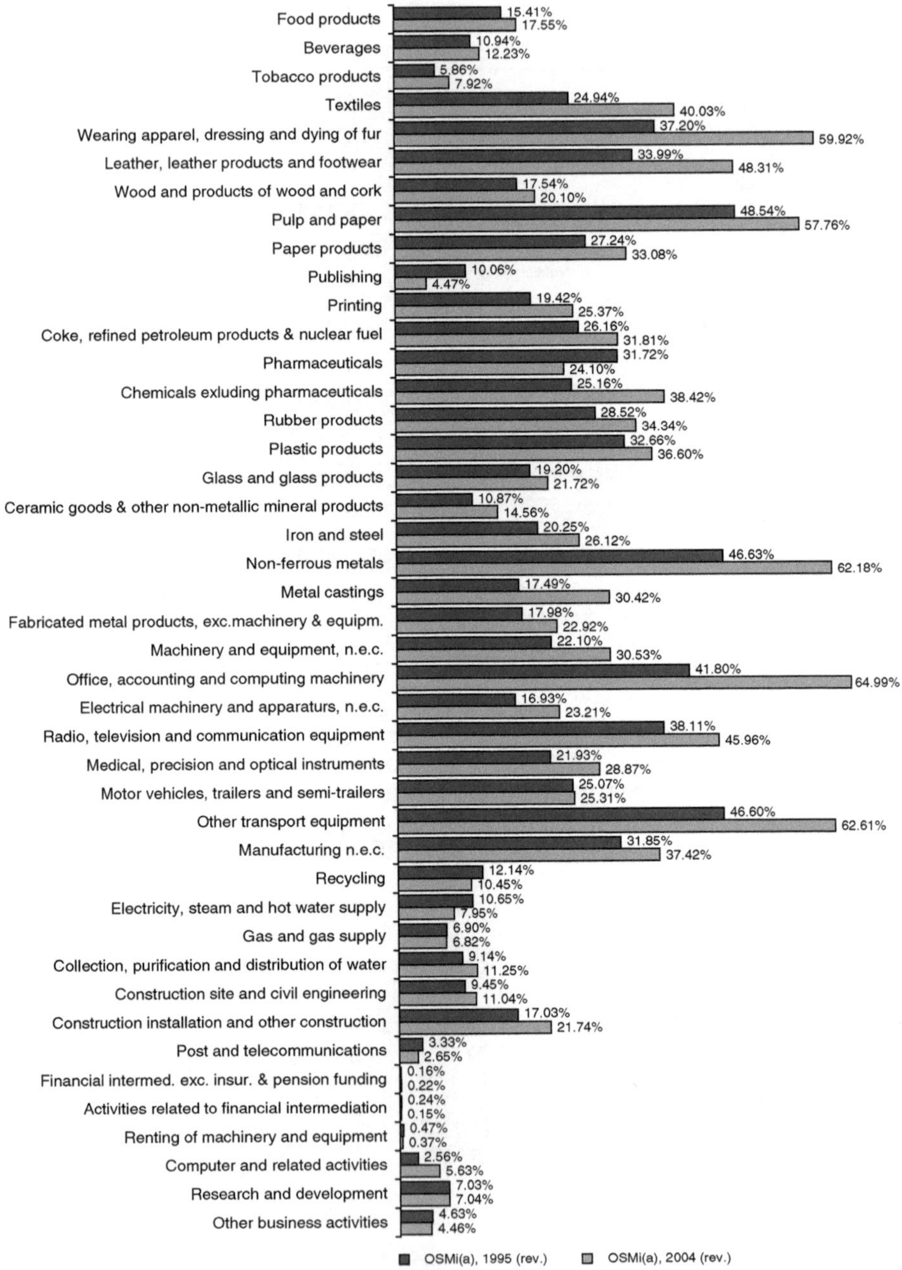

Source: own illustration. Data: Federal Statistical Office Germany, revised input–output tables

I: Global Services Attractiveness Index 2007

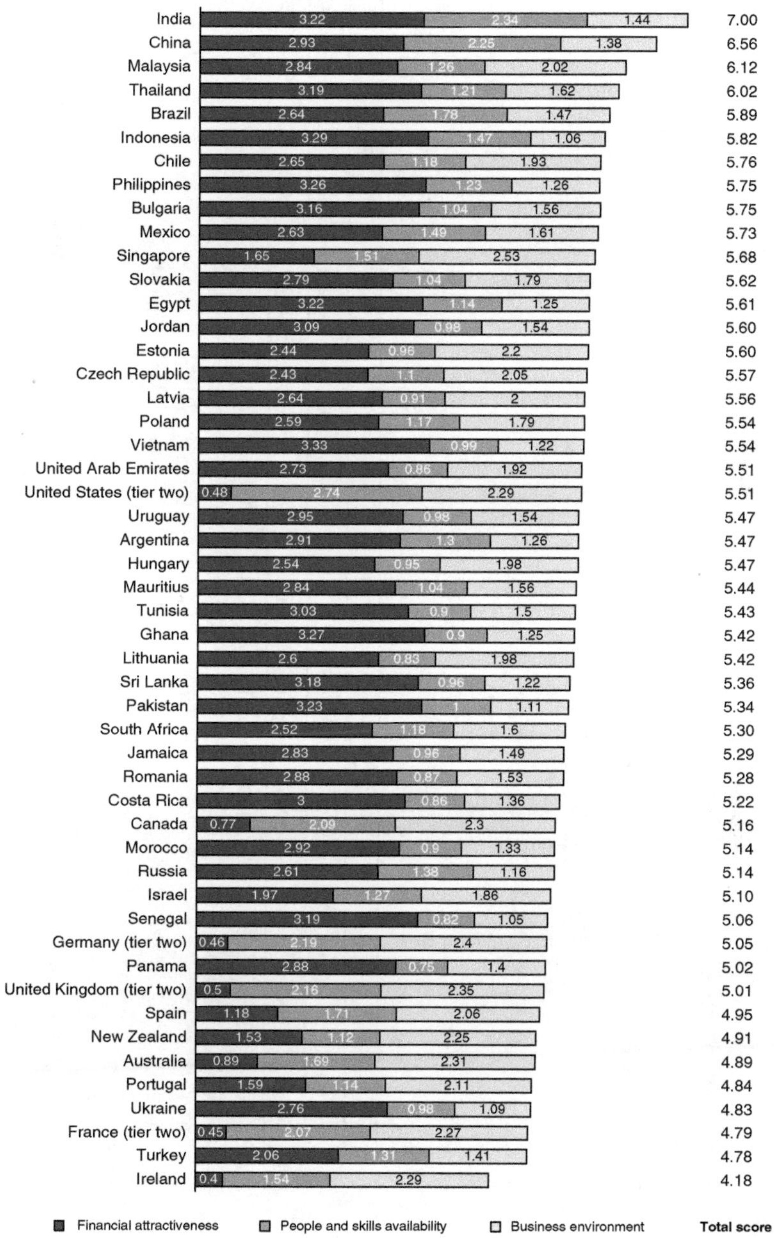

Source: A.T. Kearney, See: http://www.atkearney.com/res/shared/pdf/GSLI_2007.pdf. The weight distribution for the three categories is 40:30:30. Financial attractiveness is rated on a scale of 0–4, and the categories for people and skills availability, and business environment are on a scale of 0–3

J: Exports and Imports of Goods and Services

Goods	Exports				Imports				Balance			
	(B US$)		(% of GDP)		(B US$)		(% of GDP)		(B US$)		(% of GDP)	
	1991	2005	1991	2005	1991	2005	1991	2005	1991	2005	1991	2005
Denmark	37.7	83.3	27.6%	32.2%	34.3	75.0	25.1%	29.0%	3.5	8.3	2.5%	3.2%
France	213.4	434.4	17.2%	20.4%	230.8	476.0	18.6%	22.4%	−17.4	−41.6	−1.4%	−2.0%
Germany	402.7	977.8	22.3%	35.0%	389.1	777.4	21.5%	27.8%	13.6	200.4	0.8%	7.2%
Japan	314.5	594.9	9.2%	13.0%	236.7	515.9	6.9%	11.3%	77.8	79.1	2.3%	1.7%
United Kingdom	182.2	384.4	17.6%	17.5%	209.8	515.8	20.3%	23.5%	−27.6	−131.4	−2.7%	−6.0%
United States	421.7	904.3	7.1%	7.2%	509.2	1,732.3	8.5%	13.8%	−87.5	−828.0	−1.5%	−6.6%

Services	Exports				Imports				Balance			
	(B US$)		(% of GDP)		(B US$)		(% of GDP)		(B US$)		(% of GDP)	
	1991	2005	1991	2005	1991	2005	1991	2005	1991	2005	1991	2005
Denmark	14.3	36.3	10.4%	14.0%	10.4	33.4	7.6%	12.9%	3.8	2.9	2.8%	1.1%
France	80.1	116.0	6.5%	5.5%	63.7	106.1	5.1%	5.0%	16.4	9.9	1.3%	0.5%
Germany	64.1	154.9	3.5%	5.5%	90.0	202.9	5.0%	7.3%	−25.9	−47.9	−1.4%	−1.7%
Japan	44.8	110.2	1.3%	2.4%	86.6	134.3	2.5%	2.9%	−41.8	−24.0	−1.2%	−0.5%
United Kingdom	56.3	203.1	5.4%	9.2%	49.0	160.5	4.7%	7.3%	7.3	42.6	0.7%	1.9%
United States	162.6	376.8	2.7%	3.0%	118.1	314.6	2.0%	2.5%	44.5	62.2	0.7%	0.5%

Source: own calculations. Data: OECD International Trade by Commodities Statistics, International Monetary Fund (IMF), retrieved from: UNCTAD

Index

J

K

L

M

N

O

P

Q

R

S

T

U

V

W

Kolibri 360 GmbH
Ferdinand-Jühlke-Straße 7
99095 Erfurt, Deutschland
produktsicherheit@kolibri360.de